EVERY DAY IS A GOOD DAY FOR PIZZA.

Pizza dough is a gateway for many home bread bakers, allowing them to experiment with different tools, toppings, ingredients, timings, and shapes. Learning to bake pizza is not unlike undertaking a yoga practice, learning a musical instrument or art, or beginning a new friendship: You invest time to build a life skill—only this one comes with amazing pizza. According to master baker Tara Jensen,

INTUITION IS ACCUMULATED BY THE BODY OVER TIME. IT IS A GIFT YOU GIVE YOURSELF THROUGH PRACTICE: MAKE A LOT OF PIZZA.

This companion guides you step by step from simplest doughs to artisanal bakes. Here are 91 recipes any baker can enter, with a simple cook-along layout, and ways to explore different ingredients, techniques, flours, and heat sources for perfecting pizza. Jensen helps you set up your baking space with the right ingredients and tools, cook over fire or with an outdoor oven, trick out the oven that came with your apartment to bake an impressive pie, or start a pizza party tradition with your little ones.

Jensen also gives guidance on the perfect ratios of toppings to crust, stepping you through the build for classics such as Margherita, Clam, and Supreme Delight, as well as a collection of fancifully delicious takes including Breakfast Pizza; Delicata Squash, Shallot, and Gruyère; and a particularly luscious Pancetta and Brown Butter Pineapple pie. No book on pizza is complete without simple sauces, dips, and drizzles, such as Lemony Roasted-Garlic Cream, Hot Honey, and a fresh Uncooked Tomato Sauce. For after your pizza, Jensen offers dessert: homemade ice cream, cobbler, brownies, chocolate chip cookies, and a classic yellow birthday cake with vanilla frosting.

The first pizza bible from a woman, Pizza Practice *is a new approach and everything you need to bake your best pizzas.*

PIZZA
PRACTICE

PIZZA PRACTICE

DOUGHS, TECHNIQUES + TOPPINGS

TARA JENSEN

Foreword by Katie Parla

Photographs by Scott Suchman

CHRONICLE BOOKS
SAN FRANCISCO

Library of Congress Cataloging-in-Publication Data available.

ISBN 978-1-7972-3083-2

Manufactured in China.

Photography by Scott Suchman.
Photographs pages 116 and 123 by Ilana Freddye.
Food styling by Lisa Cherkasky.
Design by Lizzie Vaughan.
Typesetting by Taylor Roy.
Editorial direction by Sarah Billingsley.

10 9 8 7 6 5 4 3 2 1

Chronicle Books LLC
680 Second Street
San Francisco, California
94107
www.chroniclebooks.com

dedicated to

marley green

Contents

EVERYTHING YOU EVER WANTED TO KNOW ABOUT SOURDOUGH AND ABOUT MIXING, SHAPING, AND BAKING PERFECTLY PILLOWY PIZZA IN WOOD-FIRED AND HOME OVENS

3: SAUCES, DRIZZLES, AND DIPS
174

4: PIZZA CROWD-PLEASERS
196

SAUCED PIES 198

WHITE PIES 236

SEASONAL PIES 268

PITA, FOCACCIA, AND PIZZA-NIGHT DESSERTS

Foreword

Pizza has always been treated as bread's unruly cousin, fun but unserious, something you scarf down, folded, in various stages of inebriation on the sidewalk. Tara Jensen calls BS on all that. She knows pizza is every bit as technical and disciplined as bread, and she proves it in *Pizza Practice*.

This is not a book that hands you a recipe and sends you on your way. Tara maps out the practice of pizza with the precision of a career baker who has contemplated fermentation for decades. She shows you how to measure flour correctly, why water temperature matters, and how desired dough temperature keeps everything in balance. She explains bulk fermentation in plain English, then walks you through shaping and proofing until your hands respond to the dough intuitively. Her chapters on stretching, building, and baking read like field notes from the counter of a pizzeria, and they actually prepare you to succeed in your home kitchen.

The range is staggering. You get same-day supermarket flour doughs for weeknights and double-levain formulas that reward patience with deep flavor. You get pan pizza, wood-fired pizza, outdoor tabletop oven pizza. You get pita, focaccia, and even desserts, because Tara knows a real pizza night doesn't stop when the last savory pie comes out of the oven. What ties it all together is the philosophy of practice: repetition, attention, consistency. She is not telling you to make one pretty pizza and post it online. She is teaching you to become fluent in dough through steady work.

This book is also a flour education. Tara explains the wheat berry and how each part affects flavor and fermentation. She takes you inside roller-milled and stone-ground flours, heritage grains, protein structures, and hydration tests. This kind of detail lets you make informed decisions instead of buying whatever is on the supermarket shelf. That's rare in pizza writing, and essential if you want to grow beyond formula following.

And then there is Tara herself. She has been a professional baker for years, built and run wood-fired ovens, taught thousands of people, and baked her way through every variable of grain, starter, fermentation, and oven setup you can imagine. She is also a mother of three who knows what it means to fold fermentation into a chaotic household. That mix of deep technical authority and lived practicality is exactly why this book works. She can teach you baker's math and folding techniques, but she can also tell you what to do when your dough overproofs while you wrangle a screaming toddler.

There are plenty of pizza books out there, but almost none that will actually teach you to bake. Tara Jensen has done the work in ovens, bakeries, and classrooms. She knows what matters, and she knows how to teach it. That makes *Pizza Practice* an essential manual for anyone serious about the craft.

KATIE PARLA

If bread is the body of Christ, pizza is what everyone ate after the wine was gone.

NTRODUCTION

I JOKE, BUT PIZZA, THOUGH WIDELY ADORED, IS OFTEN VIEWED AS LESS SACRED AND LESS SERIOUS THAN BREAD.

Yes, there are the exceptions; the fact that you're holding this book in your hands points toward progress. But many artisanal bakers look down their nose at pizza—it's an ordinary street food—whereas bread has hymns written about it, and it sits, revered, upon the Eucharist table.

When I began hosting a monthly wood-fired pizza night at Smoke Signals, my old bakery in Marshall, North Carolina, I confessed to my bread-baking mentor that I was shocked at how popular (and lucrative) pizza was. He leaned in close and whispered, in a melancholy tone, "Tara, it's OK. Pizza comes for us all." Is the pull of ease simply too hard to escape, even for the most noble among us? As a serious-bread-baker-turned-mother-of-three, the gray area between the sanctity of bread and the convenience of pizza is where I live.

It wasn't always this way. As a young, single woman, I could afford (literally and figuratively) lofty values when it came to food. Even after getting married and becoming a mother to one child, I was still able to scrape together a new normal. Maybe not *everything* in my shopping cart was organic, and I didn't make it to the farmers' market *every* weekend, but I still fancied myself on the "right" side of the food world. Having twins blew the wheels off my ride. Not only did I have to let Jesus take the wheel, but I had to get out and walk.

Throughout my life I have turned toward baking and God in times of grief. After my twins, Poppy and Laurel, were born, I ran to church, which has always been a safe place to cry. And cry I did, week after week. Nothing prepared me for the strength I needed to withstand the chorus of a four-year-old and two newborns screaming at once. I felt like a paper bag in the wind. I needed to build up a solid spiritual core or my mind was going to warp. I also began making pizza every week, sometimes more than once, and my practices of faith and fermentation became one and the same.

There are lovely similarities between practicing faith and practicing pizza. The first step is clear: devoting time. Dedicating time, both to worship and to make dough, is key. Carving out a few hours to give thanks and slow down became nonnegotiable in my week, as did the hours needed to tend to my starter and mix doughs. It's easy to feel that we don't have enough time, but, somehow, when we decide to make the commitment, the required hours appear. Where your attention goes, energy flows.

Next is the physicality. Both prayer and pizza have their own dances. Ninety percent

of good baking is muscle memory. Maybe the same can be said of worship? The calisthenics of prayer, like the movements of folding and stretching dough, became a familiar, soothing ritual. Kneeling for confession and rising for songs carry the body along, just as the motions of mixing, shaping, and baking usher a body through the bake. New bakers often mistakenly equate *knowing* a lot about bread with being a good baker, but what makes a baker stand out is their responsiveness to the dough, which requires touch. Learn the motions, and they will lead you deeper into the process.

The third requirement is consistency. When it comes to sourdough starters, notorious for their finicky nature, the real unpredictable element is the human caretaker. The more predictable you are with your cultures and doughs, with regular feeding and use, the more they will return the favor. They will also become robust. When I first started going to church, I was in free fall, and I needed to go every week just to get to the next week. The first time I missed church a couple weekends in a row didn't faze me because I had built up the benefits not through intermittent dabbling but real, solid attendance. The same can be said of baking: Your skills don't evaporate if you've put the work in. Showing something a little love every day is better than infrequent displays of passion.

At the end of my first year of attending St. James' Episcopal Church in Leesburg, Virginia, I made the choice to be baptized. For the first time as a bread maker, I was able to eat the communion wafer. I savored the experience, excitedly kneeling while it was placed into my palm. My baptism happened on All Saints' Day, so at the end we walked to the church graveyard and read the names of those who had passed, tolling the bell every so often. I sat in a graveyard in a party dress holding gift bags, and somehow it was perfect—birth and death overlapping. Afterward, I went out for pizza.

I am in the family chapter of life. It's noisy, messy, hectic, and exhausting. Nothing is as clean and clear-cut as I once thought it was. I've been humbled to realize that using certain ingredients doesn't make you morally superior. It just means you can afford them. As a young baker, I didn't know what it meant to live life in survival mode. Now, on the floor under a pile of children, I am well acquainted with doing whatever you need to do to get through the day, even if sanity involves out-of-season strawberries.

Bread, my first love, is on hiatus in my house. Pizza has taken its place. Bread may have brought me to the altar, but pizza has quietly done the heavy lifting, showing up for dinner (and cold for breakfast on occasion) and making the values I once held so tightly more accessible, fun, and enjoyable for everyone. Overlooked but ever steady, **pizza, I love you**.

GLOSSARI
INGREDIENT

ES, TOOLS, S, AND PREP

MAKING PIZZA AT HOME is joyful and fun, yet it does take some physical and mental preparation. This chapter will help you become familiar with the key vocabulary, equipment, ingredients, and techniques I use for making delicious pizza from the comfort of my own kitchen.

HOW TO USE THIS BOOK

This book focuses on foundational recipes and repetitive practice to help you train yourself in the art of making and baking pizza, pita, and focaccia. I am here to help you find one pizza dough to master and give you other options to explore once you've gotten your feet under you. In these pages, you'll also discover my favorite foolproof focaccia, all you need to know to make pita with your kids, and an easy, no-fail recipe for a delicious birthday cake.

If you're new to pizza making, start with the recipes that call for roller-milled supermarket flour and commercial yeast so you can focus on building muscle memory and intuition. When you're ready to bring in more flavor and you have the time to be responsive to your dough, seek out the formulas that ask for a sourdough starter, levain, and freshly milled flour. These doughs will behave somewhat unpredictably, keeping you on your toes and rewarding you with incredible taste and texture.

If you're already a pizza pro, pay close attention to the sections on flour and fermentation in the early part of the book, as they will help you improve your game. Once you have a solid grasp of the ratios in pizza dough, the way the ingredients interact, and how to control the heat during a bake, I hope you'll take the final step and create a pizza that reflects a flavor and style all your own.

Pizza Jargon

If you're new to making pizza, all the baker-specific vocabulary can be just as mystifying as handling the dough. What makes matters worse is that words may have more than one meaning. Here are some introductory definitions to help get you thinking and speaking like a pizza pro.

Alveoli are the air pockets, also called bubbles or holes, in the crumb, or interior of the pizza dough (see Crumb, following).

Ash content is a term used to talk about the performance, color, texture, and flavor of flour. It is determined by incinerating a sample portion of flour. Once the organic matter has burned away, the inorganic minerals, mostly concentrated portions of bran and germ, are left behind. This residue is weighed and expressed as a percentage of the original sample flour weight. A high ash percentage indicates the flour has an abundance of bran and germ.

Autolyse describes the 30 to 60 minutes at the start of the mix when all the flour and a portion of the water—or all the water—are mixed and left to rest. Withholding the leavening and salt at this point allows the water to go toward gluten development, reducing the overall mix time. Adding water to flour also activates the enzyme protease, which breaks down protein, resulting in a relaxed, slack dough. In effect, an autolyse both strengthens and softens a dough.

Baker's math is a set of equations bakers use to write a pizza dough formula, or recipe (see also page 66). It's common to hear the term in relation to the most famous rule: The flour weight is treated as 100 percent and all other ingredients are expressed as a percentage of the flour weight. For example, if the flour is 100 g, and the water is 50 g, the water would be 50 percent. In baker's math, it is normal for the total percentage for a recipe to exceed 100 percent.

Baking steel (a.k.a. pizza steel) is a solid slab of steel placed in the oven and preheated. Pizza is baked directly on the hot steel.

Building is used to describe the process of layering sauce, cheese, and toppings on the pizza. My rule for building a pizza is "less is more," focusing on ingredients with maximum flavor and textural impact.

Bulk fermentation is the time between mixing and shaping. This is also called the first rise or the bulk proof. If the dough has a high level of prefermented flour, the bulk window will be short, under 2 hours. There may or may not be folds during this time, depending on whether the dough was mixed in a stand mixer or by hand.

Cheese flow is the way the cheese melts on the pizza. Cheese with a high moisture content, like fresh mozzarella, will spread and break easily, while cheese with a lower moisture content, like American cheese, will melt where it's placed and stay creamy longer. The shape of the cheese (squares, shreds, small balls, large slices) also dictates how it will flow on the pizza.

Crumb refers to the webby interior structure of the pizza crust. (Imagine cutting a pizza in half and looking at the cross section of the crust: That's the crumb.) It can be open and filled with irregular holes, or it can be dense and uniform. The crumb affects the texture of the pizza, making it doughy and chewy or thin and crispy.

Crust is often used to describe just the rim of the pizza, but it can also refer to the entire dough portion of the pizza, such as thin-crust pizza.

Desired dough temperature is the temperature you want the pizza dough to reach when it's done being mixed. In general, for wheat-based pizza dough, it's 80°F [27°C]. Factors that directly affect the dough temperature include the water temperature and mixing method. Often the desired dough temperature, also called the **DDT**, is spoken of in terms of adjusting the dough temperature with the addition of warming or cooling water.

Doming is used to finish off the pizza by holding it, on the peel, close to the ceiling—"in the dome"—of the oven. Positioning the pizza in the dome, where the temperature is the highest, gives the pie a final blast of intense heat, boosting caramelization and browning.

Folding is a specific set of movements done at regular intervals during bulk fermentation that builds strength in a dough. There are many types of folds, such as the coil fold, the four-quarter-turn-in-the-bowl fold, and the slap and fold. The type of fold called for is informed by the strength of the flour, the hydration of the dough, and the mixing method.

Fresh flour is stone-ground and under 2 weeks old. It has a creamy, smooth texture, thanks to the oily, perishable germ of the wheat berry, and a nutty, grassy aroma. To store freshly milled flour, which sometimes has the date it was milled stamped on the bag, seal it in a plastic bag and slip it into the freezer, where it will keep for up to 3 months. Bring the flour to room temperature before using.

High extraction is a term used by millers to describe the amount of bran present in flour. Think of the whole wheat berry and what is being "extracted" in the process of milling. If all the wheat berry is present in the flour, it's a 100 percent whole-grain flour. But if it has *most* of the original berry present, with only the largest bran flakes removed, it is considered a high-extraction flour.

Hydration refers to the amount of water in a dough. For example, if a dough is 100 percent flour at 100 g and there is 75 g of water, the hydration is 75 percent. To calculate the overall hydration, or total amount of water, add together the water in the starter, levain, and final dough.

Lactobacilli are tiny, rod-shaped microorganisms found in nature that digest simple sugars and produce lactic acids. Lactic acids in pizza dough can make for a chewy texture and a mildly tangy flavor. Commonly found on the skin of grapes, on leaves of cabbage, and on our bodies, lactic acids are also used in cultured foods, such as kimchi and yogurt.

Leoparding is the name for the pattern of tiny bubbles on the rim of the pizza that char, making a striking contrast of black spots on a golden crust—like a leopard's coat! Different from the larger crisp, charred bubbles you get in your home oven, leoparding is only achievable on pizzas baked for 2 to 3 minutes in an oven heated to around 1,000°F [540°C].

Levain is a preferment composed of flour, water, and sourdough starter. Levains may be made with various flours and hydration levels and fermented for 3 to 4 hours or longer, bubbling away for up to 12 hours. The levain is calculated as a percentage of the dough, so use all the levain prepared, leaving none behind to be perpetuated.

Pan pizza is pizza baked in a pan! It comes in various styles and shapes, the most notable of which are Detroit, grandma, and Sicilian, each with a different crust depth, pan size, and arrangement of sauce, cheese, and toppings.

Pepperoni cupping is when pepperoni slices crinkle upward at the edges in the heat of the oven and turn into small, oil-filled cups with tall, charred sides.

Pizzaiolo (or **pizzaiola**, the feminine form) is a person who makes pizza! It can also mean a chef who specializes in the craft and tradition of Italian-style pizza making.

Proofing is the stage after shaping, when the dough rises again, relaxes from any tension introduced while shaping, and takes on complex flavors from fermentation. It's not uncommon to proof pizza dough in cold temperatures of 38° to 42°F [3° to 6°C] for up to 72 hours. You can under proof, correctly proof, or over proof pizza dough. A well-proofed pizza round will feel like a pillow when gently poked, yet still maintain its shape and stretch easily. Under-proofed dough will buck back when stretched, and over-proofed dough will fall apart when extended.

Rest is the word I use to describe the 10 to 15 minutes at the beginning of the mix when the salt and possibly also the levain are held back and the flour and water come together. It's not mandatory but definitely makes mixing the dough easier and more efficient.

Roller-milled flour is flour made by crushing wheat between a series of rollers. The germ is removed, as is the bran, making the flour shelf-stable. Roller-milled flour is milled to industry specifications for ash content, protein, and moisture. Roller mills achieve consistency season to season by blending wheats from many farms.

Sifted flour is flour that has had the larger flakes of bran screened out. It is also called "gray" flour for its tan or golden hue. Sifted flours are a wonderful way to add nutrition, flavor, and texture to baked goods, as they are neither strictly white nor whole wheat.

Sourdough starter is a mixture of flour and water, refreshed daily, that's filled with wild yeast and lactic acid bacteria. It contains 1 part yeast to 100 parts lactic acid bacteria, but if you were to weigh the yeast and bacteria separately in a mature starter, they would weigh the same, because the yeast is significantly larger.

Stone-ground flour is flour made by crushing wheat berries between two large millstones. Because it contains the perishable germ oil from the wheat berry, it should be stored in the freezer.

Stretching is a series of motions that coaxes a round or relaxed pizza dough into the desired size. Pizza makers use a variety of techniques to stretch the dough, including tossing, slapping, hanging, and even rolling with a rolling pin (or a wine bottle in a pinch).

Undercarriage is a fancy term for the bottom side of the pizza that touches the hearth. The undercarriage should be crisp, golden, and spotted with patches of char and deeply browned dough. The underside of the pizza is just as important as the top!

Yeast is a single-celled microorganism that consumes simple sugars and produces gas as a by-product. It can be found in our environments, on our bodies, and in flour. The acid-tolerant yeasts that thrive in sourdough fall under the yeast species *Saccharomyces cerevisiae*, which includes different strains, including both baker's yeast and brewer's yeast.

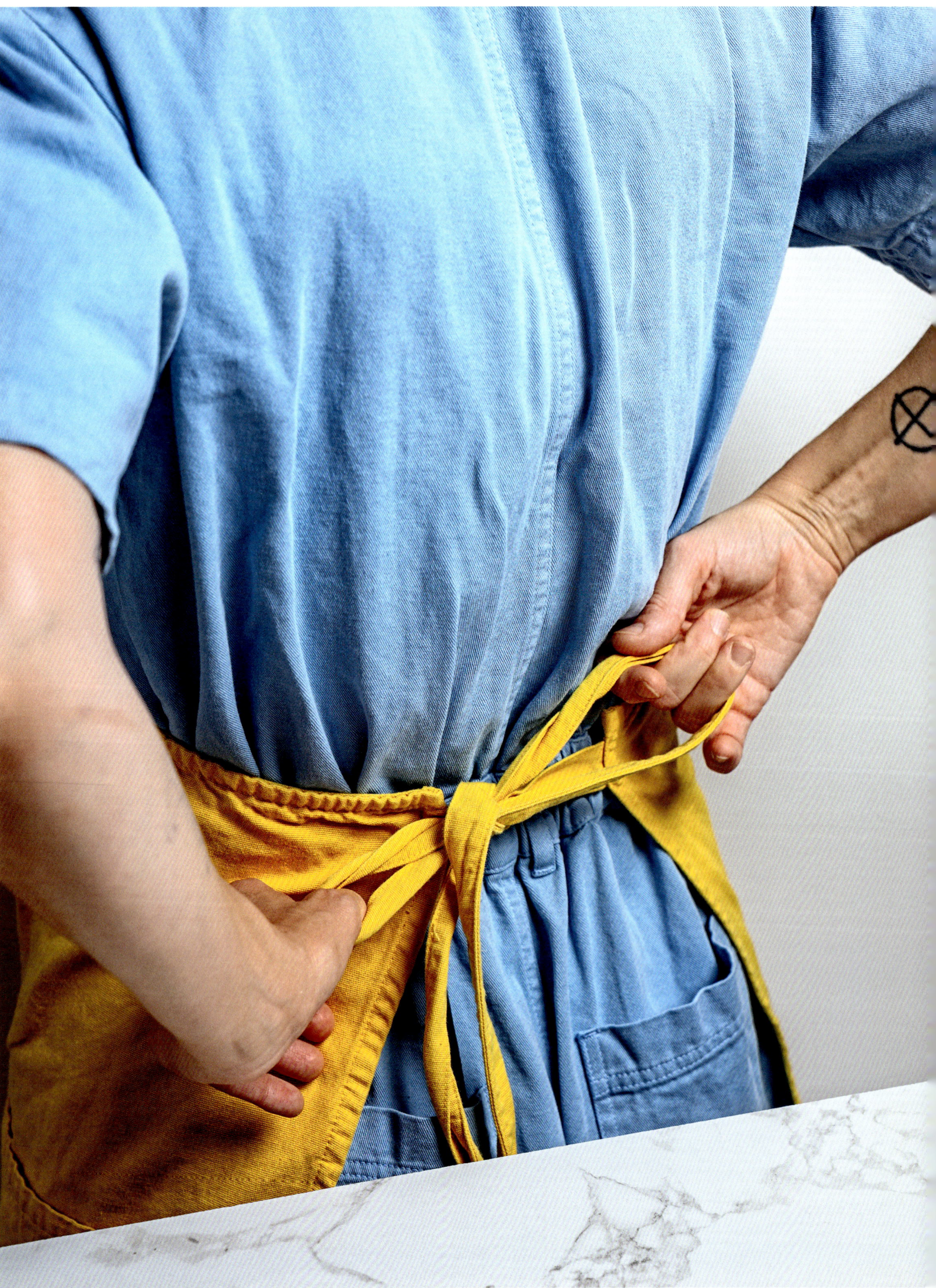

A Space to Work

I have a dedicated space in my kitchen for baking. I keep it clean and ready to go, free of clutter and my family's various bits of debris. I fight for this, and I work hard to maintain it because it's the first step to making the whole process approachable for me. My space consists of a long metal table on wheels with a metal shelf below the work surface. I keep a wine cooler set at 50°F [10°C] on the shelf. On the table itself is my KitchenAid 7 qt [6.6 L] stand mixer, my KoMo grain mill, my digital scales, a restaurant-style water pitcher, and a Brød & Taylor Sourdough Home set at 55°F [13°C].

Next to the table is a Belgian-made Rofco B40 oven with three stone decks that can bake three pizzas or twelve loaves of bread at once. On the other side of the table is a tall baker's rack. It has rungs for sheet pans and is covered with a plastic zip-up "jacket." I keep my sheet pans, parchment, cling film, aluminum foil, and bread baskets on the rack and use it to keep my proofing doughs cozy. On the wall above the table is a bulletin board and calendar where I post the recipe I'm working on and when I need to do what.

I keep roller-milled flour in 5 qt [4.7 L] Cambro storage containers in my pantry and freshly milled flour double bagged in the freezer. I have had a chest freezer on and off over the past few years just for stone-ground flour, and if you have the extra space, acquiring one is worth it.

Although I know it's not possible for everyone to have this kind of arrangement at home, I do urge you to carve out a little space for yourself. It will keep your mind focused and your pizza dough on track.

The saying "practice makes perfect" is true! The only thing standing between you and a perfect pizza is elbow grease and time. Here are suggestions to get going and stay interested . . .

SET YOURSELF UP FOR SUCCESS

Get what you need to feel excited. Maybe that's a digital scale and thermometer. Maybe it's a special journal for your notes. Spend time deciding what dough you'll make and source the ingredients.

DECIDE WHEN!

PUT IT ON THE CALENDAR!

Mark the day you'll need to feed your starter (if using) and when you'll mix and bake your pizza.

MAKE PIZZA EVEN WHEN YOU'RE NOT FEELING ESPECIALLY MOTIVATED OR CREATIVE.

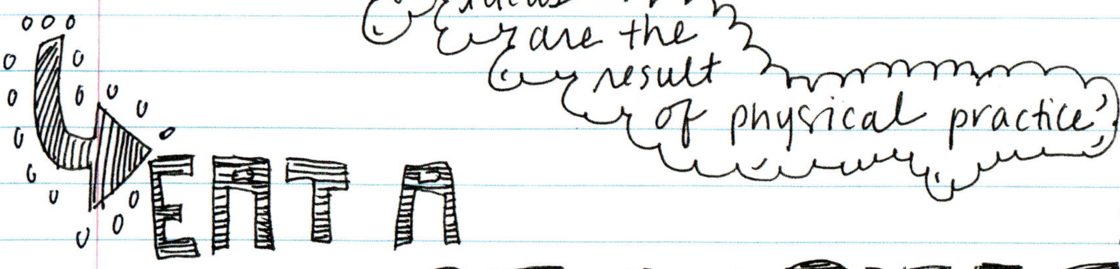

MAKE THE SAME PIZZA OVER AND OVER

Consistency is worth striving for, but it's often the goal and not the reality.

BE A PIZZA TOURIST

Look up all the places within a few hours' drive and make it a day trip. GO SOLO. Ask questions, order it all! take pictures and notes

DON'T BE AFRAID TO LOOK LIKE A FOOL

The beginner's mind is a fresh and precious place.

TAKE YOUR PRACTICE WITH YOU

* MAKE PIZZA ON VACATION!
* MAKE PIZZA IN A DIFFERENT COUNTRY!
* MAKE PIZZA FOR BREAKFAST!

ONCE YOU MASTER A ROUND PIZZA, TRY OTHER STYLES

(like pan pizza!)

TEACH SOMEONE ELSE

This is a wonderful way to share your love of food with friends, family, and community. And as you answer questions you'll solidify your own knowledge.

TOOLS AND EQUIPMENT

A good digital scale and a high-heat baking steel are nonnegotiable for the pizza recipes in this book. The scale will cure issues with inaccuracy, making sure your dough turns out the same way consistently, and the steel, when used properly, will yield a light and crispy crust every time. I use my scale for all my baking and keep my steel in the oven, using it for pies and bread when it's not being used for pizza.

I've suggested other tools and equipment here that will help your dough ferment well and improve the overall process of pizza night at home. Investments like a dough proofer can be expensive but will give you a happy, bubbly dough. Smaller items, like dough scrapers, don't need to be brand specific, and you can even find great baking tools in the paint and drywall tools aisle of your local hardware store. Also, be sure to look around and see what you already have!

A **baking steel** is a flat, food-grade plate of steel used to bake pizza and breads in a home oven. After trying a traditional ceramic pizza stone, a cast-iron stone, and a baking steel, the steel was a clear winner, with the cast iron coming in second. A baking steel is expensive but will give your crust a perfect bottom in a home oven. It's also indestructible. I clean it after each use (once it has cooled!) by scraping it with a bench knife. Occasionally I will wash it by hand with hot, soapy water and a stiff brush, then oil it and warm it in the oven to reseason it. My baking steel has become part of my oven, living on the middle rack in between bakes.

A **countertop flour mill** allows you to mill your own flour at home, achieving the freshest of fresh flour! I have a KoMo mill, and I add 10 percent home-ground flour to my pizza dough. Because the millstones on the KoMo are small, the flour is on the coarser side, particularly when milled from harder wheats. So I opt for softer wheats, such as Appalachian White or Sonora, for my home-milled flour. I also keep the wheat berries in the freezer and grind them frozen to minimize the heat added by the milling process.

Dough containers and covers are the baker's choice. They are commonly made from metal, ceramic, or food-grade plastic, and each material has its pros and cons. Ceramic holds heat well but will also keep a cold dough chilly. Metal easily transfers heat, cooling a hot dough or warming a cold one quickly. Most professional pizza shops and bakeries prefer thick plastic because it's easy to clean and transfers heat relatively slowly, which means your warm dough will stay cozy once covered.

I go back and forth between letting my pizza dough rise in a **large ceramic mixing bowl** and using the same **rectangular plastic dough box** I use for proofing dough rounds. I like the familiarity of the mixing bowl, but the rectangular shape of the box makes folding easy and efficient. I can also see the dough relaxing much better than in a bowl, which helps me choose to increase or decrease the folds and know when the dough is ready to be shaped. The proofing box comes with a lid, and I cover my bowls with shower caps.

Dough proofing boxes (a.k.a. tubs) provide a stable place with the right humidity and temperature to help pizza dough rise. I proof my dough rounds, staggered, in white, food-grade plastic dough proofing boxes. They are stackable, and the size that fits well in my fridge is 17 by 13 in [43 by 33 cm]. Each box can easily accommodate eight 250 g [8¾ oz] rounds, and the boxes can be found on various online sites under "dough proofing boxes" or "dough tubs."

If I won't be baking all four pizzas in one night, I will proof each round in its own container. I use either an inverted **round, lidded 48 oz [1.4 L] takeout container**, like the kind you might get a large salad or noodles in, or an inverted **meal-prep container**, such as an inverted **round, lidded 6 cup [1.4 L] Pyrex bowl**. Either way, the shaped dough rests on the lid, with the container covering it. It's nice for the container to be a little larger than the dough round so the dough can comfortably slope on the sides.

A **dough scraper** is a flexible plastic tool ideal for handling dough and scraping out mixing bowls. My favorite dough scraper isn't even sold for pizza or bread making. It's a small, yellow, soft scraper found in the paint aisle of a hardware store. A **bench knife** is a flat metal rectangle with a wooden handle along one long edge. It is used for dividing dough and cleaning up work surfaces. Keep the handle oiled and the blade sharp.

A **digital gram scale** and a **digital milligram scale** are must-haves for baking in general. A digital kitchen scale allows you to measure ingredients in grams, which provides greater precision and consistency than either ounces or volume measurements. I prefer a digital gram kitchen scale with a stainless-steel body and raised platform. My scale has a capacity of 8 kg [18 lb]. Although kitchen scales will weigh down to 1 gram, they often lose their accuracy below 8 g. So for yeast, salt, and other ingredients called for in very small amounts, I turn to a milligram scale, a pocket-size device that can quickly and accurately measure 0.5 g or 1 g. Clean your scales after each use and keep extra batteries on hand.

A **digital thermometer** is invaluable for ensuring the temperature of the water for your mix is correct, for checking the temperature of the dough after it's mixed, and for popping into the dough throughout bulk fermentation to make sure it's staying warm. If you're baking focaccia, you can slide it into the bread toward the end of the bake to check the internal temperature, making sure it's above 195°F [90°C] before you pull it out of the oven.

An **immersion blender**, also known as a stick or wand blender, is ideal for mixing up quick pizza sauces, dips, and drizzles.

An **infrared thermometer** is handy for checking the temperature of your baking steel or pizza stone. Just because your oven is preheated to 550°F [290°C] doesn't mean that your steel or stone is also 550°F [290°C]. If you're using a wood-fired oven or a propane-powered tabletop oven, you'll want to check the interior surfaces with this thermometer.

A **mandoline** is a flat, rectangular slicer great for prepping pizza toppings, as it yields precision with surprising speed when compared to a knife. Set the blade of your mandoline to about ¼ in [6 mm] to get the right thickness for nearly any vegetable or meat you will be using.

A **Microplane grater** is key to finishing any pizza with a final shower of freshly grated Parmesan. The razor-sharp teeth of this easy-to-use tool are also handy for zesting lemon and grating garlic.

Outdoor pizza ovens are not essential, but if you truly want restaurant-style high-heat oven temperatures (and you like to manage flames), an outdoor oven is for you. I love both my Gozney Roccbox and my Gozney Dome, and I run them off propane rather than wood. I hear great things about Ooni ovens too. All these ovens have their quirks, just like any oven, and they take practice and patience to master, but with repeated and consistent effort, an outdoor oven is well worth the investment for anyone who can afford one. **(For more on outdoor ovens, see page 127.)**

Plastic squeeze bottles are nice for drizzling olive oil or thin sauces onto a pizza after the bake, as they allow you to control both the direction and the volume of the stream.

Pizza pans are a fantastic option if you want to feed a crowd or skip the work of shaping and stretching dough into a round. You'll want a **black aluminum pan** with square edges, like the ones from Lloyd in Washington State. I originally ordered only one of these pans, but it made such a perfectly crisp and light pizza, I purchased three more. I use them for both pan pizza and focaccia, and they are in heavy rotation, paying for themselves. You can also use cast-iron skillets, cake pans, and standard sheet pans.

A **Sourdough Home**, made by Brød & Taylor, is a lifesaver when it comes to keeping my starter happy. My starter is kept at ambient room temperatures—68° to 72°F [20° to 22°C]—during the day and rests overnight in my Sourdough Home set at 55°F [13°C]. This overnight stint at a cool temperature slows down fermentation but doesn't stop it. That means I can capture the benefits of continuous fermentation (super-active, balanced acidity, ready to use quickly, floral tasting) without having to feed it more than once a day.

A **stainless-steel box grater** is a must-have for shredding low-moisture mozzarella. I use the largest holes and cold cheese for the best results.

A **stand mixer**, when used correctly, will mix a strong, smooth dough that requires less folding than a hand-mixed dough because the strength is developed during the mix rather than the folds. Any of the doughs in this book can be mixed either by hand or in a mixer. I have spent the better part of my baking career mixing by hand but have recently fallen for the efficiency and ease that a stand mixer introduces into the process. I now use it all the time! I use a KitchenAid mixer with a 7 qt [6.6 L] bowl and a dough hook for most of my pizza doughs, mixing around 1 kg [2¼ lb] dough at a time. For wetter doughs, like focaccia, I will begin with the paddle attachment, then switch to the dough hook once a shaggy dough has developed. I primarily use two speeds, 2 and 8, similar to how a commercial mixer has only "low" and "high" speeds, or speed 1 and speed 2. Keep in mind that using a mixer means that you are still smelling, touching, tasting, poking, and prodding your dough for key sensory clues to its needs and wants. **(For specific instructions on using a stand mixer, see page 84.)**

Welding gloves are the new oven mitts! I don a pair of heat-resistant, blue suede leather welding gloves in my kitchen and outside when I work with my tabletop pizza ovens. They wear well over time and protect your wrists and lower arms from burns.

A **wine cooler** can work magic on your proofing dough by slowing down fermentation without stopping it. I cold proof my dough in bulk, still in the container, or the covered, shaped rounds in a wine cooler set at 50°F [10°C]. This is a warmer temperature than the 38° to 42°F [3° to 6°C] my fridge provides, so the dough takes on more air and flavor. I bought a simple, square box-style cooler and removed the racks designed to hold bottles. I can fit two large mixing bowls, four shaped loaves of bread, or two pizza dough boxes in it.

A **wire cooling rack** is the first place a pizza lands when it is unloaded from the oven. This is essential for a crisp crust. Without air circulating under the pizza as it cools, the steam is trapped against the crust and can lead to a soggy underside.

A **wide-mouthed, restaurant-style plastic water pitcher** lives in my workspace. Initially, I use the pitcher to hold the correct-temperature water for the dough, then I leave it around to pull water from before a fold, or I dip my dough scraper or bench knife into it for a quick cleaning. I also like to rinse my hands off in the pitcher, avoiding gumming up the sink with a gluey mess.

A **wooden peel** for building the pizza and a **perforated metal peel** for rotating it on the baking steel or hearth and for transferring it from the oven to the cooling rack are great tools to own. Wooden peels absorb and transfer heat slowly, so you can work several doughs at once and you don't have to worry about them sticking. You want the peel to have a short handle for a home oven and to be about 1 in [2.5 cm] wider than the size of the pizza you are making. A perforated metal peel slides easily under the pizza and transfers heat quickly, and its long handle keeps you a comfortable distance from the heat.

INGREDIENTS

Choosing the right ingredients for pizza is important, as they directly impact the flavor, texture, and overall experience, both for the pizza maker and for the lucky friends and family who will enjoy the final pie. Since pizza is a simple food, high-quality flour, cheese, and tomatoes are crucial, as is the right combination of toppings, sauces, and cheeses.

Flour is the most important ingredient in pizza. Incredible cheese or a blazing wood-fired oven will still yield a mediocre pizza if the flour for the crust hasn't been carefully milled and well tended. ●

THE WONDERFUL WHEAT BERRY

To understand the kinds of flour you'll encounter in the following recipes, it helps to be familiar with the four major components of the wheat berry, or whole wheat kernel. The germ, endosperm, aleurone layer, and bran each bring different qualities to flour.

The germ is the smallest part of the wheat berry, just under 3 percent of the overall weight, yet it is the most nutritionally important and flavorful portion. High in vitamin B and essential fats, the germ is a dense food source for the wheat plant once it sprouts. When it is present in flour, you'll notice a hay-like aroma, a silky texture, and milky, nutty flavors in the baked dough. The germ is perishable, which is why stone-ground flour, the only kind of flour that contains the fatty germ, needs to be kept in the freezer.

The endosperm, a blend of carbohydrates, proteins, minerals, and vitamins, is 80 percent of the weight of the wheat berry. The outer layers, close to the bran, are high in enzymes, and the inner layers, near the germ, are where the proteins, gliadin and glutenin, reside. Responsible for creating gluten, gliadin gives a dough extensibility, while glutenin makes the dough elastic. Equally important are the carbohydrates, which, once broken down by enzymes, become simple sugars for yeast and bacteria to digest. Depending on the variety of the wheat, the endosperm can have high or low protein.

The aleurone layer is a thick sheath that encapsulates the endosperm. Its significance lies in its high level of enzymes. Rich in alpha-amylase, which breaks down long chains of starches, and beta-amylase, which knocks off the ends of the shorter chains, these enzymes effectively break down starches, allowing sugars to move about freely in the dough. Because the aleurone layer clings to the back of the bran, whole wheat and sifted flour (which comes in various grades according to how much bran has been screened out) will contain larger portions of this layer, much more than white flour.

The bran is the outer shell of the wheat berry and makes up 13 to 14 percent of its weight. It is a key source of insoluble fiber and antioxidants. When included in the flour, it deepens the color and makes for a toothsome texture. Thanks to the extra minerals and enzymes, the flour will also ferment quickly. The additional enzymes and the rough shape of the bran may interfere with gluten development, so doughs made with whole-grain or high-extraction flour may need extra time to absorb water and strengthen.

○ **POPULATION WHEAT FOR CLIMATE CHANGE** / Population wheats are genetically distinct varieties that are planted together, like the ORC Wakelyns Population wheat—nicknamed YQ wheat—developed by Martin Wolfe in 2002. Blended from twenty different varieties, it's chaos gardening at its best. Looking at a field of population wheat, you'll see various heights, hues, and seed-head profiles; together, these varieties make a resilient crop. The technique of planting a wide variety of grains together to see what grows best harkens back to traditional methods of interplanting. Many argue this is the future of growing grain, as the crops are better able to adapt to variations in soil and weather. These are issues we must consider as bakers experiencing the effects of climate change.

FROM BERRY TO FLOUR

Flour is milled by a series of rollers or between two stones, each method having its pros and cons. A roller mill separates the germ and bran from the endosperm and discards them both before further refining the remaining flour through a series of tightly spaced rollers, making a shelf-stable product. In contrast, a stone mill crushes the wheat between two large stones, smearing the germ through the flour and knocking the bran off. Before the 1860s, when roller mills became popular, all flour was stone-ground. Today, roller mills dominate the industry. Although my heart is with freshly milled stone-ground flours, I've grown to appreciate high-quality roller-milled flour and its availability.

Roller mills excel at shearing off the germ and stripping away the bran. Discarding these parts of the wheat berry removes fat that could go rancid and lowers the enzymes that can wreak havoc on fermentation. Stone-ground flour preserves the germ throughout the flour. Although you can find roller-milled flours that include the germ, these are specialty products you won't see on supermarket shelves. The loss of germ is the biggest differences between roller- and stone-milled flours, and also why freshly milled stone-ground flour needs to be kept in the freezer.

Roller-milled flour produces four main edible streams. The first pass, during which the grain is cracked between corrugated rollers, is called "break flour." This process separates the endosperm from the bran and germ. Next, the endosperm is passed through smooth rollers until reduced to a finer consistency. This is known as "reduction flour." These two initial passes yield what is referred to as "patent" flour, which consists of the innermost portions of the wheat berry. Patent flour can

KING ARTHUR FLOUR / King Arthur flour is unbleached and naturally aged for 2 to 4 weeks. In addition to forgoing bleaching, the flour is never brominated to speed up the aging process. King Arthur offers a signature flour, Sir Galahad, which is equivalent to a French Type 55 (T55) flour, best described as an all-purpose or low-protein bread flour with minimal enrichment of 11.7 percent protein and 0.5 percent ash. Play around with making your own T55 flour from two parts King Arthur all-purpose and one part King Arthur bread flour.

BASSINAGE FOR STONE-GROUND FLOUR / Pay close attention to how the flour from a stone-ground mill or home mill hydrates. The chunkiness of the particles poses challenges to dough hydration. Although the flour may be strong enough to hold an ample amount of water, it will need to be added slowly. Bassinage, also called double hydration, reserves 5 to 10 percent of the water in a recipe and adds it in at the end of the mix. Should you try this, it's best to mix the dough in a stand mixer fitted with a dough hook. If the dough still feels stiff or tight, you can continue to drizzle in water until you have a soft, smooth dough.

be blended to create signature bread, all-purpose, and cake flours, or it can be used alone. The remaining two passes, called "first clear flour" and "second clear flour," consist of bran and middlings. These rougher, coarser portions are often added to whole wheat or rye flours.

Abiding by strict industry standards when it comes to variables like protein, ash, and moisture, roller mills source grain from many farms and blend it, creating flours that are predictable season to season and year to year. On the downside, blending varieties masks their unique hues, textures, and aromas—in short, you can end up with flour that works great but lacks personality. If you're up for a fermentation and flavor adventure, try a single varietal flour from a stone mill. It will undoubtedly be interesting to tinker with.

Both roller mills and stone mills provide options for whole-grain and sifted flours. Whole-grain flour from a roller mill is generally reconstituted by adding the bran back into the endosperm. I use 10 to 20 percent whole-grain flour in my pizza crust, but what I really love to work with are sifted flours. A miller makes sifted flours by diverting flour through various-sized mesh screens to create beautiful flours that fall between white and whole wheat. These flours are designated with a number, such as T80 or T65. In general, the higher the number, the more bran and outer portions of the endosperm are present in the flour.

I was a flour purist before my twins were born, sourcing only freshly milled stone-ground flour. But these days if I want to bake, my experience needs to be convenient and predictable, so I blend flour from a stone mill and flour from a roller mill. I source my King Arthur flour in bulk at Costco, and once a month, I drive down a bumpy dirt road and pick up brown-paper sacks filled with freshly milled flour at a vegetable stand. Milled by local baker John Derry, this stuff is the staff of life.

If it's not obvious to you where to buy freshly milled or regional flour, start poking around a farmers' market or co-op near you. Joining organizations such as the Bread Baker's Guild of America, Common Grain Alliance, or Grow NYC Grains is also a great way to gain access to the vast network of bakers, farmers, and millers doing good work. You can, of course, find lovely stone-ground flour online **(see page 405 for resources)** as well, but that's a little like removing the germ from the flour: The social relationship is the most important aspect of sourcing local flour.

Make Your Own Sifted Flour

I really enjoy sifted, or "bolted," flours, which retain some portion of the bran and outer endosperm (and germ, if stone-milled). Here I've used the ash content of whole wheat (1 to 2 percent) and all-purpose (0.45 to 0.5 percent) flours to calculate mixes you can blend at home to approximate commercially made sifted flour. (You can also simply blend all-purpose and whole wheat flour in equal portions for a nice rustic flour!)

T85	Volume	Ingredient
30%	300 G	WHOLE WHEAT FLOUR
70%	700 G	ALL-PURPOSE FLOUR
	1 KG	

T75	Volume	Ingredient
20%	200 G	WHOLE WHEAT FLOUR
80%	800 G	ALL-PURPOSE FLOUR
	1 KG	

T65	Volume	Ingredient
10%	100 G	WHOLE WHEAT FLOUR
90%	900 G	ALL-PURPOSE FLOUR
	1 KG	

○ **WATER MAKES THE MAGIC HAPPEN /** When water is introduced to flour, the gliadins and glutenins, proteins found in the endosperm of the wheat berry that are inactive and tightly coiled when dry, become malleable, changing shape, unfolding, and bonding with one another, with water, and with oxygen. This network, or matrix, inside the dough is gluten. Gluten is magical in that it is both extensible and elastic.

○ **ASH IN FLOUR? /** The ash content of flour, which is technically an indicator of its mineral content, is determined by incinerating a sample of the flour at high heat. Once the organic matter has burned away, only the inorganic minerals remain. The ash is then weighed in relation to the weight of the flour sample and is expressed as a percentage. For example, if the flour sample weighed 100 g and the ash weighed 5 g, the ash content would be 5 percent (the weight of the ash divided by the weight of the original sample multiplied by 100). Flours with high ash will have a noticeable tan or golden hue, resulting in a darker pizza or bread. They also ferment quickly due to the higher mineral content and may require additional water to account for the water absorbed by the bran.

POWERFUL PROTEIN

The protein content of flour ranges from around 10 percent for delicate pastry flour to 11 to 12.7 percent for midrange all-purpose flour to 12.7 to 14 percent for high-gluten or bread flour. Often, the protein content of flour is expressed as a number on the flour bag, making it possible to quickly assume the best use of the flour. In general, the higher the number, the more elastic the dough will be, and the lower the number, the more fragile it will be. Yet the number printed on the bag tells only part of the story. The quality and balance of the proteins are ultimately more important than a static figure.

Proteins, long chains of molecules built from amino acids, vary in how they respond to hydration and strengthening. There are four types of proteins found in common, modern wheat: water-soluble albumins, salt-soluble globulins, alcohol-soluble prolamins (gliadins), and acid-soluble glutenins. For pizza and bread making, the most important groups are the gliadins and glutenins.

Glutenins are long chains of proteins with amino acids on each end. The acids can readily bond with other acids, yet they need oxygen to do so, which is why incorporating air as you mix will strengthen a dough. Gliadins are shorter protein chains, weakly bonding only with themselves and glutenins. They work to lubricate the glutenin coils, allowing the long chains to pass by one another without tangling, creating extensibility in a dough. If it weren't for gliadin, stretching a pizza dough would be like fighting a ball of rubber bands.

Too much elasticity or extensibility in a dough will cause problems, however: Unchecked elasticity will make a "bucky" dough that resists shaping, and excessive extensibility will make a dough that has difficulty holding any shape at all. The amount of gliadin and glutenin in any given flour stems from the variety of wheat.

The oldest wheats, einkorn, emmer, and spelt, are high in protein, which made them a valuable plant-based food source at the dawn of agriculture. Because these ancient grains don't fit easily into our modern classifications, they are typically discussed according to how many chromosomes they possess. Einkorn is a diploid with fourteen chromosomes, emmer is a tetraploid with twenty-eight chromosomes, and spelt, my favorite and the most modern of the lot, is a hexaploid, with the highest number of chromosomes at forty-two.

Besides chromosome count, bakers categorize wheat using six adjectives: hard and soft, red and white, and winter and spring. Hard wheats are high in protein and great for chewy baked goods like bagels. By contrast, soft wheats are great for making tender, creamy doughs with low volume, such as European-style hearth breads. Red wheats, which can be either hard or soft, are characterized by the ruby hue of their bran and can taste both bitter and nutty. White wheats, which can also be hard or soft, are mild and sweeter and are great for crackers, tortillas, and noodles. Winter wheats are planted in fall and harvested in the spring, and spring wheats are planted in the late spring and harvested in early autumn.

It's helpful to have a language to talk about wheat, to describe it as hard or soft, red or white, winter or spring. But these simple words fail to describe the complexity of flour and lead us to think of our most important ingredient in boxes, rather than in 3D. The care with which the grain was grown, the milling style, and the fermentation of the flour are just as critical to how the flour performs.

Lastly, the *quality* of the protein is more important than the quantity, and, in fact, we don't want a high-protein flour for pizza dough because then it would be a pain to stretch. Also, if the flour has a high level of protein but degrades quickly, it won't be suitable for a long, cold fermentation.

Slurry Test for Strength and Hydration

Hydration is the amount of water in a dough relative to the amount of flour, typically expressed as a percentage (a.k.a. baker's math). For example, 100 g flour and 70 g water equals 70 percent hydration (70/100 × 100 = 70). "High" hydration doughs—those with over 80 percent water—will produce a more open crumb, but pushed too far, the flour will ferment too quickly and fall apart. High hydration is necessary for some flours, such as whole wheat, where the bran soaks up much of the available water. To judge how much water a flour can handle, you can do this simple slurry test.

Mix 100 g of your flour sample and 80 g of water in a pint-size deli or similar container and evaluate how it feels. Is it relatively stiff? Is it somewhat dry? Or is it soupy and loose? Cover the container with a lid or kitchen towel and let it rest for an hour at room temperature.

Return to the slurry and check it again by pulling up a portion with a finger. Has it become smoother or more cohesive? Can it stretch easily without tearing? Does it feel like it could handle more water? Cover it again and let rest overnight.

Check the slurry one more time by pulling up a portion with a finger to gauge its strength. You will be able to stretch a strong, well-hydrated flour paper-thin, while a weaker flour will tear or shred. When you go to make pizza with the flour, if it held up to the test well, no alterations are necessary. However, if it fell apart, try reducing the amount of water or supplementing some of the flour with a high-protein flour, blending until you get the correct gluten development.

Heritage Wheats

Heritage wheats, with names like Turkey Red, Red Fife, and Rouge de Bourdeaux, are varieties that have been passed down from our great-grandparents to our grandparents in handfuls. They have survived due to the efforts of a few dedicated individuals and are enjoying time in the spotlight now as farmers, millers, and bakers seek out older varieties of wheat grown prior to modern plant breeding with its focus on yield. These heritage wheats evolve with each planting, with the best from each generation saved and replanted, cultivating a resilient food system.

Glorious Bubbles

The pockets of air trapped inside a dough by gluten are often talked about as being like tiny balloons, but the edge of the bubble is much more porous than the tight, impermeable wall of a balloon. If the gas bubbles really were like balloons, they couldn't travel through the dough, meet one another, and join forces, lifting the dough and opening the crumb together. Think of the gluten matrix in a dough as a tightly woven cloth with air moving through it not only by means of the gas produced by the yeast but also from the mechanical action of a stand mixer or the vigorous action of hand mixing through folding.

Shopping Around

The following chart is imperfect but gives you a good idea of how various flours may be interchanged. While we may find only all-purpose, bread, and whole wheat flour in domestic supermarkets, the baking aisle in France will have five or six different flour options—how fun!

Type of flour	United States (protein)	France (ash)	Italy (grind)
PASTRY	8% TO 9%	T45	TIPO 00
ALL-PURPOSE	9% TO 12%	T55	TIPO 0
BREAD	12% TO 14%	T80	TIPO 1
SIFTED WHOLE WHEAT	12% TO 13%	T110	TIPO 2
100% WHOLE WHEAT	13% TO 15%	T150	INTEGRALE

COMPARING FLOURS

Countries classify their flour differently, and the significant marker is not always the same. In the United States, flour is ranked according to protein levels. In France, flour is described by the ash content, denoted by the letter *T*. Italians rank flour according to the fineness of the grind, with tipo 00 being the most powdery. Sometimes there simply isn't an equivalent flour based on the type of wheat or the way it was milled, so when using a new flour, add water slowly and pay attention to how quickly the dough is fermenting. When I am testing a new flour, I always record in my baking journal how much water it took to get a pliable, supple consistency, how long it took to ferment before shaping, the proof time, and a description of the crumb so I can reference my observations later.

Are European flours better? I am regularly confronted by bread and pizza lovers who want to know why they find they can easily digest baguettes and pizzas all day long while in Europe but feel bloated when they eat the same way at home in the United States. Some of this is psychosomatic, but European wheat varietals are softer wheats with lower gluten and are grown without many of the pesticides, like Roundup, that are used freely in the United States. There may be no single answer to this question. Just remember, wherever you are in the world, always try to select bread and pizza made from good-quality, well-fermented flour.

SELECTING FLOUR

I encourage new pizza makers to start with roller-milled flour because it is predictable. That alone can make Saturday pizza night less stressful. But if you find you're interested in freshly milled regional flour, go ahead and dive in. Either way, use the same flour repeatedly so you can build knowledge of how the flour performs and gain the crucial muscle memory needed for shaping and stretching. Commit to flour you know you can find easily and that gets you excited to bake.

I use Italian 00 flour when I'm baking in a wood-fired oven or I want a treat at home. Also known as doppio zero, 00 flour is finely milled from medium-strength soft wheats. It has a powdery texture and crisp white color and bakes up into a classic-looking pizza with a golden crust. The fineness of a flour defines how much water it can absorb. The finer the flour, the less water it can accept. Dough made with 00 flour handles well between 60 and 68 percent hydration. The lower the hydration, the faster you want the pizza to bake. Otherwise, the pie will come out dry and leathery. That's why pizza made with 00 flour is baked at temperatures of around 900°F [480°C]. I like Caputo "00" Pizzeria Flour in the blue-and-white bags and King Arthur '00' Pizza Flour.

Unbleached and unbrominated all-purpose flour is my go-to for pizza dough. At 11 to 12 percent protein, it makes a dough that's enjoyable to stretch, with very little spring back, and rises nicely in the oven, with charred blisters and bubbles. I use all-purpose flour from both roller and stone mills.

Some of the dough recipes in this book call for a blend of all-purpose and bread flour. The bread flour increases the protein slightly, helping the dough maintain its structure while in the refrigerator for a long period. These doughs may need a little pause between stretches but are also somewhat indestructible, making them friendly to a beginner's hand.

High-extraction and sifted flours are beautiful for pizza. They ferment well due to the extra nutrition and enzymes, and they are so flavorful you can almost forgo toppings. Search for freshly milled stone-ground flours like a type 85 or 75. Having 15 to 25 percent of the largest flakes of bran removed means that the dough will still be toothy and robust but not so heavy that it won't spring on the hearth. I pair these types of flour with natural fermentation, using a levain to build acidity, elevating already complex flavors.

I want my pizza to taste and feel light and refreshing, so in general I don't go for bran-heavy flours. But this doesn't mean whole-grain flours have no place in pizza. Choose whole-grain flours made from soft wheats and skip those milled from hard red spring wheat. Spelt flour is my go-to flour for almost anything I want to bake with whole-grain flour. I use it for breads, cakes, cookies, and in my pizza dough. The "newest" of the ancient wheats, spelt has 14 percent protein and is incredibly extensible.

You'll also see rye flour in this book. It's another flour, like spelt, that I keep on hand, opting for freshly milled whole rye flour when I can. Rye flour is fluffy and can smell more like mushrooms or green tea than the crisp, hay-like aroma of wheat. Known for growing well in cold, rocky climates, it lacks the necessary balance of proteins needed to develop gluten, so while dough made from rye flour is not gluten-free, it can be better for those looking for flours that are gentle on their digestion. The aleurone layer extends farther into the endosperm of the rye berry, creating a flour that is rich in enzymes and minerals, which translates to quick (and flavorful) fermentation. Rye flour is used in this book in small amounts to kick-start sourdough starter and for pizza and focaccia doughs, imparting a unique savory umami flavor. I also use it in sweets, like the Rye Brownies **(page 395)** in the final chapter!

Yeast was first observed and described in the late 1600s by Dutch naturalist Antonie van Leeuwenhoek upon witnessing tiny cells moving under his microscope. It wasn't until the 1800s that French chemist Louis Pasteur linked yeast to the process of fermentation. ●

YEAST

Whether we are talking about baker's yeast cultivated in a lab or wild yeast perpetuated in a sourdough starter, the kind of yeast that ferments flour is called *Saccharomyces cerevisiae*, a single-celled fungus whose name translates to "sugar mold." Appropriately named, this microbe consumes the simple sugars that become available when flour is broken down and produces carbon monoxide and trace amounts of alcohol as a result.

Tiny Friends / Microbes, organisms too small to see with the naked eye, cover everything (yes, even this page), and their origin on the planet stretches back three billion years. Microbes helped to create the world we live in, they sustain our lives through breaking down organic matter, and they create 70 percent of the oxygen on our planet. We owe them thanks and praise!

COMMERCIAL YEAST

The yeast you purchase from the grocery store will be one of three main cultivated strains of the acid-tolerant, gas-producing *Saccharomyces cerevisiae*. Chosen for its ability to process maltose (the starchy sugar in flour) efficiently and rapidly, these microorganisms are responsible for producing the gases that raise dough. Commercial yeast, also known as baker's yeast, is propagated, harvested, dried, and packaged all within temperature-controlled, sterile environments to ensure the yeast variety is not contaminated.

Glance at the shelf in the baking aisle of most supermarkets and you'll see active dry, instant, and rapid-rise yeasts. Active dry yeast is the kind that your grandparents reached for, dissolving it in warm water with a pinch of sugar or a little honey before combining it with flour. It was the first dehydrated yeast, and the initial technology used to create it killed off a portion of the cells. Combining the granular dried yeast with warm water dissolved the unnecessary cells and activated the remaining yeast. Thanks to advancements in dehydration methods today, there are far fewer inactive cells in active dry yeast, and in most cases, you can simply add it right to the flour and mix.

As drying and dehydrating methods improved, instant yeast became available. Retaining more yeast cells, instant yeast could be added directly to the dough, with no proofing required. This is the kind of yeast I call for in the following recipes. I order Saf-instant The Original Red yeast online and keep it in the freezer in a sealed container labeled with the date. There is no need to warm up the yeast. It can be used directly from the freezer.

Rapid-rise yeast is a variation of instant yeast, and it gives one good, quick rise, but it isn't what you want for a dough that will require several rises or spend a long time in the fridge fermenting. If things move too fast, doughs can be hard to handle. Even with baker's yeast, time can be an ingredient.

FRESH YEAST

I've only ever encountered fresh, or cake, yeast in a commercial bakery setting, but you can sometimes find it, refrigerated, in supermarkets around the holidays. Cake yeast contains active, living yeast cells compressed into a block (20 to 30 percent moisture removed) that smells sweet and has the texture of a pencil eraser. It's perishable, lasting for about 2 weeks, while dry yeast can remain viable for up to 2 years.

Bakers use fresh yeast because it gives a slightly better and longer rise than dry yeast and imparts a sweet note to the final taste. You may either add it directly to the dough or proof it in warm water first. Should you choose to proof it, remember to subtract the water you use to proof the yeast from the water called for in the dough. To swap in fresh yeast for active dry or instant yeast in any of the dough recipes, multiply the dry yeast amount by 3 to get the weight you will need for the fresh yeast (for example, 12 g fresh yeast to every 4 g dry yeast).

How to Check Old Yeast / Not sure if your yeast is still good? Stir a little of it into some 100°F [38°C] water and wait for the telltale bubbles before using. The best way to ensure your yeast is functional is to store it in the freezer, buy only what you need, and bake often.

NATURAL YEAST

Wild yeast was cultivated and used for fermenting by brewers and bakers in ancient Egypt. Today, it is found in natural wines, beers, and in baked goods made with a sourdough starter—a batter-like mixture of flour and water that contains yeast and lactic acid bacteria. The yeast in a sourdough starter comes from the flour itself—even more so if there's a little bran involved—from the baker's hands, and from the environment in which the starter is maintained. Essentially, if it occurs spontaneously in nature, it's wild yeast.

Grains, just like grapes and cabbages, have an assortment of yeasts and lactic acid bacteria living on their skins. When a portion of bran is present in the flour you use to tend your sourdough starter, you may have a more diverse population of yeasts, finding a few more species than if you were to use only white flour. What these various yeasts eat and produce will vary, as will the temperature zones in which they flourish. Over time, as your starter acidifies, certain varieties of *Saccharomyces cerevisiae* will become dominant.

○ **LACTIC AND ACETIC ACIDS /** Lactic acid weakens a dough, which makes it easier to stretch. But too much lactic acid can cause problems, turning your starter or dough into a runny soup or a slack mess. Acetic acid causes the opposite effect, tightening. Too much acetic acid built up in a dough can make for a leathery and unpleasantly chewy texture. Proper fermentation will curb these undesired qualities, so take care of your starter: Feed it daily and keep it at room temperature.

LACTIC ACID BACTERIA

There are over one hundred species of lactic acid bacteria found on vegetables, in dairy products, on meat, and even in our stomachs. Like yeast, lactic acid bacteria thrive in warm conditions, and in bread and pizza dough, they consume the simple sugars, releasing lactic acid (and trace amounts of gas) into the dough. This process is used to flavor and preserve some of our most beloved foods: cheese, yogurt, kimchi, pickles, and, of course, pizza. The acid is a key preservative in fermented foods. By lowering the pH, the bread dough, kimchi, or yogurt becomes inhospitable to bad bacteria. Lactic acid will also break down gluten over time through producing the enzyme protease, making a dough soft and light.

Lactic acid bacteria (LAB) generally fall under two classifications, homofermentive and heterofermentive. Homofermentive LAB prefer warm temperatures of 86° to 95°F [30° to 35°C] and produce only lactic acid. Heterofermentive LAB like slightly cooler temperatures of 59° to 72°F [15° to 22°C] and produce lactic acid, acetic acid, ethanol, and trace amounts of carbon dioxide. If your practice is to keep your starter at room temperature, you will get more of the milky lactic acid flavor, and if you store it mostly at fridge temps, you will encourage a colony of heterofermentive LAB.

The most popular example of a heterofermentive LAB is *Lactobacillus sanfranciscensis*, the strain of LAB found in a tangy San Franciscan sourdough. The population of lactic acid bacteria you'll find in your starter will depend on the flour you use, the environment in which you maintain it, and the times and temperatures used in refreshing and fermenting.

8 CUPS 2 QTS.

Water is an important ingredient in pizza dough, so much so you'll see people travel with it, import it, or swear that it's what makes their dough superior. I get it. ●

WATER

I spent a few years teaching bread workshops in a remote setting using spring water that came directly out of the mountainside, and I've never had more lively bread. And yet I've also flown around the world, stopping in big cities, suburban towns, my parents' kitchen in Florida, and everywhere in between, using whatever water was available, and I've never had an issue with water that's too hard or soft to make a nice pizza. In short, you don't need to buy bottled water or stress too much about the water. Anything that you would drink is good enough for making dough.

What Does Water Do? / When water is added to flour, an incredible cascade of reactions begins. It makes the dough homogenous and malleable so the enzymes can start moving around and begin breaking down the complex starches and proteins. The gliadin and glutenin are able to start making connections, forming gluten, and the yeast and bacteria can begin to access sugars and start making gas and acids.

Salt seasons a dough, bringing out flavor, and works to slow down fermentation so it doesn't get out of hand. ●

SALT

Salt draws water away from the yeast that require it to metabolize sugars and reproduce, slowing down fermentation. Other available water in a dough is bound up with the proteins and starches in a weblike network of gluten. As the salt is worked into the dough, it pulls water away from the gluten matrix and the dough becomes taut. You'll know if you've forgotten the salt because your dough will be loose, will bubble right out of the tub, and will taste chalky.

Salt also makes the dough taste good! It's important to season dough just as you would any baked good or dish. I prefer to use sea salt. Diamond Crystal kosher salt, while excellent for cooking, is too coarse for dough unless it's dissolved first. I use two brands, Redman Real Salt fine sea salt and Celtic fine sea salt, both of which dissolve easily. The pizza, focaccia, and pita recipes in this book are all salted between 2 and 3 percent.

Finishing salts can add a nice dimension to a baked pizza or focaccia. Try flaky sea salt (such as Maldon brand), black Hawaiian, or various smoked salts. Consider the salinity of the toppings, cheese included, before you season further. Low-moisture and aged cheeses, such as Parmigiano-Reggiano, have a high salt content, so you may want to skip adding more as a finish if you've selected a salty cheese.

PREPPING FOR PIZZA

A clean kitchen bathed in afternoon light, with good music humming and a pile of fresh ingredients to wash, peel, and chop, is a sacred space. I love the rhythmic handwork and small tasks that pizza prep invites, and I prefer to do it solo, although it's also fun to have the whole family join in, tearing up basil leaves and shredding cheese. Delicate vegetables will degrade in the fridge, and shredding cheese too far in advance can cause it to clump, but you can do most of your pizza prep up to 4 days ahead of baking.

I shop for ingredients the weekend before, prepare the cheese and other toppings on Wednesday, make the sauce and levain on Thursday, mix and shape the dough on Friday, and bring everything out and bake my pizzas on Saturday. This workflow allows me to make midweek pan pizza or focaccia with leftover topping bits and leaves breathing room at the end of the week for spontaneity. Maybe I will whip up ranch dressing from scratch or take a day trip to a farm for an ultra-seasonal ingredient.

If possible, find a local farmers' market and make it a habit to select your toppings there. If you're stuck with the supermarket, you can still buy seasonally. Many grocery stores even have a local produce section. I work with what the grocery store does best: finding toppings that were *meant* to be shelf-stable, such as condiments, pickles, and other fermented foods.

Uncooked toppings need to be sliced thinly enough to cook in the 8 to 10 minutes that it takes for the crust to bake. I recommend using a mandoline to slice toppings that you might usually use a chef's knife to slice. This small, simple tool is my go-to, and I prepare everything with it: pepperoni and other meats, onions, potatoes, carrots, squash, peppers, fennel, and so on. I also use it to shave toppings to a thickness of two stacked quarters for adding to the pizza mid- or post-bake.

Tomato sauce, cheese, pepperoni—these toppings are what you think of when you think "pizza," and you'll want to keep them on hand.

TOPPING STAPLES

AS WITH EVERYTHING THAT GOES INTO PIZZA

QUALITY MATTERS

Hearty toppings will need care beyond just being properly cut. For example, gently roast mushrooms, winter squashes, beets, and potatoes, and wilt or quick sauté bitter greens, bacon, asparagus, leeks, and zucchini. You can also use the confit method for potatoes or garlic, cooking them in oil to tenderize them. (Save the oil for drizzling over the pizza when it's done.) If you have the time, toast any nuts that will go on your pizza or focaccia, as it will bring out their oils.

On the opposite end, delicate toppings that will burn or otherwise suffer in the intense oven heat, such as flower petals, fresh herbs, burrata cheese, and greens like arugula, should always be added after the pizza comes out of the oven.

How Thin Is Too Thin? / While toppings need to be sliced thinly enough to cook properly in a short amount of time, they also need to have enough moisture to prevent them from shriveling up in the oven. I pack radishes, carrots, red onions, and the like in water if they are sliced more than 48 hours in advance. Drain and pat dry before placing on your pizza. You can also make **Refrigerator Pickles (page 195)** for a crunchy, zippy twist.

CANNED TOMATOES

No matter where you live, it's hard to find good tomatoes year-round, so I make an uncooked pizza sauce with canned San Marzano tomatoes when tomatoes are out of season and a roasted sauce when juicy, flavorful tomatoes fill market bins. I prefer the uncooked sauce, but years of pizza parties have proven that most people go for the cooked sauce, which has a nostalgic pasta sauce flavor. Try both and decide for yourself.

San Marzano is the name for both a variety of tomato and a small area in the Campania region in southern Italy. San Marzano tomatoes are sought after for pizza because they are plump, sweet, and have fewer seeds than other varieties. Prized for its volcanic soils—said to enhance a balanced sweetness and acidity in the tomatoes—San Marzano has been granted protected designation of origin (PDO) status (in Italian, *denominazione di origine protetta*, or DOP), so if a can of tomatoes is truly from San Marzano, you'll see PDO or DOP on the label. Try a can if you never have but don't get hung up on this detail. A number of great domestic canned tomato brands are available, such as Bianco DiNapoli, which uses California-grown tomatoes (a project between pizza all-star Chris Bianco and farmer Rob DiNapoli) and San Merican. I mail order Bianco DiNapoli (biancodinapoli.com) and pick up San Merican tomatoes in the stores in my area.

MOZZARELLA

Mozzarella cheese is a fresh cheese made from either cow's milk or, more famously, water buffalo milk. The milk splits into curds when an acid, such as citric acid or vinegar, is added to it, and the proteins tangle together into a solid mass, leaving behind the whey. The curds are then shredded and salt and boiling water are added. This seasons and melts the curds, turning them into what looks like a giant melted marshmallow.

Through the process of kneading, or turning with a large, long wooden paddle, the curds reform as a stringy, stretchy material that is then made into various shapes, such as balls, knots, braids, and sometimes even little animals. Once the shapes are formed, the mozzarella can be enjoyed right away.

Grocery store "fresh" mozzarella will still be floral and milky, but it can also veer toward chalky, chewy, and firm, melting in globs rather than swirls. In contrast, artisanal mozzarella is tender, creamy, grassy, and salty, but it can also be so flowy it runs off the pizza! If you can find handmade fresh mozzarella where you live, buy it! If you can't, choose fresh cheese packed in water over presliced logs.

I use a combination of fresh mozzarella packed in water from the farmers' market and low-moisture mozzarella bought at the supermarket in blocks, which I then shred myself.

Try adding fresh mozzarella halfway through the bake or even post-bake. If the cheese is really tender, it will lose its integrity in the high heat of the oven. Burrata, an oval of fresh mozzarella with an interior of cream and stracciatella (small shreds, or "rags") is delicate and should always go on after the bake.

Low-moisture mozzarella is firm, releases little water as it cooks, and boasts a tangier, saltier flavor than its milky, creamy sibling. Low-moisture mozzarella is key to classic New York slices, as it releases its oil in the heat of the oven, creating tiny puddles of orange grease. Stay away from preshredded mozzarella, which is covered in chalky powder to prevent clumping. It can mute the flavor of the cheese.

Go with the Flow / The cheese you select for topping your pizza will flow—or melt—in a certain way depending on its fat content and moisture level. Hard cheeses don't spread much, while softer cheeses can ooze everywhere. To control how the cheese melts, drain and blot any cheese packed in water or brine, alternate between the cheese and the sauce as you build the pizza, putting the cheese down first and then the sauce, and, finally, if using a particularly moist, fresh, delicate, or fatty cheese, add it mid-bake or after the pizza comes out of the oven.

OTHER CHEESES

I grate Parmesan on almost all my pizzas after they come out of the oven. Parmesan, a golden-hued aged cheese made from cow's milk, adds a salty, nutty flavor to each bite. Pecorino romano, another hard cheese, is made from sheep's milk in Italy, while domestic versions are crafted from cow's milk. Also known simply as romano, it has a beautiful straw color and a rich, salty intensity.

Made from the milk of cows, goats, sheep, or water buffalo, ricotta is a fresh cheese fashioned from the whey (the watery portion and tiny bits of curd that remain after the cheese solids have been removed) left over from making other cheeses. The whey is heated, an acid is added and sometimes also a little whole milk or cream, resulting in curds. The curds are drained, leaving behind ricotta. Supermarket ricotta is generally made from cow's milk and comes in two versions, part-skim and whole milk. I prefer whole-milk ricotta for its intense floral sweetness and rich creaminess.

Made from cow's milk, domestic fontina is buttery, pungent, and tastes ultra nutty. It boasts a 45 percent fat content and a strong, savory flavor, and I pair it with fall and winter flavors like figs and charred Brussels sprouts. It is a great melting cheese with a medium flow, making it ideal for pairing with fresh mozzarella.

Sliced American cheese, an emulsified blend of Cheddar, Colby, and Jack cheeses, is in my house because my children love it. One day when I was out of mozzarella, I grabbed American cheese for a pan pizza and have never looked back. It melts into a beautiful blanket, and, honestly, it's kind of perfect. You could also try sliced provolone or Swiss. To adjust for the fat content, add sliced cheese halfway through the bake to avoid burnt spots.

Get creative with your cheese selections and use up odds and ends. You don't need to stick to traditional mozzarella. When I make pizza on the fly, I'll often end up using pulled-apart string cheese and dollops of cottage cheese. I've even used a little sour cream and Parmesan for a white sauce when I don't have **Crème Fraîche (page 188)** on hand.

PEPPERONI

I love a good pepperoni pizza, and I use both flat and cupping pepperoni. Cupping pepperoni curls up into a little goblet of grease with crispy, singed edges, resulting in a bacon-like crunch with every bite. The puckering is caused by several factors: the casing material, the thickness of the individual slices, and the direction of the heat in the oven.

Pepperoni is sold in either a natural casing, like pig intestine, or a fibrous casing made from paper. A natural casing is thick and resists expansion, so when it is stuffed, the sausage meat is driven down the middle and up the sides to form a U shape. A paper-like fibrous casing relaxes when it is stuffed, so the meat is more uniformly shaped inside, unfolding flat on the pizza. While a natural casing is completely edible, you need to peel off

and discard a fibrous casing. Brands like the Ezzo Sausage Company, based in Ohio, make both kinds of pepperoni, natural casing and fibrous casing. To top your pizza with cupping pepperoni, make sure you purchase pepperoni with a natural casing, slice it thin to medium thick—about ⅛ in [4 mm]—and use the broiler at the end of the bake to encourage the edges to curl.

OTHER MEATS

Some meats, such as bacon, are precooked before going onto a pizza. I cook bacon about 80 percent of the way to done, so that it finishes off on top of the pizza. (See cooking instructions to the right.) Then I pop it onto the pizza, where it finishes cooking and crisps. Raw sausage can go either way, depending on how much is used, how long the pizza will bake, and how you build the pizza. If used sparingly (not in the style of a "supreme" topping) in dime-size bits, raw sausage will fully cook during the bake. If you plan to cover it with cheese or will be baking in a high-heat oven, precook the sausage. Most smoked and cured meats don't need to be precooked.

Cooking Bacon / Preheat the oven to 400°F [200°C], line a sheet pan with parchment paper, and top a plate with a paper towel. Arrange the bacon strips in a single layer on the sheet pan, making sure they don't overlap. Bake the bacon for 8 to 10 minutes, rotating the pan halfway through. Watch for the bacon to curl and turn crispy just on the edges. Thicker bacon slices will need the full time, while thinner slices may need less. Use tongs to transfer the bacon to the towel-lined plate, then let cool. Using your hands, crumble the cooled bacon into various shapes and sizes, dropping them onto a clean plate or into a small bowl. Set aside until needed. The bacon can be cooked up to 2 days in advance and stored in an airtight container in the fridge. Bring to room temperature before adding to the pizza.

VEGETABLES

Anything goes in the vegetable world, if prepared well. I began hosting pizza nights while I was also organic farming, and I'd bring home crates of misshapen carrots, peppers with a rotten tip, tomatoes with a bruised shoulder. They all went on pizzas. Practicing vegetable-forward pizzas was both a personal commitment to eating seasonally and economical for my bakery. If getting to a farmers' market is hard for you, look for roadside produce stands. Several farms in my area have self-serve stores open daily with an honor system for payment. I live by these alternatives to the supermarket.

Pizza Salad / I always prep a little more than I will need to top a pizza, such as an extra sliced tomato, a few more chunks of roasted squash, or one more fried eggplant, and then I toss these extras into a salad after pizza night. My favorite combination is banana peppers, pepperoni, shredded mozzarella, olive oil, and mixed greens. You can also mix up a huge bowl of leafy greens to have out at your pizza party and invite guests to mix in toppings.

EGGS

Eggs on pizza are delicious but precarious. They can slosh off, and you don't get to taste the yolk and the white together. I've adopted pizza guru Anthony Falco's method of using squeeze bottles to squirt the egg in a lattice pattern over the top of a baked pizza just pulled from the oven. I separate the whites and yolks, whisk them each with a little salt, and keep them in squeeze bottles, refrigerated, for up to 3 days before using.

OLIVE OIL

I use olive oil in dough and as a garnish. The olive variety, when the olives are harvested, how the oil is extracted, and how the oil is processed all play an important role in the quality and taste of the final oil. Made by milling olives into a paste, olive oil is extracted by layering the mash between stones, then pressing the stones together. As the olive mash is crushed, the oil is released, making its way out from between the stones and down into a collection system. A modern version of the same task sends the mash through a centrifuge, extracting the oil through high-speed spinning.

Extra-virgin olive is made from the first cold pressing. Cold pressing olives, just like cold milling flour, preserves the integrity of the oil—its flavor and nutrients. The oil is tasted by professionally trained tasters for any impurities and then graded. Extra-virgin olive oil can taste grassy, buttery, peppery, fruity, floral, or pungent. The steps necessary to certify the oil as extra virgin, along with the process itself, often make extra-virgin oil an expensive choice.

Once pressed, the oil faces labeling regulations that differ depending on where the oil was made. To find extra-virgin oil worth spending your money on, look for a darkly tinted glass bottle or a tin that includes the date when the olives were harvested and/or the oil was pressed and the best-by date. Olive oil is a perishable product and should be used within a year of its creation. This is part of the joy of olive oil, and while it is special, it should be enjoyed every day.

Tasting Olive Oil / Pour a tablespoon or two of olive oil into a stemless wineglass or similar glass, cup your hand around it, and rub the bottom or sides of the glass to gently heat the oil. This will release the fragrance. Swirl the oil in the glass and watch how it cascades down the inside wall. Next, breathe in the oil for your first "taste," then huff the oil, inhaling deeply with your nose over the glass. Now, with both your nose and mouth (open), you might start to taste the oil on your tongue. Slurp a bit of the oil as if it were soup, purposefully incorporating some air into your mouth. Swirl the oil around your mouth and then swallow it, making note of how much it tickled—or burned—your throat. What did you taste and how did it feel? Rinse your mouth with water and move on to the next oil. After sampling each oil, have fun taking notes and encouraging friends to join you!

EVERYTHIN
WANTED TO
SOURDOUGH

G YOU EVER
NOW ABOUT
AND ABOUT

MIXING, SHAPI

PERFECTLY P

IN WOOD-FIRE

AND HOME OVENS

G, AND BAKING
LOWY PIZZA

THIS NEXT SECTION is an informative walk through the nuts and bolts of a recipe, or formula as bakers call it, and a comprehensive look at the overall process of making pizza that you can refer back to when you need more detail or guidance than a recipe includes.

I'll also share tips and tricks I use to manage the dough, such as creating a dough proofer **(see page 88)** and using a wine cooler to slow fermentation **(see page 30)**, and how I like to bake my pizzas in both my kitchen oven and in a blazing outdoor wood-fired one.

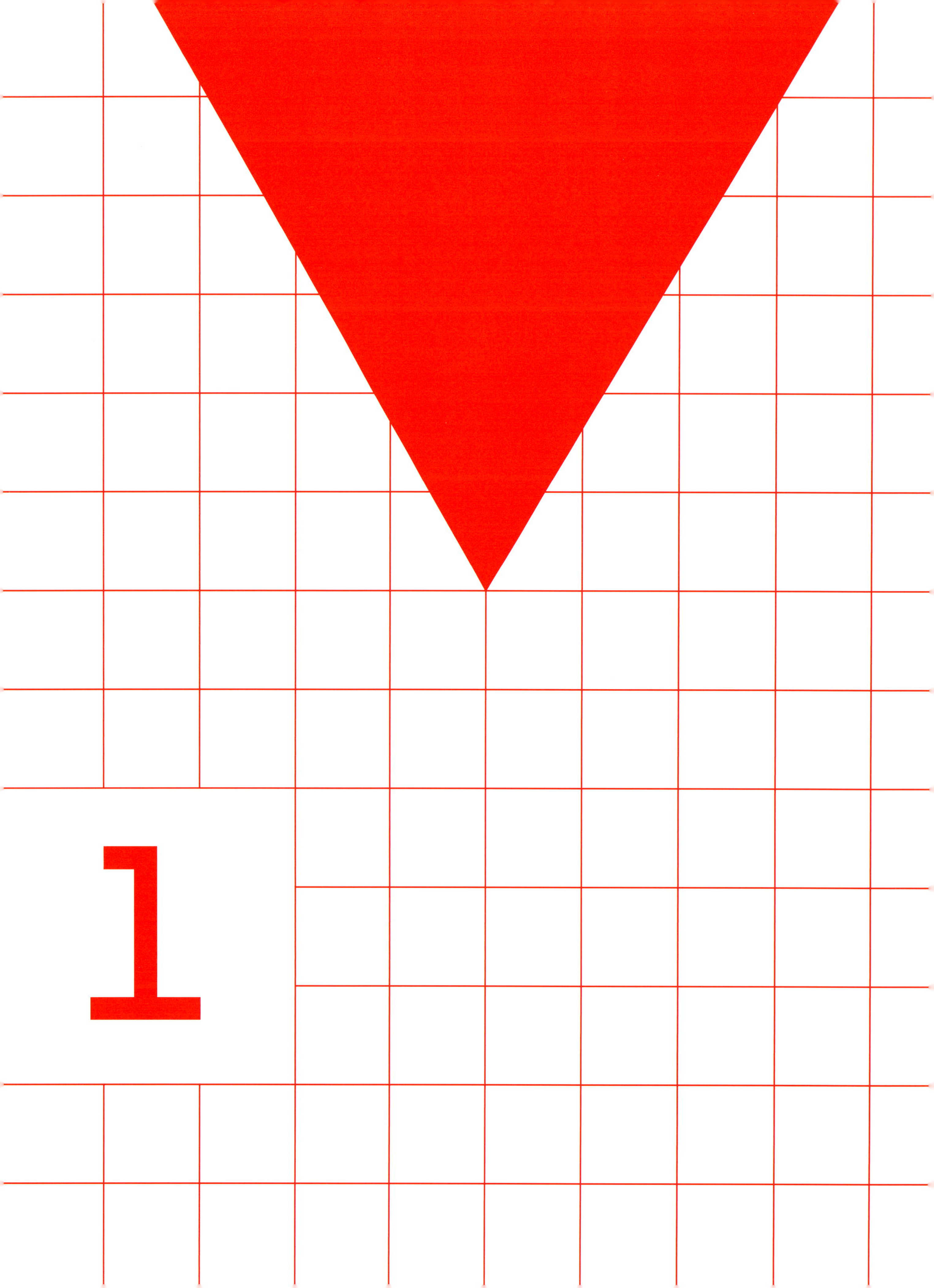
1

The beginning is when you will need to invest the most time in your pizza making. That's when you are developing muscle memory and becoming familiar with all the various ingredients.

Once you have learned one dough well, you can take pauses in pizza making and still retain the skill. At the start, commit and practice seriously. You can even write it on the calender and set a reminder on your phone. If you can carve out the time, then the rest is easy!

Weighing for Success

Weighing ingredients is crucial for consistency and precision in baking. Pounds and grams measure weight and cups and liters measure volume. If you are working with a solid such as flour and you use a cup, the measure will be slightly different every time you scoop. This fluctuation can result in dry and crumbly doughs, among other problems, which is why I use weight rather than volume for baking.

All the recipes in this book call for ingredients by weight as the primary measurement. I prefer the kilograms and grams of the metric system over the pounds and ounces of the British imperial or US customary system because they retain accuracy to very small amounts and work well for increasing or decreasing a recipe with ease. I use **both a gram scale and a milligram scale (see page 28)**, and if you don't have them, I encourage you to get them. They are relatively inexpensive, and you will use them constantly.

I have included volume measures as a secondary choice in all the recipes. If you look closely at my volume measures, you'll notice that their equivalents with weighed measures vary across recipes. This is intentional and was done to make it easier for bakers who are more comfortable using cups and spoons. But again, just use a scale.

SPOON-AND-SWEEP METHOD / If you must use volume measures, there is a method to the madness. First, transfer the flour from a bag to a large airtight container. Next, fluff up the flour with a whisk or a few stirs of a spoon. Spoon the flour into the cup until the flour is mounded in the middle and almost spilling over the sides. Using the spine (straight back edge) of a knife, level off the flour by sweeping the knife across the top of the cup. (You may need to do a few sweeps.) Never pack down the flour or shake the cup, as this will compact it, and you'll end up with more flour in the dough than is called for.

WHAT IS A CUP OF FLOUR? / Roller-milled flour made from commodity wheat is milled and blended to prescribed specifications, with interchangeable standards from mill to mill that specify 1 cup flour (bread or all purpose) weighs 140 g. This formula breaks down when applied to stoneground flour or regional flours, where differences in flour from mill to mill are not only expected but celebrated as part of local diversity. The stones, the grind, and the grain will all vary, making a standard cup weight almost impossible.

USING A DIGITAL SCALE

Most scales have an on and off button, a tare button, and can switch between pounds, ounces, grams, and kilograms. I prefer a scale with a weighing platform that sits above the body, rather than a flat scale, so I can easily see the number quickly. To use a digital scale, place your bowl, dough box, or other vessel on the scale, set the scale to grams, and press the tare button. Once you're looking at a zero, you can add your first ingredient. Tare after each ingredient and finish using the scale according to the recipe's instructions.

Baking by feel will never go out of style: It's the mark of a well-practiced baker. When you've practiced enough, you'll calibrate your hands to your ingredients, and you won't need to rely on exact grams. You'll know by touch what little adjustments to make along the way. It's quite magical to mix a dough with nothing but a bowl and your body, like a true artisan. But just like any artistic endeavor, it takes a lot of practice to get there. Bake regularly and you will be well on your way.

How to Read a Formula

In a typical recipe, the ingredients are listed in their order of use. This is not true in the formula for a dough, where ingredients appear according to percentages. The percentages descend from the largest to the smallest, and the ingredients are listed the same way, regardless of where they are in the timeline of the dough. You will encounter formulas in which a flour percentage defies this statement, putting 20 percent spelt above 70 percent water, but that is because the flour blend, when added together, equals 100 percent. For doughs that have preferments, such as an overnight levain, you'll see more than one formula, with the preferment listed before the dough. With just a glance, you'll be able to see the overall weight of the dough, the baker's percentages, and the DDT, or desired dough temperature.

BAKER'S MATH

Baker's math is a set of equations and guidelines bakers use to write formulas for doughs. In this system, the flour weight is treated as 100 percent and all other ingredients are expressed as a percentage of the flour weight. For example, if the flour is 100 g and the water is 50 g, the flour would be 100 percent and the water would be 50 percent. The total percentage for a recipe will exceed 100 percent. This is normal in baker's math. Look at the formula that follows to see how it works.

Yeasted Pizza Dough

DDT 80°F [27°C]

Baker's Percentage	Weight	Volume	Ingredient
100%	282 G	2¼ CUPS	ALL-PURPOSE FLOUR (11% TO 12% PROTEIN)
75%	212 G	¾ CUP + 2 TBSP	WATER, WARM
2%	6 G	1 TSP	SALT
0.25%	0.7 G	¼ TSP	INSTANT YEAST

All ingredients are measured by weight for accuracy. Volume is secondary.

- Flour is 100%. All other ingredients are expressed as a percentage of the flour weight.

↳ When added together, the total exceeds 100 percent. THIS IS NOT A MISTAKE!

* TO CALCULATE THE WEIGHT OF THE FLOUR:
  - ↳ DECIDE HOW MUCH DOUGH YOU WANT (ex: 500g)
  - ↳ CALCULATE THE TOTAL PERCENT (ex: 177%)
  - ↳ DIVIDE THE TOTAL DOUGH WEIGHT BY THE (500/177) TOTAL PERCENTAGE, THEN MULTIPLY THE (2.8 × 100) ANSWER BY 100 * TO MOVE THE DECIMAL OVER TWO PLACES * THE RESULT IS THE FLOUR WEIGHT ~ (282g flour)

CALCULATE THE WEIGHT OF THE other ingredients by placing a decimal in front of the percentage and multiply by the flour weight.

* (e.g., 75 percent beomes 0.75) (.75 × 282 = 211g)

↑ WATER ... WATER WEIGHT ↗

- If you only have the weight of the ingredient, divide the weight by the flour weight to arrive at the percentage, then × 100.

(e.g., 375 / 500 = 0.75 × 100 = 75%)

375 = water, 500 = flour

INGREDIENT PARAMETERS FOR PIZZA DOUGH

Every type of dough—pizza dough, bread dough, brioche, whatever it may be—has certain parameters for each ingredient. These parameters make the dough successful and identifiable. For example, too much water and a dough may fail to rise properly or will lose the qualities and characteristics that make it identifiable as a specific kind of dough. These somewhat flexible boundaries are expressed as ranges in percentage in a formula or recipe.

Many doughs have almost universal percentages. It's what makes a language within baking, so we can say "pizza dough" and you know it will be different than, say, "baguette dough." Pizza dough intended to be stretched into a round and baked at high temperatures needs to be extensible and hydrated properly.

In general, you will find these percentages when comparing pizza formulas. This doesn't mean there aren't outliers, but this is a good place to start if you're interested in crafting your own formula from scratch.

WATER	between 60 and 72 percent
SALT	between 2 and 2.2 or even 3 percent
YEAST	between 0.25 and 3 percent
LEVAIN (if used)	between 10 and 20 percent

Percentages are also part of the creative expression of the baker: They tell you key information about the quality of the dough, how long it will rise, and what the final crust will taste and feel like. With familiarity, you'll get a good picture of the dough with just a quick look.

I am often asked why percentages vary from formula to formula and baker to baker, particularly when it comes to how much levain or sourdough is called for. You'd really need to look at the formula to answer this. Is the dough with a small amount of levain fermented for several days, while the dough with a high percentage is baked the same day? Often the answer has to do with factors such as how long the dough will rise and the final flavor or texture the baker is after. It's not arbitrary, even though it can seem so because it varies so greatly among doughs.

Preferments

Pizza doughs can be either a yeasted straight dough, mixed all at once, or they can be mixed in stages using preferments. A preferment is a portion of the final dough that is mixed and fermented ahead of time. There are several styles of preferment, from the Italian biga to the French poolish, and they each impart their own characteristics to the final dough. I use yeasted poolishes and sponges for strength and extensibility and levains made from a sourdough starter for complex and nuanced flavor. A key benefit to using a preferment is shortening the window of bulk fermentation time without compromising the overall fermentation.

P.F.F.

The amount of flour used in the preferment is noted in a formula as prefermented flour, or "p.f.f." Bakers will look for this information because it helps them gauge how much time they will need for bulk fermenting and how long the dough will hold up in the fridge. A dough with a small portion of p.f.f.—below 12 percent—can need 5 to 6 hours before it's ready to divide and can hold up shaped in the fridge for up to 72 hours. A dough with a high p.f.f.—over 20 to 25 percent—will possibly be ready to shape within an hour. Dough with a high p.f.f., like the **Double-Levain Pizza Dough on page 166** with 40 percent p.f.f., can hold up to 24 hours, but once the acidity takes over, the dough will quickly degrade.

A sponge is made with flour, water, and a tiny portion of instant yeast. It kick-starts fermentation and can be ready in as little as 3 hours or fermented for up to 6 hours. I use 80 percent water to 100 percent flour in my sponges, but the water amount can go up or down based on a baker's preference. The more water, the faster the fermentation, so if you want to slow things down, use a sponge with 50 to 60 percent hydration relative to the flour weight. Sponges are a great way to develop more flavor in a dough while also encouraging the yeast to flourish, resulting in a light and tender crumb.

A poolish is created with equal parts flour and water and a pinch of commercial yeast. You'll find it's called for in many French doughs (most popularly the baguette), and it's a handy preferment to familiarize yourself with simply because it's a quick batter to mix up with profound effects on the final dough. (Read: minimal effort but big payoff. Sounds good—am I right?) As I mentioned earlier, commercial yeast is cultivated to burn big and burn bright, so a poolish, while being a preferment, can be ready in as little as 4 hours, or the fermentation can be extended up to 12 hours. Milder than sourdough, poolish gives a signature "nutty" taste to a dough.

LEVAIN

Levain *[la-vhon]* is a preferment made with a small portion of sourdough starter, which is then fed flour and water to scale it up for the task ahead: leavening your dough. Think of it as an "offshoot" of your starter, or of the way you propagate a new plant from a clipping. Once the levain is made, it is used entirely in the dough; none remains or is perpetuated. While it has essentially the same composition as a starter, a levain allows you to keep a small amount of starter on hand, so there's less waste. A levain is also a good way to experiment with various flours and hydration levels without disturbing your precious, predictable starter.

FLOUR FERMENTATION

In yeasted doughs, the flour is fermented solely by baker's yeast, which consumes simple sugars and produces gas and alcohol. Doughs made with levains contain both yeast and lactic acid bacteria, which make the process more complex. Lactic acid bacteria predigest the sugars and turn the dough into a probiotic food, something you don't get when using only baker's yeast. They also acidify the dough the way a yogurt or cheese is cultured and impart a tangy flavor to the final crust or slice.

If we pull back the curtain, enzymes are truly the heroes of fermentation. An enzyme is a large molecule, typically a protein, that speeds up a reaction, reducing barriers and making the transformation happen efficiently. Amylase deconstructs starches by breaking the chain between two sugar rings, releasing maltose. This process sweetens the dough, encourages browning, and increases volume by providing more available food to the yeast. Protease works on proteins by cleaving peptide bonds, which are the bonds that hold the amino acids together, through a process called hydrolysis. As the gluten network is unknit, the dough becomes softer (more malleable), slack, and relaxed. Better volume is achieved because the dough is less resistant to rising, and the interior is tender, having some of the chewiness reduced.

As you work through the doughs in this book, you'll notice each one has its own time frame for rising and proofing. That's because fermentation isn't linear. The speed at which a dough ferments depends on such factors as the amount of prefermented flour, the amount and temperature of the water, and the type of flour being used. Let's look at how to start and maintain a sourdough starter to make a levain, my preferred way of fermenting pizza dough.

Starting a Sourdough Starter

A sourdough starter is a demanding pet that you will need to pamper, starting with the container it lives in. You'll want something with enough room for the starter to double in size but not so big that it loses heat. It is ideally made from a material like glass, which will insulate the starter and keep it cozy, and the walls of the container should be clear so you can easily observe the growth. For these reasons, Weck and Ball jars are two popular choices.

I keep my starter in a quart-size deli container made from food-grade, BPA-free plastic. With so many kids underfoot, I like that it's relatively indestructible, and I use these deli containers for other things, too, like pizza toppings. Although strong acids can break down plastic over time, I don't find this a compelling reason to make the switch to glass. I transfer a small portion of starter to a clean container every morning and discard the rest in my compost. Whatever you choose to keep your starter in, be sure it is easy to clean and you have a second one on hand so you can start each feeding with a clean vessel.

A starter made from scratch should be ready to use in 7 to 10 days, but it would not be unreasonable if it took up to 14 days to rise and fall *predictably* and take on a floral, creamy essence. When you begin a starter, it takes 4 or 5 days for the mixture to acidify, killing off unwanted bacteria and creating the conditions for the lactic acid bacteria to flourish. This is when the batter-like mixture truly becomes a starter—not on day one or day two but late into that first week. Have patience because cultivating the ability to wait will serve you well as a baker.

SAY HELLO TO YOUR STARTER

Day 1

Mix 25 g bread flour and 25 g rye flour [2 Tbsp plus 2 tsp bread flour and ¼ cup rye flour] and 50 g [3 Tbsp] warm water (80°F [27°C]) in your chosen starter container. Stir vigorously with a spoon or chopstick until no dry flour is visible. At this point, the starter will resemble a very small portion of dough. Cover the container with a lid. You can fully close it, as you want the starter to stay warm. If the lid is plastic, it will expand a little if gases build up, or it might even burp itself. If you have a screw-on lid, give it just a few turns so accumulated gases can pass through while the starter stays cozy. You don't want to cover the container with just a kitchen towel because the starter will lose heat and the surface may dry out. Place a rubber band around the exterior of the container at the height of the starter. You'll use this band later to assess if your starter has risen, and if so, how much. Leave the starter at room temperature (68° to 72°F [20° to 22°C]) for 24 hours.

Day 2

It's common to see a burst of activity within the first 24 hours, but don't be fooled. This isn't the kind of stable and predictable rise and fall that will become characteristic of your starter. Check the rise and aeration: Did it surpass the rubber band and does it have any bubbles? Regardless, you will now begin daily refreshments for the rest of the life of the starter.

To refresh your starter, portion out 10 g [2 tsp] of starter into a clean container and add 50 g [5½ Tbsp] bread flour and 50 g [3 Tbsp] warm water. This will give you 110 g [½ cup] to work with. (Discard the rest.) Once your starter is established, you can scale this back even more, keeping less on hand to reduce discard. In the beginning, you want things to be thriving, so more is better. Cover tightly and leave at room temperature (68° to 72°F [20° to 22°C]) for 24 hours.

Day 3

Be prepared to see a dip in the activity of your starter. This is normal as the pH in the starter drops. Some of the bacteria making the initial fermentation (read: bubbles) won't survive moving forward, but the acid-tolerant yeast and lactic acid bacteria will.

Day 4 to Day 7

Congratulations!

Continue to refresh once a day until the starter is *at least* doubling in size within 4 to 5 hours after feeding and has a pleasant, yogurt-like aroma. These are both signs that your starter is now ready for long-term maintenance and will be strong enough to create levains to bake with.

If you're not seeing dish soap–size bubbles, the starter isn't doubling in size within a morning or afternoon, and it tastes chalky rather than slightly tangy, sorry, but you need to start over!

Do I Have to Discard? / Discarding is essential. It provides fresh food and water for the yeast and bacteria and balances the acidity. But don't despair. If you dislike waste, once your starter is established and healthy, you can collect the discard in a separate container, store it in the fridge, and use it within the week just as you would your starter. If you are feeling wasteful, remember there's no discard in a bakery or pizza shop. It just goes into the next levain or batch of dough. The discard phenomenon is a struggle only home bakers face, and there's no way around it—unless you turn your home into a bakery!

Starter Maintenance

A starter fed daily and kept at ambient room temperature will have a fundamentally different colony of lactic acid bacteria than a starter that is fed weekly or infrequently and kept in the fridge between uses. Because I want to select for the lactic acid bacteria most likely to be in a bakery or pizza kitchen (the most efficient and complex ones) where the starter is never refrigerated, I've moved away from storing my starter in the fridge and instead keep it at ambient room temperature, always above 55°F [13°C]. I maintain a small amount of starter, so the discard is minimal and doesn't deplete my flour bins. (I discard about 280 g [10 oz] per week, which amounts to 140 g [1 cup] of flour—not too awful!) I find there is less waste this way than when I kept it in the fridge and refreshed it several times at the end of the week for a weekend bake.

Consider the way a sourdough, or natural leavening, is tended in a bakery versus at home. The starter in the bakery is in continuous fermentation—refreshed once a day, possibly even twice, and likely never refrigerated. This means that even if you are diligent about feeding your starter once a week, it will certainly be decent, but it will never have the same flavors or activity that you'll find in a pizzeria or bakery because it is generally cold, and hence, the bacteria that prefer colder temperatures will dominate.

○ **WHY RYE? /** I call for a dose of rye flour on the first day of your starter's life because rye flour has more available sugars than wheat flour and because it's richer in enzymes, which speed up fermentation. If you don't have rye flour on hand or don't want to buy some for just one day (you can use the extra to make the **10 Percent Rye Pizza Dough** **on page 162**), you can either swap it out for whole wheat or spelt flour or skip it altogether and use all bread flour.

The common refrigerator temperature is 38° to 42°F [3° to 6°C], which is well below the climate preferred by the microbes in your starter. The yeast (*Saccharomyces cerevisiae*) ferments sugars efficiently between 82° and 91°F [28° and 32°C], and the lactic acid bacteria do the same between 86° and 104°F [30° and 40°C]. When your starter goes into the fridge, a portion of yeast and bacteria dies off. This means that not only are you diminishing the microbes you're trying so diligently to cultivate, you're also starting out each bake with a slightly different population.

Cold temperatures also result in unwanted acidity. The pH level influences the microbial composition and health of your starter. Baker's yeast prefers 4.5 to 6.0 pH, and lactobacilli are comfortable between 5.8 and 6.0 pH. When a starter goes into the fridge, the acidity builds up, dropping the pH unfavorably low. When your starter is properly refreshed, keeping it on the countertop will balance the pH, and you'll always have a milky, floral, pleasant aroma and flavor.

I refresh my starter every day with my first cup of coffee. It's a ritual I look forward to. Refreshing it early each morning means it will be ready in 2 to 3 hours, one of the benefits of continuous fermentation. The way you refresh your starter is essentially the same as the first week, but because you are now moving into maintenance mode and want to curb any waste, you'll shrink the total amount of your starter from 110 g [⅓ cup + 2 Tbsp] to 45 g [3 Tbsp]. Portion out 5 g [1 tsp] of starter into a clean container, add 40 g [¼ cup] bread flour and 40 g [2½ Tbsp] warm water, and stir vigorously, then cover with a lid.

If possible, keep the starter around 78° to 80°F [26° to 27°C] when you've finished mixing. If nothing is done to keep it warm, it will acclimate to the temperature of your kitchen. I keep my starter out during the day at room temperature, then transfer it to my Sourdough Home set at 55°F [13°C] for an overnight rest. Keep a notepad near your starter and jot down when it's ready each day so you can get a sense of how long it takes to peak in your kitchen.

If you don't have temperature control, like a wine cooler or a Sourdough Home, when the weather turns warm, you may need to refresh your starter every 12 hours rather than every 24 hours. If you live in a hot climate, you may need to do this year-round. You could choose to store the starter in the fridge for part of the day or overnight to reduce activity. (My concern with starter in the fridge is more when the fridge is the permanent home, rather than when it's used in hot months to avoid feeding twice a day.) If you find your starter is constantly going past its peak, collapsing, and needing to be fed more than once every 24 hours, stiffen it up by reducing the water to 70 to 75 percent.

Phases of Natural Fermentation

Fermentation happens in waves, and it accelerates to a fever pitch as time and temperature increase. The initial period of development, called lag time, runs from the moment you refresh your starter to the time it takes for the yeast and bacteria to begin to multiply. This is why you won't see much activity right after you feed your starter: reactions are just getting going.

The growth phase is when things take off: Yeast and bacteria reproduce exponentially (two split to make four and four make sixteen), so once reproduction begins, you'll see a huge uptick in activity. The lactic acid bacteria are slower to get going, the yeast cells begin reproducing first, but in the end, the bacteria win out over the yeast (about one yeast cell for every one hundred cells of lactic acid bacteria), and the mixture becomes acidified. The height of the reproductive phase is the peak of the starter. Using the starter at this juncture reduces the lag time in the levain, and using the levain at its peak reduces the lag time in the final dough.

The stationary phase occurs when the yeast and bacteria are still multiplying, but just as many are also dying off, creating a moment of stasis. This can extend for some time. When there is no more available food, and the starter is heavily polluted with acids, both the yeast and bacteria die off. This is when the starter will cave in, recede down the walls of the container, and flatten or fizzle out. Refreshment needs to happen for any further fermentation.

○ **BOOSTER FEEDING /** If your levain has gone past its peak—it has a dimple or dent in the middle, has started to collapse in on itself, or has turned loose and fizzy—you can do a quick booster feeding. A booster levain is made with the original levain, flour, and warm water in equal amounts. Because of the high ratio of levain, the booster is ready within 1 to 2 hours when kept at a warm room temperature of 72° to 78°F [22° to 26°C], a shorter time frame than if you were to simply refresh the levain with the original percentages.

○ **BAKER'S MISE EN PLACE /** Weighing out all your ingredients the night before you plan to mix reduces the chance of making mistakes and allows you to mix efficiently early in the day. I read the recipe and weigh everything out into deli containers, including the flour for the levain, a day ahead, leaving just the water to deal with before mixing.

CUSTOMIZING A LEVAIN

While the recipes in this book will tell you exactly how to make the called-for levain, if you're writing your own formula you have the option to customize your levain. I make three types of levain: a stiff one (less water than flour) that ferments overnight (8 to 12 hours) and is used first thing in the morning; a levain with equal parts flour and water that is ready in 2 to 3 hours, which I mix at breakfast and use around lunch; or a booster levain, which is equal parts levain, flour, and water.

TIMING STARTER AND LEVAIN

In all aspects of dough fermentation, you need to wait until the phase you're in is at its maximum potential before you move forward. For this reason, avoid using a just-refreshed starter to make a levain. Immediately after a starter has been fed, the yeast and bacteria are diluted and need time to repopulate. It takes my starter 2 to 3 hours to be ready (doubled in size, covered in big bubbles, and smells floral), and it stays ready to use—in a state of stasis—for several more hours. (If the discard looked good, you could absolutely use it in the levain. A huge benefit of tending a continuous starter is that there's always a little bit ready to use.) One option is to count 4 hours back from when you will be mixing the levain and refresh your starter then, so for a 10:00 a.m. mix, refresh at 6:00 a.m., making sure it stays warm the whole time.

Since I prefer to refresh my starter first thing in the morning, around 7:00 a.m., and I only want to feed it once a day, I store it in my wine cooler (set at 55°F [13°C]) or my Sourdough Home (also at 55°F [13°C]) at some point in the afternoon, pull it out before bed to mix the levain, and place the leftover starter back in the wine cooler or fridge. I don't let the starter warm up before mixing the levain or before I feed it the next morning. In this scenario, your starter is mixed and ready, and you're simply holding it in the right place for a prolonged period so you can mix your levain whenever you want. I enjoy this flexibility.

Water Temperature and Desired Dough Temperature

DDT

Target temperatures are important for optimal fermentation. For most wheat-based doughs, this temperature is 78° to 80°F [26° to 27°C]. Water is the second largest ingredient in most doughs, and it's easy to warm it or cool it quickly, so I focus on the temperature of the water when trying to arrive at the correct final dough temperature, making it ideal to tinker with. Remember, it is just as important to keep the dough within the desired temperature zone as it bulk ferments as it is to nail the water temperature.

THE PESKY FRICTION FACTOR

The friction factor is the amount of heat added to the dough through the process of mixing. I have found the friction factor variable in a DDT calculation to be most helpful in industrial settings. Commercial-grade power and speed create more potential for friction between the dough and the bowl, causing a noticeable increase in dough temperature. At home, I mix either by hand or with a stand mixer fitted with a dough hook. Neither of these mixing methods heats the dough beyond a few degrees.

I still use the friction factor in my own kitchen, but I refer to it as the "fudge factor," understanding that managing dough temperature is both an art and a science. I use a friction factor of 0° to 5°F [0° to 3°C] when mixing by hand and 3° to 7°F [2° to 4°C] when using my stand mixer.

To find the friction factor for your mixer, combine the flour, water, levain, and salt for the dough in the bowl of your stand mixer fitted with a dough hook. Turn on the mixer to the lowest speed to stir the ingredients for a few moments, just until a rough dough comes together. You may need to stop and scrape down the sides of the bowl and underneath the dough to get all the flour incorporated. Take the temperature of the dough. Now mix on the lowest speed for 2 minutes, then on speed 4 for 5 minutes. Take the temperature of the dough again. The difference between these numbers is the friction factor. In general, my friction factor is 3° to 7°F [2° to 4°C]. If you perform this test on a cold day in your kitchen, don't be alarmed if the dough temperature drops when it is mixed. Incorporating the ambient cold air will do this.

DOQAUS
HOLD
MAX
MIN
DIGITAL THERMOMETER
AUTO
OFF

Water Temperature Cheat Sheet

You can use this chart to get a near-accurate water temperature based off the flour temperature. **You can also simply use 80°F [27°C] water**, which is what I do most in practice.

Flour temperature	Use this temperature water
65°F [18°C]	90°F [32°C]
70°F [21°C]	80°F [27°C]
75°F [24°C]	70°F [21°C]
80°F [27°C]	60°F [16°C]
85°F [29°C]	50°F [10°C]
90°F [32°C]	40°F [4°C]

Turn on your tap to the hottest setting and hold the probe of a digital thermometer in the running water to see just how hot your water gets. From there you can adjust as necessary. In the summer months in the South, it's not uncommon for me to add a little ice to my water to cool it down. In the end, water temperature is a bit more of an art than a science.

WATER TEMPERATURE

Bakers use a standard equation to determine the temperature of the water, and although it generally works, it has quirks that have long bugged me. For example, when you calculate water temperature using the classic format, the preferment in the dough is not considered. That's an issue if you're using a large portion of prefermented flour, such as in the **Double-Levain Pizza Dough on page 166**. In the following calculation, room temperature is unimportant and the preferment is weighted. This is a significant departure from most water-temperature calculators, which typically include ambient room temperature and give no consideration to whether a small or a large portion of prefermented flour is being used in the dough.

This math works by figuring out how close each variable is from the desired final temperature, and from that data, it calculates the water temperature. *Thank you to Andrew Janjigian for sharing this method.*

Temperature Trick!

A + B + C =
FINAL DOUGH TEMPERATURE

A = final dough temperature – flour temperature
B = final dough temperature – friction factor
C = (final dough temperature – preferment temperature) × preferment percent

For example, if it is 20 percent levain, move the decimal over two places to make it 0.2.

Here is an example for a 78°F [26°C] dough with a friction factor of 5°F [3°C] and 20 percent levain.

A + B + C =
FINAL DOUGH TEMPERATURE

A = 78 – 75 = 3
B = 78 – 5 = 70
C = 78 – 70 = 8 × 0.2 = 1.6

3 + 70 + 1.6 = 74.6
rounded up to 75°F [24°C] water is needed

Mixing

Mixing is a series of small steps that transforms disparate ingredients into a cohesive dough. I enjoy mixing by hand and with a stand mixer fitted with a dough hook equally. Either way, the initial mixing gives the flour a chance to hydrate, jump-start the gluten development, and activate the enzymes so they can move freely throughout the dough.

- **Using a mixer:** In a commercial setting with professional equipment, most mixers have only two speeds, high and low. I try to use my KitchenAid the same way. When mixing with a mixer, start by simply aerating the flour on the lowest speed, or the stir setting. After a few rotations, begin to drizzle in the correct-temperature water and increase the speed to low (2 on a KitchenAid). Mix the dough for 2 to 3 minutes, then increase the speed to high (8 on a KitchenAid) and mix until the dough has pulled away from the sides of the bowl, is wrapped around the dough hook, and looks shiny and smooth, 4 to 5 minutes. This is called the cleanup stage and mixes the dough to a medium strength. Strength will be added through a fold or two and from the built-up acidity in the dough, which happens as the dough ferments. When done, I transfer the dough to a lightly oiled rectangular dough tub, take the temperature, and cover with a lid.

- **Mixing by hand:** Before adding the water to the bowl, I fluff up the flour with my hand in a claw shape, then I dip my hands in water (or coat them with a little olive oil), drizzle in the correct-temperature water, and work my way around the bowl a few times with my hand in the shape of a paddle, fingers together. Once the flour starts taking on the water, I switch to pinching, or grabbing and squeezing, the dough until no dry flour is visible. The final steps are the same as mixing with a mixer: Transfer to a lightly oiled container, take the temperature, and cover.

You are not going to overmix your dough at home even if you use a mixer. Overmixing is possible in a commercial bakery or pizzeria where doughs are mixed at high intensity, getting *whipped* into shape, but it's almost impossible by hand or with a tabletop mixer. In fact, most home bakers undermix their doughs.

AUTOLYSE / The autolyse mixing method was popularized by French baker and chemist Raymond Clavel in the early 1970s. In biology, autolysis describes the breakdown of a cell by its own enzymes. As cells die and stop functioning, their internal enzymes cannibalize their various parts. The breakdown of the starches and proteins in the flour through enzymes at the start of the mix led Clavel to name this window of time autolyse, after the biological phenomenon of deconstruction from within. Its history is rooted in a commercial bakery environment, but it has become popular in home baking. I use it frequently in my bread baking because I like to work with weak flours that need additional strength or whole-grain flours that hydrate slowly. It's often used when it's unnecessary.

REST, NOT AUTOLYSE

An autolyse, a resting period with only the flour and water combined, is incredibly popular and useful. It uses time rather than mechanical action to develop the gluten, break down the proteins, and give coarse flour a longer window to absorb water. An autolyse is not mandatory, however, and I don't find it necessary for most pizza doughs.

I let my doughs sit for 10 minutes without the salt. In my opinion, this is not an autolyse, so I call it a "rest," and it's simply a kind thing to do for your dough. I'll also reserve a portion of the overall water, warm it up, and mix it with the salt so the salt dissolves prior to being added to the dough. This is a *really* nice way to incorporate the salt. I find this brief pause helpful enough to make a difference in how easy the dough is to mix but not involved enough that I need to set a timer.

STRENGTHENING

Strength building happens either in the mixer or when mixing by hand through a series of folds after the dough has come together. If you use a mixer, you will have fewer folds than if you mix by hand. Hand-mixed doughs don't often reach the right amount of development until the end of the first rise, when the folds and acidity have a cumulative effect. I like a long bulk ferment with lots of folds when I'm having a lazy day around the house, but more often than not, I use my mixer to mix my doughs now.

To strengthen your dough in a mixer, try jogging it, a method I picked up at a wood-fired bakery that used a gentle diving-arm mixer. Jogging the mixer simply means mixing the dough on low speed for 2 to 3 minutes, then stopping for 8 to 10 minutes, then mixing again for another 2 to 3 minutes, and repeating this pattern until the dough is smooth, cohesive, and has built up noticeable elasticity when you stretch a little in your hands. You can use this same technique when hand mixing: Knead the dough for a few strokes, then let it rest, covered, before kneading again, repeating these steps until the dough is ready.

To check dough development, stretch a little portion with your fingers and observe the edges of the holes that develop. If they are clean, then I know the gluten is sufficiently developed. If the edges of the holes are shaggy and fragmented, the dough needs more strength building.

To build strength by hand for wet doughs like focaccia dough, I use famed England-based, Breton-born baker Richard Bertinet's slap-and-fold technique. To try the slap and fold, lightly smear water onto your work surface. Using a dough scraper, gather the dough together in the bowl and flip it out onto the damp surface. Fold the dough away from you so it looks like a taco, with a smooth side facing up and a "seam" facing away from you. Next, use both hands to pick up the right edge of the dough, rotate it 90 degrees so the top is now facing you and the seam is facing left, and then slap it down on the surface. Stretch it toward you and then fold the portion in your hand onto the dough still stuck to the work surface. Repeat slapping, stretching, and folding three or four times. The dough is ready when it has pulled into a ball with a fairly smooth top.

Some pizza doughs have relatively low hydration and are difficult to stretch sufficiently for slap and fold. I use good old-fashioned kneading for these. To knead dough, sprinkle your work surface with flour and, using a dough scraper, turn the dough out onto the surface. Using the heel of your dominant hand, push the top of the dough away from you, then fold it back on itself and rotate it 90 degrees. Again push the top away with the heel of your palm, fold the dough back on itself, and rotate it 90 degrees. Repeat this three-step action for 2 to 3 minutes, or until the dough has pulled itself into a ball.

TAKING THE DOUGH TEMPERATURE

The final step in any mix is taking the dough temperature. If you've done your due diligence, you should come out between 78° and 80°F [26° and 27°C]. If you don't do anything to keep the temperature of your dough consistent after mixing, it will quickly acclimate to room temperature, a problem if you want your dough at 80°F [27°C] and your kitchen is 71°F [22°C]. That nine-degree [five-degree] difference will have an impact on how long it takes the dough to rise. Will it be awful? No, but your time frame will veer from the recipe, which can cause needless worry.

If your dough is on the cooler side, below 75°F [24°C], put it in a warm spot, such as a proofer, above the fridge, above the dryer, or in the oven with only the oven light turned on. I use a tabletop Brød & Taylor proofer set at 80°F [27°C] to bulk ferment my dough. (I also weigh out my flour into the mixing bowl ahead of time and keep it, covered, in the proofer overnight so it's easier to get to the correct dough temperature.)

When the proofer is too small, I create a bigger version out of an old beach cooler that can hold two dough bowls or four loaves of shaped bread. You will need the following: a cooler; a temperature controller, such as the Inkbird Digital Temperature Controller 2-Stage Outlet Thermostat; a timer switch; and a heating pad or seed-germinating mat. Place the heating pad (or seed mat) on the floor of the cooler. Plug the heating pad into the timer switch and plug the timer switch into the thermostat. Plug the thermostat into an outlet and set it at the desired temperature. Tape the temperature sensor to the inside of the cooler and close the lid. Let the cooler warm up for about an hour. This is a great option for larger dough tubs or multiple dough bowls.

If your dough is on the warmer side, take the heat off by resting it in a wine cooler set at 50°F [10°C] for 5 minutes, sticking it in a fridge or a cellar or garage for a few minutes, or letting it acclimate to room temperature if your kitchen is cool.

Bulk Fermentation

The period between mixing and dividing is called bulk fermentation—*bulk* because the dough is still in a single mass. During this time, there is partying going on in the dough! The gluten matrix in the dough expands and forms new connections; the yeast reproduces, eats, and expels gas; the gas travels through the dough to join already-present pockets of air; and the lactobacilli—if a levain is involved—enhance the strength and flavor through the buildup of lactic acid. These transformations take time, so it's important not to rush this stage.

Folding

○ **HOW MANY IS TOO MANY? /** The more you fold, the stronger the dough will become and the more developed the gluten will be. You're always feeling for the sweet spot when you fold, introducing tension but not so much that you destroy the gluten networks already in place. Once you see tears on the surface, you're in danger of stretching the dough beyond its limits. If you do go too far, return the dough to the dough tub, cover, and let rest. You can either skip the next fold or give it a gentle fold, stretching less than normal.

All the doughs in this book have at least one fold during bulk fermentation. Straight doughs—doughs with baker's yeast added directly to them with no preferment—will get a long bulk fermentation and two folds. In contrast, doughs made with prefermented flour will get a slightly shorter bulk fermentation and a single fold. Remember, never move on to dividing until the dough feels soft and full of air, even if you must extend the bulk fermentation time and add an additional fold.

Folding is a dough-strengthening technique done at timed intervals during bulk fermentation. Each fold is a set of folds, with more tension early in the process and a gentler touch as the dough gains strength. The purpose of folding is to bring shorter strands of gluten into contact with longer lengths, improving dough elasticity, regulating dough temperature, and, to a small extent, introducing air into the dough. Folding also provides an opportunity to get in touch with the dough and make sure it is on track.

If the dough has been mixed in a mixer, remember that much of the strengthening has already happened and handle the dough with a light touch when folding. If the dough has been mixed by hand, you'll need to fold it more frequently and vigorously throughout bulk fermentation, keeping in mind it will also strengthen itself naturally through the buildup of acidity, which tightens gluten organically.

To fold, dip your fingers in a little water. Gently lift the dough straight up from the middle with both hands. One end will release from the container as you pull upward. Allow the loosened end to tuck under the middle of the dough and then repeat with the other side, lifting and tucking toward the middle. The dough will look like it has coiled underneath itself. Rotate the container 90 degrees (a quarter turn) and repeat the process. Continue rotating the container and folding until the dough doesn't stretch or spread and has a smooth top. Re-cover the container.

Dividing

THE FOLLOWING
PIZZA DOUGH RECIPES MAKE
FOUR ROUNDS.

IF YOU WOULD LIKE
TO MAKE A PAN PIZZA (PAGE 113),
SKIP DIVIDING THE DOUGH.

Dividing ends bulk fermentation and starts the proofing portion of the dough journey.

To divide the dough, lightly flour your work surface. Using a dough scraper, turn the dough out onto the floured surface so the top is now the bottom and you're looking at the puffy underbelly. Using a bench knife, divide the dough into four equal portions, making confident, decisive cuts. Now use the bench knife to scoop a hunk of the dough onto your digital scale. Check the weight. You're looking for the hunk to weigh 250 g [8¾ oz]. Use the bench knife to add or remove dough as needed to reach 250 g [8¾ oz]. (It's more important to have fewer bits and pieces than it is to have four portions that are exactly equal, so don't obsess here.) Set the first piece of dough aside and weigh the remaining portions. You may also skip the scale and simply eyeball the weight, accepting that each pizza will be slightly different.

Shaping

Shaping takes the dough from an unformed chunk to a smooth ball with a sealed seam on the bottom. Too much flour on the dough will inhibit the gathered seams from sticking to each other, so use a minimal amount on your work surface and resist the urge to sprinkle any flour on the dough. I keep a small mound of all-purpose flour at the top of my work area, gently patting the bottom of the dough (the portion touching the work surface or my hands) in the flour as I go.

1 Take your first portion of dough and flip it over onto your work surface. You're now looking at what will be the bottom of the round, and the part touching the work surface will become the top. Hopefully the dough is a sort of square shape already, but if not, gently pat it into one. You now have a top and a bottom, a left and a right, and a center point in the middle.

2 Bring the top edge and the bottom edge to meet in the middle and pinch them together. Now gently stretch out the left and right sides a few inches [about 5 cm] and pinch them together over the just-sealed dough. If you didn't start with a square, you will now have one. Grab the top left corner and the bottom right corner, stretch them a little, and then pinch them together. Repeat stretching and pinching with the top right corner and bottom left corner. The point where all the gathered portions of dough come together is your seam. The dough will look like a little purse or dumpling, with the seam facing up.

3 Gently flip the dough back over so you are now looking at the smooth top. On a dry, flour-free area, and with a clean, dry cupped hand (or your dough scraper), drag the dough 8 to 10 in [20 to 25 cm], making sure it doesn't roll over. Keep the top upright and the bottom seam touching the work surface. As you drag, the dough will tighten and become smooth. Let the round rest on the surface to help the seam seal while you work on the other dough portions. Repeat with the remaining dough.

Proofing

Much like bulk fermentation, proofing is a continuum, moving from when the dough is just shaped to when it's stretched and baked. During this time, the dough will take on more air, relax from the tension introduced while shaping, and develop flavor. Dough may be under proofed, correctly proofed, or over proofed, with each phase flowing into the next. Home bakers tend to chronically under proof their doughs, so I encourage you to push the proof on your dough, even over proofing it once to see how far it can really go.

Unfortunately, there is no single indicator that tells you when a dough is done proofing. The end of the proof is more of a series of changes in the dough that coalesce in "doneness." The recipes indicate proof times, but once a dough becomes familiar, you can always explore other options, extending or shortening the proofing time to fit your needs.

Proofing can be done in a range of temperatures depending on when you need or want the dough ready. I use a combination of temperatures, often leaving my dough out for an hour on the countertop, then putting it in the wine cooler overnight, or slipping it directly into the wine cooler for 24 hours and then into the fridge for 24 hours. The key is simply understanding that warmer temperatures will encourage the proof to move quickly, while cooler temperatures slow the process down.

SAME-DAY BAKE	Second rise at room temperature	68° to 72°F [20° to 22°C]
	Or at warm room temperature in a proofer	78° to 80°F [26° to 27°C]
NEXT-DAY BAKE	Directly into a wine cooler	50°F [10°C]
48 HR FERMENT	Directly into the fridge	38° to 42°F [3° to 6°C]

Crust proofed and baked in a single day will have a thin "eggshell" texture and a flour-forward flavor because it hasn't had time to take on much acidity. Dough that's undergone a longer proof in cooler temperatures will have a thicker crust that "leopards" easier and a flavor profile that goes beyond the nutty taste of wheat. This is especially true if sourdough is involved, as the enzymes have had time to free up amino acids and sugars. My sweet spot is a 24-hour proof, and if you have time, this is what I recommend.

The Poke Test / Touching the dough throughout the proof is essential. The poke test, as bakers call it, is an imperfect but incredibly useful tool to gauge the readiness of a dough for stretching and baking. To perform the poke test, gently but firmly jab the dough with your index finger. (You're not trying to break through the surface. Instead, you're pressing on the skin to test its elasticity.) If the dough quickly springs back, it needs more time. If your jab leaves an indent that rises back slowly, you're in the zone where you may choose to bake or chill the dough. If you press on the dough and meet no resistance, and you hear a little gas escape, the dough has gone too far and needs to be baked right away.

Stones, Steels, and Cast Iron

Most home ovens max out at 500° to 550°F [260° to 290°C] due to safety reasons. This may seem hot, but when you consider commercial pizza oven temperatures run about 725°F [385°C] or even 900°F [480°C], 500°F [260°C] pales in comparison. That's OK. Your oven will make great pizza with a crisp, browned crust, bubbly cheese, and properly cooked toppings, particularly if you have a pizza stone or baking steel.

Increasing the heat retention in your oven through a preheated stone or steel will bake an excellent pizza—one with an open-crumb crust and a nicely baked thin slice that doesn't flop—in just 8 to 10 minutes. If you long to cook a pizza in 3 minutes or less, invest in a **wood-fired oven** **(see page 117)**.

Clay Clay pizza stones are large, flat, unglazed clay slabs. Affordable and easy to find, they come in various shapes—round, square, rectangular—sizes, and thicknesses and are light enough to move in and out of the oven easily. Clay, made from fine soil particles, is porous, so a "stone" soaks up some of the moisture released as steam while your pizza bakes, resulting in a crisp crust. On the downside, many pizza stones can only handle heat up to 500°F [260°C], and the brittle material can crack from being heated or cooled too quickly. And since they transfer heat so readily, they need significant recovery time between pizzas.

Steel As noted earlier, a baking steel is my preferred tool for making pizza in my home oven. Steel can withstand incredibly high temperatures, is nonporous, and transfers heat quickly, making it a great material on which to bake pizzas. Similar to pizza stones, baking steels come in a variety of shapes, with square the most popular; sizes; and thicknesses, from 3⁄16 to ½ in [4.5 to 12 mm]. Steel has a quicker recovery time than clay, making it the more efficient option for multiple rounds of baking. I leave my steel in the oven between bakes to boost the thermal mass. The price point runs much higher on steel than on clay, so it's a great investment only if you love making pizza frequently.

Cast iron If you own neither a stone nor a steel, an overturned large cast-iron skillet does a terrific job of baking pizza. Cast iron heats up slower than steel, but it delivers a consistent, even heat. Both cast iron and steel are seasoned over time through repeated and frequent use, delivering a bolder bake the older they are. The darker patina of cast iron encourages better browning, and the built-in seasoning makes it virtually nonstick. Lodge makes a dedicated, circular cast-iron pizza stone that I love.

No matter what you buy, nothing will replace taking the time to get to know your oven. All ovens have their own personalities, hot spots, and quirks. By baking frequently, you'll become attuned to your oven and be able to confidently achieve the look and doneness that best suits you.

SETTING UP YOUR OVEN

Place a baking stone or steel in the center of an oven rack 8 to 10 in [20 to 25 cm] from the top of the oven. Preheat for at least 1 hour at the hottest temperature your oven will allow. I've tried many configurations, and this is the simplest setup that gets me consistent, great results. Once it comes time to bake, you'll want to keep your welding gloves, an infrared thermometer, and a wire-bristle brush (and a dustpan—not plastic!) close by so you can clean off the steel or stone as needed.

To increase thermal mass, you can purchase firebricks from your local hardware store and put them on a sheet pan under the steel or stone. Alternatively, you can place a steel or stone on a rack in the middle of the oven and then put a second steel or stone on the rack above it. When working with two baking surfaces like this, I start the pizza on the top and finish it on the bottom, capturing the radiant heat from the top to finish off the bake.

MATCHING HYDRATION WITH OVEN TEMPERATURES / The hydration of a pizza dough directly affects how long it will take to bake. Pizza doughs that will bake for a short period in a high-heat zone have a lower hydration between 60 and 68 percent. Doughs that will bake in a home oven around 500°F [260°C] do well with a hydration of 68 to 75 percent. This extra 1 to 5 percent of water yields a crust that isn't dry, even given the additional time in the oven.

The Broiler

The broiler is a great tool, and the intense heat it produces can mimic the doming achieved when a pizza is held on the peel close to the ceiling of a wood-fired oven, charring and blistering the dough. Some ovens will operate the bake mode and the broiler at the same time and others won't. Most broilers have only on and off settings, while others have high and low or allow you to set a specific temperature. Any of these broiler setups will work for pizza. In my oven, I switch from bake to high broil for the final 2 to 3 minutes. The broiler can also be used for the last 10 minutes of the preheat—right before you load the pizza—to blast the stone or steel with heat. (Make sure to turn your oven back to bake once the pizza is loaded.)

Why not just bake pizza on an inverted sheet pan? Because color equals flavor and that's what we're chasing: flavorful pizza that tastes complex. You must bake boldly to achieve a crust that boasts colorful hues of bronze, burnished red, and chestnut. Like what transpires when a baguette is baked or a steak is seared in a sizzling hot skillet, these crust colors are indicators of the Maillard reaction, a chemical process that naturally occurs between sugars and amino acids in high-heat temperatures, producing rich flavors, aromas, and colors.

Wooden vs. Metal Peel / I use a wooden peel for building and loading my pizza and a thin metal peel with a perforated surface for rotating the pizza during the bake and removing it when it's done. Wooden peels absorb heat slowly and wick away moisture. When well floured, they make the transfer into the oven a joy. Thin metal peels heat up and cool down quickly, so they excel at sliding under a pizza as it cooks. I don't recommend parchment paper for loading a pizza for two reasons: Most parchment paper is rated to only 450°F [230°C], and you want the dough in direct contact with the hot steel or stone.

Designing Workflow

The physical act of making pizza is a dance, one of my favorites to perform. To make sure everything flows properly, set up your space so you can move seamlessly from stretching to building to baking to cooling. Having everything within arm's reach or a simple pivot is essential. I love tiny pizza joints where only one or two people are making pizzas and working the oven. It's inspirational how much can be done when your workspace is well designed.

To prepare my kitchen for pizza, I clear off my counter to the right of the oven and arrange the ingredients in order of use: dough, sauce, cheese, and toppings. On the left side of the counter, I make a station for cooling, topping, and slicing post-bake. Here I put ingredients like fresh basil, a squeeze bottle of olive oil, a big hunk of Parmigiano-Reggiano, and other delicate toppings. A Microplane grater, pizza wheel or rocker cutter, cooling rack, and cutting board are set there too.

How you work is also a piece of the puzzle. Although you don't need to rush, you do need to focus and move with urgency. And finally, start with a clean kitchen. A tidy workspace cultivates an efficient, coordinated, confident bake. At my live-fire pizza pop-ups, my favorite moment is when the booth is immaculate, the fire is hot, the dough is bubbling, and I make that first beautiful pizza just for myself.

Stretching

HOW TO USE A ROLLING PIN FOR PIZZA DOUGH / Generously sprinkle your work surface with all-purpose flour and have a small bowl with more flour nearby. Working with one dough round at a time, use a rolling pin (I prefer a French-style pin, which has tapered ends) to gently roll out the dough, moving from the center outward first and then rolling diagonally. You can encourage the dough to stay in a circular shape by giving it a quarter turn clockwise as you roll. (It's OK if it isn't a perfect circle when you've finished!) If the dough resists stretching, try working more than one ball at a time, giving the resistant one a "micro" rest in between rollings. Follow the directions for topping the pizza according to individual recipes.

DUSTING AND STRETCHING FLOUR / I use either white rice flour or all-purpose flour for dusting my peel and dough. White rice flour is hard, granular, and round, and it acts like ball bearings, helping the pizza slide off the peel. (Some love semolina for the same reason.) White (or brown) rice flour does work nicely, but if I don't have it, I don't sweat it and reach for all-purpose instead. Cornmeal is too chunky and flavorful for me, and it tends to burn, so use it as a last resort.

The kind of pizza dough I like needs to be handled gently and confidently and cannot withstand being sent through the air like a Frisbee. Tossing a dough round to stretch it is sexy, but that dough is firmer than most of mine. Occasionally, I use a rolling pin (or a wine bottle!) to roll out a dough. This is handy when I bake with my children or I want a very thin crust. Otherwise, I stick to only my hands and gravity.

The intention behind shaping is to stretch the preshaped ball of dough into a circle with a defined rim and a lower, smooth center. A well-stretched dough will bake evenly, with no undercooked or overcooked sections, and won't puff up like pita on the baking stone or steel. It's difficult to stretch dough that's too cold—the proteins are tightly coiled—or too warm, when built-up acidity starts to degrade the gluten.

Besides handling difficulty, cold dough also causes baking problems. You want a room-temperature dough going onto a hot stone or steel so it doesn't shock the material or deplete the heat immediately. Dough between 68° and 70°F [20° and 21°C] is a good working temperature.

In general, I take my dough out of the fridge 2 to 3 hours ahead of pizza making. I shave some time off this in the summer and add some time in the winter. If you are making a lot of dough, you can stagger the time you bring the dough boxes or containers out so they are ready in a nice succession.

1 To stretch, use a bench scraper to flip the dough round over onto a floured peel so the top is now on the bottom. Lightly dust with flour. Create the crust with your fingertips by making a ¼ in [6 mm] indent into the dough all the way around the rim. Using the pads of your fingers and leaving the edge alone, pat down the inner circle of dough, starting at the top and working your way down. Flip the dough over and repeat the process, indenting the rim and patting down the center, then flip it back over.

2 Now slide your hands, palms facing down, under the dough and make two fists in the center. Lift your hands and the pizza into the air so it rests on the back of your knuckles. Slowly and carefully pull your hands in opposite directions, stretching the dough. Keeping the dough on the back of your hands, rotate it 90 degrees and lightly stretch again, pulling in opposite directions. These brief motions will stretch the center of the pizza and gravity will take care of the rest. If the dough is resisting, try working two rounds at a time, moving back and forth between them so each one gets a little rest while you stretch the other one. If you are making only one pizza, just give the dough a short rest. Set the resting dough on a lightly floured surface and cover with a non-terry cloth kitchen towel.

3 Once the dough is opened in the center and relaxed, make an arc with your hands and allow the dough to slide off your knuckles and hang off the back of your hands. I like to imagine the dough as a steering wheel: Keep your hands at 12 o'clock and work the dough in a circular motion to thin out and extend the portion between the center and the indented rim. When the dough is stretched to 12 in [30.5 cm], give or take, lay it back down on the peel and slide your hands out.

Building

○ **THE CALZONE /** Inevitably, you'll poke a hole in the dough while you're building the pizza. If the dough isn't covered in sauce yet, you can pinch the hole closed and try to get the pizza in the oven as quickly as possible. If the hole happens after you've added the sauce or toppings, just fold the dough over itself and press down firmly along the edge to seal it, creating a makeshift calzone. Bake the calzone directly on the stone or steel until the dough is deeply browned.

1 Once the dough is stretched and on the floured peel, quickly build the pizza. If the recipe calls for a sauce, spoon the amount you'll need onto the middle of the pizza and, using the back of the spoon, spread the sauce evenly over the dough, leaving 1 in [2.5 cm] naked around the raised edge of the crust. Use restraint and try not to over sauce the pizza or you'll end up with a gummy layer or a soggy center. I have a special sauce spoon that I use religiously, as I know that two spoonfuls will give me the perfect amount, and it's shallow, so there's a nice wide surface for spreading the sauce.

2 Finish building the pizza with the called-for cheese and toppings. When making up your own pizzas, follow the same rule as for the sauce, using ingredients sparingly and as a highlight to the crust. Too much cheese and you run the risk of a watery mess or an undercooked crust. Too little cheese and the sauce will reduce too much from prolonged heat exposure. When it comes to toppings, remember that being creative doesn't have to mean a wild assortment of ingredients. A few simple, in-season elements will do the trick. The dough is the star when it comes to pizza, and the toppings are there to add fat, brightness, and salt, complementing the fermentation. Add the toppings and give the pizza a final shake, making sure it will slide, then get to the oven.

Baking

1. Make sure your oven is on as high as it will go and preheat the baking stone or steel for a solid hour before baking. When I have the time, I will preheat my steel for up to 2 hours before making pizza. Ovens vary wildly from brand to brand, so keep an oven thermometer in the baking chamber and use an infrared thermometer to take the temperature of the stone or steel. Use the outlined bake times as a suggestion, but in general, if the oven is properly preheated, the pizza should bake in under 10 minutes.

2. Getting the pizza into the oven is a culminating moment, and you can feel the excitement, but don't let your nerves get the best of you: stay focused and limber. Be silly and do some jumping jacks or wiggle your body. Trust me, it will all be much easier if you're moving fluidly and confidently.

3. To load the pizza, go in parallel to the stone or steel, touch the end of the peel down to the farthest edge of the stone or steel, then gently tilt the peel and, with a graceful jerk, slide the peel out from under the pizza. Avoid tilting the peel at a steep angle or the dough will haphazardly fold over itself, and you'll end up with a messy variation of a calzone. Do not shuffle the pizza onto the stone or steel, which can create wrinkles and result in the dough cooking unevenly.

4. Once the pizza is loaded into the oven, distract yourself by having some wine or stepping outside for a minute so you're not tempted to keep opening the oven door. When you check back, 4 to 5 minutes into the bake, you should see the crust browning and the cheese melting. Use a metal peel to rotate the pizza 180 degrees, taking note of any hot spots in the oven. As you rotate, peek at the undercarriage of the pizza. It should still be golden and not too dark yet. Add any mid-bake toppings, then close the door and bake for another 4 to 5 minutes.

5. When the pizza is done, the crust will be deeply browned, the bubbles will be slightly charred, and the cheese will be browned. When you inspect the undercarriage, it will have tiny spots of char on a golden-brown background. This is perfect. Slide the metal peel under the pizza and transfer it to a wire rack to cool for 5 to 6 minutes. The moment the pizza comes out of the oven, I *lightly* drizzle on the olive oil, going around the rim once and over the pizza, and if the recipe calls for Parmesan, I grate it over the top. Once cooled, slide the pizza onto a cutting board and top with anything delicate, like fresh basil or arugula, then cut and enjoy!

WHAT CAUSES OVEN SPRING? /

It's commonly said that the rise of your dough when it hits a hot surface is due to the last gasp of yeast, but fermentation accounts for almost none of the spring that you see. A third of the visible overall rise is a direct result of evaporation. When the water in the dough begins evaporating, the carbon dioxide in the water is forced out, traveling through the dough to join the alveoli (air pockets) already present from fermentation and from the air incorporated while mixing. This is why wetter doughs have a more open crumb: There is more air in the dough overall, in various forms.

Evaluation

Now that you've made a pizza, step back and evaluate it before going forward. Some adjustments can be made in the moment, like stretching the dough thinner or using less sauce. Other tweaks, such as correctly fermenting the dough, will need to be addressed the next time you mix dough.

- **Was the dough properly fermented?** The edge should be light, airy, deeply browned with charred bubbles, and crisp. If the edge of the pizza is too low, pale, and dense, make sure your sourdough is thriving, your levain is well risen, and your yeast has not expired. Also, check that the oven temperature is getting hot enough to encourage a good spring.

- **Is there a balance between the cheese and the toppings?** If you've used too many toppings and the pizza is underbaked or soggy, practice restraint on your following pizzas. The cheese should be deeply browned but not burnt or greasy. If the cheese has separated, it may have gotten too hot, so try adding it halfway through the bake. If the cheese and sauce have melted together, they are out of balance. The mozzarella should be white islands with a rosy color on the edges. To correct the balance, try using less mozzarella and a blend of both fresh and low moisture.

- **Is the undercarriage cooked through?** If the crust remains pale, make sure your stone or steel is properly preheated. If it burns, make sure you're not using too much flour on the peel. If the toppings and crust are baking at different rates, adjust accordingly, reducing the amount of ingredients you're putting on the pizza or decreasing the heat of the stone or steel you're baking on. This difference in cooking times can easily show up on the first pizza when the stone or steel is ripping hot. After making a pizza on it, some of the heat will be absorbed, and subsequent pizzas will take a little longer to bake, even after giving the stone or steel a moment to recover.

Pan pizza hits you with comfort and crunch all at once. It's like bread and pizza had a delicious baby, and it's what I turn to for feeding a crowd or a weeknight dinner. ●

PAN PIZZA

Besides the crispy golden edges and soft, airy interior, pan pizza is a lovely style to make with children because they feel like chefs simply by sprinkling on the cheese. Plus, you're not panicking about whether the dough is sticking to the peel. It's a slower vibe. Any of the pizza doughs in this book can become a pan pizza with a few adjustments.

1 First, bulk ferment the dough in a lightly oiled rectangular tub, rather than a round bowl. Dough will conform to the shape it's given, so starting it out in a rectangle will mean you'll already have four corners of dough ready to go into the four corners of the pan. I use my dough proofing boxes for this task.

2 Second, skip dividing the dough into rounds. Transfer the dough to the fridge after its folds are done and let it rest there for at least 2 hours or up to 24 hours, or according to the time frame in the dough recipe. Bring the dough to room temperature before attempting to stretch it.

3 Choose your pan size. This will determine the thickness of the final crust. Four rounds of dough combined equals 1 kg [2¼ lb], enough to fill one 12 by 16 in [30.5 by 40.5 cm] sheet pan or two 6 by 12 in [15 by 30.5 cm] sheet pans. Black steel pans, like Lloyd pans made in Washington State, are excellent for pan pizza. My preferred pans are the 8 by 10 in [20 by 25 cm], the 12 by 12 in [30.5 by 30.5 cm], and, my most used, the 16 by 16 in [40.5 by 40.5 cm]. Lloyd pans are pre-seasoned and don't need to be oiled.

4 Plan for and prepare twice the amount of sauce and toppings for your pan pizza, or divide the top of the pizza in half and top each half with a different set of toppings. There's more surface area and less crust on a pan pizza, so make sure you bulk up. If you end up with extra toppings, you can toss them into a salad or save them in the fridge for a future focaccia.

5 Drizzle your sheet pan with olive oil and turn the dough out with a dough scraper, being careful not to degas it. With the pads of your fingertips, gently coax the dough toward the corners 1 to 2 in [2.5 to 5 cm], then cover the pan with a lid (many pizza pans come with lids!) or cling film and rest for 30 minutes. When you return to the dough, you can continue pressing and pushing with your fingers, or pick up the dough on the back of your hands and pull in opposite directions to stretch the dough between them. The pizza should be proofed and ready to bake in 2 to 3 hours.

○ **CARING FOR YOUR PANS /** Treat steel pans as you would cast-iron pans. Lloyd pans come pre-seasoned, but if your pan isn't, simply wipe it well with a light coating of vegetable oil and heat for an hour in a preheated 500°F [260°C] oven. To clean the pans after use, let them cool completely, then gently scrape away any debris with a dough scraper. If bits of pizza are stuck to the pan, run the pan under warm water and use a nonabrasive sponge or cloth to dislodge the stubborn remains. Prepare the pan for the next bake by wiping it dry, applying a thin coat of oil, and heating it for 30 to 40 minutes in a preheated 400°F [200°C] oven.

○ **CAKE PANS /** With a little prep, you can use round cake pans 9 in [23 cm] in diameter for baking pizza. (I've even baked pizza in a cast-iron skillet!) To bake pizza dough in a round cake pan, cut a circle of parchment the diameter of the pan, lightly spray the bottom and sides of the pan with nonstick cooking spray, lay the parchment circle on the pan bottom, and spray the parchment. Proof the dough directly on the parchment in the pan. Top and bake the pizza, then let cool to the touch in the pan on a wire rack, gently lift the pizza from the pan, peel off and discard the parchment, and serve.

6 Bake the pizza for 10 minutes in a preheated oven at 500°F [260°C] on a preheated baking steel or stone, then rotate the pizza, lower the heat to 450°F [230°C], and continue to bake until the underside is crispy and browned, the cheese, if using, is melted, and the edges are golden, 10 to 15 minutes longer. The total bake time depends on the thickness of the dough and on the toppings, so be sure to bake the pizza thoroughly, and remember, there's flavor in a bold bake.

7 Remove the pizza from the oven and use a wide metal spatula to lift it out of the pan and slide it onto a wire rack. Let cool for a few minutes to allow the dough and cheese to set. Top with any post-bake frills, such as hot honey or fresh basil, before serving.

Par-Bake Option / You can par-bake a pan pizza either naked or with just a thin layer of sauce for 8 to 10 minutes at 450° to 475°F [230° to 245°C]. This gives some of the moisture a chance to evaporate, drying out the surface before it's topped. I like to include a thin sauce layer on the par-bake so the top is a little weighted, and then do another layer of sauce before I add the cheese and toppings. If you're making the pizza upside down (cheese first, then sauce), you can include a light sprinkle of cheese to help the crust rise evenly, then add the toppings, cheese, and sauce last.

The crust can be par-baked up to 48 hours ahead of making the final pizza. Follow the whole process, then when you remove it, let it cool completely, tightly wrap it in cling film, and freeze it. Let it thaw in the fridge overnight before using.

I am in my element when baking wood-fired pizzas, and there's real grit and joy involved in the process, which is more akin to a ritual than a method. ●

ALL YOU EVER WANTED TO KNOW ABOUT WOOD-FIRED PIZZA

Essay

WOOD-FIRED PIZZA LIFE ● He scoffed at the price, "Sixteen dollars for a cheese pizza?" I wavered for a moment, wondering if I was off my rocker charging that much, then I felt the splinters in my hand, the sweat dripping down the back of my neck, and the pavement beneath my already-tired feet and said, "Yeah." I didn't bother to rattle off any fancy facts about the long, natural fermentation or the carefully sourced cheeses with specific moisture contents, and I only half-heartedly glanced behind me at the roaring 750°F [400°C] wood-fired oven hitched to the back of my truck. "OK," he said, "take my money. You're the only food here."

Then the dance began. A light sprinkle of flour on the table, followed by a scraper up and under the puffy, yielding dough, flipping it onto the dusted surface. My hands were moving in silent synchronicity, patting out a ring around the edge and then moving from twelve o'clock to six o'clock on the circle, pressing out the largest bubbles. Turning the dough over, I repeated the same gentle but firm pressing and patting, echoing a potter with a disk of clay. Finally maneuvering the dough onto the back of my hands and pulling them apart, I skillfully stretched it until it was thin and taut—like the surface of a balloon—and then returned it to its initial floury resting place.

The red sauce, glistening in the afternoon sun, covered the dough almost to the edge. A quarter-size piece of white-as-a-sheet fresh mozzarella placed in the middle was quickly surrounded with a circle of six more pieces. Next, a handful of shredded low-moisture mozzarella obscured any spots where the maroon tomato sauce still showed. And then the scraping of wood on metal as the peel shimmied under the pizza like a rough hand sliding under a crisp sheet.

My favorite moment came next: swiveling from the table to the oven and sliding the pizza from the peel onto the hearth with a single motion, like a magician pulling a tablecloth from under a setting of fine-china tableware. The crust almost immediately jerked to life, as if the spirit of the Holy Ghost was inspiring it to rise, blooming and unfolding and begging to look like dinner. I waited for the precise moment when the bottom had baked just enough for me to slide the peel under it to turn it and the side facing the fire wasn't yet charred. Too soon and the pizza would fold in on itself as I pulled it toward me. Too late and someone was going to call it burnt and ask for their sixteen bucks back.

I forced myself to look around the parking lot for two minutes. I noticed there was still a heap of corn and squash on my neighbor's table, but the honey and cinnamon rolls across the aisle had disappeared. At the end of the lot near the creek, a few kids scratched out a hopscotch game with big, colorful sticks of chalk. I licked my lips looking at some watermelons and then turned the pizza. It was perfect. Tiny, blistered bubbles of char stood out against a golden crust, like the spotting on a leopard. The cheese was beginning to bubble and turn brown, and tiny rivers of oil were collecting against white clouds of cheese, looking like tributaries and deltas of deliciousness.

I squinted into the haze and announced, "Your pizza's almost ready." It had been about four minutes since he had ordered. A few more spins, each time bringing the pizza from the back of the oven toward the front to position a different part of the crust next to the flame, and then it was back on the peel and a quick slide onto a paper plate. It was lovingly covered in a blanket of freshly grated Parmesan and then kissed with a thousand flecks of pink sea salt before it was drizzled with a spiral of fruity olive oil. Barely able to touch it, I cut it into quarters with a pair of kitchen scissors and handed it to the doubtful but hungry onlooker, calling out, "Have a nice day." I genuinely hoped he would.

He had been my only customer so far, and I was feeling lonely, like a mime waiting for a passerby to drop a coin into my cup so I could start pretending I was climbing a wall or walking down a nonexistent staircase. I was the new kid in town, and wood-fired pizza—and my prices—were under scrutiny here where Pizza Hut was still king. I left my tent and bought a nice-looking bag of greasy beans and a can of pickled corn, which, of course, I thought would taste good on a pizza. A few clouds rolled overhead and the fiddlers began to play those high lonesome tunes that made me cry confusing tears that weren't quite sad but not quite happy.

The customer came back and showed me an empty plate splattered like a Jackson Pollock painting with green-gold olive oil and dotted with a few spots of charred dough where the pizza had been so hot it stuck to the paper. "That," he said, "was the best pizza I've eaten in my life."

MASONRY OVENS

Masonry ovens are made from clay, stone, or brick and can withstand temperatures of over 1,000°F [540°C] without cracking or warping. They work either through cooking with a live fire, like when a pizza is placed next to a rolling flame, or through retained heat, like when bread is loaded into an empty chamber and is baked by drawing heat from the charged, hot mass around it. I am often asked if wood-fired ovens are the best way to bake. Ultimately what's best depends on the needs of the baker and the style of pizza or bread being made, but cooking or baking with fire is, without question, my *favorite* way to go.

The high temperatures in a wood-fired oven evoke flavors and textures electric and gas ovens simply can't replicate. Yet just because the oven *can* reach 900°F [480°C] doesn't mean you need to bake your pizzas that hot. Unless you're making an authentic Neapolitan pizza, which must be baked in under 90 seconds, it's generally unnecessary to get an oven that blazing. I prefer a temperature range of 700° to 725°F [370° to 385°C] for my pizza. It bakes up into a beautiful golden crust with charred bubbles and a light texture in 5 to 8 minutes, a perfectly reasonable bake time.

Should you come upon a masonry oven in the wild, the construction materials, mass, and shape are all clues to whether it is primarily used for baking bread or pizza. Although you can make pizza in a bread oven and bread in a pizza oven, certain characteristics make one choice more efficient than the other.

A long, deep rectangular oven with thick walls and a low, vaulted dome is built for baking rows of bread with the door closed using retained heat. An oven with a circular footprint is designed for keeping a live fire to one side and having the flame roll over the dome, baking pizza with the door open. The circular oven ensures that heat flows uniformly in the chamber, following the curve and cooking evenly with minimal heat escaping.

Black and White Burning Ovens

Black burning ovens, also called direct fired ovens, have a fire built in the same chamber in which the baking takes place. The soot from the fire turns the ceiling black (the soot burns off), and the coals are also dark, earning the oven its name. White ovens have the wood, fire, and coals in an external firebox, often below the hearth in the front. Pizza ovens are almost always black burning, with a live flame going continuously throughout the bake.

In both styles of oven, heat is generated through combustion, with pieces of wood or wood pellets as the fuel and oxygen as the catalyst. When the wood or pellets are ignited, complex molecules break down into simpler compounds and release waves of heat. Volatile gases, tar, and charcoal mix with air in a secondary combustion that generates even more heat. You can see this secondary combustion in a very hot oven when the gases in the air ignite like glowing blue northern lights that snake through the chamber.

In addition to intense direct heat, wood-fired ovens also make use of conductive, convective, and radiant heat simultaneously to bake dough quickly and thoroughly. Radiant heat moves through the air, warming any object in its path. Convection transfers heat through the movement of a fluid, such as gases or liquids. Electric-powered convection ovens use fans to speed up the transfer of heat, while a masonry oven accomplishes the same task though the swirling release of moisture as it evaporates from the baking dough. Finally, conductive heat moves through physical contact, such as when a pizza dough starts to puff immediately from contact with the hearth.

British Thermal Units

A British thermal unit, or BTU, is a unit of measurement for heat energy. It's useful here to compare how much heat is released when different types of wood are burned. A pound of dry wood set afire on average releases around 8,500 BTUs. (One BTU is roughly equivalent to the amount of heat energy generated when a kitchen match is lit.) The density of wood, however, varies greatly, and for this reason, hardwoods, like oak or ash, put out more BTUs than softer, lighter woods, such as spruce.

WOOD

You need an abundance of dry hardwood in several thicknesses to fire your oven well. Common varieties I've used in the Southeast include hickory, birch, beech, locust, cherry, walnut, and oak. Hardwoods burn well, have a high BTU, and make chunky coals, which is insurance that the fire won't dissipate without warning. Soft woods, such as pine and poplar, burn fast and bright, leaving mostly ash, so they are best for starting a fire but not for sustaining one. The residue left from soft woods can also clog a chimney with oily creosote, causing an unwanted fire.

Wet wood will sputter, smoke, and spit moisture onto the hearth, making the whole experience unpleasant, so buy (or cure yourself) seasoned firewood with 15 to 20 percent moisture. Here's a quick test to gauge the moisture in your firewood: Knock two logs together. They should feel light and sound hollow, like thumping the bottom of a fully baked loaf of bread. If you hear a dull thud, the wood needs more time. You can also purchase a digital moisture reader for greater accuracy and more assurance.

Along with the wood being dry, you'll want wood in three different sizes for an easy firing. I gauge by circumference, with plenty of kindling as thick as my thumb, medium cuts as wide as my wrist, and larger pieces with a girth as big as my forearm. The kindling is necessary for the initial fire and to keep the live fire going with a bright flame. The medium and larger pieces get the oven up to baking temperature and make coals. Collect any slivers or splinters created while chopping wood; these make incredible tinder for starting the fire.

Source the wood for your oven with the same care you use to source your flour. Just like tapping into a network of millers and farmers, the relationships you build with your wood sources are meaningful. When I ran my wood-fired bakery, I would drive once a week to a furniture maker to collect his kiln-dried shavings to use as tinder, and we would enjoy small talk over a hot cup of coffee. Thanks to the popularity of tabletop pizza ovens post-pandemic, you can now buy firewood in big-box stores or even online. But seeking out your region's best cooking wood and the people who supply it is part of the fun.

Curing Wood / Green hardwood, freshly cut, takes a year to season properly. If you have the time and space, cutting and curing your own firewood is a nice, economical process. Start by splitting large rounds into manageable logs and then stack them loosely off the ground on a pallet. Keep the wood protected from the rain with a tarp, but leave the ends exposed to the sun and breezes to dry out. Check the wood at around 3 months, 6 months, and then at a year. Softer woods will lose moisture sooner than hardwoods. As you pull from your pile, rotate so the driest wood is burned first.

HELPFUL EQUIPMENT

The following is a short list of tools I find indispensable when it comes to working a wood-fired oven. Some of these tools have migrated into my kitchen, like the welding gloves and infrared thermometer. To browse good sources for these items, **see Tool and Equipment Suppliers on page 404**.

Andirons. Used in pairs, these metal supports lift the firewood off the chamber floor so air can circulate underneath, making for a clean burn. You can find them in antique shops and at estate sales, or grab a plain pair online for under $50.

Ash bucket. If your oven doesn't have a built-in ash slot (some do), you'll need a receptacle for the ash and a place to store hot coals if you need the oven to be empty in a hurry.

Brush. A long-handled brush with wire or brass bristles is ideal for cleaning up debris from pizza baking. I prefer a brush that also features a scraper for more intense cleaning.

Hoe and poker. I use a steel hoe for moving larger pieces of firewood in the chamber and a long, wooden poker for lifting pieces of wood or busting through coals and ash to make air channels. My poker is an old broom handle with a singed pointed end and a smooth handle worn soft from years of use.

Infrared thermometer. An infrared thermometer records temperatures without physical contact, making it a safe and accurate way to measure the *surface* temperatures inside the chamber.

Long-handled shovel. A shovel with a good reach is excellent for raking out the ash when the firing is over.

Long-reach lighter. A long lighter ensures safety when lighting the initial fire.

Newspaper or brown-paper bags. These are good for starting the fire.

Peels. I use a wooden peel for loading and a metal peel for rotating and unloading.

Rag mop. I tie a wet flour-sack towel to the end of the poker and quickly swab down the hearth where the pizzas will bake right before the bake begins. (Yes, it sizzles a little. Just go fast and dunk it in some water when you're done.)

Rake. A rake is handy for managing coals and ash and, like a shovel, can be used for dragging out the ash into a heat-safe container at the end of the firing.

Welding gloves. Made from suede and with a heatproof liner, welding gloves are great protection for your forearms while working the oven.

PREHEAT THE OVEN

Wood-fired ovens work most efficiently when fired daily or at least every other day. Frequent firings keep the chamber dry and heat stored in the masonry, essentials for wood-fired baking. If the base temperature never drops below 200° to 400°F [95° to 200°C], getting it back up to 600° to 725°F [315° to 385°C] should take only a few hours.

If your oven is cold and neglected, preheat it with a small-to-medium fire for a few hours the day *before* you plan to fire it for pizza making. A preheat before the final firing will drive out any moisture and begin to warm the oven materials so they can efficiently absorb the heat when you want to bring the oven up to a high baking temperature relatively quickly. Starting with a hot, dry chamber also helps maintain a consistent temperature, so you'll use less firewood. Lastly, it's much easier to predict when the oven will be ready for a party if it's already warm. Cold starts make for an unpredictable bake in general.

FIRING THE OVEN

Start by placing two pieces of kindling 6 to 8 in [15 to 20 cm] long into the chamber parallel to each other. Next, stack two pieces on top, positioning them perpendicular to the first pieces as if building a log cabin. Repeat, adding kindling in alternating directions until the stack is five to six stories high. Crumple dry newspaper and stuff it into the center of the square, leaving room for airflow to help the wood ignite. Light the newspaper and let the kindling catch. If you have tinder—dry wood shavings or slivers from chopping wood—add it now. Once the fire is established, add two or three pieces of kindling at a time. When coals have formed, use a rake to push the fire deeper into the chamber, toward the center of the oven.

Initially the fire may be smoky, but once the oven is burning hot enough, the smoke will clear. You may also notice the dome turn black, but by the end of the firing, 3 to 4 hours later, it should be completely clean, as the soot will be incinerated by the high heat.

Continue to feed the fire gradually, moving to medium-size pieces of wood. Make sure each log catches before adding more, and avoid having more than 30 percent of the chamber full of wood: Too much wood at once can restrict airflow and cool down the oven. If a log rolls out of place or you notice the fire smoking, use a poker or fireplace tongs to adjust the wood and stoke the fire. It should take about an hour for the fire to grow strong enough that you can safely wander away without fear it will die out.

Once you've reached live fire baking temperatures (roughly 3 to 4 hours from a preheated start)—the dome of the oven is white, the flames roll toward the center, and the internal temperature is 600° to 725°F [315° to 385°C]—take a few minutes to clean up your space, wipe things down, and make sure everything you need is within arm's reach. You'll now transition from building the fire to sustaining it while baking.

Use a long-handled metal peel, hoe, or the scraper end of a wire-bristle brush to push the fire to one side of the oven, depending on your dominant hand. I am right-handed, so I push the coals and fire to the right wall and load to the left. Clean up the hearth with a bristle brush and allow the surface heat to mellow before loading the first pizza. As you bake your pizzas, add a few pieces of kindling every now and again to keep the flame rolling and stop to brush down the hearth periodically.

Depending on the wood quality, preheating, and firing, the oven can either be too hot or too cold when the dough is ready. If the hearth is ripping hot, it will scorch the bottom of the pizza. Put the proofing dough back in the fridge to rest. To take down the heat, refrain from adding any additional wood, sear vegetables like red peppers and onions on a sheet pan or cast-iron pan with the oven door open, or, of course, simply pour yourself a tasty drink and wait. Bring the pizza dough back out when you're 10° to 15°F [6° to 8°C] from your target temperature. If instead you've struggled with the firing or began from a cold start and the oven failed to get to temperature in the expected time frame, return the dough to the fridge and build up your fire to a strong blaze.

LOADING

Make your pizza on a floured wooden peel and give it a shimmy shake to make sure it will slide off. If any part is stuck, lift the edge and toss a little all-purpose or rice flour underneath. Look at where you want the pizza to bake and place the peel there. Holding the peel at a 35-degree angle, swiftly slide the pizza off the peel and onto the hearth. If the peel is at too much of an angle, the pizza will fold over on itself and make a mess rather than drop gracefully onto the hot floor. Practice loading the pizza in a single fluid motion. Shuffling will cause wrinkles, making ridges of undercooked dough.

When considering where to place the pizza, keep in mind that not only is the live fire hot (obviously) but the walls and dome give off intense heat, too, so if the pizza is close to the wall, it will cook quickly. Pizzas are baked with an open door, and it's exciting to watch the pizza as it puffs up and colors. The open door also provides you with a cool zone if you need to reposition a pizza that's baking too fast.

BAKING

When the pizza hits the hearth, the rim should spring up within 30 seconds. Let the pizza bake in the same spot until it's firm enough to rotate 90 degrees so a new section of the crust can bake close to the flame. To rotate, assuming the live fire is on the left, slide the long-handled metal peel under the right side of the pizza, toward the back, then pull the pizza toward you so the charred part is now in the back. Continue to go under the pizza on the right, pulling it toward you to rotate, until it has completed a full circle, directing each new section of crust toward the flames. Depending on the hydration of the dough, the quality of the fire, and the size of the pizza, a pizza can be done in less than 90 seconds or take several minutes. As mentioned earlier, I like a comfortable bake time of 5 to 8 minutes at 725°F [385°C].

To finish your bake, dome the pizza. Lift the pizza on the metal peel so that it's within a few inches from the oven ceiling. Known as doming, this little trick at the end of the bake gives an incredible last blast of high heat, much like a broiler would, achieving perfect char, sauce reduction, and caramelization.

When the pizza is done—the rim has risen and is deeply browned, the cheese is melted, and the sauce is bubbly—remove it from the oven wearing welding gloves and using the metal peel. Transfer it to a wire rack and add any post-bake extra toppings, such as flaky salt or grated Parmesan, then let cool for a few minutes so the cheese can set. Slide the pizza onto a cutting board and cut it with a rocker cutter, pizza wheel, or scissors and serve warm. Use the bristle brush to clean up the hearth before the next pizza. Stoke the fire and check to see if you need to add more wood.

EVALUATION

Now that you've made a wood-fired pizza, step back and evaluate it before going forward. Some adjustments can be made in the moment, like bringing down or raising the heat or using less sauce. Other tweaks, like correctly fermenting or proofing the dough, will need to be addressed the next time you mix the dough. These are the questions I use to guide me in my wood-fired pizza check-in:

Check the undercarriage of the pizza. Is it burnt? Lower the heat by leaving the door open. If you can sacrifice a dough round, **roll it out into a pita (see page 303)** and use it to test the heat, absorbing some of the initial shock. You can also bake a focaccia in a sheet pan to take heat off the hearth. If you have nothing to bake waiting in the wings, leave the door open for a bit and let time mellow the heat, using an infrared thermometer to check it periodically.

Is the pizza too blond? Chill the dough and bring up the oven temperature. If the oven is already at baking temperature, make sure you are loading the pizza deep enough into the oven and close enough to the live fire. Also, check that you have a fire with rolling flames, not just hot coals, in one side of the chamber.

Is the crust well risen and deeply browned with irregular, charred bubbles? If not, check the oven temperature and make sure you're baking the pizza close enough to the live fire and turning it to expose each section to the heat. Also, be sure to adequately bulk ferment and proof the dough next time. It needs to be pillowy and full of air before you shape it and again before you stretch it to bake.

Did the sauce bubble and thicken well? If not, use less sauce next time, so it has a chance to reduce and turn velvety in the oven. Also, refrain from using watery toppings or overloading the pizza, which can cause the sauce to turn into a gummy layer between the dough and the cheese.

Did the cheese melt and brown evenly? If not, give the pizza more time in the oven or dome the pizza for the final 3 to 4 minutes so it browns fully. Then adjust the oven temperature as needed before the next bake, adding kindling to raise the heat or spreading out the coals to disperse the intensity of the heat. Also, be sure to give the hearth a chance to reheat after each pizza. One of the joys of wood-fire baking is staying on top of the subtle changes occurring between the dough and the fire, a truly fun and rewarding experience.

If you're interested in the look and flavor of wood-fired pizza but don't want to chop wood, Gozney and Ooni make wonderful, totally-worth-the-spend outdoor tabletop pizza ovens. ●

OUTDOOR TABLETOP OVENS

GOZNEY is a United Kingdom–based company, and its ovens are known for their durability, high performance, and innovative design, catering to both home chefs and professional cooks. Scotland-based **OONI** focuses on portable pizza ovens that are compact, versatile, affordable, and easy to use. I own two Gozney ovens, the Roccbox and the Dome, and I love using them.

Both the Gozney Roccbox ($500) and the Ooni Koda 12 ($399) can reach up to 950°F [510°C] by directing a live flame onto a low dome of insulated metal above a clay hearth. This creates the definitive look of a wood-fired pizza: tall rim, charred spots, deep browning of the crust. They also produce all the flavors that come from a wood-fired bake: a pronounced nuttiness, a malty bitterness, and notes of toasted hay. If you're looking for complex flavor at home, you need this level of high heat. Here are some tips for success with a new tabletop oven.

- Matching the hydration of the dough with the length of the bake is important. Pizza baked in a high-heat oven needs to have the water in the dough evaporate quickly and also have enough water to achieve a delicate crumb (unless you want a cracker crust). Neapolitan-style doughs with roughly 60 to 65 percent hydration bake in 90 seconds at extremely high temperatures of 800° to 900°F [430° to 480°C], while a Detroit-style pizza may have 80 percent hydration and bake at 475°F [245°C] for 25 to 35 minutes. In short, choose a dough with 68 to 72 percent hydration for a live flame bake.

- Unlike having a large baking stone or steel for baking your pizza, the hearth in a tabletop oven is small and the space above narrow, so use 200 to 220 g [7 to 7¾ oz] dough rounds and stretch the pizzas 2 to 3 in [5 to 7.5 cm] smaller than the width of the hearth. This will also provide loading and rotating room. The peel that comes with the oven is a good guide. For example, the Roccbox comes with a 12 in [30.5 cm] peel, so you should stretch the dough to 10 in [25 cm].

- You'll need to choose among gas, wood pellets, or kindling for fuel. I haven't used wood pellets myself, but I have both the original kindling and gas-powered attachments for the Roccbox. Being a wood-fired baker, I immediately dismissed the propane hookup and went for the kindling attachment. But perhaps *because* I am a wood-fired baker, I was frustrated by the tiny pieces of kindling and the amount necessary to reach (and sustain) the level of heat I needed, so I abandoned the kindling. I have used the propane attachment since and been happy.

- Just like a larger wood-fired oven, the Roccbox needs to build up heat in the floor and the dome for successful baking. This is accomplished through a preheat of at least an hour before the oven is ready to use. Regardless of what the sales materials say, it's always good to give ovens like this time to heat up to avoid a major temperature difference between the floor and the dome. The flame is blasted from the back of the oven, over the dome, and the floor is heated up by proxy, so while the top may be scorching, if the bottom isn't saturated with heat, your pizza will be charred on top but the undercarriage will remain undercooked.

- The flame is shooting from the back in the Roccbox and from the back and sides in the Ooni Koda. These are the hot spots you must manage and negotiate as you try to bake your pizza evenly. As you bake, practice using the knobs that increase or decrease the gas so you can learn the dance. They're often in an awkward spot, and it's good to know you're just going to have to move between the knob and the peel while you bake. Lower the flame, load the pizza, bake until you can get a peel under the crust, 2 to 3 minutes, and then rotate the pizza a quarter turn, increase the flame, and finish baking, rotating as needed.

- You'll need to rotate the pizza regularly during the bake to make sure the edge of the pizza next to the flame isn't burning. Begin by loading the pizza near the front of the oven, then, after rotating, push it toward the back third. Try not to fuss with your pizza too much, rotating it only three or four times at evenly paced intervals. The stone will need a few minutes of recovery time before baking the next pizza.

- I've gotten the crisp crust I prefer by placing a baking steel on my backyard grill, preheating the steel and the oven simultaneously, and starting the pizza on the steel, topping it, and then finishing it off in the oven. This pretty much turns the tabletop oven into a very expensive broiler.

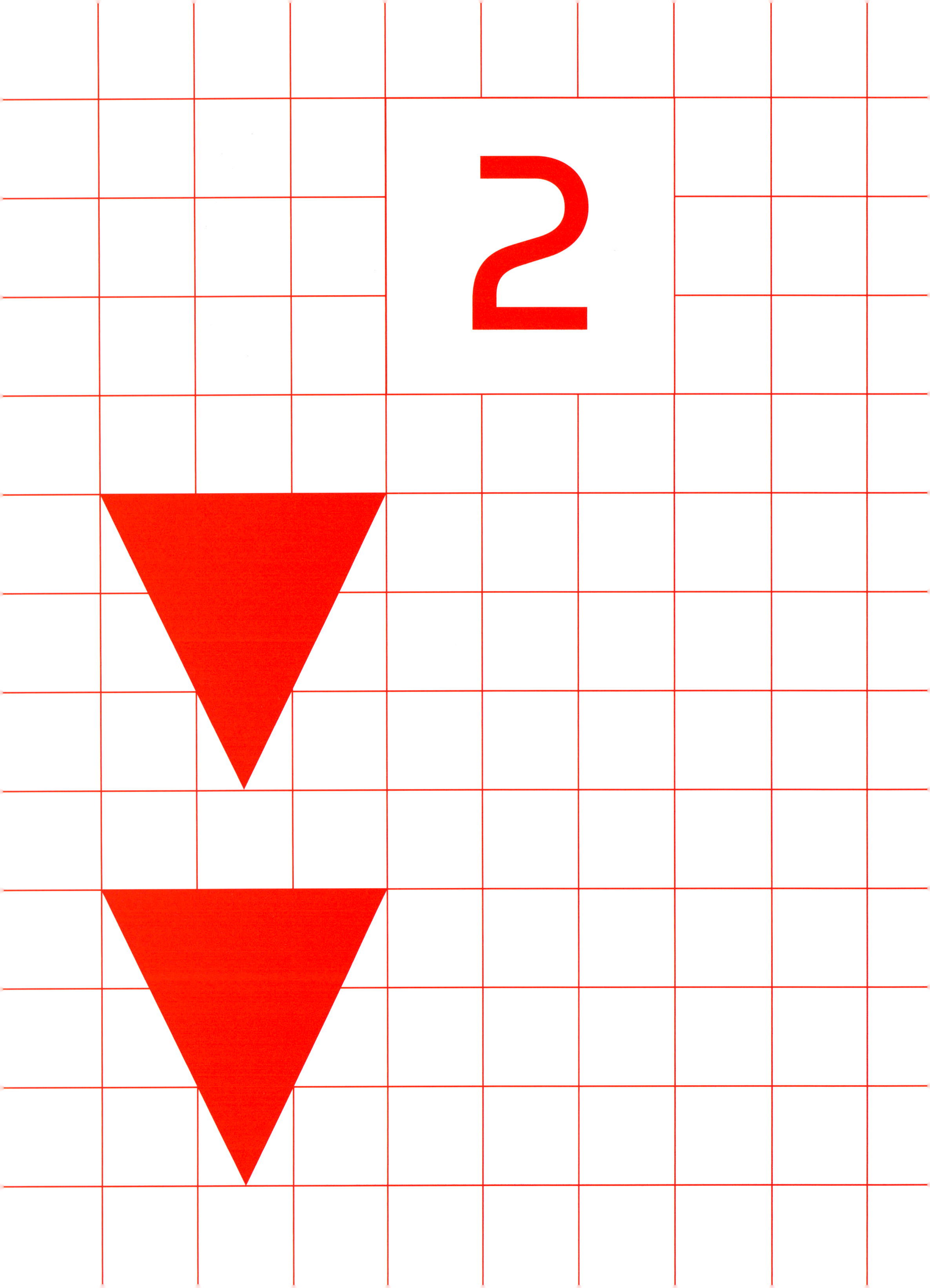
2

PIZZA DOUGH RECIPES

The recipes in this chapter move from a same-day yeasted dough to a dough made with natural leavening and multiple days of fermentation. The middle ground between these styles is explored with yeasted preferments, like **Pizza Dough with Poolish (page 149)**. You'll want to stock your pantry with a good all-purpose flour and make sure you have two digital scales, one for grams and one for milligrams, for the best results.

Pick a dough and make it several times before you move on to another recipe. The first time you make a dough, you're just getting to know it. The second time, you're seeing what needs to be adjusted, and the third go-round, you tweak it, maybe a little more water or more proof time. Intuition is data accumulated by the body over time, so if you want to accelerate your proficiency, make a lot of pizza. I can't give you intuition. That is a gift you give yourself through the discipline of practice. But I can provide solid recipes for you to build on.

FLEXIBLE SCHEDULES

Most of the following doughs and time frames are quite flexible. Once you have a grasp on how the dough should feel at each stage, you can experiment. You may want to try chilling the dough as a whole portion in the fridge overnight and dividing it the following day, or leave the shaped rounds in the fridge for an extra 24 hours. Each dough recipe includes an example time frame, but these time frames are suggestions, not hard rules. As you look at these examples, think about the time between each step and make it work for you. For example, you may decide to mix a starter or levain and leave it to ferment during the day rather than at night.

USE DIGITAL SCALES

The recipes in this book were all written and tested in grams, using both a gram scale and a milligram scale. For accuracy and success, I urge you to use weights when measuring your ingredients, as volume measurements are inherently imprecise. To write the recipes in this book, I converted the gram amount for each kind of flour, such as all-purpose or whole wheat, into a volume measurement. Because a cup of roller-milled white flour will not weigh the same as a cup of freshly milled stone-ground white flour (the latter will be heavier), you will notice fluctuations in the volume amounts based on the type of flour used.

VOLUME MEASUREMENTS

Volume measurements have been rounded for ease. If you opt to use volume measures, you may end up with slightly more dough. First weigh the four 250 g [8¾ oz] portions called for in a recipe, then use any extra dough bits to make smaller practice pizzas. **To learn more about scales and how to properly use volume measures, see page 65.**

SAME-DAY PIZZA DOUGH

Baker's Percentage	Weight	Volume	Ingredient
100%	560 G	4 CUPS	ALL-PURPOSE FLOUR (11% TO 12% PROTEIN)
72%	403 G	1⅔ CUPS	WATER, WARM
2.2%	12 G	2 TSP	SALT
0.25%	1.4 G	¼ TSP	INSTANT YEAST
			ALL-PURPOSE FLOUR FOR KNEADING

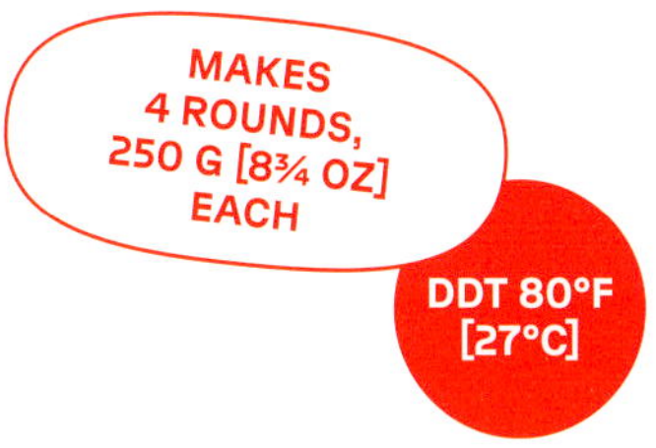

Ready from bowl to bake in 6 hours, this is my go-to dough for an impromptu pizza dinner. Mix the dough as early as you can in the morning and keep it warm throughout the entire process. Although great to use on the day it's made, the dough will hold up well in the fridge for up to 48 hours.

Example Time Frame	
7:00 A.M.	MIX DOUGH
8:00 A.M.	FOLD
9:00 A.M.	FOLD
10:00 A.M.	DIVIDE, SHAPE, AND PROOF

Ready a restaurant-style wide-mouthed water pitcher half full of warm water. **To get the precise temperature, use the chart on page 82**, or just use 80°F [27°C]. You'll use water from this pitcher for mixing the dough and then later for wetting your fingers when folding.

In a large mixing bowl, combine the all-purpose flour and yeast. Quickly stir with a dry hand to blend and aerate, then add the water. Next, using your dominant hand in the shape of a claw, agitate the flour and water into a dough. You can use your free hand to stabilize the bowl. Once a sticky dough has formed, grab and squeeze it several times to bring it into a cohesive, shaggy mass. Cover with a shower cap or lid and let rest for 10 minutes.

Return to the bowl and sprinkle the salt over the dough. With your hands in the shape of crab claws, pinch in the salt. You'll feel the dough tighten. Stop once you have felt the salt dissolve.

When all the ingredients are incorporated, using a dough scraper, turn the dough out onto a lightly floured work surface. Using the heel of your dominant hand, push the top of the dough away from you, then fold it back on itself and rotate it 90 degrees. Push, fold, and rotate again. Repeat this three-step action for 2 to 3 minutes. A simple kneading is sufficient. It doesn't have to be lengthy, as even a few strokes will help the gluten absorb water and strengthen. Use as much flour as you need while you work but no more than is necessary. Stop kneading as soon as the dough resists. **CONT'D**

Transfer the dough to a lightly oiled rectangular dough tub or clean mixing bowl and cover with a lid. The dough has now entered bulk fermentation, or the first rise, and will be given two folds before being divided and shaped. Find a warm place for the dough to rise where the temperature will stay around 80°F [27°C] the whole time.

An hour after mixing, fold the dough. To fold, dip your fingers into the warm water in the pitcher. Gently lift the dough straight up from the middle with both hands. One end will release from the container as you pull upward. Allow the loosened end to tuck under the middle of the dough and then repeat with the other side, lifting and tucking toward the middle. The dough will look like it has coiled underneath itself. Rotate the container a quarter turn and repeat the process. Continue rotating the container and folding until the dough doesn't stretch or spread and has a smooth top. Cover and let rest for 1 hour.

Repeat the folding process and then cover the container and let rest for another hour.

During the hour following the second fold, return to the dough every now and then, uncover the container, and investigate it. It's ready to divide into individual rounds when it smells yeasty, has risen about 20 percent in the bowl, and slowly springs back when gently prodded. Once the dough is relaxed and feels soft like a pillow, move on to dividing. If it needs a little more time, give it an extra 30 minutes. **(If making a pan pizza, see page 113.)**

To divide the dough, lightly flour your work surface. Using the dough scraper, turn the dough out onto the floured surface so the top is now the bottom and you're looking at the puffy underbelly. Using a bench knife, divide the dough into four equal portions, making confident, decisive cuts. Now use the bench knife to scoop a hunk of the dough onto the digital scale. Check the weight: You're looking for the hunk to weigh 250 g [8¾ oz]. Use the bench knife to add or remove dough as needed to reach 250 g [8¾ oz]. (It's more important to have fewer bits and pieces than it is to have four portions that are exactly equal, so don't obsess here.) Set the first piece of dough aside and weigh the remaining portions. You may also skip the scale and simply eyeball the weight, accepting that each pizza will be slightly different.

To form a dough portion into a ball, bring the top edge and the bottom edge to meet in the middle and pinch them together. Now gently stretch out the left and right sides and pinch them together over the just-sealed dough. You'll now have a square of dough. Grab the top left corner and the bottom right corner, stretch them a little, and then pinch them together. Repeat stretching and pinching with the top right corner and bottom left corner. The point where all the gathered portions of dough come together is your seam. The dough will look like a little purse or dumpling. Seal the seam by gently flipping the dough over and dragging it 8 to 10 in [20 to 25 cm] on a dry, flour-free area of the work surface, either cupped in the palm of your hand held in a C shape or nestled against the inside edge of the dough scraper. As you drag, you'll see the dough noticeably tighten and become smooth. Place the ball seam-side down on a flour-free area of the work surface. Shape the remaining dough.

If you plan to make all the pizzas at once, stagger the rounds in a clean, unoiled dough box, spacing them 1 to 2 in [2.5 to 5 cm] apart. If you want to bake them one at a time, place each round in its own inverted takeout container or meal-prep container, with the dough ball resting on the lid covered by the bottom or bowl, or in a lightly oiled deli container.

FOR PROOFING, TOPPING, AND BAKING INSTRUCTIONS, SEE PAGES 96 TO 108.
FOR FREEZING INSTRUCTIONS, SEE PAGE 173.

24-HOUR PIZZA DOUGH WITH SPELT FLOUR

Baker's Percentage	Weight	Volume	Ingredient
80%	464 G	3¼ CUPS	ALL-PURPOSE FLOUR (11% TO 12% PROTEIN)
20%	116 G	1 CUP + 2 TBSP	SPELT FLOUR
68%	394 G	1½ CUPS + 2 TBSP	WATER, WARM
2.2%	13 G	2¼ TSP	SALT
2%	12 G	2¼ TSP	OLIVE OIL (EVOO)
0.25%	1.5 G	¼ TSP	INSTANT YEAST
			ALL-PURPOSE FLOUR FOR KNEADING

Made with 20 percent spelt flour and a few glugs of olive oil, this dough yields an incredible crust with minimal effort. The spelt flour adds extensibility to the dough, making it easy to stretch, and the olive oil tenderizes the crumb and contributes to bold browning in the oven. Best after a 24-hour cold proof, the dough bakes up with hints of toasty caramel and a toothy, tuggy bite.

Example Time Frame	
9:00 A.M.	MIX DOUGH
10:00 A.M.	FOLD
11:00 A.M.	FOLD
12:00 P.M.	DIVIDE, SHAPE, AND MOVE TO FRIDGE

Ready a restaurant-style wide-mouthed water pitcher half full of warm water. **To get the precise temperature, use the chart on page 82**, or just use 80°F [27°C]. You'll use water from this pitcher for mixing the dough and then later for wetting your fingers when folding.

In a large mixing bowl, combine the all-purpose flour, spelt flour, and yeast. Quickly stir with a dry hand to blend and aerate, then add the olive oil and water. Next, using your dominant hand in the shape of a claw, agitate the flour and water into a dough. You can use your free hand to stabilize the bowl. Once a sticky dough has formed, grab and squeeze it several times to bring it into a cohesive, shaggy mass. Cover with a shower cap or lid and let rest for 10 minutes.

Return to the bowl and sprinkle the salt over the dough. With your hands in the shape of crab claws, pinch in the salt. You'll feel the dough tighten. Stop once you have felt the salt dissolve.

When all the ingredients are incorporated, using a dough scraper, turn the dough out onto a lightly floured work surface. Using the heel of your dominant hand, push the top of the dough away from you, then fold it back on itself and rotate it 90 degrees. Push, fold, and rotate again. Repeat this three-step action for 2 to 3 minutes.

A simple kneading is sufficient. It doesn't have to be lengthy, as even a few strokes will help the gluten absorb water and strengthen. Use as much flour as you need while you work but no more than is necessary. Stop kneading as soon as the dough resists.

Transfer the dough to a lightly oiled rectangular dough tub or clean mixing bowl and cover with a lid. The dough has now entered bulk fermentation, or the first rise, and will be given two folds before being divided and shaped. Find a warm place for the dough to rise where the temperature will stay around 80°F [27°C] the whole time.

An hour after mixing, fold the dough. To fold, dip your fingers into the warm water in the pitcher. Gently lift the dough straight up from the middle with both hands. One end will release from the container as you pull upward. Allow the loosened end to tuck under the middle of the dough and then repeat with the other side, lifting and tucking toward the middle. The dough will look like it has coiled underneath itself. Rotate the container a quarter turn and repeat the process. Continue rotating the container and folding until the dough doesn't stretch or spread and has a smooth top. Cover and let rest for 1 hour.

Repeat the folding process and then cover the container and let rest for another hour.

During the hour following the second fold, return to the dough every now and then, uncover the container, and investigate it. It's ready to divide into individual rounds when it smells yeasty, has risen about 20 percent in the bowl, and slowly springs back when gently prodded. Once the dough is relaxed and feels soft like a pillow, move on to dividing. If it needs a little more time, give it an extra 30 minutes. **(If making a pan pizza, see page 113.)**

To divide the dough, lightly flour your work surface. Using the dough scraper, turn the dough out onto the floured surface so the top is now the bottom and you're looking at the puffy underbelly. Using a bench knife, divide the dough into four equal portions, making confident, decisive cuts. Now use the bench knife to scoop a hunk of the dough onto the digital scale. Check the weight: You're looking for the hunk to weigh 250 g [8¾ oz]. Use the bench knife to add or remove dough as needed to reach 250 g [8¾ oz]. (It's more important to have fewer bits and pieces than it is to have four portions that are exactly equal, so don't obsess here.) Set the first piece of dough aside and weigh the remaining portions. You may also skip the scale and simply eyeball the weight, accepting that each pizza will be slightly different. **CONT'D**

To form a dough portion into a ball, bring the top edge and the bottom edge to meet in the middle and pinch them together. Now gently stretch out the left and right sides and pinch them together over the just-sealed dough. You'll now have a square of dough. Grab the top left corner and the bottom right corner, stretch them a little, and then pinch them together. Repeat stretching and pinching with the top right corner and bottom left corner. The point where all the gathered portions of dough come together is your seam. The dough will look like a little purse or dumpling. Seal the seam by gently flipping the dough over and dragging it 8 to 10 in [20 to 25 cm] on a dry, flour-free area of the work surface, either cupped in the palm of your hand held in a C shape or nestled against the inside edge of the dough scraper. As you drag, you'll see the dough noticeably tighten and become smooth. Place the ball seam-side down on a flour-free area of the work surface. Shape the remaining dough.

If you plan to make all the pizzas at once, stagger the rounds in a clean, unoiled dough box, spacing them 1 to 2 in [2.5 to 5 cm] apart. If you want to bake them one at a time, place each round in its own inverted takeout container or meal-prep container, with the dough ball resting on the lid covered by the bottom or bowl, or in a lightly oiled deli container. Refrigerate the rounds for at least 2 hours or up to 24 hours.

FOR PROOFING, TOPPING,
AND BAKING INSTRUCTIONS,
SEE PAGES 96 TO 108.
FOR FREEZING INSTRUCTIONS,
SEE PAGE 173.

WHOLE WHEAT PIZZA DOUGH

Baker's Percentage	Weight	Volume	Ingredient
100%	548 G	4¾ CUPS	WHOLE WHEAT FLOUR
70%	384 G	1½ CUPS + 1½ TBSP	WATER, WARM
5%	26 G	1 TBSP + 2 TSP	OLIVE OIL (EVOO)
5%	26 G	1 TBSP + 1 TSP	HONEY
2.2%	12 G	2 TSP	SALT
0.25%	1.4 G	¼ TSP	INSTANT YEAST
			WHOLE WHEAT FLOUR FOR KNEADING

MAKES 4 ROUNDS, 250 G [8¾ OZ] EACH

DDT 80°F [27°C]

Stone-ground whole wheat flour contains the germ, endosperm, and bran of the wheat berry. The germ is the fatty, aromatic portion of the berry, like the yolk of an egg, and it makes the dough creamy and packed with flavor. The honey sweetens the bitterness that the bran can add, and the olive oil softens the dough. If you have freshly milled stone-ground flour, use it. But if you don't, supermarket whole wheat flour works well too. Opt for a soft wheat, if possible, rather than a strong one, or try a sifted flour, like a T85 **(see page 36 for more on sifted flours)**.

Example Time Frame	
9:00 A.M.	MIX DOUGH
10:00 A.M.	FOLD
11:00 A.M.	FOLD
12:00 P.M.	DIVIDE, SHAPE, AND MOVE TO FRIDGE

Ready a restaurant-style wide-mouthed water pitcher half full of warm water. **To get the precise temperature, use the chart on page 82**, or just use 80°F [27°C]. You'll use water from this pitcher for mixing the dough and then later for wetting your fingers when folding.

In a large mixing bowl, combine the whole wheat flour and yeast. Quickly stir with a dry hand to blend and aerate, then add the water, olive oil, and honey. Next, using your dominant hand in the shape of a claw, agitate the flour and water into a dough. You can use your free hand to stabilize the bowl. Once a sticky dough has formed, grab and squeeze it several times to bring it into a cohesive, shaggy mass. Cover with a shower cap or lid and let rest for 10 minutes.

Return to the bowl and sprinkle the salt over the dough. With your hands in the shape of crab claws, pinch in the salt. You'll feel the dough tighten. Stop once you have felt the salt dissolve.

When all the ingredients are incorporated, using a dough scraper, turn the dough out onto a lightly floured work surface. Using the heel of your dominant hand, push the top of the dough away from you, then fold it back on itself and rotate it 90 degrees. Push, fold, and rotate again. **CONT'D**

Repeat this three-step action for 2 to 3 minutes. A simple kneading is sufficient. It doesn't have to be lengthy, as even a few strokes will help the gluten absorb water and strengthen. Use as much flour as you need while you work but no more than is necessary. Stop kneading as soon as the dough resists.

Transfer the dough to a lightly oiled rectangular dough tub or clean mixing bowl and cover with a lid. The dough has now entered bulk fermentation, or the first rise, and will be given two folds before being divided and shaped. Find a warm place for the dough to rise where the temperature will stay around 80°F [27°C] the whole time.

An hour after mixing, fold the dough. To fold, dip your fingers into the warm water in the pitcher. Gently lift the dough straight up from the middle with both hands. One end will release from the container as you pull upward. Allow the loosened end to tuck under the middle of the dough and then repeat with the other side, lifting and tucking toward the middle. The dough will look like it has coiled underneath itself. Rotate the container a quarter turn and repeat the process. Continue rotating the container and folding until the dough doesn't stretch or spread and has a smooth top. Cover and let rest for 1 hour.

Repeat the folding process and then cover the container and let rest for another hour.

During the hour following the second fold, return to the dough every now and then, uncover the container, and investigate it. It's ready to divide into individual rounds when it smells yeasty, has risen about 20 percent in the bowl, and slowly springs back when gently prodded. Once the dough is relaxed and feels soft like a pillow, move on to dividing. If it needs a little more time, give it an extra 30 minutes. **(If making a pan pizza, see page 113.)**

To divide the dough, lightly flour your work surface. Using the dough scraper, turn the dough out onto the floured surface so the top is now the bottom and you're looking at the puffy underbelly. Using a bench knife, divide the dough into four equal portions, making confident, decisive cuts. Now use the bench knife to scoop a hunk of the dough onto the digital scale. Check the weight: You're looking for the hunk to weigh 250 g [8¾ oz]. Use the bench knife to add or remove dough as needed to reach 250 g [8¾ oz]. (It's more important to have fewer bits and pieces than it is to have **CONT'D** four portions that are exactly equal, so don't obsess here.) Set the first piece of dough aside and weigh the remaining portions. You may also skip the scale and simply eyeball the weight, accepting that each pizza will be slightly different.

To form a dough portion into a ball, bring the top edge and the bottom edge to meet in the middle and pinch them together. Now gently stretch out the left and right sides and pinch them together over the just-sealed dough. You'll now have a square of dough. Grab the top left corner and the bottom right corner, stretch them a little, and then pinch them together. Repeat stretching and pinching with the top right corner and bottom left corner. The point where all the gathered portions of dough come together is your seam. The dough will look like a little purse or dumpling. Seal the seam by gently flipping the dough over and dragging it 8 to 10 in [20 to 25 cm] on a dry, flour-free area of the work surface, either cupped in the palm of your hand held in a C shape or nestled against the inside edge of the dough scraper. As you drag, you'll see the dough noticeably tighten and become smooth. Place the ball seam-side down on a flour-free area of the work surface. Shape the remaining dough.

If you plan to make all the pizzas at once, stagger the rounds in a clean, unoiled dough box, spacing them 1 to 2 in [2.5 to 5 cm] apart. If you want to bake them one at a time, place each round in its own inverted takeout container or meal-prep container, with the dough ball resting on the lid covered by the bottom or bowl, or in a lightly oiled deli container. Refrigerate the rounds for at least 2 hours or up to 48 hours.

FOR PROOFING, TOPPING,
AND BAKING INSTRUCTIONS,
SEE PAGES 96 TO 108.
FOR FREEZING INSTRUCTIONS,
SEE PAGE 173.

KID'S PITZA DOUGH

Baker's Percentage	Weight	Volume	Ingredient
50%	325 G	2¼ CUPS	ALL-PURPOSE FLOUR (11% TO 12% PROTEIN)
50%	325 G	2¾ CUPS + 2 TBSP	WHOLE WHEAT FLOUR
40%	260 G	1 CUP + 1 TBSP	PLAIN YOGURT, WHOLE-MILK, AT ROOM TEMPERATURE
12%	78 G	¼ CUP + 1½ TBSP	OLIVE OIL (EVOO)
2%	13 G	2¼ TSP	SALT
0.5%	3 G	¾ TSP	INSTANT YEAST
			ALL-PURPOSE FLOUR FOR KNEADING

MAKES 4 ROUNDS, 250 G [8¾ OZ] EACH

This dough was originally our household pita bread. Then my daughter and I decided we wanted pizza instead, and *pitza* was born. The yogurt makes the dough soft, easy for tiny mouths to teethe on. Skip Greek yogurt for this recipe—it's too thick. If you can find soft whole wheat flour, use it. If not, supermarket whole wheat flour, which tends to be milled from a hard wheat, works too. The dough is sticky and benefits from being chilled before being shaped and rolled out.

Example Time Frame	
7:00 A.M.	MIX DOUGH
8:00 A.M.	FOLD
9:00 A.M.	FOLD
10:00 A.M.	MOVE TO FRIDGE
7:00 A.M. (FOLLOWING DAY)	DIVIDE AND SHAPE

To get your kids involved, pre-weigh the ingredients into separate containers, like deli containers or cereal bowls, and then let them combine the all-purpose flour, whole wheat flour, and yeast in a large mixing bowl. Have them quickly stir (with clean, dry hands) to blend and aerate the dry ingredients, then add the yogurt and olive oil. Use your hands to hold down the bowl while your young bakers grab and squeeze the ingredients several times to bring them into a cohesive, shaggy mass. Use a dough scraper to scrape any dough on their hands (or yours) back into the mixing bowl. Cover the bowl with a shower cap or lid and let rest for 10 minutes.

Return to the bowl and sprinkle the salt over the dough. With your little ones' hands in the shape of crab claws, have them pinch in the salt. You should see the dough tighten. Have them stop once they feel the salt dissolve. A minute or two of pinching should do it.

When all the ingredients are incorporated, using the dough scraper, turn the dough out onto a lightly floured work surface. With the heel of your dominant hand, push the top of the dough away from you, then fold it back on itself and rotate it 90 degrees. Push, fold, and rotate again. Repeat this three-step action for 2 to 3 minutes. A simple kneading is sufficient. It doesn't have to be lengthy, as even a few strokes will help the gluten absorb moisture and strengthen. You can start off the process and let your helpers finish the final few strokes. Use as much flour as you need while you work but no more than is necessary. Stop kneading as soon as the dough resists.

CONT'D

Transfer the dough to a lightly oiled rectangular dough tub or clean mixing bowl and cover with a lid. The dough has now entered bulk fermentation, or the first rise, and will be given two folds before being divided and shaped. Find a warm place for the dough to rise where the temperature will stay around 80°F [27°C] the whole time. This is a great time to go on a hunt in your house for a nice warm place to put the dough.

Ready a restaurant-style wide-mouthed water pitcher half full of warm water. You'll use this water to wet fingers when folding.

An hour after mixing, fold the dough. To fold, dip your fingers into the warm water in the pitcher. Gently lift the dough straight up from the middle with both hands. One end will release from the container as you pull upward. Allow the loosened end to tuck under the middle of the dough and then repeat with the other side, lifting and tucking toward the middle. The dough will look like it has coiled underneath itself. Rotate the container a quarter turn and repeat the process. Continue rotating the container and folding until the dough doesn't stretch or spread and has a smooth top. Cover, give the bowl a little pat, and let the dough rest for 1 hour.

Repeat the folding process and then cover the container. Transfer the dough to the fridge overnight or for up to 24 hours.

The following morning, bring out the dough and let it warm up for 10 to 15 minutes. Using the dough scraper, turn the dough out onto a lightly floured surface so the top is now the bottom and you're looking at the puffy underbelly. You or a helper can now divide the dough. Using a bench scraper, cut it into four equal portions, making confident, decisive cuts. Skip the scale here and simply eyeball the weight, accepting that each pitza will be slightly different.

To form a dough portion into a ball, bring the top edge and the bottom edge to meet in the middle and pinch them together. (Little fingers are great at pinching!) Now gently stretch out the left and right sides and pinch them together over the just-sealed dough. You'll now have a square of dough. Grab the top left corner and the bottom right corner, stretch them a little, and then pinch them together. Repeat stretching and pinching with the top right corner and bottom left corner. The point where all the gathered portions of dough come together is your seam. The dough will look like a little purse or dumpling. Seal the seam by gently flipping the dough over and dragging it 8 to 10 in [20 to 25 cm] on a dry, flour-free area of the work surface, either cupped in the palm of your hand held in a C shape or nestled against the inside edge of the dough scraper. As you drag, you'll see the dough noticeably tighten and become smooth. Place the ball seam-side down on a flour-free area of the work surface. Shape the remaining dough.

If you plan to make all the pitzas at once, stagger the rounds in a clean, unoiled dough box, spacing them 1 to 2 in [2.5 to 5 cm] apart. If you want to bake them one at a time, place each round in its own inverted takeout container or meal-prep container, with the dough ball resting on the lid covered by the bottom or bowl, or in a lightly oiled deli container. You can choose to refrigerate the dough overnight again (or up to another 24 hours), or leave it out at room temperature for a same-day bake.

FOR PROOFING, TOPPING,
AND BAKING INSTRUCTIONS,
SEE PAGES 96 TO 108.
FOR FREEZING INSTRUCTIONS,
SEE PAGE 173.

PIZZA DOUGH WITH A 3-HOUR SPONGE

Sponge

Baker's Percentage	Weight	Volume	Ingredient
100%	124 G	¾ CUP + 2 TBSP	ALL-PURPOSE FLOUR (11% TO 12% PROTEIN)
60%	74 G	⅓ CUP	WATER
0.2%	0.4 G	PINCH	INSTANT YEAST

Dough

Baker's Percentage	Weight	Volume	Ingredient
100%	496 G	3½ CUPS	ALL-PURPOSE FLOUR (11% TO 12% PROTEIN)
60%	297 G	1¼ CUPS	WATER, WARM
40%	198 G	¾ CUP	SPONGE
2%	10 G	1¾ TSP	SALT
0.25%	1 G	¼ TSP	INSTANT YEAST
			ALL-PURPOSE FLOUR FOR KNEADING

A sponge is a preferment, a portion of the final dough that is mixed in advance and left to ferment. This simple step starts to unlock flavors in the flour and break down a portion of the stretchy proteins present, creating a supple dough. It is a great method to try if you want to get more complicated but aren't up to tending a sourdough culture.

TO MAKE THE SPONGE: In a quart-size deli or similar container, combine the all-purpose flour, water, and yeast. Stir thoroughly with a spoon until it forms a stiff ball. You may need to use the back of the spoon to press and "knead" it together. Try to keep most of it in the container and not on the spoon. Cover with a lid and ferment for 3 hours at room temperature (68° to 72°F [20° to 22°C]). It's ready to use when it has doubled in size, smells yeasty, and is full of bubbles.

TO MAKE THE DOUGH: Ready a restaurant-style wide-mouthed water pitcher half full of warm water. **To get the precise temperature, use the chart on page 82**, or just use 80°F [27°C]. You'll use water from this pitcher for mixing the dough and later for wetting your fingers when folding.

Example Time Frame	
8:00 A.M.	MIX SPONGE
11:00 A.M.	MIX DOUGH
12:00 P.M.	FOLD
1:00 P.M.	DIVIDE, SHAPE, AND MOVE TO FRIDGE

In a large mixing bowl, combine the all-purpose flour and yeast. Quickly stir with a dry hand to blend and aerate, then add the sponge and the water. Next, using your dominant hand in the shape of a claw, agitate the flour and water into a dough. You can use your free hand to stabilize the bowl. Once a rough, sticky dough has formed, grab and squeeze it several times to bring it into a cohesive, shaggy mass. Cover with a shower cap or lid and let rest for 10 minutes.

Return to the bowl and sprinkle the salt over the dough. With your hands in the shape of crab claws, pinch in the salt. You'll feel the dough tighten. Stop once you have felt the salt dissolve.

When all the ingredients are incorporated, using a dough scraper, turn the dough out onto a lightly floured work surface. With the heel of your dominant hand, push the top of the dough away from you, then fold it back on itself and rotate it 90 degrees. Push, fold, and rotate again. Repeat this three-step action for 2 to 3 minutes. A simple kneading is sufficient. It doesn't have to be lengthy, as even a few strokes will help the gluten absorb water and strengthen. Use as much flour as you need while you work but no more than is necessary. Stop kneading as soon as the dough resists.

Transfer the dough to a lightly oiled rectangular dough tub or clean mixing bowl and cover with a lid. The dough has now entered bulk fermentation, or the first rise, and will be given a single fold before being divided and shaped. Find a warm place for the dough to rise where the temperature will stay around 80°F [27°C] the whole time.

An hour after mixing, fold the dough. To fold, dip your fingers into the warm water in the pitcher. Gently lift the dough straight up from the middle with both hands. One end will release from the container as you pull upward. Allow the loosened end to tuck under the middle of the dough and then repeat with the other side, lifting and tucking toward the middle. The dough will look like it has coiled underneath itself. Rotate the container a quarter turn and repeat the process. Continue rotating the container and folding until the dough doesn't stretch or spread and has a smooth top. Cover and let rest for 1 hour. **CONT'D**

During the hour following the fold, return to the dough every now and then, uncover the container, and investigate it. It's ready to divide into individual rounds when it smells yeasty, has risen about 20 percent in the bowl, and slowly springs back when gently prodded. Once the dough is relaxed and feels soft like a pillow, move on to dividing. If it needs a little more time, give it an extra 30 minutes. **(If making a pan pizza, see page 113.)**

To divide the dough, lightly flour your work surface. Using a dough scraper, turn the dough out onto the floured surface so the top is now the bottom and you're looking at the puffy underbelly. Using a bench knife, divide the dough into four equal portions, making confident, decisive cuts. Now use the bench knife to scoop a hunk of the dough onto the digital scale. Check the weight: You're looking for the hunk to weight 250 g [8¾ oz]. Use the bench knife to add or remove dough as needed to reach 250 g [8¾ oz]. (It's more important to have fewer bits and pieces than it is to have four portions that are exactly equal, so don't obsess here.) Set the first piece of dough aside and weigh the remaining portions. You may also skip the scale and simply eyeball the weight, accepting that each pizza will be slightly different.

To form a dough portion into a ball, bring the top edge and the bottom edge to meet in the middle and pinch them together. Now gently stretch out the left and right sides and pinch them together over the just-sealed dough. You'll now have a square of dough. Grab the top left corner and the bottom right corner, stretch them a little, and then pinch them together. Repeat stretching and pinching with the top right corner and bottom left corner. The point where all the gathered portions of dough come together is your seam. The dough will look like a little purse or dumpling. Seal the seam by gently flipping the dough over and dragging it 8 to 10 in [20 to 25 cm] on a dry, flour-free area of the work surface, either cupped in the palm of your hand held in a C shape or nestled against the inside edge of the dough scraper. As you drag, you'll see the dough noticeably tighten and become smooth. Place the ball seam-side down on a flour-free area of the work surface. Shape the remaining dough.

If you plan to make all the pizzas at once, stagger the rounds in a clean, unoiled dough box, spacing them 1 to 2 in [2.5 to 5 cm] apart. If you want to bake them one at a time, place each round in its own inverted takeout container or meal-prep container, with the dough ball resting on the lid covered by the bottom or bowl, or in a lightly oiled deli container. Refrigerate the rounds for at least 2 hours or up to 48 hours.

FOR PROOFING, TOPPING, AND BAKING INSTRUCTIONS, SEE PAGES 96 TO 108. FOR FREEZING INSTRUCTIONS, SEE PAGE 173.

PIZZA DOUGH WITH POOLISH

Poolish

Baker's Percentage	Weight	Volume	Ingredient
100%	88 G	½ CUP + 2 TBSP	ALL-PURPOSE FLOUR (11% TO 12% PROTEIN)
100%	88 G	¼ CUP + 2 TBSP	WATER
0.2%	0.2 G	PINCH	INSTANT YEAST

Dough

Baker's Percentage	Weight	Volume	Ingredient
100%	500 G	3½ CUPS	ALL-PURPOSE FLOUR (11% TO 12% PROTEIN)
63%	315 G	1⅓ CUPS	WATER, WARM
35%	175 G	¾ CUP	POOLISH
2%	10 G	1¾ TSP	SALT
0.25%	1 G	¼ TSP	INSTANT YEAST
			ALL-PURPOSE FLOUR FOR KNEADING

A poolish is a yeasted preferment made from equal parts water and flour. Mixed and left to ferment overnight before using, it transforms an ordinary dough into a nutty-flavored, sweetly aromatic, stretchy dough. The poolish should be used at its peak, around the 10- to 12-hour mark. This is a very forgiving, good-for-beginners dough.

Example Time Frame	
8:00 P.M. (PREVIOUS NIGHT)	MIX POOLISH
8:00 A.M.	MIX DOUGH
9:00 A.M.	FOLD
10:00 A.M.	DIVIDE, SHAPE, AND MOVE TO FRIDGE

TO MAKE THE POOLISH: In a quart-size deli or similar container, combine the all-purpose flour, water, and yeast. Stir thoroughly with a spoon. The poolish will be loose and sticky. Try to keep most of it in the container and not on the spoon. Cover with a lid and ferment for 10 to 12 hours at room temperature (68° to 72°F [20° to 22°C]). It's ready to use when it has doubled in size, smells yeasty, and is full of bubbles.

TO MAKE THE DOUGH: Ready a restaurant-style wide-mouthed water pitcher half full of warm water. **To get the precise temperature, use the chart on page 82**, or just use 80°F [27°C]. You'll use water from this pitcher for mixing the dough and later for wetting your fingers when folding.

In a large mixing bowl, combine the all-purpose flour and yeast. Quickly stir with a dry hand to blend and aerate, then add the poolish and water. Next, using your dominant hand in the shape of a claw, agitate the flour and water into a dough. You can use your free hand to stabilize the bowl. CONT'D

Once a rough, sticky dough has formed, grab and squeeze it several times to bring it into a cohesive, shaggy mass. Cover with a shower cap or lid and let rest for 10 minutes.

Return to the bowl and sprinkle the salt over the dough. With your hands in the shape of crab claws, pinch in the salt. You'll feel the dough tighten. Stop once you have felt the salt dissolve.

When all the ingredients are incorporated, using a dough scraper, turn the dough out onto a lightly floured work surface. With the heel of your dominant hand, push the top of the dough away from you, then fold it back on itself and rotate it 90 degrees. Push, fold, and rotate again. Repeat this three-step action for 2 to 3 minutes. A simple kneading is sufficient. It doesn't have to be lengthy, as even a few strokes will help the gluten absorb water and strengthen. Use as much flour as you need while you work but no more than is necessary. Stop kneading as soon as the dough resists.

Transfer the dough to a lightly oiled rectangular dough tub or clean mixing bowl and cover with a lid. The dough has now entered bulk fermentation, or the first rise, and will be given a single fold before being divided and shaped. Find a warm place for the dough to rise where the temperature will stay around 80°F [27°C] the whole time.

An hour after mixing, fold the dough. To fold, dip your fingers into the warm water in the pitcher. Gently lift the dough straight up from the middle with both hands. One end will release from the container as you pull upward. Allow the loosened end to tuck under the middle of the dough and then repeat with the other side, lifting and tucking toward the middle. The dough will look like it has coiled underneath itself. Rotate the container a quarter turn and repeat the process. Continue rotating the container and folding until the dough doesn't stretch or spread and has a smooth top. Cover and let rest for 1 hour.

During the hour following the fold, return to the dough every now and then, uncover the container, and investigate it. It's ready to divide into individual rounds when it smells yeasty, has risen about 20 percent in the bowl, and slowly springs back when gently prodded. Once the dough is relaxed and feels soft like a pillow, move on to dividing. If it needs a little more time, give it an extra 30 minutes. **(If making a pan pizza, see page 113.)**

To divide the dough, lightly flour your work surface. Using the dough scraper, turn the dough out onto the floured surface so the top is now the bottom and you're looking at the puffy underbelly. Using a bench knife, divide the dough into four equal portions, making confident, decisive cuts. Now use the bench knife to scoop a hunk of the dough onto the digital scale. Check the weight: You're looking for the hunk to weigh 250 g [8¾ oz]. Use the bench knife to add or remove dough as needed to reach 250 g [8¾ oz]. (It's more important to have fewer bits and pieces than it is to have four portions that are exactly equal, so don't obsess here.) Set the first piece of dough aside and weigh the remaining portions. You may also skip the scale and simply eyeball the weight, accepting that each pizza will be slightly different.

To form a dough portion into a ball, bring the top edge and the bottom edge to meet in the middle and pinch them together. Now gently stretch out the left and right sides and pinch them together over the just-sealed dough. You'll now have a square of dough. Grab the top left corner and the bottom right corner, stretch them a little, and then pinch them together. Repeat stretching and pinching with the top right corner and bottom left corner. The point where all the gathered portions of dough come together is your seam. The dough will look like a little purse or dumpling. Seal the seam by gently flipping the dough over and dragging it 8 to 10 in [20 to 25 cm] on a dry, flour-free area of the work surface, either cupped in the palm of your hand held in a C shape or nestled against the inside edge of the dough scraper. As you drag, you'll see the dough noticeably tighten and become smooth. Place the ball seam-side down on a flour-free area of the work surface. Shape the remaining dough.

If you plan to make all the pizzas at once, stagger the rounds in a clean, unoiled dough box, spacing them 1 to 2 in [2.5 to 5 cm] apart. If you want to bake them one at a time, place each round in its own inverted takeout container or meal-prep container, with the dough ball resting on the lid covered by the bottom or bowl, or in a lightly oiled deli container. Refrigerate the rounds for at least 2 hours or up to 48 hours.

FOR PROOFING, TOPPING,
AND BAKING INSTRUCTIONS,
SEE PAGES 96 TO 108.
FOR FREEZING INSTRUCTIONS,
SEE PAGE 173.

"00" PIZZA DOUGH

Levain

Baker's Percentage	Weight	Volume	Ingredient
100%	26 G	3 TBSP	ALL-PURPOSE FLOUR (11% TO 12% PROTEIN)
100%	26 G	1¾ TBSP	WATER
10%	3 G	¾ TSP	SOURDOUGH STARTER

Dough

Baker's Percentage	Weight	Volume	Ingredient
100%	556 G	4¾ CUPS	00 FLOUR
68%	377 G	1½ CUPS	WATER, WARM
10%	56 G	¼ CUP	LEVAIN
2.2%	12 G	2¼ TSP	SALT
0.25%	1.4 G	¼ TSP	INSTANT YEAST
			ALL-PURPOSE FLOUR FOR KNEADING

Doppio zero (00) Italian flour is the finest grind of flour you can get in Italy, and it's used here to make an incredibly light, pillowy crust with a crisp exterior. Imported Italian brands at the supermarket will likely be made from soft wheat, and domestic brands, such as King Arthur '00' Pizza flour, are typically made from a blend of hard and soft wheats. This dough can be stretched paper-thin and is excellent for a high-heat oven, like an outdoor tabletop pizza oven.

TO MAKE THE LEVAIN: In a pint-size deli or similar container, combine the all-purpose flour, water, and sourdough starter. Stir thoroughly with a spoon. The levain will be loose and sticky. Try to keep most of it in the container and not on the spoon. Cover with a lid and ferment for 8 to 10 hours at room temperature (68° to 72°F [20° to 22°C]). It's ready to use when it has doubled in size, smells like yogurt, and is full of bubbles.

TO MAKE THE DOUGH: Ready a restaurant-style wide-mouthed water pitcher half full of warm water. **To get the precise temperature, use the chart on page 82**, or just use 80°F [27°C]. You'll use water from this pitcher for mixing the dough and later for wetting your fingers when folding.

In a large mixing bowl, combine the 00 flour and yeast. Quickly stir with a dry hand to aerate, then add the levain and water. Next, using your dominant hand in the shape of a claw, agitate the levain, flour, and water into a dough. You can use your free hand to stabilize the bowl. Once a rough, sticky dough has formed, grab and squeeze it several times to bring it into a cohesive, shaggy mass. Cover with a shower cap or lid and let rest for 10 minutes.

Example Time Frame

9:00 P.M. (PREVIOUS NIGHT)	MIX LEVAIN
7:00 A.M.	MIX DOUGH
8:00 A.M.	FOLD
9:00 A.M.	DIVIDE, SHAPE, AND MOVE TO FRIDGE

Return to the bowl and sprinkle the salt over the dough. With your hands in the shape of crab claws, pinch in the salt. You'll feel the dough tighten. Stop once you have felt the salt dissolve.

When all the ingredients are incorporated, using a dough scraper, turn the dough out onto a lightly floured work surface. Using the heel of your dominant hand, push the top of the dough away from you, then fold it back on itself and rotate it 90 degrees. Push, fold, and rotate again. Repeat this three-step action for 2 to 3 minutes. A simple kneading is sufficient. It doesn't have to be lengthy, as even a few strokes will help the gluten absorb water and strengthen. Use as much flour as you need while you work but no more than is necessary. Stop kneading as soon as the dough resists.

Transfer the dough to a lightly oiled rectangular dough tub or clean mixing bowl and cover with a lid. The dough has now entered bulk fermentation, or the first rise, and will be given a single fold before being divided and shaped. Find a warm place for the dough to rise where the temperature will stay around 80°F [27°C] the whole time.

An hour after mixing, fold the dough. To fold, dip your fingers into the warm water in the pitcher. Gently lift the dough straight up from the middle with both hands. One end will release from the container as you pull upward. Allow the loosened end to tuck under the middle of the dough and then repeat with the other side, lifting and tucking toward the middle. The dough will look like it has coiled underneath itself. Rotate the container a quarter turn and repeat the process. Continue rotating the container and folding until the dough doesn't stretch or spread and has a smooth top. Cover and let rest for 1 hour.

During the hour following the fold, return to the dough every now and then, uncover the container, and investigate it. It's ready to divide into individual rounds when it smells yeasty, has risen about 20 percent in the bowl, and slowly springs back when gently prodded. Once the dough is relaxed and feels soft like a pillow, move on to dividing. If it needs a little more time, give it an extra 30 minutes. **(If making a pan pizza, see page 113.)** **CONT'D**

To divide the dough, lightly flour your work surface. Using the dough scraper, turn the dough out onto the floured surface so the top is now the bottom and you're looking at the puffy underbelly. Using a bench knife, divide the dough into four equal portions, making confident, decisive cuts. Now use the bench knife to scoop a hunk of the dough onto the digital scale. Check the weight: You're looking for the hunk to weigh 250 g [8¾ oz]. Use the bench knife to add or remove dough as needed to reach 250 g [8¾ oz]. (It's more important to have fewer bits and pieces than it is to have four portions that are exactly equal, so don't obsess here.) Set the first piece of dough aside and weigh the remaining portions. You may also skip the scale and simply eyeball the weight, accepting that each pizza will be slightly different.

To form a dough portion into a ball, bring the top edge and the bottom edge to meet in the middle and pinch them together. Now gently stretch out the left and right sides and pinch them together over the just-sealed dough. You'll now have a square of dough. Grab the top left corner and the bottom right corner, stretch them a little, and then pinch them together. Repeat stretching and pinching with the top right corner and bottom left corner. The point where all the gathered portions of dough come together is your seam. The dough will look like a little purse or dumpling. Seal the seam by gently flipping the dough over and dragging it 8 to 10 in [20 to 25 cm] on a dry, flour-free area of the work surface, either cupped in the palm of your hand held in a C shape or nestled against the inside edge of the dough scraper. As you drag, you'll see the dough noticeably tighten and become smooth. Place the ball seam-side down on a flour-free area of the work surface. Shape the remaining dough.

If you plan to make all the pizzas at once, stagger the rounds in a clean, unoiled dough box, spacing them 1 to 2 in [2.5 to 5 cm] apart. If you want to bake them one at a time, place each round in its own inverted takeout container or meal-prep container, with the dough ball resting on the lid covered by the bottom or bowl, or in a lightly oiled deli container. Refrigerate the rounds for at least 2 hours or up to 24 hours.

FOR PROOFING, TOPPING,
AND BAKING INSTRUCTIONS,
SEE PAGES 96 TO 108.
FOR FREEZING INSTRUCTIONS,
SEE PAGE 173.

HYBRID YEAST AND NATURAL LEAVENING PIZZA DOUGH

Levain

Baker's Percentage	Weight	Volume	Ingredient
100%	56 G	⅓ CUP + 1 TBSP	ALL-PURPOSE FLOUR (11% TO 12% PROTEIN)
80%	45 G	3 TBSP	WATER
10%	6 G	1½ TSP	SOURDOUGH STARTER

MAKES 4 ROUNDS, 250 G [8¾ OZ] EACH

DDT 80°F [27°C]

Dough

Baker's Percentage	Weight	Volume	Ingredient
80%	420 G	3 CUPS	ALL-PURPOSE FLOUR (11% TO 12% PROTEIN)
20%	105 G	¾ CUP	BREAD FLOUR (12% TO 14% PROTEIN)
68%	358 G	1⅓ CUPS + 2 TBSP	WATER, WARM
20%	105 G	⅓ CUP + 2 TBSP	LEVAIN
2.2%	13 G	2 TSP	SALT
0.1%	0.5 G	PINCH	INSTANT YEAST
			ALL-PURPOSE FLOUR FOR KNEADING

Slightly chewy, crisp, and complex, this dough is my sourdough, or naturally leavened, version of a Neapolitan-like crust, and my go-to for weekend pizza nights. Made with an overnight levain, the final dough has a mellow, cultured flavor from the sourdough and a pillowy, light crumb thanks to the dose of commercial yeast. **To learn how to create a sourdough starter, see page 72.**

Example Time Frame

11:00 P.M. (PREVIOUS NIGHT)	MIX LEVAIN
7:00 A.M.	MIX DOUGH
8:00 A.M.	FOLD
9:00 A.M.	DIVIDE, SHAPE, AND MOVE TO FRIDGE

TO MAKE THE LEVAIN: In a pint-size deli or similar container, combine the all-purpose flour, water, and sourdough starter. Stir thoroughly with a spoon. The levain will be stiff and sticky. Try to keep most of it in the container and not on the spoon. Cover with a lid and ferment for 8 to 10 hours at room temperature (68° to 72°F [20° to 22°C]). It's ready to use when it has doubled in size, smells like yogurt, and is full of bubbles.

TO MAKE THE DOUGH: Ready a restaurant-style wide-mouthed water pitcher half full of warm water. **To get the precise temperature, use the chart on page 82**, or just use 80°F [27°C]. You'll use water from this pitcher for mixing the dough and later for wetting your fingers when folding.

In a large mixing bowl, combine the all-purpose flour, bread flour, and yeast. Quickly stir with a dry hand to blend and aerate, then add the levain and water. Next, using your dominant hand in the shape of a claw, agitate the levain, flour, and water into a dough. You can use your free hand to stabilize the bowl. Once a sticky dough has formed, grab and squeeze it several times to bring it into a cohesive, shaggy mass. Cover with a shower cap or lid and let rest for 10 minutes.

Return to the bowl and sprinkle the salt over the dough. With your hands in the shape of crab claws, pinch in the salt. You'll feel the dough tighten. Stop once you have felt the salt dissolve.

When all the ingredients are incorporated, using a dough scraper, turn the dough out onto a lightly floured work surface. Using the heel of your dominant hand, push the top of the dough away from you, then fold it back on itself and rotate it 90 degrees. Push, fold, and rotate again. Repeat this three-step action for 2 to 3 minutes. A simple kneading is sufficient. It doesn't have to be lengthy, as even a few strokes will help the gluten absorb water and strengthen. Use as much flour as you need while you work but no more than is necessary. Stop kneading as soon as the dough resists.

Transfer the dough to a lightly oiled rectangular dough tub or clean mixing bowl and cover with a lid. The dough has now entered bulk fermentation, or the first rise, and will be given a single fold before being divided and shaped. Find a warm place for the dough to rise where the temperature will stay around 80°F [27°C] the whole time.

An hour after mixing, fold the dough. To fold, dip your fingers into the warm water in the pitcher. Gently lift the dough straight up from the middle with both hands. One end will release from the container as you pull upward. Allow the loosened end to tuck under the middle of the dough and then repeat with the other side, lifting and tucking toward the middle. The dough will look like it has coiled underneath itself. Rotate the container a quarter turn and repeat the process. Continue rotating the container and folding until the dough doesn't stretch or spread and has a smooth top. Cover and let rest for 1 hour.

During the hour following the fold, return to the dough every now and then, uncover the container, and investigate it. It's ready to divide into individual rounds when it smells yeasty, has risen about 20 percent in the bowl, and slowly springs back when gently prodded. Once the dough is relaxed and feels soft like a pillow, move on to dividing. If it needs a little more time, give it an extra 30 minutes. **(If making a pan pizza, see page 113.)** **CONT'D**

To divide the dough, lightly flour your work surface. Using the dough scraper, turn the dough out onto the floured surface so the top is now the bottom and you're looking at the puffy underbelly. Using a bench knife, divide the dough into four equal portions, making confident, decisive cuts. Now use the bench knife to scoop a hunk of the dough onto the digital scale. Check the weight: You're looking for the hunk to weigh 250 g [8¾ oz]. Use the bench knife to add or remove dough as needed to reach 250 g [8¾ oz]. (It's more important to have fewer bits and pieces than it is to have four portions that are exactly equal, so don't obsess here.) Set the first piece of dough aside and weigh the remaining portions. You may also skip the scale and simply eyeball the weight, accepting that each pizza will be slightly different.

To form a dough portion into a ball, bring the top edge and the bottom edge to meet in the middle and pinch them together. Now gently stretch out the left and right sides and pinch them together over the just-sealed dough. You'll now have a square of dough. Grab the top left corner and the bottom right corner, stretch them a little, and then pinch them together. Repeat stretching and pinching with the top right corner and bottom left corner. The point where all the gathered portions of dough come together is your seam. The dough will look like a little purse or dumpling. Seal the seam by gently flipping the dough over and dragging it 8 to 10 in [20 to 25 cm] on a dry, flour-free area of the work surface, either cupped in the palm of your hand held in a C shape or nestled against the inside edge of the dough scraper. As you drag, you'll see the dough noticeably tighten and become smooth. Place the ball seam-side down on a flour-free area of the work surface. Shape the remaining dough.

If you plan to make all the pizzas at once, stagger the rounds in a clean, unoiled dough box, spacing them 1 to 2 in [2.5 to 5 cm] apart. If you want to bake them one at a time, place each round in its own inverted takeout container or meal-prep container, with the dough ball resting on the lid covered by the bottom or bowl, or in a lightly oiled deli container. Refrigerate the rounds for at least 2 hours or up to 24 hours.

FOR PROOFING, TOPPING,
AND BAKING INSTRUCTIONS,
SEE PAGES 96 TO 108.
FOR FREEZING INSTRUCTIONS,
SEE PAGE 173.

NATURALLY LEAVENED PIZZA DOUGH

Levain

Baker's Percentage	Weight	Volume	Ingredient
100%	50 G	5¾ TBSP	ALL-PURPOSE FLOUR (11% TO 12% PROTEIN)
100%	50 G	3¼ TBSP	WATER
10%	5 G	1 TSP	SOURDOUGH STARTER

Dough

Baker's Percentage	Weight	Volume	Ingredient
80%	404 G	3⅓ CUPS + 2 TBSP	HIGH-EXTRACTION OR SIFTED FLOUR (11% TO 12% PROTEIN)
20%	101 G	⅔ CUP	ALL-PURPOSE FLOUR (11% TO 12% PROTEIN)
72%	364 G	1½ CUPS	WATER, WARM
20%	101 G	6¾ TBSP	LEVAIN
4%	20 G	1½ TBSP	OLIVE OIL (EVOO)
2.2%	12 G	2 TSP	SALT
			ALL-PURPOSE FLOUR FOR KNEADING

If you're new to tending a sourdough starter, this dough is a great place to get comfortable with the rhythm of sourdough baking. I call for keeping a small amount of starter that is fed daily. The starter is then used to make an overnight levain. You do not need to feed your starter after you mix the levain. Simply refresh as normal the next day. **(For instructions on how to refresh, see page 75.)** Once you get used to the routine, the extra effort will seem worth it, as you will have captured the tasty, cultured flavor and chewy tug for which sourdough is celebrated. **CONT'D**

Example Time Frame	
9:00 P.M. (PREVIOUS NIGHT)	MIX LEVAIN
7:00 A.M.	MIX DOUGH
8:00 A.M.	FOLD
10:00 A.M.	DIVIDE, SHAPE, AND MOVE TO FRIDGE

TO MAKE THE LEVAIN: In a pint-size deli or similar container, combine the all-purpose flour, water, and sourdough starter. Stir thoroughly with a spoon. The levain will be loose and sticky. Try to keep most of it in the container and not on the spoon. Cover with a lid and ferment for 8 to 10 hours at room temperature (68° to 72°F [20° to 22°C]). It's ready to use when it has doubled in size, smells like yogurt, and is full of bubbles.

TO MAKE THE DOUGH: Ready a restaurant-style wide-mouthed water pitcher half full of warm water. **To get the precise temperature, use the chart on page 82**, or just use 80°F [27°C]. You'll use water from this pitcher for mixing the dough and later for wetting your fingers when folding.

In a large mixing bowl, combine the high-extraction flour and all-purpose flour. Quickly stir with a dry hand to blend and aerate, then add the levain, olive oil, and water. Next, using your dominant hand in the shape of a claw, agitate the levain, flour, and water into a dough. You can use your free hand to stabilize the bowl. Once a rough, sticky dough has formed, grab and squeeze it several times to bring it into a cohesive, shaggy mass. Cover with a shower cap or lid and let rest for 10 minutes.

Return to the bowl and sprinkle the salt over the dough. With your hands in the shape of crab claws, pinch in the salt. You'll feel the dough tighten. Stop once you have felt the salt dissolve.

When all the ingredients are incorporated, using a dough scraper, turn the dough out onto a lightly floured work surface. Using the heel of your dominant hand, push the top of the dough away from you, then fold it back on itself and rotate it 90 degrees. Push, fold, and rotate again. Repeat this three-step action for 2 to 3 minutes. A simple kneading is sufficient. It doesn't have to be lengthy, as even a few strokes will help the gluten absorb water and strengthen. Use as much flour as you need while you work but no more than is necessary. Stop kneading as soon as the dough resists.

Transfer the dough to a lightly oiled rectangular dough tub or clean mixing bowl and cover with a lid. The dough has now entered bulk fermentation, or the first rise, and will be given a single fold before being divided and shaped. Find a warm place for the dough to rise where the temperature will stay around 80°F [27°C] the whole time.

An hour after mixing, fold the dough. To fold, dip your fingers into the warm water in the pitcher. Gently lift the dough straight up from the middle with both hands. One end will release from the container as you pull upward. Allow the loosened end to tuck under the middle of the dough and then repeat with the other side, lifting and tucking toward the middle. The dough will look like it has coiled underneath itself. Rotate the container a quarter turn and repeat the process. Continue rotating the container and folding until the dough doesn't stretch or spread and has a smooth top. Cover and let rest for 2 hours.

During the 2 hours following the fold, return to the dough every now and then, uncover the container, and investigate it. It's ready to divide into individual rounds when it smells yeasty, has risen about 20 percent in the bowl, and slowly springs back when gently prodded. Once the dough is relaxed and feels soft like a pillow, move on to dividing. If it needs a little more time, give it an extra 30 minutes. **(If making a pan pizza, see page 113.)**

To divide the dough, lightly flour your work surface. Using the dough scraper, turn the dough out onto the floured surface so the top is now the bottom and you're looking at the puffy underbelly. Using a bench knife, divide the dough into four equal portions, making confident, decisive cuts. Now use the bench knife to scoop a hunk of the dough onto the digital scale. Check the weight: You're looking for the hunk to weigh 250 g [8¾ oz]. Use the bench knife to add or remove dough to reach 250 g [8¾ oz]. (It's more important to have fewer bits and pieces than it is to have four portions that are exactly equal, so don't obsess here.) Set the first piece of dough aside and weigh the remaining portions. You may also skip the scale and simply eyeball the weight, accepting that each pizza will be slightly different.

To form a dough portion into a ball, bring the top edge and the bottom edge to meet in the middle and pinch them together. Now gently stretch out the left and right sides and pinch them together over the just-sealed dough. You'll now have a square of dough. Grab the top left corner and the bottom right corner, stretch them a little, and then pinch them together. Repeat stretching and pinching with the top right corner and bottom left corner. The point where all the gathered portions of dough come together is your seam. The dough will look like a little purse or dumpling. Seal the seam by gently flipping the dough over and dragging it 8 to 10 in [20 to 25 cm] on a dry, flour-free area of the work surface, either cupped in the palm of your hand held in a C shape or nestled against the inside edge of the dough scraper. As you drag, you'll see the dough noticeably tighten and become smooth. Place the ball seam-side down on a flour-free area of the work surface. Shape the remaining dough.

If you plan to make all the pizzas at once, stagger the rounds in a clean, unoiled dough box, spacing them 1 to 2 in [2.5 to 5 cm] apart. If you want to bake them one at a time, place each round in its own inverted takeout container or meal-prep container, with the dough ball resting on the lid covered by the bottom or bowl, or in a lightly oiled deli container. Refrigerate the rounds for at least 2 hours or up to 24 hours.

FOR PROOFING, TOPPING,
AND BAKING INSTRUCTIONS,
SEE PAGES 96 TO 108.
FOR FREEZING INSTRUCTIONS,
SEE PAGE 173.

10 PERCENT RYE PIZZA DOUGH

Levain

Baker's Percentage	Weight	Volume	Ingredient
100%	42 G	5 TBSP	BREAD FLOUR (12% TO 14% PROTEIN)
80%	34 G	2¼ TBSP	WATER
10%	4 G	¾ TSP	SOURDOUGH STARTER

Dough

Baker's Percentage	Weight	Volume	Ingredient
50%	270 G	1¾ CUPS + 3 TBSP	ALL-PURPOSE FLOUR (11% TO 12% PROTEIN)
40%	216 G	1½ CUPS	BREAD FLOUR (12% TO 14% PROTEIN)
10%	54 G	½ CUP	RYE FLOUR
68%	367 G	1½ CUPS	WATER, WARM
15%	81 G	¼ CUP + 1 TBSP	LEVAIN
2.2%	12 G	2 TSP	SALT
			ALL-PURPOSE FLOUR FOR KNEADING

Rye flour is light and fluffy and smells woodsy and dank (in the best way!). These earthy qualities come through in this pizza dough and make it the perfect complement to seasonal pizza toppings, such as bitter spring greens or roasted Kuri squash. For the best results, look for freshly milled stone-ground whole-grain rye flour, though supermarket rye flour will suffice. Light or medium rye flour will yield a milder flavor. This dough is inherently sticky, so having experience handling dough is helpful.

TO MAKE THE LEVAIN: In a pint-size deli or similar container, combine the bread flour, water, and sourdough starter. Stir thoroughly with a spoon. The levain will be a little stiff and sticky. Try to keep most of it in the container and not on the spoon. Cover with a lid and ferment for 8 to 10 hours at room temperature (68° to 72°F [20° to 22°C]). It's ready to use when it has doubled in size, smells like yogurt, and is full of bubbles.

TO MAKE THE DOUGH: Ready a restaurant-style wide-mouthed water pitcher half full of warm water. **To get the precise temperature, use the chart on page 82**, or just use 80°F [27°C]. You'll use water from this pitcher for mixing the dough and later for wetting your fingers when folding.

Example Time Frame

11:00 P.M. (PREVIOUS NIGHT)	MIX LEVAIN
7:00 A.M.	MIX DOUGH
8:00 A.M.	FOLD
10:00 A.M.	DIVIDE, SHAPE, AND MOVE TO FRIDGE

In a large mixing bowl, combine the all-purpose flour, bread flour, and rye flour. Quickly stir with a dry hand to blend and aerate, then add the levain and water. Next, using your dominant hand in the shape of a claw, agitate the levain, flour, and water into a dough. You can use your free hand to stabilize the bowl. Once a rough, sticky dough has formed, grab and squeeze it several times to bring it into a cohesive, shaggy mass. Cover with a shower cap or lid and let rest for 10 minutes.

Return to the bowl and sprinkle the salt over the dough. With your hands in the shape of crab claws, pinch in the salt. You'll feel the dough tighten. Stop once you have felt the salt dissolve.

When all the ingredients are incorporated, using a dough scraper, turn the dough out onto a lightly floured work surface. Using the heel of your dominant hand, push the top of the dough away from you, then fold it back on itself and rotate it 90 degrees. Push, fold, and rotate again. Repeat this three-step action for 2 to 3 minutes. A simple kneading is sufficient. It doesn't have to be lengthy, as even a few strokes will help the gluten absorb water and strengthen. Use as much flour as you need while you work but no more than is necessary. Stop kneading as soon as the dough resists.

Transfer the dough to a lightly oiled rectangular dough tub or clean mixing bowl and cover with a lid. The dough has now entered bulk fermentation, or the first rise, and will be given a single fold before being divided and shaped. Find a warm place for the dough to rise where the temperature will stay around 80°F [27°C] the whole time.

An hour after mixing, fold the dough. To fold, dip your fingers into the warm water in the pitcher. Gently lift the dough straight up from the middle with both hands. One end will release from the container as you pull upward. Allow the loosened end to tuck under the middle of the dough and then repeat with the other side, lifting and tucking toward the middle. The dough will look like it has coiled underneath itself. Rotate the container a quarter turn and repeat the process. Continue rotating the container and folding until the dough doesn't stretch or spread and has a smooth top. Cover and let rest for 2 hours. **CONT'D**

During the 2 hours following the fold, return to the dough every now and then, uncover the container, and investigate it. It's ready to divide into individual rounds when it smells yeasty, has risen about 20 percent in the bowl, and slowly springs back when gently prodded. Once the dough is relaxed and feels soft like a pillow, move on to dividing. If it needs a little more time, give it an extra 30 minutes. **(If making a pan pizza, see page 113.)**

To divide the dough, lightly flour your work surface. Using the dough scraper, turn the dough out onto the floured surface so the top is now the bottom and you're looking at the puffy underbelly. Using a bench knife, divide the dough into four equal portions, making confident, decisive cuts. Now use the bench knife to scoop a hunk of the dough onto the digital scale. Check the weight: You're looking for the hunk to weigh 250 g [8¾ oz]. Use the bench knife to add or remove dough as needed to reach 250 g [8¾ oz]. (It's more important to have fewer bits and pieces than it is to have four portions that are exactly equal, so don't obsess here.) Set the first piece of dough aside and weigh the remaining portions. You may also skip the scale and simply eyeball the weight, accepting that each pizza will be slightly different.

To form a dough portion into a ball, bring the top edge and the bottom edge to meet in the middle and pinch them together. Now gently stretch out the left and right sides and pinch them together over the just-sealed dough. You'll now have a square of dough. Grab the top left corner and the bottom right corner, stretch them a little, and then pinch them together. Repeat stretching and pinching with the top right corner and bottom left corner. The point where all the gathered portions of dough come together is your seam. The dough will look like a little purse or dumpling. Seal the seam by gently flipping the dough over and dragging it 8 to 10 in [20 to 25 cm] on a dry, flour-free area of the work surface, either cupped in the palm of your hand held in a C shape or nestled against the inside edge of the dough scraper. As you drag, you'll see the dough noticeably tighten and become smooth. Place the ball seam-side down on a flour-free area of the work surface. Shape the remaining dough.

If you plan to make all the pizzas at once, stagger the rounds in a clean, unoiled dough box, spacing them 1 to 2 in [2.5 to 5 cm] apart. Refrigerate the rounds for at least 2 hours or up to 24 hours.

FOR PROOFING, TOPPING, AND BAKING INSTRUCTIONS, SEE PAGES 96 TO 108.
FOR FREEZING INSTRUCTIONS, SEE PAGE 173.

DOUBLE-LEVAIN PIZZA DOUGH

Levain 1

Baker's Percentage	Weight	Volume	Ingredient
100%	55 G	½ CUP	HIGH-EXTRACTION OR SIFTED FLOUR (11% TO 12% PROTEIN)
70%	39 G	2½ TBSP	WATER
10%	6 G	1½ TSP	SOURDOUGH STARTER

Levain 2

Baker's Percentage	Weight	Volume	Ingredient
100%	100 G	¾ CUP + 2 TBSP	HIGH-EXTRACTION OR SIFTED FLOUR (11% TO 12% PROTEIN)
100%	100 G	⅓ CUP + 1 TBSP	WATER, WARM (80°F [27°C])
100%	100 G	⅓ CUP	LEVAIN 1

Dough

Baker's Percentage	Weight	Volume	Ingredient
100%	416 G	3½ CUPS + 3 TBSP	HIGH-EXTRACTION OR SIFTED FLOUR (11% TO 12% PROTEIN)
70%	295 G	1¼ CUPS	LEVAIN 2
68%	283 G	1 CUP + 3 TBSP	WATER, WARM
2.2%	9 G	1½ TSP	SALT
			ALL-PURPOSE FLOUR FOR KNEADING

Example Time Frame

9:00 P.M. (PREVIOUS NIGHT)	MIX LEVAIN 1
7:00 A.M.	MIX LEVAIN 2
9:00 A.M.	MIX DOUGH
10:30 A.M.	FOLD
11:30 A.M.	DIVIDE, SHAPE, AND MOVE TO FRIDGE

Doughs made with 100 percent natural leavening can be tough and sour—side effects from too much lactic acid built up in the dough. Even though this dough contains no commercial yeast, it bakes up light because it's developed over time, in stages, to favor yeast growth over bacterial reproduction. The final dough acts like a yeasted dough, rising joyfully fast. If you don't have high-extraction flour or sifted flour, swap in all-purpose flour. **(To make your own sifted flour, see page 36.)**

TO MAKE THE LEVAIN 1: In a pint-size deli or similar container, combine the high-extraction flour, water, and sourdough starter. Stir thoroughly with a spoon. The levain will be a little stiff and sticky. Try to keep most of it in the container and not on the spoon. Cover with a lid and ferment for 8 to 10 hours at room temperature (68° to 72°F [20° to 22°C]). It's ready to use when it's doubled in size and bubbly.

TO MAKE THE LEVAIN 2: In a medium mixing bowl, combine the high-extraction flour, water, and the first levain. Mix thoroughly with a spoon until no dry flour is visible. Cover with a shower cap or lid and ferment at room temperature (68° to 72°F [20° to 22°C]) for 2 hours. It's ready to use when it has doubled in size and has plenty of surface bubbles. If it is going slowly, give it more time.

TO MAKE THE DOUGH: Ready a restaurant-style wide-mouthed water pitcher half full of warm water. **To get the precise temperature, use the chart on page 82**, or just use 80°F [27°C]. You'll use water from this pitcher for mixing the dough and later for wetting your fingers when folding.

In a large mixing bowl, weigh the high-extraction flour. Quickly stir with a dry hand to aerate, then add the levain 2 and the water. Next, using your dominant hand in the shape of a claw, agitate the levain, flour, and water into a dough. You can use your free hand to stabilize the bowl. Once a rough, sticky dough has formed, grab and squeeze it several times to bring it into a cohesive, shaggy mass. Cover with a shower cap or lid and let rest for 10 minutes.

Return to the bowl and sprinkle the salt over the dough. With your hands in the shape of crab claws, pinch in the salt. You'll feel the dough tighten. Stop once you have felt the salt dissolve.

When all the ingredients are incorporated, using a dough scraper, turn the dough out onto a lightly floured work surface. Using the heel of your dominant hand, push the top of the dough away from you, then fold it back on itself and rotate it 90 degrees. Push, fold, and rotate again. Repeat this three-step action for 2 to 3 minutes. A simple kneading is sufficient. It doesn't have to be lengthy, as even a few strokes will help the gluten absorb water and strengthen. Use as much flour as you need while you work but no more than is necessary. Stop kneading as soon as the dough resists. **CONT'D**

Transfer the dough to a lightly oiled rectangular dough tub or clean mixing bowl and cover with a lid. The dough has now entered bulk fermentation, or the first rise, and will be given a single fold before being divided and shaped. Find a warm place for the dough to rise where the temperature will stay around 80°F [27°C] the whole time.

An hour and a half after mixing, fold the dough. To fold, dip your fingers into the warm water in the pitcher. Gently lift the dough straight up from the middle with both hands. One end will release from the container as you pull upward. Allow the loosened end to tuck under the middle of the dough and then repeat with the other side, lifting and tucking toward the middle. The dough will look like it has coiled underneath itself. Rotate the container a quarter turn and repeat the process. Continue rotating the container and folding until the dough doesn't stretch or spread and has a smooth top. Cover and let rest for 1 hour.

During the 1 hour following the fold, return to the dough every now and then, uncover the container, and investigate it. It's ready to divide into individual rounds when it smells yeasty, has risen about 20 percent in the bowl, and slowly springs back when gently prodded. Once the dough is relaxed and feels soft like a pillow, move on to dividing. If it needs a little more time, give it an extra 30 minutes. **(If making a pan pizza, see page 113.)**

To divide the dough, lightly flour your work surface. Using the dough scraper, turn the dough out onto the floured surface so the top is now the bottom and you're looking at the puffy underbelly. Using a bench knife, divide the dough into four equal portions, making confident, decisive cuts. Now use the bench knife to scoop a hunk of the dough onto the digital scale. Check the weight: You're looking for the hunk to weigh 250 g [8¾ oz]. Use the bench knife to add or remove dough as needed to reach 250 g [8¾ oz]. (It's more important to have fewer bits and pieces than it is to have four portions that are exactly equal, so don't obsess here.) Set the first piece of dough aside and weigh the remaining portions. You may also skip the scale and simply eyeball the weight, accepting that each pizza will be slightly different.

To form a dough portion into a ball, bring the top edge and the bottom edge to meet in the middle and pinch them together. Now gently stretch out the left and right sides and pinch them together over the just-sealed dough. You'll now have a square of dough. Grab the top left corner and the bottom right corner, stretch them a little, and then pinch them together. Repeat stretching and pinching with the top right corner and bottom left corner. The point where all the gathered portions of dough come together is your seam. The dough will look like a little purse or dumpling. Seal the seam by gently flipping the dough over and dragging it 8 to 10 in [20 to 25 cm] on a dry, flour-free area of the work surface, either cupped in the palm of your hand held in a C shape or nestled against the inside edge of the dough scraper. As you drag, you'll see the dough noticeably tighten and become smooth. Place the ball seam-side down on a flour-free area of the work surface. Shape the remaining dough.

If you plan to make all the pizzas at once, stagger the rounds in a clean, unoiled dough box, spacing them 1 to 2 in [2.5 to 5 cm] apart. If you want to bake them one at a time, place each round in its own inverted takeout container or meal-prep container, with the dough ball resting on the lid covered by the bottom or bowl, or in a lightly oiled deli container. Refrigerate the rounds for at least 2 hours or up to 24 hours.

FOR PROOFING, TOPPING, AND BAKING INSTRUCTIONS, SEE PAGES 96 TO 108.
FOR FREEZING INSTRUCTIONS, SEE PAGE 173.

Leftover Pizza Dough / More than once I have made pizza dough and didn't get to finish it either because the day got away from me or something else came up for dinner. If I've abandoned the dough in the fridge as a whole portion, still in the bulk-fermentation phase, I make stromboli. If the dough has already been divided into rounds, I make "pizza bread."

STROMBOLI

1 RECIPE	PIZZA DOUGH **(any of the doughs on pages 133 to 166)**
	FILLINGS OF CHOICE (SUCH AS TOMATO OR OTHER SAUCE; THINLY SLICED DELI MEATS, CHEESES, AND RAW OR COOKED VEGETABLES; LEAFY GREENS)
1	LARGE EGG YOLK, LIGHTLY BEATEN
2 TBSP	UNSALTED BUTTER, MELTED

MAKES TWO 12 IN [30.5 CM] LONG STROMBOLI

Preheat the oven to 400°F [200°C]. Line a sheet pan with parchment paper.

Sprinkle your work surface with all-purpose flour. Turn out the dough onto the floured surface and flour the dough lightly. Using a bench knife, cut the dough into two equal portions. Roll out each portion into a rectangle about 10 by 16 in [25 by 40.5 cm] and ¼ in [6 mm] thick.

Layer your fillings onto each rectangle, leaving a 1 in [2.5 cm] border uncovered on all four sides. Start with a light brushing of sauce and add the meats, cheeses, and vegetables. Make sure the fillings are no more than about 1 in [2.5 cm] high or the dough will be difficult to shape. Brush the naked edges with the egg yolk.

Starting at a long side of one rectangle, roll up the dough into a cylinder, working slowly to make sure the dough is wrapped tightly around the filling. Tuck the ends underneath the roll and transfer to the parchment-lined pan. Repeat with the second rectangle and fillings. Brush the stromboli with the butter and then cut four or five slits crosswise in the top of each stromboli, spacing the slits about ½ in [12 mm] apart.

Bake until the crust is deeply browned, the cheese is visibly bubbly through the slits, and an instant-read thermometer inserted into the center registers 200°F [95°C], 25 to 30 minutes. Transfer to a wire rack to cool for 5 to 10 minutes before cutting and serving.

PIZZA BREAD

4	PIZZA DOUGH ROUNDS **(any of the doughs on pages 133 to 166)**
	ALL-PURPOSE FLOUR FOR SPRINKLING

MAKES TWO 9 BY 4 IN [23 BY 10 CM] LOAVES

Lightly spray the bottom and sides of two 9 by 4 in [23 by 10 cm] Pullman pans or similar-size loaf pans with nonstick cooking spray.

Sprinkle your work surface with all-purpose flour and turn out the proofed dough onto the flour. Stack two rounds on top of each other and gently but firmly roll them into a cylinder shape, applying pressure in the middle to help the bulk of the dough extend. This is your first loaf. Transfer it to one of the pans, seam-side down. Repeat stacking the rounds and rolling them into a loaf with the remaining two rounds. Move to the second pan. Cover each pan with a shower cap or drape with a (non-terry cloth) kitchen towel and proof the dough in a warm place (80°F [27°C]) until it rises to 1 in [2.5 cm] below the pan rim, 2 to 3 hours. About 20 minutes before you're ready to bake, preheat the oven to 500°F [260°C].

Bake the loaves for 10 minutes, then lower the heat to 450°F [230°C] and continue to bake until the loaves are deeply browned, have pulled away from the pan sides, and an instant-read thermometer inserted into the center of each loaf registers 200°F [95°C], 20 to 25 minutes more. Turn the loaves out onto wire racks and let cool completely, 2 to 3 hours.

Slice and enjoy. The bread will keep in a paper bag inside a cloth bag on your counter for up to 3 days. You can also slice the loaves, freeze the slices, and revive them one or two at a time in a toaster oven.

Freezing Pizza Dough / Freeze pizza dough after it's been shaped into individual rounds. Thaw the dough in the refrigerator overnight (8 to 12 hours) and then continue proofing according to the recipe instructions.

I recommend making a whole pizza and freezing it on a parchment paper–lined sheet pan. I do this when I've made four dough rounds and only plan to bake two. I follow the process all the way to building the pizza, then top it on the parchment-lined pan, cover it tightly with cling film, and freeze it. Bake directly from frozen in a preheated oven according to the recipe instructions, adding an additional 8 to 10 minutes to the bake time.

3

SAUCES, DRIZZLES, AND DIPS

The golden wheat flavor of a well-made pizza crust matched with an unfussy tomato sauce can be downright refreshing. My two pizza sauces are simple, one made from just a can of whole or crushed San Marzano tomatoes and the other from roasted fresh tomatoes in the summer. Other recipes in this chapter, like the **Crème Fraîche (page 188)**, **Herby Olive Oil Drizzle (page 182)**, and **Lemony Roasted-Garlic Cream (page 186)**, can be used as a pizza sauce or as a dip for crisp, chewy crusts. You'll find yourself making these dressings even when it's not pizza night, so keep a few plastic squeeze bottles on hand for storage and easy application.

PRACTICAL MANIFESTATION

Experts say there is a way to manifest your dreams that doesn't involve charging crystals in the full moon (although that can't hurt). To manifest your desires practically, first write down what you want in a single sentence. Then say it out loud. Then close your eyes and visualize yourself doing or receiving what you desire. Try this once a day for a month. When we write things down, say them out loud, and visualize them, we prime our minds to start taking action.

UNCOOKED TOMATO SAUCE

Weight	Volume	Ingredient
794 G	ONE 28 OZ CAN	WHOLE PEELED TOMATOES
5 G	1 TSP	SALT

A pizza sauce made from canned tomatoes should be a balance of tart and sweet, with a silky, plush texture. Crushing the whole tomatoes in a blender releases excess water into the sauce, interfering with the naturally velvety texture. To avoid this, crush the tomatoes by hand or pass them through a food mill. Inspect the tomatoes before you process them, as some brands are thick or runny right from the start.

Pour the entire contents of the tomato can into a quart-size deli or similar container and add the salt. Blend briefly with an immersion blender or use your hands to squeeze and crush the tomatoes into their can liquid. Stop the immersion blender before the tomatoes get bubbly or frothy. When crushing by hand, work the sauce just until the large tomato chunks are gone and the texture is still irregular, with small bits of whole tomato throughout.

Tightly cover the container and refrigerate for at least 3 hours before using. This gives the sauce time to thicken and improve in flavor, taking on the salt. The sauce will keep in the fridge for up to 5 days. Stir well and bring to room temperature before using. Any unused sauce can be frozen for up to 4 weeks. Thaw in the refrigerator before using.

ROASTED HEIRLOOM TOMATO SAUCE

Weight	Volume	Ingredient
794 G	1¾ LB (4 OR 5)	HEIRLOOM TOMATOES, CUT INTO CHUNKS
140 G	1 CUP	YELLOW ONION, CHOPPED
20 G	1½ TBSP	OLIVE OIL (EVOO), PLUS MORE IF NEEDED TO THIN
10 G	2	GARLIC CLOVES, CHOPPED
5 G	1 TSP	SALT
2 G	1 TSP	RED PEPPER FLAKES
1 G	1 TSP	OREGANO, DRIED
2 G	1 TSP	LEMON ZEST, GRATED

MAKES 980 G [4 CUPS]

Roasting tomatoes brings out their sweetness and makes for a delicious, thick sauce that resembles a store-bought pizza sauce. Make this sauce in the summer when heirloom tomatoes are abundant and freeze some for the winter months. Cherokee Purple, Brandywine, and German Johnson are some of the best tomato varieties to use for this recipe. You can blend cherry, slicer, and paste tomatoes together too. I wing the amounts, adding a little more or less of what I have on hand, and I let any extra tomato juice evaporate. Here is a solid place to start.

Preheat the oven to 400°F [200°C].

In a medium mixing bowl, combine the tomatoes, onion, olive oil, garlic, salt, red pepper flakes, oregano, and lemon zest and toss together gently, coating the tomato chunks with the oil and seasonings. Transfer the tomato mixture to a sheet pan and spread into a somewhat even layer.

Roast until the tomatoes are bubbly and slightly thickened, 45 minutes to 1 hour. You don't want to roast them until they are jammy, as the sauce still needs to spread. If the sauce becomes too thick, splash in a few tablespoons of water. Remove from the oven and let cool to room temperature.

Divide the sauce between two quart-size deli or similar containers and blend with an immersion blender until the ingredients are smooth and uniform (if you prefer a slightly chunky sauce, stop just short of smooth). If the sauce needs thinning, stream in a little olive oil as you blend. You should be able to spoon the final sauce. Cover tightly and refrigerate for at least 3 hours before using. This will give the flavors time to meld and deepen. The sauce will keep in the fridge for up to 5 days. Bring to room temperature and stir well before using. Any unused sauce can be frozen for up to 4 weeks. Thaw in the refrigerator before using.

ANYTHING GREEN GOES PESTO

Weight	Volume	Ingredient
70 G	½ CUP + 1 TBSP	PINE NUTS
5 G	1	GARLIC CLOVE
31 G	2 TBSP	LEMON JUICE
1 G	¼ TSP	SALT
1 G	½ TSP	BLACK PEPPER
40 G	2 CUPS	BASIL LEAVES, FRESH, FIRMLY PACKED (OR ARUGULA, SPINACH, OR DANDELION GREENS)
56 G	¼ CUP	OLIVE OIL (EVOO), PLUS MORE IF NEEDED TO THIN
25 G	¼ CUP	PARMESAN, GRATED

No doubt basil makes a classic pesto, but I've found almost any green can be substituted. Try using watercress, arugula, flat-leaf parsley, or spinach either in place of or in combination with basil. No matter the greenery, this pesto is creamy, bright, and a crowd-pleaser. Pine nuts are soft, oily, and traditional, but you can swap them out for walnuts in a pinch.

In a food processor, combine the pine nuts, garlic, lemon juice, salt, and pepper and pulse until the nuts and garlic are well chopped. Add the basil and pulse until combined. Then, with the processor running on low speed, stream in the olive oil. Finally, add the Parmesan and pulse a few times to mix. Stream in more olive oil on low speed if needed to achieve a spreadable consistency. If your food processor has only on, off, and pulse settings, use the pulse setting in short bursts for 2 to 3 minutes for adding the olive oil.

Transfer the pesto to a pint-size deli or similar container and cover tightly. Let the sauce rest in the refrigerator for 2 to 3 hours to thicken and take on flavor before using. Although the pesto will keep in the fridge for up to 5 days, it will lose its bright green color over time. Stir well and bring to room temperature before using. Any unused sauce can be frozen for up to 4 weeks. Thaw in the refrigerator before using.

HERBY OLIVE OIL DRIZZLE

Weight	Volume	Ingredient
224 G	1 CUP	OLIVE OIL (EVOO)
	5 SPRIGS	ROSEMARY, FRESH
	4 SPRIGS	THYME, FRESH
	3 SPRIGS	OREGANO, FRESH
	2 SPRIGS	SAGE, FRESH

MAKES 224 G
[1 CUP]

The herbs in this drizzle deliver a classic Italian vibe. Use more or less of your favorite players, and keep them on the stems for maximum flavor. This is a nice sauce for a white pizza or an elegant drizzle post-bake. It is also good on leftover pasta, toast, or as a salad dressing.

In a medium saucepan, combine the olive oil, rosemary, thyme, oregano, and sage. Bring to a simmer over medium-low heat and cook gently for 10 minutes. Remove from the heat and let cool to room temperature.

Strain the cooled oil into a squeeze bottle and discard the herbs and stems. Use immediately or store at room temperature (68° to 72°F [20° to 22°C]) for up to 3 days.

HOT HONEY

Weight	Volume	Ingredient
340 G	1 CUP + 1 TBSP	HONEY, CLOVER OR OTHER LIGHT, MILD TYPE
14 G	1	JALAPEÑO CHILE, THINLY SLICED (KEEP THE SEEDS)
5 TO 10 G	1 TO 2 TSP	DISTILLED WHITE VINEGAR

Hot honey is an easy way to elevate almost anything. I drizzle this home-made version on peanut butter toast, salads, and, of course, on pepperoni pizza hot from the oven. It is the perfect marriage of sweetness and heat, so if you haven't jumped on the hot honey bandwagon yet, here's your invitation. The heat of jalapeños can vary from chile to chile, so try one and add more to increase the spiciness if desired. Wear gloves while you slice the jalapeño, as it contains capsaicin, a natural chemical compound that can irritate your skin.

In a medium saucepan, combine the honey and jalapeño. Bring to a gentle simmer over medium heat, stirring frequently with a heat-safe flexible spatula and taking care to not let the honey come to a boil. Remove from the heat and let the honey cool and rest for 30 minutes before tasting. If you'd like more kick, add extra jalapeño or let the honey infuse longer.

Strain the mixture through a fine-mesh sieve into a pint jar and discard any seeds or bits of jalapeño. Stir in the vinegar until evenly combined. Use the honey immediately or cap tightly and store in the refrigerator for up to 1 week. (If you leave it in your pantry at room temperature, you run the risk of creating a fermented food, which is not what the recipe intends.) Stir well and bring to room temperature before using.

LEMONY ROASTED-GARLIC CREAM

Weight	Volume	Ingredient
200 G	7 OZ	GARLIC CLOVES, PEELED AND GERM REMOVED
112 G	½ CUP	OLIVE OIL (EVOO)
1 G	¼ TSP	SALT
357 G	1½ CUPS	HEAVY CREAM
125 G	½ CUP	RICOTTA, WHOLE-MILK
2 G	1 TSP	LEMON ZEST, GRATED

MAKES 840 G [3½ CUPS]

Smooth and rich, this garlic cream works wonders as a white sauce on pizza and is also perfect folded into a bowl of fresh pasta. Roasting the garlic confit-style brings out its natural sweetness, which is typically masked by the pungent punch garlic is best known for. The lemon zest brightens up the cream, but if you don't have it, you can still make the recipe. Reserve the confit oil and use it as a drizzle over a baked pizza or to dress a salad.

In a medium saucepan, combine the garlic cloves and olive oil. Bring to a simmer over medium-low heat and cook gently until the garlic is golden and you can easily smoosh the cloves with the back of a spoon, 30 to 40 minutes. Remove from the heat and let the garlic and oil cool to room temperature.

Drain the garlic through a fine-mesh sieve placed over a small bowl and transfer the garlic to a food processor. (Transfer the oil to a squeeze bottle and save for other uses.) Add the salt, cream, ricotta, and lemon zest and blend on low speed until smooth and creamy, 3 to 4 minutes. Stop the processor and scrape down the sides and along the bottom of the bowl with a flexible spatula if you notice the garlic clinging to the surfaces. If your food processor has only on, off, and pulse settings, use the pulse setting in short bursts for 4 to 5 minutes until the sauce is smooth.

Transfer to a quart-size deli or similar container and cover tightly. Let the cream rest for 2 to 3 hours in the fridge to thicken and take on flavor before using. (It tastes best after 24 hours.) The cream will keep in the fridge for up to 1 week. Stir well and bring to room temperature before using.

SPICY MAYO DRIZZLE

Weight	Volume	Ingredient
220 G	1 CUP	MAYONNAISE
60 G	¼ CUP	SRIRACHA
10 G	2 TSP	LIME JUICE
1 G	PINCH	SALT

MAKES 290 G [1¼ CUPS]

This all-purpose spicy mayo is not only perfect for pizza but also for sandwiches, burgers, french fries, and tacos. Look for Japanese mayonnaise, such as Kewpie brand, which is sweeter and thinner than beloved domestic brands like Duke's. (If you can't find Japanese mayo, don't worry. Just be sure to use mayonnaise, not Miracle Whip.) I jokingly refer to this as a "super sauce," and I think you will too.

In a medium mixing bowl, whisk together the mayonnaise, sriracha, lime juice, and salt. Taste and add more sriracha to increase the heat if desired.

Transfer to a squeeze bottle and use immediately or store in the refrigerator for up to 3 weeks. Shake and bring to room temperature before using.

CRÈME FRAÎCHE

Weight	Volume	Ingredient
478 G	2 CUPS	HEAVY CREAM
28 G	2 TBSP	BUTTERMILK

MAKES 515 G [2¼ CUPS]

Crème fraîche is incredibly easy to make, but it requires planning. A staple of French cooking, crème fraîche was historically made from fresh cow's milk left to culture outside of refrigeration. The natural bacteria would not only prevent it from spoiling but also thicken and flavor the crème. Today, most milk is pasteurized, so the lactic acid bacteria are introduced by buttermilk.

In a medium mixing bowl, gently whisk together the cream and buttermilk until blended. Cover with cling film and allow to thicken at room temperature (68° to 72°F [20° to 22°C]) to the desired texture. It's perfect at 10 to 12 hours.

Transfer to an airtight container and store in the fridge for up to 2 weeks. It will continue to mature and culture, so check the taste as the days go by and use it before you lose it. Stir well and bring to room temperature before using.

RANCH DRESSING

Weight	Volume	Ingredient
120 G	⅓ CUP + 2 TBSP	MAYONNAISE
121 G	½ CUP	BUTTERMILK
122 G	½ CUP	SOUR CREAM
5 G	1	GARLIC CLOVE, GRATED
5 G	1 TSP	LEMON JUICE
56 G	¼ CUP	OLIVE OIL (EVOO)
0.5 G	¼ TSP	DILL, DRIED
2 G	1 TSP	CHIVES, DRIED
0.5 G	½ TSP	PARSLEY, DRIED
1 G	½ TSP	ONION POWDER
0.5 G	PINCH	SALT
0.5 G	¼ TSP	BLACK PEPPER

MAKES 434 G [1¾ CUPS]

One of America's most iconic dressings and dips, savory, tangy ranch has been doused, drizzled, and poured over everything from pasta dishes to chicken wings to, yes, pizza. I like it as both a drizzle over a pepperoni pizza and in a small cup for dunking crust. I've been making this dressing since my first bread baking workshops in 2016, thanks to my friend Ilana Freddye, who introduced me to the heaven that I now know as homemade ranch.

In a large mixing bowl, whisk together the mayonnaise, buttermilk, sour cream, garlic, and lemon juice until blended. While your dominant hand is still whisking, use your free hand to slowly stream in the olive oil until the mixture is emulsified, about 1 minute. Using a flexible spatula, fold in the dill, chives, parsley, onion powder, salt, and pepper. Taste and adjust with salt and pepper if needed. Thin with a little water (15 to 30 g [1 to 2 Tbsp]) if necessary.

Transfer to a jar or squeeze bottle and let rest in the fridge for 4 to 5 hours or up to overnight to allow the flavors to meld and deepen before using. The dressing will keep in the fridge for up to 2 weeks. Shake and bring to room temperature before using.

CAESAR DRESSING

Weight	Volume	Ingredient
112 G	½ CUP	VEGETABLE OIL
28 G	2 TBSP	OLIVE OIL (EVOO)
19 G	1	LARGE EGG YOLK
3 G	½ TSP	DIJON MUSTARD
3 G	½ TSP	ANCHOVY PASTE
15 G	1 TBSP	LEMON JUICE
5 G	1	GARLIC CLOVE
5 G	1 TSP	PARMESAN, GRATED
1 G	PINCH	SALT
0.5 G	¼ TSP	BLACK PEPPER

MAKES 191 G [¾ CUP]

A good Caesar dressing should taste briny and have a kick from black pepper. I am a huge fan of using this classic for dunking crust and, of course, as a dressing for a simple green salad. I prefer to make the dressing by hand, but you can use a food processor. It comes together quickly, and once you try this recipe, you won't go back to any other Caesar.

In a small bowl, combine the vegetable oil and olive oil and set aside.

In a medium mixing bowl, whisk together the egg yolk, mustard, anchovy paste, and lemon juice until a smooth, uniform mixture forms. While your dominant hand is still whisking, use your free hand to slowly stream in the oils until the mixture is emulsified, about 1 minute. Grate in the garlic, then, using a flexible spatula, fold in the Parmesan, salt, and pepper. Taste and adjust the salt and lemon juice if needed. Thin with a little water (15 to 30 g [1 to 2 Tbsp]) if necessary.

Transfer to a jar or squeeze bottle and let rest in the fridge for 4 to 5 hours or up to overnight to allow the flavors to meld and complexify. The dressing will keep in the fridge for up to 2 weeks. Shake and bring to room temperature before using.

HOMEMADE HUMMUS

Weight	Volume	Ingredient
200 G	1 CUP + 2 TBSP	CHICKPEAS, DRIED
2 G	½ TSP	BAKING SODA
100 G	½ CUP	TAHINI
12 G	2	GARLIC CLOVES, MINCED
30 G	2 TBSP	LEMON JUICE
4 G	¾ TSP	GROUND CUMIN
4 G	¾ TSP	SALT

MAKES 394 G [1¾ CUPS]

This hummus has a silky texture and bold flavor, a result of using some of the reserved cooking liquid from the beans in the final whipping of the chickpeas. If you're short on time, you can swap out the dried beans for canned chickpeas. Just remember to reserve some of the liquid from the can. Serve the hummus in cute cups for dipping your pizza crust, layer it on fresh pitas from Chapter 5, or scoop it in a bowl, top it with a drizzle of olive oil, and set a basket of **Za'atar Pita Chips (page 325)** alongside.

Weigh the dried chickpeas into a medium mixing bowl or other container and add room-temperature water to cover. Cover the bowl and let the beans soak overnight at room temperature (68° to 72°F [20° to 22°C]). It's OK if they soak up all the water. You don't need to keep adding more.

The next morning, drain off any remaining water and then rinse the beans under cool running water. Fill a medium stockpot about half full with water. Set it on the stovetop, turn on the heat to medium-low, and bring the water to a gentle boil. Add the chickpeas and baking soda. The baking soda, which helps the skins slide off the chickpeas, will create a little bloom.

Cook the chickpeas until tender when tested with the tines of a fork, about 1 hour. Add water to the pot as needed to keep the chickpeas covered and adjust the heat as needed to keep the water at a gentle boil. When the chickpeas are ready, remove the pot from the heat and let the chickpeas cool in the liquid. You want the chickpeas slightly warm but cool enough to handle for the next step.

Drain the chickpeas through a fine-mesh sieve held over a bowl. Reserve about 240 g [1 cup] of the cooking liquid for the hummus. Transfer the chickpeas to a large bowl and quickly rub them between your hands to remove the skins. Discard the skins. (This is the kind of task that is best done to a really good song.)

In a food processor, combine the tahini and 44 g [3 Tbsp] of the cooking liquid and process until the mixture is well blended and loose. Add the garlic, lemon juice, cumin, salt, and chickpeas and blend on medium speed until smooth and creamy. If your food processor has only on, off, and pulse settings, use the pulse setting in short bursts for 2 to 3 minutes. The hummus will be whipped and fluffy.

Stop the food processor and scrape down the sides of the bowl and around the blade as needed with a flexible spatula. Adjust the consistency with the reserved cooking liquid as needed to achieve a silky texture. Use your finger to swoop the hummus. Is it too stiff? Add more cooking liquid by drizzling in 14 g [1 Tbsp] at a time. Is it too loose? Add some tahini 15 g [1 Tbsp] at a time. Chilling the hummus will help thicken it, too, so don't worry too much here.

Transfer to an airtight container, cover, and refrigerate. Serve chilled. It will keep for up to 5 days.

REFRIGERATOR PICKLES

Weight	Volume	Ingredient
455 G	1 LB	CARROTS
455 G	1 LB	CUCUMBERS
455 G	1 LB	RED ONIONS
16 G	4	GARLIC CLOVES, PEELED (OPTIONAL)
14 G	2 TBSP	PEPPERCORNS, PINK OR BLACK
	4	BAY LEAVES, DRIED (OPTIONAL)
240 G	1 CUP	WATER
240 G	1 CUP	DISTILLED WHITE VINEGAR
12 G	1 TBSP	GRANULATED SUGAR
6 G	1 TSP	SALT

MAKES FOUR 240 ML [½ PT] JARS

I have regularly made these pickles during bountiful summer months, and I was delighted to begin putting them on pizzas for a crunchy, fresh bite. Perfect for using up odds and ends in the vegetable drawer, this process is forgiving and flexible. Additional options for tossing into the brine include dill, celery seeds, coriander seeds, and mustard seeds. Experiment and make these pickles your own.

Peel the carrots, then cut them lengthwise into long, thin strips about the width of a pencil and 3 to 4 in [7.5 to 10 cm] long. Slice the cucumbers into coins and the onions into rings.

Pack the carrots, cucumbers, and onions separately into four 240 ml [½ pt] canning or other heatproof jars or combine them together in the jars. Add the garlic cloves (if using), peppercorns, and bay leaves (if using), dividing them evenly among the jars. Set the jars aside while you make the brine.

In a small saucepan, combine the water, vinegar, sugar, and salt over medium-high heat and bring to a gentle boil, between 180° and 190°F [82° to 88°C]. Remove from the heat and stir until the sugar and salt dissolve. Pour the hot brine into the jars, dividing it evenly. (A canning funnel is helpful for this step.)

Let the jars cool on the counter for 1 hour, uncovered, then cover loosely and refrigerate. Chill for at least 3 hours before using. (Once the jars are fully cooled, you may tighten the lids.) The pickles will keep in the fridge for up to 2 weeks.

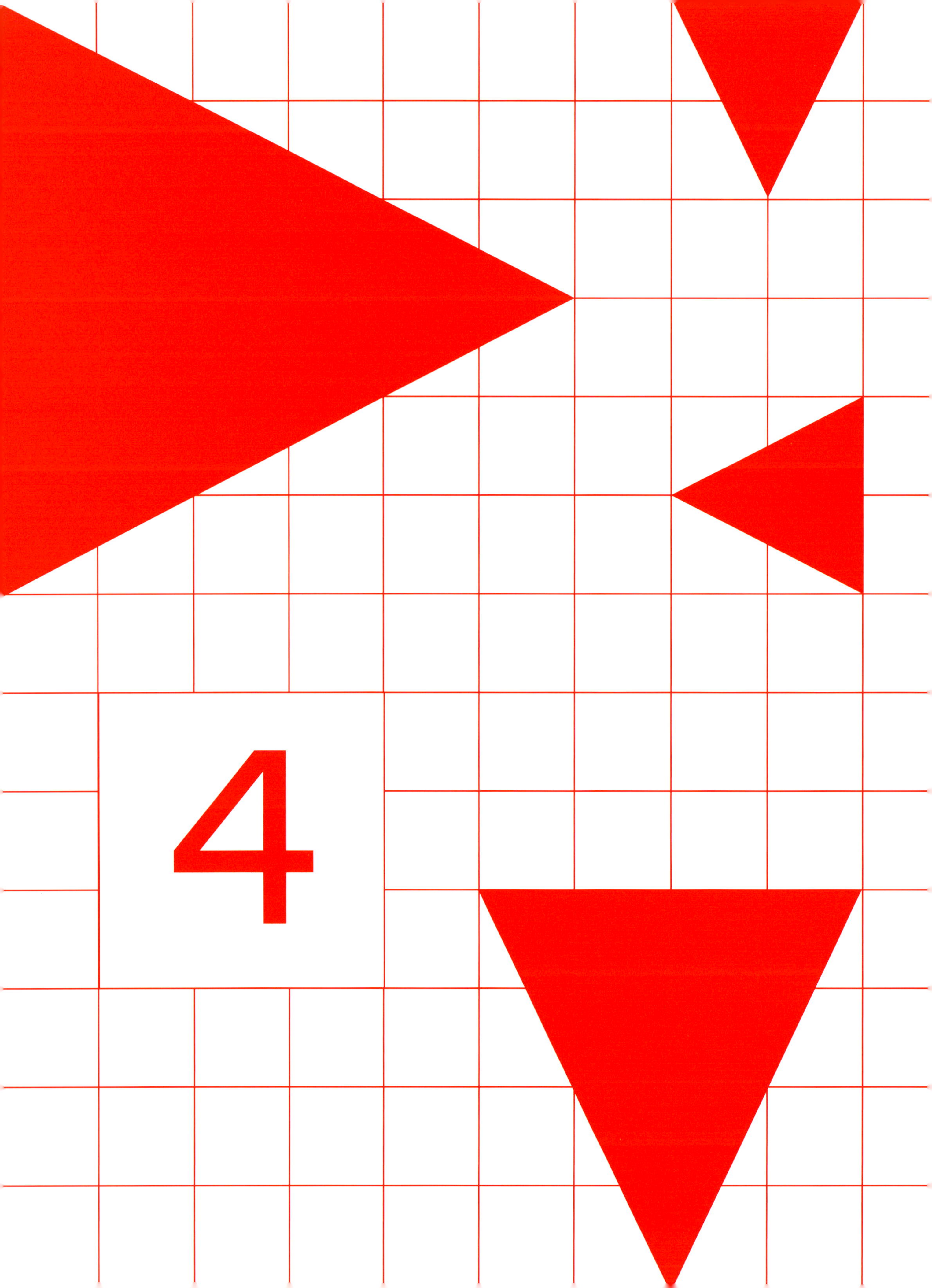
4

PIZZA CROWD-PLEASERS

Pizza is my favorite comfort food, and the following recipes are the ones I go to for familiarity. The first one, **Red Sauce Only (page 199)**, can seem fancy, but it's a pizza that my kids often request. The **Supreme Delight (page 221)** brings me right back to my mother's kitchen and the smell of yeasty dough rising, sizzling green peppers, and family movie night. I hope the pizzas in this chapter—perhaps paired with a slice of **Birthday Cake with American Buttercream (page 385)** or a scoop of **No-Churn Vanilla Ice Cream (page 400)**—bring you joy.

Friendly Reminders

BEFORE YOU GET STARTED:

- **If possible, shred cheese yourself.** Pre-shredded cheeses contain anticaking agents that make them taste chalky.
- **Don't forget to season the toppings before they go on the pizza.** Although almost every pizza I make is finished with a sprinkle of salt, a drizzle of olive oil, and a snowfall of Parmesan, you still need to salt anything you are cooking to go on top.
- **I have listed any topping prep to be done ahead of time because that's how I get it done with three kids underfoot.** If you have the time, go ahead and move that block around. For example, you can fry the eggplant while the dough is proofing.
- **Finally, when stretching the dough, work diligently on getting the center paper-thin and the edge nice and even.** Build the ingredients gently, leaving space for them to melt and cook. Less is more. On a trip to Paris in 2024, I ate at Oobatz, a trendy wine-and-pizza spot with well-deserved recognition, and the pizzas were ethereal—every flavor just a fleeting kiss. Pizza often gets a bad rap for being so filling, but you can make a pizza that leaves everyone wanting more just by topping it delicately and with intention.

BAKE TIMES

If your pizza isn't done in 8 to 10 minutes, continue baking for an additional 3 to 4 minutes, checking to make sure the undercarriage is not burning by lifting the pizza with a metal peel and looking. The cheese should be melted and browned and the crust deeply golden with a few spots of char. (Char is not the same thing as burnt! Char is delicious.)

If the bottom is getting dark but the top isn't done yet, slide the peel under the pizza and finish the pizza off by holding it near the top of the oven. If the pizza is taking upward of 15 minutes to bake, check the temperature of your steel or stone—it should be at least 525°F [275°C]—and the general temperature of your oven.

Tangy tomato sauce is a luscious and velvety base that complements almost any cheese or crust. You can make it with a can of good tomatoes, salt, and your bare

SAUCED PIES

hands, or go for something more complex, like the Roasted Heirloom Tomato Sauce on page 178. Every bite of a perfectly sauced pie is a satisfying contrast of texture and flavors. ●

RED SAUCE ONLY

Weight	Volume	Ingredient
	1	DOUGH ROUND **(any of the doughs in Chapter 2)**
125 G	½ CUP	ROASTED HEIRLOOM TOMATO SAUCE **(page 178)**
	4 OR 5	BASIL LEAVES, FRESH, TORN
6 G	1 TSP	FLAKY SALT
14 G	1 TBSP	OLIVE OIL (EVOO)
		WHITE RICE FLOUR FOR STRETCHING THE DOUGH AND DUSTING THE PEEL

This pizza, also known as rossa ("red" in Italian) or tomato pie, is a happy marriage between a velvety tomato sauce and a crisp wheat crust. With nothing to mask the flavors of the sauce or the dough, it's important to choose the tomatoes wisely and to ferment the dough properly. This pizza is spread with a little extra sauce so it can reduce during baking.

If the pizza dough is refrigerated, remove it from the fridge 2 to 3 hours before you plan to bake. Proof the dough on the counter until it's slightly puffy and room temperature. By the end of proofing, it should feel soft and full of gas. While you wait, set up where you'll be stretching and building the pizza **(see Designing Workflow, page 101)** and position a cooling rack, cutting board, and pizza wheel or rocker cutter near the oven. Ready a 9 or 10 in [23 or 25 cm] cake pan half full of white rice flour and set it aside.

An hour before baking, position an oven rack 6 to 8 in [15 to 20 cm] from the top of the oven and set a baking steel or stone on it. Preheat the oven to 550°F [290°C] or as hot as the oven will allow.

Sprinkle a wooden peel with a little white rice flour and set it aside. Slide a dough scraper under the dough round and flip it over into the cake pan of white rice flour. Turn it over two or three times, then transfer it to the peel, handling it gently.

Use your fingertips to indent a ring ¼ in [6 mm] deep all the way around the rim of the dough. Flip the dough over and repeat, pressing an indent around the outer edge. Next, use the pads of your fingers to lightly press down on the inner circle of the dough, going from 12 o'clock at the top to 6 o'clock at the bottom. Flip the dough over and repeat. Return the dough to the original side up. You'll now use gravity to stretch it into its final shape.

CONT'D

Slide clean, dry hands under the dough and make two fists in the center. Lift your hands and the pizza into the air parallel to your chin. Slowly move your fists in opposite directions to stretch the center of the pizza. Rotate the dough 90 degrees and carefully pull it in opposite directions again. Now arc your hands and let the dough slide down and hang off the back of your knuckles. Guide the dough in a circular motion, keeping it moving over the back of your hands and letting gravity do the final pulling. If the dough is resisting, give it a short rest on the peel and try again.

Lay the dough back on the peel and spoon the tomato sauce onto the middle. Use the back of the spoon to spread the sauce evenly over the dough, stopping at the indented rim. Shimmy the peel a few times to make sure the pizza moves freely and can easily slide off the peel. If the dough is stuck, quickly lift it with the dough scraper and toss a little white rice flour underneath.

Open the oven door and slide the pizza onto the steel by holding the peel at a slight angle and sliding it out from under the pizza in one fluid motion. It can help to match the edge of the peel with the far edge of the steel. Avoid shuffling the peel under the pizza.

Close the oven door and bake the pizza for 5 to 6 minutes. Open the door and check on the pizza. Chances are it will need to be rotated. Spin it 180 degrees with a metal peel or use a pair of long metal tongs to adjust the direction. Close the door and bake for an additional 4 to 5 minutes. The pizza is done when the crust is a burnished red, golden in spots, and the bubbles are slightly charred. The sauce should be bubbling.

Slide the metal peel under the pizza and transfer it to the wire rack. Scatter the basil over the top, dust with the flaky salt, and drizzle with the olive oil. Let cool for 5 to 6 minutes, then move the pizza to the cutting board and cut into eight wedges with the pizza wheel or rocker cutter. Serve immediately.

FOR STORAGE AND WARMING: Any uneaten pizza can be stored in an airtight container in the fridge for up to 5 days. To serve, reheat directly on a preheated baking steel or stone (500°F [260°C]) until the cheese is bubbly, 2 to 5 minutes.

SLICED CHEESE

Weight	Volume	Ingredient
	1	DOUGH ROUND **(any of the doughs in Chapter 2)**
56 G	¼ CUP	UNCOOKED TOMATO SAUCE **(page 177)**
170 G	6 OZ	AMERICAN CHEESE, SLICED
5 G	2 TBSP	PARMESAN
2 G	¼ TSP	SALT
14 G	1 TBSP	OLIVE OIL (EVOO)
		WHITE RICE FLOUR FOR STRETCHING THE DOUGH AND DUSTING THE PEEL

MAKES ONE 12 IN [30.5 CM] PIZZA

Made in desperation one afternoon when there was no mozzarella in the house, this pizza is topped with the sliced cheese I typically reserve for my kids' lunches. It turns out that the emulsifiers in processed cheese are good at something: melting it into a beautiful, creamy blanket. My daughter and I both love this pizza, and when I have the time, we make some **Ranch Dressing (page 189)** in advance for dipping the toasty crust bits. If you don't have American cheese, you could try sliced Swiss or provolone.

If the pizza dough is refrigerated, remove it from the fridge 2 to 3 hours before you plan to bake. Proof the dough on the counter until it's slightly puffy and room temperature. By the end of proofing, it should feel soft and full of gas. While you wait, set up where you'll be stretching and building the pizza **(see Designing Workflow, page 101)** and position a cooling rack, cutting board, and pizza wheel or rocker cutter near the oven. Ready a 9 or 10 in [23 or 25 cm] cake pan half full of white rice flour and set it aside.

An hour before baking, position an oven rack 6 to 8 in [15 to 20 cm] from the top of the oven and set a baking steel or stone on it. Preheat the oven to 550°F [290°C] or as hot as the oven will allow.

Sprinkle a wooden peel with a little white rice flour and set it aside. Slide a dough scraper under the dough round and flip it over into the cake pan of white rice flour. Turn it over two or three times, then transfer it to the peel, handling it gently.

Use your fingertips to indent a ring ¼ in [6 mm] deep all the way around the rim of the dough. Flip the dough over and repeat, pressing an indent around the outer edge. Next, use the pads of your fingers to lightly press down on the inner circle of the dough, going from 12 o'clock at the top to 6 o'clock at the bottom. Flip the dough over and repeat. Return the dough to the original side up. You'll now use gravity to stretch it into its final shape.

CONT'D

Slide clean, dry hands under the dough and make two fists in the center. Lift your hands and the pizza into the air parallel to your chin. Slowly move your fists in opposite directions to stretch the center of the pizza. Rotate the dough 90 degrees and carefully pull it in opposite directions again. Now arc your hands and let the dough slide down and hang off the back of your knuckles. Guide the dough in a circular motion, keeping it moving over the back of your hands and letting gravity do the final pulling. If the dough is resisting, give it a short rest on the peel and try again.

Lay the dough back on the peel and spoon the tomato sauce onto the middle. Use the back of the spoon to spread the sauce evenly over the dough, stopping at the indented rim. Shimmy the peel a few times to make sure the pizza moves freely and can easily slide off the peel. If the dough is stuck, quickly lift it with the dough scraper and toss a little white rice flour underneath.

Open the oven door and slide the pizza onto the steel by holding the peel at a slight angle and sliding it out from under the pizza in one fluid motion. It can help to match the edge of the peel with the far edge of the steel. Avoid shuffling the peel under the pizza.

Close the oven door and bake the pizza for 5 to 6 minutes. Open the door and use a peel to remove the pizza. Cover the entire surface with the American cheese, breaking the squares into smaller pieces to fit around the outer edge. Slide the pizza back onto the steel, rotating the direction if necessary. Close the door and bake for an additional 4 to 5 minutes. The pizza is done when the crust is a burnished red, golden in spots, and the bubbles are slightly charred. The cheese should be melted, browned, and rosy where it meets the sauce.

Slide the metal peel under the pizza and transfer it to the wire rack. Grate the Parmesan on top. Dust with the salt and drizzle with the olive oil. Let cool for 5 to 6 minutes, then move the pizza to the cutting board and cut into eight wedges with the pizza wheel or rocker cutter. Serve immediately.

FOR STORAGE
AND WARMING INFORMATION,
SEE PAGE 200.

THREE CHEESES

Weight	Volume	Ingredient
	1	DOUGH ROUND **(any of the doughs in Chapter 2)**
56 G	¼ CUP	UNCOOKED TOMATO SAUCE **(page 177)**
55 G	2 OZ	CHEDDAR, SHREDDED
55 G	2 OZ	MOZZARELLA, LOW-MOISTURE, SHREDDED
55 G	2 OZ	FONTINA, SHREDDED
5 G	2 TBSP	PARMESAN
0.5 G	½ TSP	PARSLEY, DRIED
2 G	¼ TSP	SALT
14 G	1 TBSP	OLIVE OIL (EVOO)
		WHITE RICE FLOUR FOR STRETCHING THE DOUGH AND DUSTING THE PEEL

Making your own cheese blend is one of the simplest things you can do to improve your pizza. I like to consider the sharpness or funkiness of the cheeses and the "flow factor"—how much the cheese will spread as it melts. Try any combination of these cheeses: Monterey Jack, fontina, mozzarella, goat, provolone, Asiago, and Cheddar. Aim for a selection that yields a buttery, tangy, well-balanced flavor.

If the pizza dough is refrigerated, remove it from the fridge 2 to 3 hours before you plan to bake. Proof the dough on the counter until it's slightly puffy and room temperature. By the end of proofing, it should feel soft and full of gas. While you wait, set up where you'll be stretching and building the pizza **(see Designing Workflow, page 101)** and position a cooling rack, cutting board, and pizza wheel or rocker cutter near the oven. Ready a 9 or 10 in [23 or 25 cm] cake pan half full of white rice flour and set it aside.

An hour before baking, position an oven rack 6 to 8 in [15 to 20 cm] from the top of the oven and set a baking steel or stone on it. Preheat the oven to 550°F [290°C] or as hot as the oven will allow.

Sprinkle a wooden peel with a little white rice flour and set it aside. Slide a dough scraper under the dough round and flip it over into the cake pan of white rice flour. Turn it over two or three times, then transfer it to the peel, handling it gently.

Use your fingertips to indent a ring ¼ in [6 mm] deep all the way around the rim of the dough. Flip the dough over and repeat, pressing an indent around the outer edge. Next, use the pads of your fingers to lightly press down on the inner circle of the dough, going from 12 o'clock

CONT'D

at the top to 6 o'clock at the bottom. Flip the dough over and repeat. Return the dough to the original side up. You'll now use gravity to stretch it into its final shape.

Slide clean, dry hands under the dough and make two fists in the center. Lift your hands and the pizza into the air parallel to your chin. Slowly move your fists in opposite directions to stretch the center of the pizza. Rotate the dough 90 degrees and carefully pull it in opposite directions again. Now arc your hands and let the dough slide down and hang off the back of your knuckles. Guide the dough in a circular motion, keeping it moving over the back of your hands and letting gravity do the final pulling. If the dough is resisting, give it a short rest on the peel and try again.

Lay the dough back on the peel and spoon the tomato sauce onto the middle. Use the back of the spoon to spread the sauce evenly over the dough, stopping at the indented rim. Scatter the Cheddar, mozzarella, and fontina over the sauce. Shimmy the peel a few times to make sure the pizza moves freely and can easily slide off the peel. If the dough is stuck, quickly lift it with the dough scraper and toss a little white rice flour underneath.

Open the oven door and slide the pizza onto the steel by holding the peel at a slight angle and sliding it out from under the pizza in one fluid motion. It can help to match the edge of the peel with the far edge of the steel. Avoid shuffling the peel under the pizza.

Close the oven door and bake the pizza for 5 to 6 minutes. Open the door and check on the pizza. Chances are it will need to be rotated. Spin it 180 degrees with a metal peel or use a pair of long metal tongs to adjust the direction. Close the door and bake for an additional 4 to 5 minutes. The pizza is done when the crust is a burnished red, golden in spots, and the bubbles are slightly charred. The cheese should be melted, browned, and rosy where it meets the sauce.

Slide the metal peel under the pizza and transfer it to the wire rack. Grate the Parmesan on top. Dust with the parsley and salt and drizzle with the olive oil. Let cool for 5 to 6 minutes, then move the pizza to the cutting board and cut into eight wedges with the pizza wheel or rocker cutter. Serve immediately.

FOR STORAGE AND WARMING INFORMATION, SEE PAGE 200.

MARGHERITA

Weight	Volume	Ingredient
	1	DOUGH ROUND "00" PIZZA DOUGH (page 152) OR any of the doughs in Chapter 2
56 G	¼ CUP	UNCOOKED TOMATO SAUCE (page 177)
55 G	2 OZ	MOZZARELLA, FRESH, TORN INTO ½ IN [12 MM] PIECES
114 G	½ CUP	CHERRY TOMATOES, HALVED
5 G	2 TBSP	PARMESAN
2 G	¼ TSP	SALT
14 G	1 TBSP	OLIVE OIL (EVOO)
	6	BASIL LEAVES, FRESH, TORN
		WHITE RICE FLOUR FOR STRETCHING THE DOUGH AND DUSTING THE PEEL

If I go out to eat at a pizza joint and it offers a Margherita, I must order it. It's so simple that it's a perfect measure of how good any of the other pizzas will be. Besides that, it's elegant and delicious. This is my twist on the Margherita, with cherry tomatoes delivering a juicy pop with each bite. For the tastiest result, visit your local farmers' market for the cherry tomatoes and basil and use high-quality fresh cow's milk mozzarella. If you have a wood-fired oven or a tabletop pizza oven, this is *the* pizza to master first.

If the pizza dough is refrigerated, remove it from the fridge 2 to 3 hours before you plan to bake. Proof the dough on the counter until it's slightly puffy and room temperature. By the end of proofing, it should feel soft and full of gas. While you wait, set up where you'll be stretching and building the pizza (see Designing Workflow, page 101) and position a cooling rack, cutting board, and pizza wheel or rocker cutter near the oven. Ready a 9 or 10 in [23 or 25 cm] cake pan half full of white rice flour and set it aside.

An hour before baking, position an oven rack 6 to 8 in [15 to 20 cm] from the top of the oven and set a baking steel or stone on it. Preheat the oven to 550°F [290°C] or as hot as the oven will allow.

Sprinkle a wooden peel with a little white rice flour and set it aside. Slide a dough scraper under the dough round and flip it over into the cake pan of white rice flour. Turn it over two or three times, then transfer it to the peel, handling it gently.

Use your fingertips to indent a ring ¼ in [6 mm] deep all the way around the rim of the dough. Flip the dough over and repeat, pressing an indent around the outer edge. Next, use the pads of your fingers to lightly press down on the inner circle of the dough, going from 12 o'clock

CONT'D

at the top to 6 o'clock at the bottom. Flip the dough over and repeat. Return the dough to the original side up. You'll now use gravity to stretch it into its final shape.

Slide clean, dry hands under the dough and make two fists in the center. Lift your hands and the pizza into the air parallel to your chin. Slowly move your fists in opposite directions to stretch the center of the pizza. Rotate the dough 90 degrees and carefully pull it in opposite directions again. Now arc your hands and let the dough slide down and hang off the back of your knuckles. Guide the dough in a circular motion, keeping it moving over the back of your hands and letting gravity do the final pulling. If the dough is resisting, give it a short rest on the peel and try again.

Lay the dough back on the peel and spoon the tomato sauce onto the middle. Use the back of the spoon to spread the sauce evenly over the dough, stopping at the indented rim. Scatter the mozzarella over the sauce and top with the cherry tomatoes. Shimmy the peel a few times to make sure the pizza moves freely and can easily slide off the peel. If the dough is stuck, quickly lift it with the dough scraper and toss a little white rice flour underneath.

Open the oven door and slide the pizza onto the steel by holding the peel at a slight angle and sliding it out from under the pizza in one fluid motion. It can help to match the edge of the peel with the far edge of the steel. Avoid shuffling the peel under the pizza.

Close the oven door and bake the pizza for 5 to 6 minutes. Open the door and check on the pizza. Chances are it will need to be rotated. Spin it 180 degrees with a metal peel or use a pair of long metal tongs to adjust the direction. Close the door and bake for an additional 4 to 5 minutes. The pizza is done when the crust is a burnished red, golden in spots, and the bubbles are slightly charred. The cheese should be melted, browned, and bubbly and the tomatoes slightly cooked.

Slide the metal peel under the pizza and transfer it to the wire rack. Grate the Parmesan on top. Dust with the salt, drizzle with the olive oil, and top with the basil. Let cool for 5 to 6 minutes, then move the pizza to the cutting board and cut into eight wedges with the pizza wheel or rocker cutter. Serve immediately.

FOR STORAGE AND WARMING INFORMATION, SEE PAGE 200.

BURRATA

Weight	Volume	Ingredient
	1	DOUGH ROUND **(any of the doughs in Chapter 2)**
56 G	¼ CUP	UNCOOKED TOMATO SAUCE **(page 177)**
115 G	4 OZ	BURRATA, TORN INTO PIECES
5 G	2 TBSP	PARMESAN
2 G	¼ TSP	SALT
14 G	1 TBSP	OLIVE OIL (EVOO)
	6	BASIL LEAVES, FRESH, TORN
		WHITE RICE FLOUR FOR STRETCHING THE DOUGH AND DUSTING THE PEEL

Burrata has a firm outer layer of mozzarella and an almost spreadable interior packed with stracciatella and cream. It is so delicate and rich that it breaks down in the intense heat of the oven, so it's added after the pizza comes out. You can either tear it into pieces, which I prefer, or you can serve it intact with a knife so it's an interactive experience. Mark this as a nice pie for a happy-hour pizza party or an early Sunday get-together.

If the pizza dough is refrigerated, remove it from the fridge 2 to 3 hours before you plan to bake. Proof the dough on the counter until it's slightly puffy and room temperature. By the end of proofing, it should feel soft and full of gas. While you wait, set up where you'll be stretching and building the pizza **(see Designing Workflow, page 101)** and position a cooling rack, cutting board, and pizza wheel or rocker cutter near the oven. Ready a 9 or 10 in [23 or 25 cm] cake pan half full of white rice flour and set it aside.

An hour before baking, position an oven rack 6 to 8 in [15 to 20 cm] from the top of the oven and set a baking steel or stone on it. Preheat the oven to 550°F [290°C] or as hot as the oven will allow.

Sprinkle a wooden peel with a little white rice flour and set it aside. Slide a dough scraper under the dough round and flip it over into the cake pan of white rice flour. Turn it over two or three times, then transfer it to the peel, handling it gently.

Use your fingertips to indent a ring ¼ in [6 mm] deep all the way around the rim of the dough. Flip the dough over and repeat, pressing an indent around the outer edge. Next, use the pads of your fingers to lightly press down on the inner circle of the dough, going from 12 o'clock at the top to 6 o'clock at the bottom. Flip the dough over and repeat. Return the dough to the original side up. You'll now use gravity to stretch it into its final shape. **CONT'D**

Slide clean, dry hands under the dough and make two fists in the center. Lift your hands and the pizza into the air parallel to your chin. Slowly move your fists in opposite directions to stretch the center of the pizza. Rotate the dough 90 degrees and carefully pull it in opposite directions again. Now arc your hands and let the dough slide down and hang off the back of your knuckles. Guide the dough in a circular motion, keeping it moving over the back of your hands and letting gravity do the final pulling. If the dough is resisting, give it a short rest on the peel and try again.

Lay the dough back on the peel and spoon the tomato sauce onto the middle. Use the back of the spoon to spread the sauce evenly over the dough, stopping at the indented rim. Shimmy the peel a few times to make sure the pizza moves freely and can easily slide off the peel. If the dough is stuck, quickly lift it with the dough scraper and toss a little white rice flour underneath.

Open the oven door and slide the pizza onto the steel by holding the peel at a slight angle and sliding it out from under the pizza in one fluid motion. It can help to match the edge of the peel with the far edge of the steel. Avoid shuffling the peel under the pizza.

Close the oven door and bake the pizza for 5 to 6 minutes. Open the door and check on the pizza. Chances are it will need to be rotated. Spin it 180 degrees with a metal peel or use a pair of long metal tongs to adjust the direction. Close the door and bake for an additional 4 to 5 minutes. The pizza is done when the crust is a burnished red, golden in spots, and the bubbles are slightly charred. The sauce should be bubbling.

Slide the metal peel under the pizza and transfer it to the wire rack. Scatter the burrata over the pizza and grate the Parmesan on top. Dust with the salt, drizzle with the olive oil, and top with the basil. Let cool for 5 to 6 minutes, then move the pizza to the cutting board and cut into eight wedges with the pizza wheel or rocker cutter. Serve immediately.

FOR STORAGE
AND WARMING INFORMATION,
SEE PAGE 200.

PEPPERONI

Weight	Volume	Ingredient
	1	DOUGH ROUND (any of the doughs in Chapter 2)
56 G	¼ CUP	ROASTED HEIRLOOM TOMATO SAUCE (page 178) OR UNCOOKED TOMATO SAUCE (page 177)
55 G	2 OZ	MOZZARELLA, FRESH, TORN INTO ½ IN [12 MM] PIECES
55 G	2 OZ	MOZZARELLA, LOW-MOISTURE, SHREDDED
55 G	2 OZ	PEPPERONI, THINLY SLICED
5 G	2 TBSP	PARMESAN
2 G	¼ TSP	SALT
14 G	1 TBSP	OLIVE OIL (EVOO)
		HOT HONEY (page 185) FOR DRIZZLING (OPTIONAL)
		RANCH DRESSING (page 189) FOR SERVING (OPTIONAL)
		WHITE RICE FLOUR FOR STRETCHING THE DOUGH AND DUSTING THE PEEL

MAKES ONE 12 IN [30.5 CM] PIZZA

Pepperoni is one of the most-requested pizza toppings in the world. It's salty, sweet, spicy, and comforting. This popular pie is the perfect occasion pizza, making it one to master. It's easy to dress up, too, such as drizzling it with Hot Honey (page 185) after it bakes or serving it with Ranch Dressing (page 189) for dunking. I like dusting Parmesan and red pepper flakes on mine. Use the Roasted Heirloom Tomato Sauce (page 178) for the classic flavor profile, or opt for the Uncooked Tomato Sauce (page 177) if you want it to taste refreshing.

If the pizza dough is refrigerated, remove it from the fridge 2 to 3 hours before you plan to bake. Proof the dough on the counter until it's slightly puffy and room temperature. By the end of proofing, it should feel soft and full of gas. While you wait, set up where you'll be stretching and building the pizza (see Designing Workflow, page 101) and position a cooling rack, cutting board, and pizza wheel or rocker cutter near the oven. Ready a 9 or 10 in [23 or 25 cm] cake pan half full of white rice flour and set it aside.

An hour before baking, position an oven rack 6 to 8 in [15 to 20 cm] from the top of the oven and set a baking steel or stone on it. Preheat the oven to 550°F [290°C] or as hot as the oven will allow.

Sprinkle a wooden peel with a little white rice flour and set it aside. Slide a dough scraper under the dough round and flip it over into the cake pan of white rice flour. Turn it over two or three times, then transfer it to the peel, handling it gently. CONT'D

Use your fingertips to indent a ring ¼ in [6 mm] deep all the way around the rim of the dough. Flip the dough over and repeat, pressing an indent around the outer edge. Next, use the pads of your fingers to lightly press down on the inner circle of the dough, going from 12 o'clock at the top to 6 o'clock at the bottom. Flip the dough over and repeat. Return the dough to the original side up. You'll now use gravity to stretch it into its final shape.

Slide clean, dry hands under the dough and make two fists in the center. Lift your hands and the pizza into the air parallel to your chin. Slowly move your fists in opposite directions to stretch the center of the pizza. Rotate the dough 90 degrees and carefully pull it in opposite directions again. Now arc your hands and let the dough slide down and hang off the back of your knuckles. Guide the dough in a circular motion, keeping it moving over the back of your hands and letting gravity do the final pulling. If the dough is resisting, give it a short rest on the peel and try again.

Lay the dough back on the peel and spoon the tomato sauce onto the middle. Use the back of the spoon to spread the sauce evenly over the dough, stopping at the indented rim. Top the sauce with the fresh mozzarella and low-moisture mozzarella and scatter the pepperoni on top. Shimmy the peel a few times to make sure the pizza moves freely and can easily slide off the peel. If the dough is stuck, quickly lift it with the dough scraper and toss a little white rice flour underneath.

Open the oven door and slide the pizza onto the steel by holding the peel at a slight angle and sliding it out from under the pizza in one fluid motion. It can help to match the edge of the peel with the far edge of the steel. Avoid shuffling the peel under the pizza.

Close the oven door and bake the pizza for 5 to 6 minutes. Open the door and check on the pizza. Chances are it will need to be rotated. Spin it 180 degrees with a metal peel or use a pair of long metal tongs to adjust the direction. Close the door and bake for an additional 4 to 5 minutes. The pizza is done when the crust is a burnished red, golden in spots, and the bubbles are slightly charred. The cheese should be melted and browned and the pepperoni slightly curled.

Slide the metal peel under the pizza and transfer it to the wire rack. Grate the Parmesan on top. Dust with the salt and drizzle with the olive oil and hot honey (if using). Let cool for 5 to 6 minutes, then move the pizza to the cutting board and cut into eight wedges with the pizza wheel or rocker cutter. Serve immediately. Accompany with the ranch for dunking, if desired.

FOR STORAGE AND WARMING INFORMATION, SEE PAGE 200.

SAUTÉED MUSHROOM AND BLACK OLIVE

MAKES ONE 12 IN [30.5 CM] PIZZA

Mushroom Topping

Weight	Volume	Ingredient
28 G	2 TBSP	OLIVE OIL (EVOO)
170 G	6 OZ (7 TO 8)	CREMINI MUSHROOMS, THINLY SLICED
2 G	¼ TSP	SALT

Assembly

Weight	Volume	Ingredient
	1	DOUGH ROUND **(any of the doughs in Chapter 2)**
60 G	¼ CUP	CRÈME FRAÎCHE **(page 188)**
55 G	2 OZ	MOZZARELLA, LOW-MOISTURE, SHREDDED
55 G	2 OZ	BLACK OLIVES, PITTED AND SLICED
5 G	2 TBSP	PARMESAN
2 G	¼ TSP	SALT
0.5 G	½ TSP	PARSLEY, DRIED
14 G	1 TBSP	OLIVE OIL (EVOO)
		WHITE RICE FLOUR FOR STRETCHING THE DOUGH AND DUSTING THE PEEL

White button, cremini, and portabella mushrooms are different strains of the same species, *Agaricus bisporus*. Here, I call for cremini (also marketed as baby bellas), which are brown and are firmer and a little more flavorful than their white button cousin. I love them for their savory, umami taste and pleasing color. Pair them with nice deli black olives for a high-end experience or go for big canned olives to keep this pie old-school. You'll need to make the **Crème Fraîche (page 188)** a day in advance of your bake, so plan ahead.

TO MAKE THE MUSHROOM TOPPING: Line a plate with a paper towel and set it near the stove. In a large skillet, heat the olive oil over medium-low heat until it glistens. Add the mushrooms, turning them in the oil with a heat-safe flexible spatula until coated, then let cook undisturbed for 1 minute. Stir gently, season with the salt, and continue cooking, stirring occasionally, until golden and browned on the edges, 4 to 5 minutes. Transfer to the towel-lined plate and let cool. The mushrooms can be cooked up to 2 days in advance and stored in an airtight container in the fridge. Bring to room temperature before adding to the pizza.

TO ASSEMBLE THE PIZZA: If the pizza dough is refrigerated, remove it from the fridge 2 to 3 hours before you plan to bake. Proof the dough on the counter until it's slightly puffy and room temperature. By the end of proofing, it should feel soft and full of gas. While you wait, set up where you'll be stretching and building the pizza **(see Designing Workflow, page 101)** and position a cooling rack, cutting board, and pizza wheel or rocker cutter near the oven. Ready a 9 or 10 in [23 or 25 cm] cake pan half full of white rice flour and set it aside.

An hour before baking, position an oven rack 6 to 8 in [15 to 20 cm] from the top of the oven and set a baking steel or stone on it. Preheat the oven to 550°F [290°C] or as hot as the oven will allow.

Sprinkle a wooden peel with a little white rice flour and set it aside. Slide a dough scraper under the dough round and flip it over into the cake pan of white rice flour. Turn it over two or three times, then transfer it to the peel, handling it gently.

Use your fingertips to indent a ring ¼ in [6 mm] deep all the way around the rim of the dough. Flip the dough over and repeat, pressing an indent around the outer edge. Next, use the pads of your fingers to lightly press down on the inner circle of the dough, going from 12 o'clock at the top to 6 o'clock at the bottom. Flip the dough over and repeat. Return the dough to the original side up. You'll now use gravity to stretch it into its final shape.

Slide clean, dry hands under the dough and make two fists in the center. Lift your hands and the pizza into the air parallel to your chin. Slowly move your fists in opposite directions to stretch the center of the pizza. Rotate the dough 90 degrees and carefully pull it in opposite directions again. Now arc your hands and let the dough slide down and hang off the back of your knuckles. Guide the dough in a circular motion, keeping it moving over the back of your hands and letting gravity do the final pulling. If the dough is resisting, give it a short rest on the peel and try again.

Lay the dough back on the peel and spoon the crème fraîche onto the middle. Use the back of the spoon to spread it evenly over the dough, stopping at the indented rim. Top with the mozzarella and scatter the cooked mushrooms and the olives evenly over the top. Shimmy the peel a few times to make sure the pizza moves freely and can easily slide off the peel. If the dough is stuck, quickly lift it with the dough scraper and toss a little white rice flour underneath. **CONT'D**

Open the oven door and slide the pizza onto the steel by holding the peel at a slight angle and sliding it out from under the pizza in one fluid motion. It can help to match the edge of the peel with the far edge of the steel. Avoid shuffling the peel under the pizza.

Close the oven door and bake the pizza for 5 to 6 minutes. Open the door and check on the pizza. Chances are it will need to be rotated. Spin it 180 degrees with a metal peel or use a pair of long metal tongs to adjust the direction. Close the door and bake for an additional 4 to 5 minutes. The pizza is done when the crust is a burnished red, golden in spots, and the bubbles are slightly charred. The cheese should be melted and browned.

Slide the metal peel under the pizza and transfer it to the wire rack. Grate the Parmesan on top. Dust with the salt and parsley and drizzle with the olive oil. Let cool for 5 to 6 minutes, then move the pizza to the cutting board and cut into eight wedges with the pizza wheel or rocker cutter. Serve immediately.

FOR STORAGE
AND WARMING INFORMATION,
SEE PAGE 200.

JALAPEÑO AND BACON

Weight	Volume	Ingredient
	1	DOUGH ROUND (any of the doughs in Chapter 2)
56 G	¼ CUP	UNCOOKED TOMATO SAUCE (page 177)
55 G	2 OZ	MOZZARELLA, LOW-MOISTURE, SHREDDED
55 G	2 OZ	COLBY, SHREDDED
84 G	3 OR 4	JALAPEÑO CHILES, SEEDED AND THINLY SLICED
230 G	7 OR 8 STRIPS	BACON, COOKED AND CRUMBLED (see page 265)
5 G	2 TBSP	PARMESAN
2 G	¼ TSP	SALT
14 G	1 TBSP	OLIVE OIL (EVOO)
		CRÈME FRAÎCHE (page 188) FOR TOPPING (OPTIONAL)
		WHITE RICE FLOUR FOR STRETCHING THE DOUGH AND DUSTING THE PEEL

Sweet, spicy, and salty, this pizza hits all the flavor notes and is elevated by dollops of Crème Fraîche (page 188) after the bake—optional, of course. The creaminess of the mozzarella takes the edge off the jalapeños, making the pizza refreshing rather than mouth burning. Not all bacon is the same. Here, I'm sticking with American-style pork bacon, but feel free to experiment. Cook the bacon while the dough is proofing so it's ready to go when you're building the pizza.

If the pizza dough is refrigerated, remove it from the fridge 2 to 3 hours before you plan to bake. Proof the dough on the counter until it's slightly puffy and room temperature. By the end of proofing, it should feel soft and full of gas. While you wait, set up where you'll be stretching and building the pizza (see Designing Workflow, page 101) and position a cooling rack, cutting board, and pizza wheel or rocker cutter near the oven. Ready a 9 or 10 in [23 or 25 cm] cake pan half full of white rice flour and set it aside.

An hour before baking, position an oven rack 6 to 8 in [15 to 20 cm] from the top of the oven and set a baking steel or stone on it. Turn the heat up to 550°F [290°C] or as hot as the oven will allow.

Sprinkle a wooden peel with a little white rice flour and set it aside. Slide a dough scraper under the dough round and flip it over into the cake pan of white rice flour. Turn it over two or three times, then transfer it to the peel, handling it gently.

Use your fingertips to indent a ring ¼ in [6 mm] deep all the way around the rim of the dough. Flip the dough over and repeat, pressing an indent around the outer edge. Next, use the pads of your fingers to lightly CONT'D press down on the inner circle of the dough, going from 12 o'clock at the top to 6 o'clock at the bottom. Flip the dough over and repeat. Return the dough to the original side up. You'll now use gravity to stretch it into its final shape.

Slide clean, dry hands under the dough and make two fists in the center. Lift your hands and the pizza into the air parallel to your chin. Slowly move your fists in opposite directions to stretch the center of the pizza. Rotate the dough 90 degrees and carefully pull it in opposite directions again. Now arc your hands and let the dough slide down and hang off the back of your knuckles. Guide the dough in a circular motion, keeping it moving over the back of your hands and letting gravity do the final pulling. If the dough is resisting, give it a short rest on the peel and try again.

Lay the dough back on the peel and spoon the tomato sauce onto the middle. Use the back of the spoon to spread the sauce evenly over the dough, stopping at the indented rim. Top with the mozzarella and Colby and then scatter the jalapeños and bacon over the top. Shimmy the peel a few times to make sure the pizza moves freely and can easily slide off the peel. If the dough is stuck, quickly lift it with the dough scraper and toss a little white rice flour underneath.

Open the oven door and slide the pizza onto the steel by holding the peel at a slight angle and sliding it out from under the pizza in one fluid motion. It can help to match the edge of the peel with the far edge of the steel. Avoid shuffling the peel under the pizza.

Close the oven door and bake the pizza for 5 to 6 minutes. Open the door and check on the pizza. Chances are it will need to be rotated. Spin it 180 degrees with a metal peel or use a pair of long metal tongs to adjust the direction. Close the door and bake for an additional 4 to 5 minutes. The pizza is done when the crust is a burnished red, golden in spots, and the bubbles are slightly charred. The cheese should be melted and browned and the jalapeños cooked.

Slide the metal peel under the pizza and transfer it to the wire rack to cool. Grate the Parmesan on top. Dust with the salt, drizzle with the olive oil, and finish with dollops of crème fraîche, if desired. Let cool for 5 to 6 minutes, then move the pizza to the cutting board and cut into eight wedges with the pizza wheel or rocker cutter. Serve immediately.

FOR STORAGE AND WARMING INFORMATION, SEE PAGE 200.

SUPREME DELIGHT

Mushroom and Bell Pepper Toppings

Weight	Volume	Ingredient
42 G	3 TBSP	OLIVE OIL (EVOO)
113 G	4 OZ	BUTTON MUSHROOMS, SLICED
3 G	½ TSP	SALT
90 G	½ CUP	GREEN BELL PEPPER, SLICED
62 G	½ CUP	RED ONION, SLICED

MAKES ONE 12 IN [30.5 CM] PIZZA

Assembly

Weight	Volume	Ingredient
	1	DOUGH ROUND **(any of the doughs in Chapter 2)**
56 G	¼ CUP	ROASTED HEIRLOOM TOMATO SAUCE **(page 178)**
55 G	2 OZ	MOZZARELLA, LOW-MOISTURE, SHREDDED
113 G	4 OZ	ITALIAN SAUSAGE, CASING REMOVED, PINCHED INTO DIME-SIZE PIECES
30 G	2 OZ	PEPPERONI, THINLY SLICED
2 G	¼ TSP	SALT
		WHITE RICE FLOUR FOR STRETCHING THE DOUGH AND DUSTING THE PEEL

A supreme pizza must have two meats, typically pepperoni and sausage, plus mushrooms, bell peppers, and onions. You'll also find it with olives, banana peppers, and seasoned beef, depending on where you live. Popularized by chain pizza restaurants in the 1960s, the real credit goes to Italian Americans who created pizzas with whatever was on hand. The flavor of the bell peppers and sausage is nostalgic and delicious when done well.

TO MAKE THE MUSHROOM AND BELL PEPPER TOPPINGS: Line a plate with a paper towel and set it near the stove. In a medium skillet, heat 28 g [2 Tbsp] of the olive oil over medium-low heat until it glistens. Add the mushrooms, turning them in the oil with a heat-safe flexible spatula until coated, then let cook undisturbed for 1 minute. Stir gently, season with a pinch of the salt, saving the rest for seasoning the bell pepper and onion later, and continue cooking over medium-low heat, stirring occasionally, until golden and browned on the edges, 4 to 5 minutes. Transfer to the towel-lined plate and let cool.

Add the remaining 14 g [1 Tbsp] olive oil to the skillet over medium-low heat. Add the bell pepper and onion and cook, stirring occasionally, until slightly softened, 2 to 3 minutes. Dust with the remaining salt, then transfer to the plate with the mushrooms and let cool. The mushrooms, pepper, and onion can be cooked up to 48 hours in advance and stored in an airtight container in the fridge. Bring to room temperature before adding to the pizza. **CONT'D**

TO ASSEMBLE THE PIZZA: If the pizza dough is refrigerated, remove it from the fridge 2 to 3 hours before you plan to bake. Proof the dough on the counter until it's slightly puffy and room temperature. By the end of proofing, it should feel soft and full of gas. While you wait, set up where you'll be stretching and building the pizza **(see Designing Workflow, page 101)** and position a cooling rack, cutting board, and pizza wheel or rocker cutter near the oven. Ready a 9 or 10 in [23 or 25 cm] cake pan half full of white rice flour and set it aside.

An hour before baking, position an oven rack 6 to 8 in [15 to 20 cm] from the top of the oven and set a baking steel or stone on it. Preheat the oven to 550°F [290°C] or as hot as the oven will allow.

Sprinkle a wooden peel with a little white rice flour and set it aside. Slide a dough scraper under the dough round and flip it over into the cake pan of white rice flour. Turn it over two or three times, then transfer it to the peel, handling it gently.

Use your fingertips to indent a ring ¼ in [6 mm] deep all the way around the rim of the dough. Flip the dough over and repeat, pressing an indent around the outer edge. Next, use the pads of your fingers to lightly press down on the inner circle of the dough, going from 12 o'clock at the top to 6 o'clock at the bottom. Flip the dough over and repeat. Return the dough to the original side up. You'll now use gravity to stretch it into its final shape.

Slide clean, dry hands under the dough and make two fists in the center. Lift your hands and the pizza into the air parallel to your chin. Slowly move your fists in opposite directions to stretch the center of the pizza. Rotate the dough 90 degrees and carefully pull it in opposite directions again. Now arc your hands and let the dough slide down and hang off the back of your knuckles. Guide the dough in a circular motion, keeping it moving over the back of your hands and letting gravity do the final pulling. If the dough is resisting, give it a short rest on the peel and try again.

Lay the dough back on the peel and spoon the tomato sauce onto the middle. Use the back of the spoon to spread the sauce evenly over the dough, stopping at the indented rim. Top the sauce with the mozzarella and scatter the mushrooms, bell pepper, onion, sausage, and pepperoni evenly over the top. Shimmy the peel a few times to make sure the pizza moves freely and can easily slide off the peel. If the dough is stuck, quickly lift it with the dough scraper and toss a little white rice flour underneath. **CONT'D**

Open the oven door and slide the pizza onto the steel by holding the peel at a slight angle and sliding it out from under the pizza in one fluid motion. It can help to match the edge of the peel with the far edge of the steel. Avoid shuffling the peel under the pizza.

Close the oven door and bake the pizza for 5 to 6 minutes. Open the door and check on the pizza. Chances are it will need to be rotated. Spin it 180 degrees with a metal peel or use a pair of long metal tongs to adjust the direction. Close the door and bake for an additional 4 to 5 minutes. The pizza is done when the crust is a burnished red, golden in spots, and the bubbles are slightly charred. The cheese should be melted and browned, the sausage cooked, and the pepperoni slightly curled.

Slide the metal peel under the pizza and transfer it to the wire rack. Dust with the salt. Let cool for 5 to 6 minutes, then move the pizza to the cutting board and cut into eight wedges with the pizza wheel or rocker cutter. Serve immediately.

FOR STORAGE AND WARMING INFORMATION, SEE PAGE 200.

PANCETTA AND BROWN BUTTER PINEAPPLE

Pancetta and Pineapple Toppings

Weight	Volume	Ingredient
113 G	4 OZ	PANCETTA, DICED
28 G	2 TBSP	UNSALTED BUTTER
100 G	½ CUP	PINEAPPLE, CUT INTO SMALL WEDGES AND WELL DRAINED

Assembly

Weight	Volume	Ingredient
	1	DOUGH ROUND **(any of the doughs in Chapter 2)**
56 G	¼ CUP	UNCOOKED TOMATO SAUCE **(page 177)**
57 G	2 OZ	MOZZARELLA, LOW-MOISTURE, SHREDDED
57 G	2 OZ	MONTEREY JACK, SHREDDED
0.5 G	½ TSP	PARSLEY, DRIED
1 G	½ TSP	RED PEPPER FLAKES
2 G	¼ TSP	SALT
14 G	1 TBSP	OLIVE OIL (EVOO)
		HOT HONEY **(page 185)** FOR DRIZZLING (OPTIONAL)
		WHITE RICE FLOUR FOR STRETCHING THE DOUGH AND DUSTING THE PEEL

MAKES ONE 12 IN [30.5 CM] PIZZA

Pancetta is made from a slab of pork belly, which is cured with salt and spices and rolled into a log. While it can be eaten raw, it is often cooked, which highlights its rich, deep meaty flavor. Here, the pancetta is cooked until crispy and paired with pineapple for a savory, salty, sweet experience that transcends the argument over whether pineapple should be on a pizza or not. Dusted with red pepper flakes and parsley, this is a perfect poolside summer pie. Drizzle on **Hot Honey (page 185)** for an extra kick.

TO MAKE THE PANCETTA AND PINEAPPLE TOPPINGS: Line a plate with a paper towel and set it near the stove. Put the pancetta into a cold medium skillet and place over medium heat. Cook, stirring occasionally with a heat-safe flexible spatula, until the pancetta is browned and almost crispy, 5 to 8 minutes. Transfer to the towel-lined plate to cool.

Poor off all but about 1 Tbsp of the fat from the pan and return the pan to medium heat. Add the butter, let it melt, and then add the pineapple wedges. Cook for 3 to 4 minutes, then flip the wedges over and cook on the second side for 3 to 4 minutes, basting them occasionally with the butter and fat to enhance their flavor. The pineapple is done when the edges are browned. Transfer to the plate with the pancetta and let cool. The pancetta and pineapple can be **CONT'D** cooked up to 48 hours in advance and stored in an airtight container in the fridge. Bring to room temperature before adding to the pizza.

TO ASSEMBLE THE PIZZA: If the pizza dough is refrigerated, remove it from the fridge 2 to 3 hours before you plan to bake. Proof the dough on the counter until it's slightly puffy and room temperature. By the end of proofing, it should feel soft and full of gas. While you wait, set up where you'll be stretching and building the pizza **(see Designing Workflow, page 101)** and position a cooling rack, cutting board, and pizza wheel or rocker cutter near the oven. Ready a 9 or 10 in [23 or 25 cm] cake pan half full of white rice flour and set it aside.

An hour before baking, position an oven rack 6 to 8 in [15 to 20 cm] from the top of the oven and set a baking steel or stone on it. Preheat the oven to 550°F [290°C] or as hot as the oven will allow.

Sprinkle a wooden peel with a little white rice flour and set it aside. Slide a dough scraper under the dough round and flip it over into the cake pan of white rice flour. Turn it over two or three times, then transfer it to the peel, handling it gently.

Use your fingertips to indent a ring ¼ in [6 mm] deep all the way around the rim of the dough. Flip the dough over and repeat, pressing an indent around the outer edge. Next, use the pads of your fingers to lightly press down on the inner circle of the dough, going from 12 o'clock at the top to 6 o'clock at the bottom. Flip the dough over and repeat. Return the dough to the original side up. You'll now use gravity to stretch it into its final shape.

Slide clean, dry hands under the dough and make two fists in the center. Lift your hands and the pizza into the air parallel to your chin. Slowly move your fists in opposite directions to stretch the center of the pizza. Rotate the dough 90 degrees and carefully pull it in opposite directions again. Now arc your hands and let the dough slide down and hang off the back of your knuckles. Guide the dough in a circular motion, keeping it moving over the back of your hands and letting gravity do the final pulling. If the dough is resisting, give it a short rest on the peel and try again. **CONT'D**

Lay the dough back on the peel and spoon the tomato sauce onto the middle. Use the back of the spoon to spread the sauce evenly over the dough, stopping at the indented rim. Top with the mozzarella and Monterey Jack and scatter the pancetta and pineapple evenly over the top. Shimmy the peel a few times to make sure the pizza moves freely and can easily slide off the peel. If the dough is stuck, quickly lift it with the dough scraper and toss a little white rice flour underneath.

Open the oven door and slide the pizza onto the steel by holding the peel at a slight angle and sliding it out from under the pizza in one fluid motion. It can help to match the edge of the peel with the far edge of the steel. Avoid shuffling the peel under the pizza.

Close the oven door and bake the pizza for 5 to 6 minutes. Open the door and check on the pizza. Chances are it will need to be rotated. Spin it 180 degrees with a metal peel or use a pair of long metal tongs to adjust the direction. Close the door and bake for an additional 4 to 5 minutes. The pizza is done when the crust is a burnished red, golden in spots, and the bubbles are slightly charred. The cheese should be melted and the pancetta and pineapple nicely browned.

Slide the metal peel under the pizza and transfer it to the wire rack. Dust with the parsley, red pepper flakes, and salt and drizzle with the olive oil and hot honey (if using). Let cool for 5 to 6 minutes, then move the pizza to the cutting board and cut into eight wedges with the pizza wheel or rocker cutter. Serve immediately.

FOR STORAGE AND WARMING INFORMATION, SEE PAGE 200.

CARAMELIZED ONION, SAUSAGE, AND MAPLE

MAKES ONE 12 IN [30.5 CM] PIZZA

Caramelized Onion Topping

Weight	Volume	Ingredient
45 G	3 TBSP	UNSALTED BUTTER
70 G	½ CUP	YELLOW ONION, LARGE, THINLY SLICED
2 G	¼ TSP	SALT

Assembly

Weight	Volume	Ingredient
	1	DOUGH ROUND **(any of the doughs in Chapter 2)**
56 G	¼ CUP	UNCOOKED TOMATO SAUCE **(page 177)**
55 G	2 OZ	MOZZARELLA, FRESH, TORN INTO ½ IN [12 MM] PIECES
85 G	3 OZ	ITALIAN SAUSAGE, CASING REMOVED, PINCHED INTO DIME-SIZE PIECES
14 G	1 TBSP	MAPLE SYRUP
2 G	¼ TSP	SALT
		WHITE RICE FLOUR FOR STRETCHING THE DOUGH AND DUSTING THE PEEL

I was an organic vegetable farmer once upon a time, and onions were one of my favorite things to grow. We'd start the seeds in the greenhouse in February, transplant the wispy, thin green blades in the spring, and harvest the glorious bulbous onions in the late summer when the stalks turned brown and fell over. Our barn would be filled with braided onions hanging from the rafters, drying in the fading heat. This pizza is my nod to those dusty barn days and the wonderful world of onions.

TO MAKE THE CARAMELIZED ONION TOPPING: In a medium skillet, melt the butter over low heat until it is gently bubbling. Add the onion, season with the salt, and cook, stirring frequently to avoid burning, until soft, translucent, and deeply browned, 25 to 30 minutes. Add a splash of water if the onion begins sticking to the pan. Transfer to a plate to cool. The onion can be cooked up to 48 hours in advance and stored in an airtight container in the fridge. Bring to room temperature before adding to the pizza.

TO ASSEMBLE THE PIZZA: If the pizza dough is refrigerated, remove it from the fridge 2 to 3 hours before you plan to bake. Proof the dough on the counter until it's slightly puffy and room temperature. By the end of proofing, it should feel soft and full of gas. While you wait, set up where you'll be stretching and building the pizza **(see Designing Workflow, page 101)** and position a cooling rack, cutting board, and pizza wheel or rocker

CONT'D

cutter near the oven. Ready a 9 or 10 in [23 or 25 cm] cake pan half full of white rice flour and set it aside.

An hour before baking, position an oven rack 6 to 8 in [15 to 20 cm] from the top of the oven and set a baking steel or stone on it. Preheat the oven to 550°F [290°C] or as hot as the oven will allow.

Sprinkle a wooden peel with a little white rice flour and set it aside. Slide a dough scraper under the dough round and flip it over into the cake pan of white rice flour. Turn it over two or three times, then transfer it to the peel, handling it gently.

Use your fingertips to indent a ring ¼ in [6 mm] deep all the way around the rim of the dough. Flip the dough over and repeat, pressing an indent around the outer edge. Next, use the pads of your fingers to lightly press down on the inner circle of the dough, going from 12 o'clock at the top to 6 o'clock at the bottom. Flip the dough over and repeat. Return the dough to the original side up. You'll now use gravity to stretch it into its final shape.

Slide clean, dry hands under the dough and make two fists in the center. Lift your hands and the pizza into the air parallel to your chin. Slowly move your fists in opposite directions to stretch the center of the pizza. Rotate the dough 90 degrees and carefully pull it in opposite directions again. Now arc your hands and let the dough slide down and hang off the back of your knuckles. Guide the dough in a circular motion, keeping it moving over the back of your hands and letting gravity do the final pulling. If the dough is resisting, give it a short rest on the peel and try again.

Lay the dough back on the peel and spoon the tomato sauce onto the middle. Use the back of the spoon to spread the sauce evenly over the dough, stopping at the indented rim. Top with the mozzarella and scatter the caramelized onion and sausage evenly over the top. Shimmy the peel a few times to make sure the pizza moves freely and can easily slide off the peel. If the dough is stuck, quickly lift it with the dough scraper and toss a little white rice flour underneath.

Open the oven door and slide the pizza onto the steel by holding the peel at a slight angle and sliding it out from under the pizza in one fluid motion. It can help to match the edge of the peel with the far edge of the steel. Avoid shuffling the peel under the pizza. **CONT'D**

Close the oven door and bake the pizza for 5 to 6 minutes. Open the door and check on the pizza. Chances are it will need to be rotated. Spin it 180 degrees with a metal peel or use a pair of long metal tongs to adjust the direction. Close the door and bake for an additional 4 to 5 minutes. The pizza is done when the crust is a burnished red, golden in spots, and the bubbles are slightly charred. The cheese should be melted and browned and the sausage cooked.

Slide the metal peel under the pizza and transfer it to the wire rack. Drizzle with the maple syrup and dust with the salt. Let cool for 5 to 6 minutes, then move the pizza to the cutting board and cut into eight wedges with the pizza wheel or rocker cutter. Serve immediately.

FOR STORAGE AND WARMING INFORMATION, SEE PAGE 200.

PICKLE

Weight	Volume	Ingredient
	1	DOUGH ROUND **(any of the doughs in Chapter 2)**
56 G	¼ CUP	UNCOOKED TOMATO SAUCE **(page 177)**
55 G	2 OZ	MOZZARELLA, LOW-MOISTURE, SHREDDED
140 G	1 CUP	PICKLE SLICES
5 G	2 TBSP	PARMESAN
9 G	2 SPRIGS	DILL, FRESH, CHOPPED
2 G	¼ TSP	SALT
14 G	1 TBSP	OLIVE OIL (EVOO)
		WHITE RICE FLOUR FOR STRETCHING THE DOUGH AND DUSTING THE PEEL

This pizza is unusual, but it works. The combination of rich cheese and sour pickles isn't unlike adding capers or briny olives to a pizza. You can use store-bought pickle spears or make your own using the **Refrigerator Pickles recipe on page 195**. This is one of my favorite pizzas!

If the pizza dough is refrigerated, remove it from the fridge 2 to 3 hours before you plan to bake. Proof the dough on the counter until it's slightly puffy and room temperature. By the end of proofing, it should feel soft and full of gas. While you wait, set up where you'll be stretching and building the pizza **(see Designing Workflow, page 101)** and position a cooling rack, cutting board, and pizza wheel or rocker cutter near the oven. Ready a 9 or 10 in [23 or 25 cm] cake pan half full of white rice flour and set it aside.

An hour before baking, position an oven rack 6 to 8 in [15 to 20 cm] from the top of the oven and set a baking steel or stone on it. Preheat the oven to 550°F [290°C] or as hot as the oven will allow.

Sprinkle a wooden peel with a little white rice flour and set it aside. Slide a dough scraper under the dough round and flip it over into the cake pan of white rice flour. Turn it over two or three times, then transfer it to the peel, handling it gently.

Use your fingertips to indent a ring ¼ in [6 mm] deep all the way around the rim of the dough. Flip the dough over and repeat, pressing an indent around the outer edge. Next, use the pads of your fingers to lightly press down on the inner circle of the dough, going from 12 o'clock at the top to 6 o'clock at the bottom. Flip the dough over

CONT'D

and repeat. Return the dough to the original side up. You'll now use gravity to stretch it into its final shape.

Slide clean, dry hands under the dough and make two fists in the center. Lift your hands and the pizza into the air parallel to your chin. Slowly move your fists in opposite directions to stretch the center of the pizza. Rotate the dough 90 degrees and carefully pull it in opposite directions again. Now arc your hands and let the dough slide down and hang off the back of your knuckles. Guide the dough in a circular motion, keeping it moving over the back of your hands and letting gravity do the final pulling. If the dough is resisting, give it a short rest on the peel and try again.

Lay the dough back on the peel and spoon the tomato sauce onto the middle. Use the back of the spoon to spread the sauce evenly over the dough, stopping at the indented rim. Scatter the mozzarella over the dough, then distribute the pickle slices evenly over the top. Shimmy the peel a few times to make sure the pizza moves freely and can easily slide off the peel. If the dough is stuck, quickly lift it with the dough scraper and toss a little white rice flour underneath.

Open the oven door and slide the pizza onto the steel by holding the peel at a slight angle and sliding it out from under the pizza in one fluid motion. It can help to match the edge of the peel with the far edge of the steel. Avoid shuffling the peel under the pizza.

Close the oven door and bake the pizza for 5 to 6 minutes. Open the door and check on the pizza. Chances are it will need to be rotated. Spin it 180 degrees with a metal peel or use a pair of long metal tongs to adjust the direction. Close the door and bake for an additional 4 to 5 minutes. The pizza is done when the crust is a burnished red, golden in spots, and the bubbles are slightly charred. The cheese should be melted and browned.

Slide the metal peel under the pizza and transfer it to the wire rack. Grate the Parmesan on top. Sprinkle on the dill, dust with the salt, and drizzle with the olive oil. Let cool for 5 to 6 minutes, then move the pizza to the cutting board and cut into eight wedges with the pizza wheel or rocker cutter. Serve immediately.

FOR STORAGE AND WARMING INFORMATION, SEE PAGE 200.

Pizzas without tomato sauce allow the dough to take center stage and mingle with the flavors of the cheese for a creamy, delicate experience. ●

WHITE PIES

White pizzas can be sophisticated and elegant, but the last thing they are is white. Their cheese should brown properly during baking, and they are often given a fancy, colorful finish of parsley and red pepper flakes or maybe a drizzle of yellow hot honey.

White pizzas may bake a few minutes faster than red ones because they don't have a tomato sauce that needs reducing. The absence of the weight of a tomato sauce also means it's important to stretch the dough well and to top it evenly so it doesn't rise like a pita.

Some of the following recipes call for a drizzle of olive oil before the cheese and toppings. If you like, you can carefully spread the oil with the back of a spoon or with a soft-bristled pastry brush.

Golden Crust Trick / To bring out the color of the crust, I do one swoop around the rim with a drizzle of olive oil while the pie is still hot from the oven. This makes the crust shine and turn burnished gold. It's rejuvenating to the dough that may have lost moisture in the bake and makes it extra delicious. It's a win-win!

BIANCA

Weight	Volume	Ingredient
	1	DOUGH ROUND **(any of the doughs in Chapter 2)**
55 G	2 OZ	MOZZARELLA, FRESH, TORN INTO ½ IN [12 MM] PIECES
55 G	2 OZ	PROVOLONE, SHREDDED
60 G	¼ CUP	RICOTTA, WHOLE-MILK
5 G	2 TBSP	PARMESAN
2 G	¼ TSP	SALT
		RED PEPPER FLAKES FOR FINISHING (OPTIONAL)
14 G	1 TBSP	OLIVE OIL (EVOO)
		WHITE RICE FLOUR FOR STRETCHING THE DOUGH AND DUSTING THE PEEL

MAKES ONE 12 IN [30.5 CM] PIZZA

There is always room at my table for a pizza made with cream and ricotta. Small-batch artisanal ricotta is smooth, cloud-like, and delicately flavored, while the ricotta sold in most supermarkets is aged to a firmer, grainier state. Either will work here. The fresh mozzarella keeps this pizza creamy, and the provolone adds a nice sharpness. Top with red pepper flakes if you enjoy a little heat.

If the pizza dough is refrigerated, remove it from the fridge 2 to 3 hours before you plan to bake. Proof the dough on the counter until it's slightly puffy and room temperature. By the end of proofing, it should feel soft and full of gas. While you wait, set up where you'll be stretching and building the pizza **(see Designing Workflow, page 101)** and position a cooling rack, cutting board, and pizza wheel or rocker cutter near the oven. Ready a 9 or 10 in [23 or 25 cm] cake pan half full of white rice flour and set it aside.

An hour before baking, position an oven rack 6 to 8 in [15 to 20 cm] from the top of the oven and set a baking steel or stone on it. Preheat the oven to 550°F [290°C] or as hot as the oven will allow.

Sprinkle a wooden peel with a little white rice flour and set it aside. Slide a dough scraper under the dough round and flip it over into the cake pan of white rice flour. Turn it over two or three times, then transfer it to the peel, handling it gently.

Use your fingertips to indent a ring ¼ in [6 mm] deep all the way around the rim of the dough. Flip the dough over and repeat, pressing an indent around the outer edge. Next, use the pads of your fingers to lightly press down on the inner circle of the dough, going from 12 o'clock at the top to 6 o'clock at the bottom. Flip the dough

CONT'D

over and repeat. Return the dough to the original side up. You'll now use gravity to stretch it into its final shape.

Slide clean, dry hands under the dough and make two fists in the center. Lift your hands and the pizza into the air parallel to your chin. Slowly move your fists in opposite directions to stretch the center of the pizza. Rotate the dough 90 degrees and carefully pull it in opposite directions again. Now arc your hands and let the dough slide down and hang off the back of your knuckles. Guide the dough in a circular motion, keeping it moving over the back of your hands and letting gravity do the final pulling. If the dough is resisting, give it a short rest on the peel and try again.

Lay the dough back on the peel and scatter the mozzarella and provolone evenly over the pizza. Dollop with the ricotta. Shimmy the peel a few times to make sure the pizza moves freely and can easily slide off the peel. If the dough is stuck, quickly lift it with the dough scraper and toss a little white rice flour underneath.

Open the oven door and slide the pizza onto the steel by holding the peel at a slight angle and sliding it out from under the pizza in one fluid motion. It can help to match the edge of the peel with the far edge of the steel. Avoid shuffling the peel under the pizza.

Close the oven door and bake the pizza for 5 to 6 minutes. Open the door and check on the pizza. Chances are it will need to be rotated. Spin it 180 degrees with a metal peel or use a pair of long metal tongs to adjust the direction. Close the door and bake for an additional 4 to 5 minutes. The pizza is done when the crust is a burnished red, golden in spots, and the bubbles are slightly charred. The cheese should be melted and browned.

Slide the metal peel under the pizza and transfer it to the wire rack. Grate the Parmesan on top. Dust with the salt and red pepper flakes (if using) and drizzle with the olive oil. Let cool for 5 to 6 minutes, then move the pizza to the cutting board and cut into eight wedges with the pizza wheel or rocker cutter. Serve immediately.

FOR STORAGE AND WARMING: Any uneaten pizza can be stored in an airtight container in the fridge for up to 5 days. To serve, reheat directly on a preheated baking steel or stone (500°F [260°C]) until the cheese is bubbly, 2 to 5 minutes.

GARLIC CREAM

Weight	Volume	Ingredient
	1	DOUGH ROUND **(any of the doughs in Chapter 2)**
56 G	¼ CUP	LEMONY ROASTED-GARLIC CREAM **(page 186)**
55 G	2 OZ	MOZZARELLA, FRESH, TORN INTO ½ IN [12 MM] PIECES
55 G	2 OZ	FONTINA, SHREDDED
2 G	1 TSP	OREGANO, FRESH, FINELY CHOPPED
2 G	1 TSP	THYME, FRESH, FINELY CHOPPED
2 G	1 TSP	PARSLEY, FRESH, FINELY CHOPPED
2 G	1 TSP	ROSEMARY, FRESH, FINELY CHOPPED
5 G	2 TBSP	PARMESAN
2 G	¼ TSP	SALT
14 G	1 TBSP	OLIVE OIL (EVOO)
		WHITE RICE FLOUR FOR STRETCHING THE DOUGH AND DUSTING THE PEEL

MAKES ONE 12 IN [30.5 CM] PIZZA

Raw garlic can have a sharp, pungent taste, so I prefer to transform it through gentle cooking or deep roasting, both of which will take the edge off. When roasted, it turns into what I call garlic "candy." This pizza calls for my **Lemony Roasted-Garlic Cream (page 186)**, which can be made several days in advance. Serve this pie in chilly seasons when the richness feels comforting rather than heavy.

If the pizza dough is refrigerated, remove it from the fridge 2 to 3 hours before you plan to bake. Proof the dough on the counter until it's slightly puffy and room temperature. By the end of proofing, it should feel soft and full of gas. While you wait, set up where you'll be stretching and building the pizza **(see Designing Workflow, page 101)** and position a cooling rack, cutting board, and pizza wheel or rocker cutter near the oven. Ready a 9 or 10 in [23 or 25 cm] cake pan half full of white rice flour and set it aside.

An hour before baking, position an oven rack 6 to 8 in [15 to 20 cm] from the top of the oven and set a baking steel or stone on it. Preheat the oven to 550°F [290°C] or as hot as the oven will allow.

Sprinkle a wooden peel with a little white rice flour and set it aside. Slide a dough scraper under the dough round and flip it over into the cake pan of white rice flour. Turn it over two or three times, then transfer it to the peel, handling it gently.

Use your fingertips to indent a ring ¼ in [6 mm] deep all the way around the rim of the dough. Flip the dough over and repeat, pressing an indent around the outer edge. Next, use the pads of your fingers to lightly press down on the inner circle of the dough, going from 12 o'clock at the top to 6 o'clock at the bottom. Flip the dough over and repeat. Return the dough to the original side up. You'll now use gravity to stretch it into its final shape.

Slide clean, dry hands under the dough and make two fists in the center. Lift your hands and the pizza into the air parallel to your chin. Slowly move your fists in opposite directions to stretch the center of the pizza. Rotate the dough 90 degrees and carefully pull it in opposite directions again. Now arc your hands and let the dough slide down and hang off the back of your knuckles. Guide the dough in a circular motion, keeping it moving over the back of your hands and letting gravity do the final pulling. If the dough is resisting, give it a short rest on the peel and try again.

Lay the dough back on the peel and spoon the garlic cream onto the middle. Use the back of the spoon to spread the garlic cream evenly over the dough, stopping at the indented rim. Scatter the mozzarella, fontina, oregano, thyme, parsley, and rosemary evenly over the top. Shimmy the peel a few times to make sure the pizza moves freely and can easily slide off the peel. If the dough is stuck, quickly lift it with the dough scraper and toss a little white rice flour underneath.

Open the oven door and slide the pizza onto the steel by holding the peel at a slight angle and sliding it out from under the pizza in one fluid motion. It can help to match the edge of the peel with the far edge of the steel. Avoid shuffling the peel under the pizza.

Close the oven door and bake the pizza for 5 to 6 minutes. Open the door and check on the pizza. Chances are it will need to be rotated. Spin it 180 degrees with a metal peel or use a pair of long metal tongs to adjust the direction. Close the door and bake for an additional 4 to 5 minutes. The pizza is done when the crust is a burnished red, golden in spots, and the bubbles are slightly charred. The cheese should be melted and browned.

Slide the metal peel under the pizza and transfer it to the wire rack. Grate the Parmesan on top. Dust with the salt and drizzle with the olive oil. Let cool for 5 to 6 minutes, then move the pizza to the cutting board and cut into eight wedges with the pizza wheel or rocker cutter. Serve immediately.

FOR STORAGE AND WARMING INFORMATION, SEE PAGE 238.

CLAM

MAKES ONE 12 IN [30.5 CM] PIZZA

Clam Topping

Weight	Volume	Ingredient
910 G	2 LB	CLAMS, LITTLENECK

Assembly

Weight	Volume	Ingredient
	1	DOUGH ROUND **(any of the doughs in Chapter 2)**
28 G	2 TBSP	HERBY OLIVE OIL DRIZZLE **(page 182)**
55 G	2 OZ	MOZZARELLA, FRESH, TORN INTO ½ IN [12 MM] PIECES
7 G	1	GARLIC CLOVE, MINCED
5 G	2 TBSP	PARMESAN
2 G	2 TSP	OREGANO, DRIED
2 G	¼ TSP	SALT
		WHITE RICE FLOUR FOR STRETCHING THE DOUGH AND DUSTING THE PEEL

I grew up in Maine, and seafood was a staple of my diet, particularly during my college years in Bar Harbor, a charming oceanfront town. There, clams, scallops, and lobster all made it onto pizzas, the briny, fishy flavors matched with garlic, herbs, and a squeeze of fresh lemon. This recipe calls for fresh clams, but tinned ones can be used in a pinch. I've never had the patience for shucking and instead prefer to open clams by briefly heating them in the oven.

TO PREPARE THE CLAM TOPPING: Preheat the oven to 350°F [180°C]. Line a large sheet pan with parchment paper. Rinse the clams well under cold running water, scrubbing them with a brush. Discard any that fail to close to the touch.

Arrange the clams in a single layer on the parchment-lined pan. Bake the clams just until they open, 5 to 6 minutes. Don't leave them in the oven too long, as you only want to open them, not cook them. Remove from the oven and let cool to the touch. Toss out any clams that didn't open. Using a butter knife, pry each clam fully open and dislodge the meat from the shell, dropping the meat into a medium bowl. Cover the bowl and set it aside until the clams are cool. Transfer the cooled clams to an airtight container and refrigerate. They will keep for up to 24 hours. Bring to room temperature before adding to the pizza. CONT'D

TO ASSEMBLE THE PIZZA: If the pizza dough is refrigerated, remove it from the fridge 2 to 3 hours before you plan to bake. Proof the dough on the counter until it's slightly puffy and room temperature. By the end of proofing, it should feel soft and full of gas. While you wait, set up where you'll be stretching and building the pizza **(see Designing Workflow, page 101)** and position a cooling rack, cutting board, and pizza wheel or rocker cutter near the oven. Ready a 9 or 10 in [23 or 25 cm] cake pan half full of white rice flour and set it aside.

An hour before baking, position an oven rack 6 to 8 in [15 to 20 cm] from the top of the oven and set a baking steel or stone on it. Preheat the oven to 550°F [290°C] or as hot as the oven will allow.

Sprinkle a wooden peel with a little white rice flour and set it aside. Slide a dough scraper under the dough round and flip it over into the cake pan of white rice flour. Turn it over two or three times, then transfer it to the peel, handling it gently.

Use your fingertips to indent a ring ¼ in [6 mm] deep all the way around the rim of the dough. Flip the dough over and repeat, pressing an indent around the outer edge. Next, use the pads of your fingers to lightly press down on the inner circle of the dough, going from 12 o'clock at the top to 6 o'clock at the bottom. Flip the dough over and repeat. Return the dough to the original side up. You'll now use gravity to stretch it into its final shape.

Slide clean, dry hands under the dough and make two fists in the center. Lift your hands and the pizza into the air parallel to your chin. Slowly move your fists in opposite directions to stretch the center of the pizza. Rotate the dough 90 degrees and carefully pull it in opposite directions again. Now arc your hands and let the dough slide down and hang off the back of your knuckles. Guide the dough in a circular motion, keeping it moving over the back of your hands and letting gravity do the final pulling. If the dough is resisting, give it a short rest on the peel and try again.

Lay the dough back on the peel and drizzle the herby olive oil evenly over it, working from the middle to the edge and stopping at the indented rim. Scatter the mozzarella, clams, and garlic evenly over the dough. Shimmy the peel a few times to make sure the pizza moves freely and can easily slide off the peel. If the dough is stuck, quickly lift it with the dough scraper and toss a little white rice flour underneath.

Open the oven door and slide the pizza onto the steel by holding the peel at a slight angle and sliding it out from under the pizza in one fluid motion. It can help to match the edge of the peel with the far edge of the steel. Avoid shuffling the peel under the pizza.

Close the oven door and bake the pizza for 5 to 6 minutes. Open the door and check on the pizza. Chances are it will need to be rotated. Spin it 180 degrees with a metal peel or use a pair of long metal tongs to adjust the direction. Close the door and bake for an additional 4 to 5 minutes. The pizza is done when the crust is a burnished red, golden in spots, and the bubbles are slightly charred. The cheese should be melted and the clams should be browned and crispy on the edges.

Slide the metal peel under the pizza and transfer it to the wire rack. Grate the Parmesan on top. Dust with the oregano and salt. Let cool for 5 to 6 minutes, then move the pizza to the cutting board and cut into eight wedges with the pizza wheel or rocker cutter. Serve immediately.

FOR STORAGE AND WARMING INFORMATION, SEE PAGE 238.

CAESAR SALAD

Weight	Volume	Ingredient
	1	DOUGH ROUND **(any of the doughs in Chapter 2)**
110 TO 165 G	2 TO 3 CUPS	ROMAINE LETTUCE, ROUGHLY CHOPPED
30 G	2 TBSP	CAESAR DRESSING **(page 190)**
5 G	2 TBSP	PARMESAN
20 G	¼ CUP	ASIAGO
55 G	2 OZ	MOZZARELLA, FRESH, TORN INTO ½ IN [12 MM] PIECES
40 G	1 CUP	CROUTONS
2 G	¼ TSP	SALT
0.5 G	¼ TSP	BLACK PEPPER
14 G	1 TBSP	OLIVE OIL (EVOO)
	1	LEMON WEDGE
		WHITE RICE FLOUR FOR STRETCHING THE DOUGH AND DUSTING THE PEEL

Crunchy, creamy, and cheesy—Caesar salad is good not only as a pizza side but also as a topping. In fact, any salad can become a pizza topping, mounded on by the handful after the crust is baked. This recipe calls for romaine, the classic Caesar lettuce, but mix up the greens to your liking, such as blending sweet, bitter, and spicy for a bold twist.

If the pizza dough is refrigerated, remove it from the fridge 2 to 3 hours before you plan to bake. Proof the dough on the counter until it's slightly puffy and room temperature. By the end of proofing, it should feel soft and full of gas. While you wait, set up where you'll be stretching and building the pizza **(see Designing Workflow, page 101)** and position a cooling rack, cutting board, and pizza wheel or rocker cutter near the oven. Ready a 9 or 10 in [23 or 25 cm] cake pan half full of white rice flour and set it aside.

An hour before baking, position an oven rack 6 to 8 in [15 to 20 cm] from the top of the oven and set a baking steel or stone on it. Preheat the oven to 550°F [290°C] or as hot as the oven will allow.

In a medium mixing bowl, toss together the romaine and half of the Caesar dressing. Grate the Parmesan and Asiago on top and gently toss again. Set the salad aside.

Sprinkle a wooden peel with a little white rice flour and set it aside. Slide a dough scraper under the dough round and flip it over into the cake pan of white rice flour. Turn it over two or three times, then transfer it to the peel, handling it gently.

Use your fingertips to indent a ring ¼ in [6 mm] deep all the way around the rim of the dough. Flip the dough over and repeat, pressing an indent around the outer edge. Next, use the pads of your fingers to lightly press down on the inner circle of the dough, going from 12 o'clock at the top to 6 o'clock at the bottom. Flip the dough over and repeat. Return the dough to the original side up. You'll now use gravity to stretch it into its final shape.

Slide clean, dry hands under the dough and make two fists in the center. Lift your hands and the pizza into the air parallel to your chin. Slowly move your fists in opposite directions to stretch the center of the pizza. Rotate the dough 90 degrees and carefully pull it in opposite directions again. Now arc your hands and let the dough slide down and hang off the back of your knuckles. Guide the dough in a circular motion, keeping it moving over the back of your hands and letting gravity do the final pulling. If the dough is resisting, give it a short rest on the peel and try again.

Lay the dough back on the peel and scatter the mozzarella evenly over the pizza. Shimmy the peel a few times to make sure the pizza moves freely and can easily slide off the peel. If the dough is stuck, quickly lift it with the dough scraper and toss a little white rice flour underneath.

Open the oven door and slide the pizza onto the steel by holding the peel at a slight angle and sliding it out from under the pizza in one fluid motion. It can help to match the edge of the peel with the far edge of the steel. Avoid shuffling the peel under the pizza.

Close the oven door and bake the pizza for 5 to 6 minutes. Open the door and check on the pizza. Chances are it will need to be rotated. Spin it 180 degrees with a metal peel or use a pair of long metal tongs to adjust the direction. Close the door and bake for an additional 4 to 5 minutes. The pizza is done when the crust is a burnished red, golden in spots, and the bubbles are slightly charred. The cheese should be melted and browned.

Slide the metal peel under the pizza and transfer it to the wire rack. Top with a handful of the dressed salad, saving any extra on a separate plate to enjoy on its own, add the croutons, then dust with the salt and pepper and drizzle with the olive oil. Let cool for 5 to 6 minutes, then move to the cutting board and cut into eight wedges with the pizza wheel or rocker cutter. Set the lemon wedge in the middle, for squeezing over the entire pizza, and serve immediately. This pizza doesn't hold up well in the refrigerator or reheat well, so be sure to enjoy it all in one sitting!

EGGPLANT

Eggplant Topping

Weight	Volume	Ingredient
35 G	¼ CUP	ALL-PURPOSE FLOUR
50 G	1	LARGE EGG
60 G	1 CUP	PANKO (BREAD CRUMBS)
230 G	8 OZ	EGGPLANT, CUT CROSSWISE INTO ¼ IN [6 MM] COINS
42 TO 56 G	3 TO 4 TBSP	OLIVE OIL (EVOO)
2 G	¼ TSP	SALT

Assembly

Weight	Volume	Ingredient
	1	DOUGH ROUND **(any of the doughs in Chapter 2)**
60 G	¼ CUP	CRÈME FRAÎCHE **(page 188)**
55 G	2 OZ	MOZZARELLA, FRESH, TORN INTO ½ IN [12 MM] PIECES
5 G	2 TBSP	PARMESAN
2 G	¼ TSP	SALT
	5	BASIL LEAVES, FRESH, TORN
		SPICY MAYO DRIZZLE **(page 187)** FOR FINISHING (OPTIONAL)
		WHITE RICE FLOUR FOR STRETCHING THE DOUGH AND DUSTING THE PEEL

MAKES ONE 12 IN [30.5 CM] PIZZA

Imagine crispy fried eggplant in a sea of bubbling mozzarella. Hungry yet? You'll want to choose an eggplant that is long and thin for this pizza topping, not squat and bulbous. I prefer slim, petite Fairy Tale eggplants or long, slender Japanese varieties. Their shapes make them both perfect candidates for frying. Finishing the pie with **Spicy Mayo Drizzle (page 187)** is optional but recommended. For a special treat, include the mayo at the table, too, for dipping the crust.

TO MAKE THE EGGPLANT TOPPING: Line up three medium shallow bowls for dredging the eggplant. Add the flour to the bowl on the far right, crack the egg into the middle bowl, and put the panko in the third bowl, on the far left. Whisk the egg with a fork. Place a medium plate near the bowls. Dredge an eggplant round in the flour, coating both sides and tapping off the excess; dip it in the egg, letting any extra egg run off; and then coat evenly with the panko. Transfer the breaded eggplant to the plate and repeat with the remaining rounds. The breaded rounds will keep in an airtight container in the fridge for up to 48 hours. Bring to room temperature before frying and adding to the pizza.

Set a medium plate near the stove. In a large skillet, warm 42 g [3 Tbsp] of the olive oil over medium heat until it glistens. Working in batches to avoid crowding, add the eggplant slices in a single layer and sprinkle with some of the salt. Cook until deeply golden on the bottom, 2 to 3 minutes. Flip and fry until golden on the second side, 2 to 3 minutes more. Transfer to the plate and repeat with the remaining eggplant rounds until all the rounds are fried, adding more olive oil to the pan if needed. Let cool, cover, and set aside until you're ready to top the pizza.

TO ASSEMBLE THE PIZZA: If the pizza dough is refrigerated, remove it from the fridge 2 to 3 hours before you plan to bake. Proof the dough on the counter until it's slightly puffy and room temperature. By the end of proofing, it should feel soft and full of gas. While you wait, set up where you'll be stretching and building the pizza **(see Designing Workflow, page 101)** and position a cooling rack, cutting board, and pizza wheel or rocker cutter near the oven. Ready a 9 or 10 in [23 or 25 cm] cake pan half full of white rice flour and set it aside.

An hour before baking, position an oven rack 6 to 8 in [15 to 20 cm] from the top of the oven and set a baking steel or stone on it. Preheat the oven to 550°F [290°C] or as hot as the oven will allow.

Sprinkle a wooden peel with a little white rice flour and set it aside. Slide a dough scraper under the dough round and flip it over into the cake pan of white rice flour. Turn it over two or three times, then transfer it to the peel, handling it gently.

Use your fingertips to indent a ring ¼ in [6 mm] deep all the way around the rim of the dough. Flip the dough over and repeat, pressing an indent around the outer edge. Next, use the pads of your fingers to lightly press down on the inner circle of the dough, going from 12 o'clock at the top to 6 o'clock at the bottom. Flip the dough over and repeat. Return the dough to the original side up. You'll now use gravity to stretch it into its final shape.

Slide clean, dry hands under the dough and make two fists in the center. Lift your hands and the pizza into the air parallel to your chin. Slowly move your fists in opposite directions to stretch the center of the pizza. Rotate the dough 90 degrees and carefully pull it in opposite directions again. Now arc your hands and let the dough slide down and hang off the back of your knuckles. Guide the dough in a circular motion, keeping it moving over the back of your hands and letting gravity do the final pulling. If the dough is resisting, give it a short rest on the peel and try again. **CONT'D**

Lay the dough back on the peel and spoon the crème fraîche onto the middle. Use the back of the spoon to spread it evenly over the dough, stopping at the indented rim. Top with the mozzarella, then scatter the fried eggplant evenly over the top. Shimmy the peel a few times to make sure the pizza moves freely and can easily slide off the peel. If the dough is stuck, quickly lift it with the dough scraper and toss a little white rice flour underneath.

Open the oven door and slide the pizza onto the steel by holding the peel at a slight angle and sliding it out from under the pizza in one fluid motion. It can help to match the edge of the peel with the far edge of the steel. Avoid shuffling the peel under the pizza.

Close the oven door and bake the pizza for 5 to 6 minutes. Open the door and check on the pizza. Chances are it will need to be rotated. Spin it 180 degrees with a metal peel or use a pair of long metal tongs to adjust the direction. Close the door and bake for an additional 4 to 5 minutes. The pizza is done when the crust is a burnished red, golden in spots, and the bubbles are slightly charred. The cheese should be melted and browned and the eggplant crispy.

Slide the metal peel under the pizza and transfer it to the wire rack. Grate the Parmesan on top. Dust with the salt, top with the basil, and finish with a drizzle of the mayo (if using). Let cool for 5 to 6 minutes, then move the pizza to the cutting board and cut into eight wedges with the pizza wheel or rocker cutter. Serve immediately.

FOR STORAGE AND WARMING INFORMATION, SEE PAGE 238.

FIG, DATE, AND MASCARPONE

Weight	Volume	Ingredient
	1	DOUGH ROUND **(any of the doughs in Chapter 2)**
55 G	2 OZ	MOZZARELLA, FRESH, TORN INTO ½ IN [12 MM] CHUNKS
57 G	¼ CUP	MASCARPONE
60 G	3 TBSP	FIG JAM
38 G	¼ CUP	DATES, PITTED AND CHOPPED
5 G	2 TBSP	PARMESAN
2 G	¼ TSP	SALT
14 G	1 TBSP	OLIVE OIL (EVOO)
		WHITE RICE FLOUR FOR STRETCHING THE DOUGH AND DUSTING THE PEEL

MAKES ONE 12 IN [30.5 CM] PIZZA

I'm decidedly *not* a dessert pizza person. This pie is as close as I will comfortably go to the edge, and with good reason: It's delicious and moody and deep. At our house, we call it the Meredith, named for my friend and business partner who brought this trinity of toppings during one of our *many* meetings before Dough Baby, our pizza shop, opened. The fig jam and mascarpone are dolloped on at whim, and the dates sit on top, melting into a fruit candy in the oven.

If the pizza dough is refrigerated, remove it from the fridge 2 to 3 hours before you plan to bake. Proof the dough on the counter until it's slightly puffy and room temperature. By the end of proofing, it should feel soft and full of gas. While you wait, set up where you'll be stretching and building the pizza **(see Designing Workflow, page 101)** and position a cooling rack, cutting board, and pizza wheel or rocker cutter near the oven. Ready a 9 or 10 in [23 or 25 cm] cake pan half full of white rice flour and set it aside.

An hour before baking, position an oven rack 6 to 8 in [15 to 20 cm] from the top of the oven and set a baking steel or stone on it. Preheat the oven to 550°F [290°C] or as hot as the oven will allow.

Sprinkle a wooden peel with a little white rice flour and set it aside. Slide a dough scraper under the dough round and flip it over into the cake pan of white rice flour. Turn it over two or three times, then transfer it to the peel, handling it gently. **CONT'D**

Use your fingertips to indent a ring ¼ in [6 mm] deep all the way around the rim of the dough. Flip the dough over and repeat, pressing an indent around the outer edge. Next, use the pads of your fingers to lightly press down on the inner circle of the dough, going from 12 o'clock at the top to 6 o'clock at the bottom. Flip the dough over and repeat. Return the dough to the original side up. You'll now use gravity to stretch it into its final shape.

Slide clean, dry hands under the dough and make two fists in the center. Lift your hands and the pizza into the air parallel to your chin. Slowly move your fists in opposite directions to stretch the center of the pizza. Rotate the dough 90 degrees and carefully pull it in opposite directions again. Now arc your hands and let the dough slide down and hang off the back of your knuckles. Guide the dough in a circular motion, keeping it moving over the back of your hands and letting gravity do the final pulling. If the dough is resisting, give it a short rest on the peel and try again.

Lay the dough back on the peel and scatter the mozzarella over the top. Dollop on the mascarpone and fig jam and then sprinkle on the dates. Shimmy the peel a few times to make sure the pizza moves freely and can easily slide off the peel. If the dough is stuck, quickly lift it with the dough scraper and toss a little white rice flour underneath.

Open the oven door and slide the pizza onto the steel by holding the peel at a slight angle and sliding it out from under the pizza in one fluid motion. It can help to match the edge of the peel with the far edge of the steel. Avoid shuffling the peel under the pizza.

Close the oven door and bake the pizza for 5 to 6 minutes. Open the door and check on the pizza. Chances are it will need to be rotated. Spin it 180 degrees with a metal peel or use a pair of long metal tongs to adjust the direction. Close the door and bake for an additional 4 to 5 minutes. The pizza is done when the crust is a burnished red, golden in spots, and the bubbles are slightly charred. The cheese should be melted and browned and the jam bubbling.

FOR STORAGE AND WARMING INFORMATION, SEE PAGE 238.

Slide the metal peel under the pizza and transfer it to the wire rack. Grate the Parmesan on top. Dust with the salt and drizzle with the olive oil. Let cool for 5 to 6 minutes, then move the pizza to the cutting board and cut into eight wedges with the pizza wheel or rocker cutter. Serve immediately.

BRUSSELS SPROUT AND WALNUT

MAKES ONE 12 IN [30.5 CM] PIZZA

Brussels Sprout Topping

Weight	Volume	Ingredient
90 G	3¼ OZ	BRUSSELS SPROUTS
42 TO 56 G	3 TO 4 TBSP	OLIVE OIL (EVOO)
2 G	¼ TSP	SALT

Assembly

Weight	Volume	Ingredient
	1	DOUGH ROUND **(any of the doughs in Chapter 2)**
14 G	1 TBSP	OLIVE OIL (EVOO)
60 G	¼ CUP	RICOTTA, WHOLE-MILK
28 G	¼ CUP	WALNUTS, CHOPPED AND TOASTED
2 G	¼ TSP	SALT
		WHITE RICE FLOUR FOR STRETCHING THE DOUGH AND DUSTING THE PEEL

Brussels sprouts are fibrous and bitter when raw but tender and sweet when roasted or sautéed. In this recipe, a mix of whole and shredded Brussels sprout leaves cook along with the pizza, roasting deliciously in the high oven heat. Gently toast the walnuts on a parchment-lined sheet pan or in a skillet over low heat to release the oils. A thin stream of **Herby Olive Oil Drizzle (page 182)** makes a great finishing touch.

TO MAKE THE BRUSSELS SPROUT TOPPING: Chop off the stem end of each sprout and discard the first layer of leaves. Peel off the next two layers of leaves and set aside whole. Using the large holes on a box grater, shred the remainder of each sprout. Transfer the sprouts—whole and shredded leaves—to a large mixing bowl, add 42 g [3 Tbsp] of the olive oil and the salt, and toss to mix well, adding the remaining olive oil if needed to coat evenly. Let sit for 10 minutes, then drain the sprouts and transfer to an airtight container. Store in the refrigerator for up to 48 hours. Bring to room temperature before adding to the pizza. **CONT'D**

TO ASSEMBLE THE PIZZA: If the pizza dough is refrigerated, remove it from the fridge 2 to 3 hours before you plan to bake. Proof the dough on the counter until it's slightly puffy and room temperature. By the end of proofing, it should feel soft and full of gas. While you wait, set up where you'll be stretching and building the pizza **(see Designing Workflow, page 101)** and position a cooling rack, cutting board, and pizza wheel or rocker cutter near the oven. Ready a 9 or 10 in [23 or 25 cm] cake pan half full of white rice flour and set it aside.

An hour before baking, position an oven rack 6 to 8 in [15 to 20 cm] from the top of the oven and set a baking steel or stone on it. Preheat the oven to 550°F [290°C] or as hot as the oven will allow.

Sprinkle a wooden peel with a little white rice flour and set it aside. Slide a dough scraper under the dough round and flip it over into the cake pan of white rice flour. Turn it over two or three times, then transfer it to the peel, handling it gently.

Use your fingertips to indent a ring ¼ in [6 mm] deep all the way around the rim of the dough. Flip the dough over and repeat, pressing an indent around the outer edge. Next, use the pads of your fingers to lightly press down on the inner circle of the dough, going from 12 o'clock at the top to 6 o'clock at the bottom. Flip the dough over and repeat. Return the dough to the original side up. You'll now use gravity to stretch it into its final shape.

Slide clean, dry hands under the dough and make two fists in the center. Lift your hands and the pizza into the air parallel to your chin. Slowly move your fists in opposite directions to stretch the center of the pizza. Rotate the dough 90 degrees and carefully pull it in opposite directions again. Now arc your hands and let the dough slide down and hang off the back of your knuckles. Guide the dough in a circular motion, keeping it moving over the back of your hands and letting gravity do the final pulling. If the dough is resisting, give it a short rest on the peel and try again.

Lay the dough back on the peel and drizzle the olive oil evenly over it, working from the middle to the edge and stopping at the indented rim. Dollop with the ricotta, then scatter the Brussels sprouts evenly over the pizza. Shimmy the peel a few times to make sure the pizza moves freely and can easily slide off the peel. If the dough is stuck, quickly lift it with the dough scraper and toss a little white rice flour underneath.

Open the oven door and slide the pizza onto the steel by holding the peel at a slight angle and sliding it out from under the pizza in one fluid motion. It can help to match the edge of the peel with the far edge of the steel. Avoid shuffling the peel under the pizza.

Close the oven door and bake the pizza for 5 to 6 minutes. Open the door and check on the pizza. Chances are it will need to be rotated. Spin it 180 degrees with a metal peel or use a pair of long metal tongs to adjust the direction. Close the door and bake for an additional 4 to 5 minutes. The pizza is done when the crust is a burnished red, golden in spots, and the bubbles are slightly charred. The Brussels sprouts should be slightly charred and crispy.

Slide the metal peel under the pizza and transfer it to the wire rack. Sprinkle the walnuts on top and dust with the salt. Let cool for 5 to 6 minutes, then move the pizza to the cutting board and cut into eight wedges with the pizza wheel or rocker cutter. Serve immediately.

FOR STORAGE AND WARMING INFORMATION, SEE PAGE 238.

CONFIT POTATOES AND ROSEMARY

Confit Potato Topping

Weight	Volume	Ingredient
570 G	4	YUKON GOLD POTATOES, SKIN ON
56 G	¼ CUP	OLIVE OIL (EVOO)
2 G	¼ TSP	SALT

MAKES ONE 12 IN [30.5 CM] PIZZA

Assembly

Weight	Volume	Ingredient
	1	DOUGH ROUND **(any of the doughs in Chapter 2)**
28 G	2 TBSP	OIL, RESERVED FROM COOKING THE POTATOES
55 G	2 OZ	MOZZARELLA, FRESH, TORN INTO ½ IN [12 MM] PIECES
55 G	2 OZ	CHEDDAR, SHARP, CUBED
2 G	1 TSP	ROSEMARY, FRESH, CHOPPED
5 G	2 TBSP	PARMESAN
2 G	¼ TSP	SALT
		WHITE RICE FLOUR FOR STRETCHING THE DOUGH AND DUSTING THE PEEL

Confit potatoes (potatoes gently cooked in olive oil) on pizza were one of my favorite toppings at the monthly pizza night at my old bakery. That's because they taste like candy, they are not too labor-intensive, and they can be made a couple of days in advance of using. I recommend Yukon gold potatoes, famous for their buttery richness, firm texture, and, of course, golden glow. Save the oil and use it, cooled to room temperature, for dressing the pizza. You will have more slices of potato than needed for pizza, but they are also great for breakfast, in a salad, or as a midnight snack.

TO MAKE THE CONFIT POTATO TOPPING: Using a mandoline or chef's knife, slice the potatoes crosswise into slices ¼ in [6 mm] thick. In a large nonstick skillet, combine the potatoes and olive oil and sprinkle with the salt. Place over medium heat, cover, and cook gently until the potato slices begin to sizzle and brown on the bottom, about 10 minutes. Uncover, flip the potato slices with a pair of tongs, re-cover, and cook gently for 10 minutes more. Uncover and test the potatoes. They should be firm but yield to the tines of a fork. Using a slotted utensil, transfer the cooked potatoes to a plate to cool. Let the oil cool, then strain through a fine-mesh sieve into a container, cover, and keep at room temperature until needed. When the potatoes are cool, store in an airtight container in the fridge for up to 48 hours. Bring to room temperature before adding to the pizza. **CONT'D**

TO ASSEMBLE THE PIZZA: If the pizza dough is refrigerated, remove it from the fridge 2 to 3 hours before you plan to bake. Proof the dough on the counter until it's slightly puffy and room temperature. By the end of proofing, it should feel soft and full of gas. While you wait, set up where you'll be stretching and building the pizza **(see Designing Workflow, page 101)** and position a cooling rack, cutting board, and pizza wheel or rocker cutter near the oven. Ready a 9 or 10 in [23 or 25 cm] cake pan half full of white rice flour and set it aside.

An hour before baking, position an oven rack 6 to 8 in [15 to 20 cm] from the top of the oven and set a baking steel or stone on it. Preheat the oven to 550°F [290°C] or as hot as the oven will allow.

Sprinkle a wooden peel with a little white rice flour and set it aside. Slide a dough scraper under the dough round and flip it over into the cake pan of white rice flour. Turn it over two or three times, then transfer it to the peel, handling it gently.

Use your fingertips to indent a ring ¼ in [6 mm] deep all the way around the rim of the dough. Flip the dough over and repeat, pressing an indent around the outer edge. Next, use the pads of your fingers to lightly press down on the inner circle of the dough, going from 12 o'clock at the top to 6 o'clock at the bottom. Flip the dough over and repeat. Return the dough to the original side up. You'll now use gravity to stretch it into its final shape.

Slide clean, dry hands under the dough and make two fists in the center. Lift your hands and the pizza into the air parallel to your chin. Slowly move your fists in opposite directions to stretch the center of the pizza. Rotate the dough 90 degrees and carefully pull it in opposite directions again. Now arc your hands and let the dough slide down and hang off the back of your knuckles. Guide the dough in a circular motion, keeping it moving over the back of your hands and letting gravity do the final pulling. If the dough is resisting, give it a short rest on the peel and try again.

Lay the dough back on the peel and drizzle the reserved oil evenly over it, working from the middle to the edge and stopping at the indented rim. Scatter the mozzarella and Cheddar over the pizza, dust with the rosemary, and finish with a single layer of potatoes. Shimmy the peel a few times to make sure the pizza moves freely and can easily slide off the peel. If the dough is stuck, quickly lift it with the dough scraper and toss a little white rice flour underneath.

Open the oven door and slide the pizza onto the steel by holding the peel at a slight angle and sliding it out from under the pizza in one fluid motion. It can help to match the edge of the peel with the far edge of the steel. Avoid shuffling the peel under the pizza.

Close the oven door and bake the pizza for 5 to 6 minutes. Open the door and check on the pizza. Chances are it will need to be rotated. Spin it 180 degrees with a metal peel or use a pair of long metal tongs to adjust the direction. Close the door and bake for an additional 4 to 5 minutes. The pizza is done when the crust is a burnished red, golden in spots, and the bubbles are slightly charred. The cheese should be melted and browned and the potatoes crispy on the edges and tender in the center.

Slide the metal peel under the pizza and transfer it to the wire rack. Grate the Parmesan on top and dust with the salt. Let cool for 5 to 6 minutes, then move the pizza to the cutting board and cut into eight wedges with the pizza wheel or rocker cutter. Serve immediately.

FOR STORAGE AND
WARMING INFORMATION,
SEE PAGE 238.

BANANA PEPPER, ARTICHOKE, AND FETA

Weight	Volume	Ingredient
	1	DOUGH ROUND **(any of the doughs in Chapter 2)**
56 G	¼ CUP	LEMONY ROASTED-GARLIC CREAM **(page 186)**
55 G	2 OZ	MOZZARELLA, FRESH, TORN INTO ½ IN [12 MM] PIECES
55 G	2 OZ	FETA, CRUMBLED
84 G	½ CUP	ARTICHOKE HEARTS, MARINATED OR WATER PACKED, HALVED LENGTHWISE
60 G	½ CUP	BANANA PEPPERS, SLICED
5 G	2 TBSP	PARMESAN
0.5 G	¼ TSP	OREGANO, DRIED
2 G	¼ TSP	SALT
		WHITE RICE FLOUR FOR STRETCHING THE DOUGH AND DUSTING THE PEEL

MAKES ONE 12 IN [30.5 CM] PIZZA

I am a huge fan of crunchy, zippy banana peppers. Here, they are matched with the mellow flavor of artichoke, which has a clean, fresh taste that's a mix of asparagus, broccoli, and celery. The feta adds some saltiness. If you can find locally produced feta at a farmers' market, use it. Skip red sauce for this pizza and go for the **Lemony Roasted-Garlic Cream (page 186)**. Or you can even just use a light drizzle of olive oil for the "sauce."

If the pizza dough is refrigerated, remove it from the fridge 2 to 3 hours before you plan to bake. Proof the dough on the counter until it's slightly puffy and room temperature. By the end of proofing, it should feel soft and full of gas. While you wait, set up where you'll be stretching and building the pizza **(see Designing Workflow, page 101)** and position a cooling rack, cutting board, and pizza wheel or rocker cutter near the oven. Ready a 9 or 10 in [23 or 25 cm] cake pan half full of white rice flour and set it aside.

An hour before baking, position an oven rack 6 to 8 in [15 to 20 cm] from the top of the oven and set a baking steel or stone on it. Preheat the oven to 550°F [290°C] or as hot as the oven will allow.

Sprinkle a wooden peel with a little white rice flour and set it aside. Slide a dough scraper under the dough round and flip it over into the cake pan of white rice flour. Turn it over two or three times, then transfer it to the peel, handling it gently.

Use your fingertips to indent a ring ¼ in [6 mm] deep all the way around the rim of the dough. Flip the dough over and repeat, pressing an indent around the outer edge. Next, use the pads of your fingers to lightly press down on the inner circle of the dough, going from 12 o'clock at the top to 6 o'clock at the bottom. Flip the dough over and repeat. Return the dough to the original side up. You'll now use gravity to stretch it into its final shape.

Slide clean, dry hands under the dough and make two fists in the center. Lift your hands and the pizza into the air parallel to your chin. Slowly move your fists in opposite directions to stretch the center of the pizza. Rotate the dough 90 degrees and carefully pull it in opposite directions again. Now arc your hands and let the dough slide down and hang off the back of your knuckles. Guide the dough in a circular motion, keeping it moving over the back of your hands and letting gravity do the final pulling. If the dough is resisting, give it a short rest on the peel and try again.

Lay the dough back on the peel and spoon the garlic cream onto the middle. Use the back of the spoon to spread the sauce evenly over the dough, stopping at the indented rim. Top with the mozzarella and feta. Scatter the artichoke hearts and banana peppers evenly over the top. Shimmy the peel a few times to make sure the pizza moves freely and can easily slide off the peel. If the dough is stuck, quickly lift it with the dough scraper and toss a little white rice flour underneath.

Open the oven door and slide the pizza onto the steel by holding the peel at a slight angle and sliding it out from under the pizza in one fluid motion. It can help to match the edge of the peel with the far edge of the steel. Avoid shuffling the peel under the pizza.

Close the oven door and bake the pizza for 5 to 6 minutes. Open the door and check on the pizza. Chances are it will need to be rotated. Spin it 180 degrees with a metal peel or use a pair of long metal tongs to adjust the direction. Close the door and bake for an additional 4 to 5 minutes. The pizza is done when the crust is a burnished red, golden in spots, and the bubbles are slightly charred. The cheese should be melted and browned and the artichoke hearts and banana peppers cooked.

Slide the metal peel under the pizza and transfer it to the wire rack. Grate the Parmesan on top. Dust with the oregano and salt. Let cool for 5 to 6 minutes, then move the pizza to the cutting board and cut into eight wedges with the pizza wheel or rocker cutter. Serve immediately.

FOR STORAGE AND WARMING INFORMATION, SEE PAGE 238.

S
P

BREAKFAST

Egg and Bacon Toppings

Weight	Volume	Ingredient
60 G	2	EGG WHITES, LARGE
36 G	2	EGG YOLKS, LARGE
5 G	¾ TSP	SALT
113 G	4 OZ	BACON

MAKES ONE 12 IN [30.5 CM] PIZZA

Assembly

Weight	Volume	Ingredient
	1	DOUGH ROUND **(any of the doughs in Chapter 2)**
55 G	2 OZ	MOZZARELLA, LOW-MOISTURE, SHREDDED
55 G	2 OZ	CHEDDAR, SHREDDED
14 G	1 TBSP	MAPLE SYRUP
2 G	¼ TSP	THYME LEAVES, FRESH
		WHITE RICE FLOUR FOR STRETCHING THE DOUGH AND DUSTING THE PEEL

Eggs on a pizza can be tricky. I often see them cracked whole on a pizza, which is charming, but that can end in calamity when the egg flies off and hits the baking steel before the dough does. Plus, you don't get a bit of white and yolk in each bite with the whole-egg method. I've taken to separating the white from the yolk, dressing the naked pizza with the white and drizzling on the yolk as the pizza comes out of the oven. If you're worried about undercooked yolk, you could take the pizza out a few minutes shy of being done, douse it, and return it to the oven for the end of the bake.

TO MAKE THE EGG AND BACON TOPPINGS: Put the egg whites and the egg yolks in two different squeeze bottles. Add half of the salt to the whites and the remaining half to the yolks. Screw the lids on the bottles, shake well, and refrigerate. The egg whites and yolks can be prepared up to 24 hours in advance. Bring to room temperature before adding to the pizza.

One and a half hours before you want to bake your pizza, preheat the oven to 400°F [200°C], line a sheet pan with parchment paper, and top a plate with a paper towel. Arrange the bacon strips in a single layer on the sheet pan, making sure they don't overlap. Bake the bacon for 15 to 20 minutes, rotating the pan back to front halfway through baking for even cooking. Watch for the bacon to curl and turn crispy and remove it before it begins to burn. Thicker bacon strips will need the full time, while thinner strips may need less time. Use tongs to transfer the bacon to the towel-lined plate, then let cool. **CONT'D**

Position an oven rack 6 to 8 in [15 to 20 cm] from the top of the oven and set a baking steel or stone on it. Raise the oven temperature to 550°F [290°C] or as hot as the oven will allow.

Return to the bacon and use your hands to crumble it into pieces of various shapes and sizes, dropping them onto a clean plate or into a small bowl. Set aside until needed. The bacon can be cooked up to 2 days in advance and stored in an airtight container in the fridge. Bring to room temperature before adding to the pizza

TO ASSEMBLE THE PIZZA: If the pizza dough is refrigerated, remove it from the fridge 2 to 3 hours before you plan to bake. Proof the dough on the counter until it's slightly puffy and room temperature. By the end of proofing, it should feel soft and full of gas. While you wait, set up where you'll be stretching and building the pizza **(see Designing Workflow, page 101)** and position a cooling rack, cutting board, and pizza wheel or rocker cutter near the oven. Ready a 9 or 10 in [23 or 25 cm] cake pan half full of white rice flour and set it aside.

Sprinkle a wooden peel with a little white rice flour and set it aside. Slide a dough scraper under the dough round and flip it over into the cake pan of white rice flour. Turn it over two or three times, then transfer it to the peel, handling it gently.

Use your fingertips to indent a ring ¼ in [6 mm] deep all the way around the rim of the dough. Flip the dough over and repeat, pressing an indent around the outer edge. Next, use the pads of your fingers to lightly press down on the inner circle of the dough, going from 12 o'clock at the top to 6 o'clock at the bottom. Flip the dough over and repeat. Return the dough to the original side up. You'll now use gravity to stretch it into its final shape.

Slide clean, dry hands under the dough and make two fists in the center. Lift your hands and the pizza into the air parallel to your chin. Slowly move your fists in opposite directions to stretch the center of the pizza. Rotate the dough 90 degrees and carefully pull it in opposite directions again. Now arc your hands and let the dough slide down and hang off the back of your knuckles. Guide the dough in a circular motion, keeping it moving over the back of your hands and letting gravity do the final pulling. If the dough is resisting, give it a short rest on the peel and try again.

Lay the dough back on the peel and drizzle on the egg whites, working from the middle to the edge and stopping at the indented rim. Scatter the mozzarella and Cheddar over the dough, then evenly distribute the bacon over the top. Shimmy the peel a few times to make sure the pizza moves freely and can easily slide off the peel. If the dough is stuck, quickly lift it with the dough scraper and toss a little white rice flour underneath.

Open the oven door and slide the pizza onto the steel by holding the peel at a slight angle and sliding it out from under the pizza in one fluid motion. It can help to match the edge of the peel with the far edge of the steel. Avoid shuffling the peel under the pizza.

Close the oven door and bake the pizza for 5 to 6 minutes. Open the door and check on the pizza. Chances are it will need to be rotated. Spin it 180 degrees with a metal peel or use a pair of long metal tongs to adjust the direction. Close the door and bake for an additional 4 to 5 minutes. The pizza is done when the crust is a burnished red, golden in spots, and the bubbles are slightly charred. The cheese should be melted and browned.

Slide the metal peel under the pizza and transfer it to the wire rack. Drizzle with the egg yolk and maple syrup and dust with the thyme. Let cool for 5 to 6 minutes, then move the pizza to the cutting board and cut into eight wedges with the pizza wheel or rocker cutter. Serve immediately.

FOR STORAGE AND
WARMING INFORMATION,
SEE PAGE 238.

Eating seasonally has kept me grounded in my life. Like watching the sun rise and set, certain ingredients come and go throughout the year. ●

SEASONAL PIES

The arrival of the first bitter greens of spring is always exciting, and I rejoice when the strawberries ripen because it means my neighbor will soon be leaving me baskets of fresh eggs—a colorful array in pale blue, speckled brown, and seafoam green. In the sweaty summer, small mountains of peppers, tomatoes, and eggplants take over the clay bowls on my counter. In the cool-weather months, crops like broccoli and kale fill my canvas totes at the market, looking better than bridal bouquets.

Fresh produce grown in good soil by loving hands is what makes me feel wealthy. I encourage you to seek out these toppings at your local farmers' market not only because they will taste infinitely better than what you will find at the grocery store but also because supporting small-scale farms builds food security for us all.

HERBY ARUGULA WITH PISTACHIO

Arugula Topping

Weight	Volume	Ingredient
20 G	1 CUP	ARUGULA
4 G	2 TSP	SAGE, FRESH, CHOPPED
4 G	2 TSP	MINT, FRESH, CHOPPED
	5	BASIL LEAVES, FRESH, CHOPPED
4 G	2 TSP	CHIVES, FRESH, CHOPPED
4 G	2 TSP	DILL, FRESH, CHOPPED
5 G	1 TSP	LEMON JUICE
2 G	¼ TSP	SALT

MAKES ONE 12 IN [30.5 CM] PIZZA

Assembly

Weight	Volume	Ingredient
	1	DOUGH ROUND **(any of the doughs in Chapter 2)**
56 G	¼ CUP	ANYTHING GREEN GOES PESTO **(page 181)**
55 G	2 OZ	MOZZARELLA, FRESH, TORN IN ½ IN [12 MM] PIECES
2 G	¼ TSP	SALT
15 G	2 TBSP	PISTACHIOS, CHOPPED
15 G	2 TBSP	RED ONION, PICKLED **(see Refrigerator Pickles, page 195)**
		WHITE RICE FLOUR FOR STRETCHING THE DOUGH AND DUSTING THE PEEL

Peppery and spicy, arugula is a delicate salad green that is tender enough to eat raw scattered on top of a pizza. Here, it is tossed with fresh herbs, an accent I like to add to all my salads when possible. If you don't have fresh herbs, swap them out for dried, using them in slightly smaller amounts. Make the salad right before the pizza goes into the oven, and allow the pizza to cool a bit before adding the greens.

TO ASSEMBLE THE PIZZA: If the pizza dough is refrigerated, remove it from the fridge 2 to 3 hours before you plan to bake. Proof the dough on the counter until it's slightly puffy and room temperature. By the end of proofing, it should feel soft and full of gas. While you wait, set up where you'll be stretching and building the pizza **(see Designing Workflow, page 101)** and position a cooling rack, cutting board, and pizza wheel or rocker cutter near the oven. Ready a 9 or 10 in [23 or 25 cm] cake pan half full of white rice flour and set it aside.

CONT'D

An hour before baking, position an oven rack 6 to 8 in [15 to 20 cm] from the top of the oven and set a baking steel or stone on it. Preheat the oven to 550°F [290°C] or as hot as the oven will allow.

WHILE THE DOUGH PROOFS AND THE OVEN HEATS, MAKE THE ARUGULA TOPPING: In a medium mixing bowl, combine the arugula, sage, mint, basil, chives, and dill. Add the lemon juice and salt, toss well, and set aside until the pizza is done baking.

Sprinkle a wooden peel with a little white rice flour and set it aside. Slide a dough scraper under the dough round and flip it over into the cake pan of white rice flour. Turn it over two or three times, then transfer it to the peel, handling it gently.

Use your fingertips to indent a ring ¼ in [6 mm] deep all the way around the rim of the dough. Flip the dough over and repeat, pressing an indent around the outer edge. Next, use the pads of your fingers to lightly press down on the inner circle of the dough, going from 12 o'clock at the top to 6 o'clock at the bottom. Flip the dough over and repeat. Return the dough to the original side up. You'll now use gravity to stretch it into its final shape.

Slide clean, dry hands under the dough and make two fists in the center. Lift your hands and the pizza into the air parallel to your chin. Slowly move your fists in opposite directions to stretch the center of the pizza. Rotate the dough 90 degrees and carefully pull it in opposite directions again. Now arc your hands and let the dough slide down and hang off the back of your knuckles. Guide the dough in a circular motion, keeping it moving over the back of your hands and letting gravity do the final pulling. If the dough is resisting, give it a short rest on the peel and try again.

Lay the dough back on the peel and spoon the pesto onto the middle. Use the back of the spoon to spread the pesto, working from the middle to the edge and stopping at the indented rim. Scatter the mozzarella over the top. Shimmy the peel a few times to make sure the pizza moves freely and can easily slide off the peel. If the dough is stuck, quickly lift it with the dough scraper and toss a little white rice flour underneath.

Open the oven door and slide the pizza onto the steel by holding the peel at a slight angle and sliding it out from under the pizza in one fluid motion. It can help to match the edge of the peel with the far edge of the steel. Avoid shuffling the peel under the pizza.

Close the oven door and bake the pizza for 5 to 6 minutes. Open the door and check on the pizza. Chances are it will need to be rotated. Spin it 180 degrees with a metal peel or use a pair of long metal tongs to adjust the direction. Close the door and bake for an additional 4 to 5 minutes. The pizza is done when the crust is a burnished red, golden in spots, and the bubbles are slightly charred. The cheese should be melted and browned.

Slide the metal peel under the pizza and transfer it to the wire rack. Let cool for about 1 minute or so, then dust with the salt and top with the arugula salad, pistachios, and red onion. Let cool for 4 to 5 minutes longer, then move the pizza to the cutting board and cut into eight wedges with the pizza wheel or rocker cutter. Serve immediately.

FOR STORAGE AND WARMING: Any uneaten pizza can be stored in an airtight container in the fridge for up to 5 days. To serve, reheat directly on a preheated baking steel or stone (500°F [260°C]) until the cheese is bubbly, 2 to 5 minutes.

NETTLES AND CREAM

Weight	Volume	Ingredient
	1	DOUGH ROUND (any of the doughs in Chapter 2)
120 G	½ CUP	HEAVY CREAM
2 G	¼ TSP	SALT
	1	LEMON
55 G	2 OZ (2 LARGE HANDFULS)	NETTLE LEAVES, TRIMMED AND CLEANED (SEE HEADNOTE)
60 G	¼ CUP	CRÈME FRAÎCHE (page 188)
55 G	2 OZ	MOZZARELLA, FRESH, TORN IN ½ IN [12 MM] PIECES
2 G	¼ TSP	SALT
0.5 G	½ TSP	RED PEPPER FLAKES (OPTIONAL)
14 G	1 TBSP	OLIVE OIL (EVOO)
		WHITE RICE FLOUR FOR STRETCHING THE DOUGH AND DUSTING THE PEEL

MAKES ONE 12 IN [30.5 CM] PIZZA

Known for spiky hairs that can cause a sting, nettles also have a wonderfully nutty and sweet spinach-like flavor with a cool cucumber freshness. Don gloves, then, using scissors, snip the top leaves of the earliest spring nettles, dropping them directly into a bag. Next, still wearing gloves, gently rinse the greens with cool running water and allow them to air-dry. Transfer them to an airtight container and store them in the refrigerator until you are ready to make this pizza. They will keep for up to 48 hours. The stinging hairs are still active after the nettles are rinsed, so you'll need to wear gloves to dredge the nettles through the cream. But when it's time to eat, the "danger" will have passed. The spiky hairs lose their sting in the heat of the oven. Dust the pizza with red pepper flakes for a nice finish.

If the pizza dough is refrigerated, remove it from the fridge 2 to 3 hours before you plan to bake. Proof the dough on the counter until it's slightly puffy and room temperature. By the end of proofing, it should feel soft and full of gas. While you wait, set up where you'll be stretching and building the pizza (see Designing Workflow, page 101) and position a cooling rack, cutting board, and pizza wheel or rocker cutter near the oven. Ready a 9 or 10 in [23 or 25 cm] cake pan half full of white rice flour and set it aside.

An hour before baking, position an oven rack 6 to 8 in [15 to 20 cm] from the top of the oven and set a baking steel or stone on it. Preheat the oven to 550°F [290°C] or as hot as the oven will allow.

In a medium mixing bowl, combine the cream and salt. Grate the zest from the lemon directly into the bowl (reserve the lemon for another use). Whisk to combine. Wearing gloves, dredge the nettles through the cream, then allow them to soak while you stretch the dough.

Sprinkle a wooden peel with a little white rice flour and set it aside. Slide a dough scraper under the dough round and flip it over into the cake pan of white CONT'D

rice flour. Turn it over two or three times, then transfer it to the peel, handling it gently.

Use your fingertips to indent a ring ¼ in [6 mm] deep all the way around the rim of the dough. Flip the dough over and repeat, pressing an indent around the outer edge. Next, use the pads of your fingers to lightly press down on the inner circle of the dough, going from 12 o'clock at the top to 6 o'clock at the bottom. Flip the dough over and repeat. Return the dough to the original side up. You'll now use gravity to stretch it into its final shape.

Slide clean, dry hands under the dough and make two fists in the center. Lift your hands and the pizza into the air parallel to your chin. Slowly move your fists in opposite directions to stretch the center of the pizza. Rotate the dough 90 degrees and carefully pull it in opposite directions again. Now arc your hands and let the dough slide down and hang off the back of your knuckles. Guide the dough in a circular motion, keeping it moving over the back of your hands and letting gravity do the final pulling. If the dough is resisting, give it a short rest on the peel and try again.

Lay the dough back on the peel and spoon the crème fraîche onto the middle. Use the back of the spoon to spread the crème fraîche evenly over the dough, stopping at the indented rim. Scatter the mozzarella over the top. Don your gloves again, grab the nettles, tap them against the inside of the bowl to allow any excess cream to drip off, and distribute them evenly over the cheese. Slip off the gloves, then shimmy the peel a few times to make sure the pizza moves freely and can easily slide off the peel. If the dough is stuck, quickly lift it with the dough scraper and toss a little white rice flour underneath.

Open the oven door and slide the pizza onto the steel by holding the peel at a slight angle and sliding it out from under the pizza in one fluid motion. It can help to match the edge of the peel with the far edge of the steel. Avoid shuffling the peel under the pizza.

Close the oven door and bake the pizza for 5 to 6 minutes. Open the door and check on the pizza. Chances are it will need to be rotated. Spin it 180 degrees with a metal peel or use a pair of long metal tongs to adjust the direction. Close the door and bake for an additional 4 to 5 minutes. The pizza is done when the crust is a burnished red, golden in spots, and the bubbles are slightly charred. The mozzarella should be melted and browned and the nettles crispy on the edges.

FOR STORAGE AND WARMING INFORMATION, SEE PAGE 271.

Slide the metal peel under the pizza and transfer it to the wire rack. Dust with the salt and red pepper flakes (if using) and drizzle with the olive oil. Let cool for 5 to 6 minutes, then move the pizza to the cutting board and cut into eight wedges with the pizza wheel or rocker cutter. Serve immediately.

ROASTED FENNEL AND PEA

Fennel Topping

Weight	Volume	Ingredient
250 G	1	FENNEL BULB
14 G	1 TBSP	OLIVE OIL (EVOO)
2 G	¼ TSP	SALT

MAKES ONE 12 IN [30.5 CM] PIZZA

Assembly

Weight	Volume	Ingredient
	1	DOUGH ROUND **(any of the doughs in Chapter 2)**
28 G	2 TBSP	HERBY OLIVE OIL DRIZZLE **(page 182)**
55 G	2 OZ	MOZZARELLA, FRESH, TORN INTO ½ IN [12 MM] PIECES
80 G	½ CUP	SUGAR SNAP PEAS, SHELLED
60 G	¼ CUP	RICOTTA, WHOLE-MILK
5 G	2 TBSP	PARMESAN
2 G	¼ TSP	SALT
14 G	1 TBSP	OLIVE OIL (EVOO)
	1 OR 2	FENNEL FRONDS
		WHITE RICE FLOUR FOR STRETCHING THE DOUGH AND DUSTING THE PEEL

Fresh sugar snap peas, commonly eaten pod and all, are incredibly sweet on a pizza and well worth the effort it takes to remove the peas from their pods, which "snap" when broken in half. If you want to skip the task, you can use shelled English peas, but they won't be as sweet. Paired with thinly shaved fennel bulb and plucked fronds, this pizza shouts springtime. Source the peas and fennel from the farmers' market and spend time getting the peas out of their shells the day before you make the pizza. The crust is perfect dunked in **Ranch Dressing (page 189)**.

TO MAKE THE FENNEL TOPPING: Preheat the oven to 400°F [200°C]. Line a sheet pan with parchment paper.

To prep the fennel, using a chef's knife, cut crosswise at the top, cutting the tall stalks and fronds away from the bulb. Using the knife or a mandoline, shave the tender top of the bulb into pieces the thickness of two stacked quarters. Chop the remainder of the bulb into ¼ in [6 mm] pieces. Reserve a few feathery fronds for finishing the pizza, storing them in an airtight container in the refrigerator.

Transfer the chopped and shaved fennel to a medium mixing bowl, add the olive oil and salt, and toss to coat evenly. Transfer the fennel to the parchment-lined pan, spreading it in an even layer. Bake until tender when pierced with a fork and browned on the edges, 20 to 25 minutes. Let cool completely, then transfer to an airtight container and store in the fridge for up to 24 hours. **CONT'D**

Bring the roasted fennel and the fronds to room temperature before adding to the pizza.

TO ASSEMBLE THE PIZZA: If the pizza dough is refrigerated, remove it from the fridge 2 to 3 hours before you plan to bake. Proof the dough on the counter until it's slightly puffy and room temperature. By the end of proofing, it should feel soft and full of gas. While you wait, set up where you'll be stretching and building the pizza **(see Designing Workflow, page 101)** and position a cooling rack, cutting board, and pizza wheel or rocker cutter near the oven. Ready a 9 or 10 in [23 or 25 cm] cake pan half full of white rice flour and set it aside.

An hour before baking, position an oven rack 6 to 8 in [15 to 20 cm] from the top of the oven and set a baking steel or stone on it. Preheat the oven to 550°F [290°C] or as hot as the oven will allow.

Sprinkle a wooden peel with a little white rice flour and set it aside. Slide a dough scraper under the dough round and flip it over into the cake pan of white rice flour. Turn it over two or three times, then transfer it to the peel, handling it gently.

Use your fingertips to indent a ring ¼ in [6 mm] deep all the way around the rim of the dough. Flip the dough over and repeat, pressing an indent around the outer edge. Next, use the pads of your fingers to lightly press down on the inner circle of the dough, going from 12 o'clock at the top to 6 o'clock at the bottom. Flip the dough over and repeat. Return the dough to the original side up. You'll now use gravity to stretch it into its final shape.

Slide clean, dry hands under the dough and make two fists in the center. Lift your hands and the pizza into the air parallel to your chin. Slowly move your fists in opposite directions to stretch the center of the pizza. Rotate the dough 90 degrees and carefully pull it in opposite directions again. Now arc your hands and let the dough slide down and hang off the back of your knuckles. Guide the dough in a circular motion, keeping it moving over the back of your hands and letting gravity do the final pulling. If the dough is resisting, give it a short rest on the peel and try again. **CONT'D**

Lay the dough back on the peel and drizzle the herby olive oil evenly over the dough, working from the middle to the edge and stopping at the indented rim. Scatter the mozzarella over the top. Distribute the roasted fennel and the peas evenly over the pizza and dollop the ricotta on top. Shimmy the peel a few times to make sure the pizza moves freely and can easily slide off the peel. If the dough is stuck, quickly lift it with the dough scraper and toss a little white rice flour underneath.

Open the oven door and slide the pizza onto the steel by holding the peel at a slight angle and sliding it out from under the pizza in one fluid motion. It can help to match the edge of the peel with the far edge of the steel. Avoid shuffling the peel under the pizza.

Close the oven door and bake the pizza for 5 to 6 minutes. Open the door and check on the pizza. Chances are it will need to be rotated. Spin it 180 degrees with a metal peel or use a pair of long metal tongs to adjust the direction. Close the door and bake for an additional 4 to 5 minutes. The pizza is done when the crust is a burnished red, golden in spots, and the bubbles are slightly charred. The cheese should be melted and browned and the fennel and peas cooked.

Slide the metal peel under the pizza and transfer it to the wire rack. Dust with the Parmesan and salt, drizzle with the olive oil, and scatter the fennel fronds over the top. Let cool for 5 to 6 minutes, then move the pizza to the cutting board and cut into eight wedges with the pizza wheel or rocker cutter. Serve immediately.

FOR STORAGE AND WARMING INFORMATION, SEE PAGE 271.

BLISTERED PEPPERS

Pepper Topping

Weight	Volume	Ingredient
115 G	4 OZ	JIMMY NARDELLO PEPPERS
115 G	4 OZ	SHISHITO PEPPERS
28 G	2 TBSP	OLIVE OIL (EVOO)
2 G	¼ TSP	SALT

Assembly

Weight	Volume	Ingredient
	1	DOUGH ROUND **(any of the doughs in Chapter 2)**
60 G	¼ CUP	CRÈME FRAÎCHE **(page 188)**
55 G	2 OZ	MOZZARELLA, LOW-MOISTURE, SHREDDED
2 G	¼ TSP	SALT
14 G	1 TBSP	OLIVE OIL (EVOO)
3 G	1 TBSP	CILANTRO LEAVES, FRESH, TORN
	1	LIME WEDGE
		WHITE RICE FLOUR FOR STRETCHING THE DOUGH AND DUSTING THE PEEL

MAKES ONE 12 IN [30.5 CM] PIZZA

Shishito and Jimmy Nardello are my two favorite peppers. Although the shishito is an early season pepper (from summer into early fall) and the Jimmy Nardello comes in later, there is a moment in the middle when both are abundant. Shishito peppers, a slightly spicy Japanese variety, are similar in taste to a Padrón. An Italian variety, the Jimmy Nardello develops an intense sweetness when roasted. Here, both are blistered to bring out their best qualities, resulting in an intoxicating spicy, sweet, bitter bite.

TO MAKE THE PEPPER TOPPING: Position an oven rack 6 to 8 in [15 to 20 cm] from the broiler. Turn on the broiler and preheat for 15 minutes. (If your broiler has heat settings, set it on high.) Line a sheet pan with parchment paper.

Arrange the Jimmy Nardello and shishito peppers in a single layer on the parchment-lined pan. Drizzle the peppers with the olive oil and sprinkle with the salt. Gently toss with your hands, lightly coating the peppers with the oil and salt. Broil the peppers, turning them every few minutes, until evenly charred and sizzling, 15 to 20 minutes. Remove from the oven and let cool to the touch.

Remove any large stems from the peppers. Leave the shishitos, which are small, whole. Cut the larger Jimmy Nardellos in half crosswise and discard their seeds. Store the peppers in an airtight container in the fridge for up to 48 hours. Bring to room temperature before adding to the pizza. **CONT'D**

TO ASSEMBLE THE PIZZA: If the pizza dough is refrigerated, remove it from the fridge 2 to 3 hours before you plan to bake. Proof the dough on the counter until it's slightly puffy and room temperature. By the end of proofing, it should feel soft and full of gas. While you wait, set up where you'll be stretching and building the pizza **(see Designing Workflow, page 101)** and position a cooling rack, cutting board, and pizza wheel or rocker cutter near the oven. Ready a 9 or 10 in [23 or 25 cm] cake pan half full of white rice flour and set it aside.

An hour before baking, position an oven rack 6 to 8 in [15 to 20 cm] from the top of the oven and set a baking steel or stone on it. Preheat the oven to 550°F [290°C] or as hot as the oven will allow.

Sprinkle a wooden peel with a little white rice flour and set it aside. Slide a dough scraper under the dough round and flip it over into the cake pan of white rice flour. Turn it over two or three times, then transfer it to the peel, handling it gently.

Use your fingertips to indent a ring ¼ in [6 mm] deep all the way around the rim of the dough. Flip the dough over and repeat, pressing an indent around the outer edge. Next, use the pads of your fingers to lightly press down on the inner circle of the dough, going from 12 o'clock at the top to 6 o'clock at the bottom. Flip the dough over and repeat. Return the dough to the original side up. You'll now use gravity to stretch it into its final shape.

Slide clean, dry hands under the dough and make two fists in the center. Lift your hands and the pizza into the air parallel to your chin. Slowly move your fists in opposite directions to stretch the center of the pizza. Rotate the dough 90 degrees and carefully pull it in opposite directions again. Now arc your hands and let the dough slide down and hang off the back of your knuckles. Guide the dough in a circular motion, keeping it moving over the back of your hands and letting gravity do the final pulling. If the dough is resisting, give it a short rest on the peel and try again.

Lay the dough back on the peel and spoon the crème fraîche onto the middle. Use the back of the spoon to spread it evenly over the dough, stopping at the indented rim. Scatter the mozzarella on top and distribute the peppers evenly over the top. Shimmy the peel a few times to make sure the pizza moves freely and can easily slide off the peel. If the dough is stuck, quickly lift it with the dough scraper and toss a little white rice flour underneath.

Open the oven door and slide the pizza onto the steel by holding the peel at a slight angle and sliding it out from under the pizza in one fluid motion. It can help to match the edge of the peel with the far edge of the steel. Avoid shuffling the peel under the pizza.

Close the oven door and bake the pizza for 5 to 6 minutes. Open the door and check on the pizza. Chances are it will need to be rotated. Spin it 180 degrees with a metal peel or use a pair of long metal tongs to adjust the direction. Close the door and bake for an additional 4 to 5 minutes. The pizza is done when the crust is a burnished red, golden in spots, and the bubbles are slightly charred. The cheese should be melted and browned and the peppers sizzling.

Slide the metal peel under the pizza and transfer it to the wire rack. Dust with the salt, drizzle with the olive oil, and sprinkle with the cilantro. Let cool for 5 to 6 minutes, then move the pizza to the cutting board and cut into eight wedges with the pizza wheel or rocker cutter. Set the lime wedge in the middle, for squeezing over the entire pizza, and serve immediately.

FOR STORAGE AND WARMING INFORMATION, SEE PAGE 271.

PEACH, RED ONION, AND CAPER

Weight	Volume	Ingredient
	1	DOUGH ROUND **(any of the doughs in Chapter 2)**
55 G	2 OZ	MOZZARELLA, FRESH, TORN INTO ½ IN [12 MM] PIECES
150 G	1	YELLOW PEACH, THINLY SLICED
75 G	½	RED ONION, THINLY SLICED
9 G	2 TBSP	CAPERS
2 G	¼ TSP	SALT
14 G	1 TBSP	OLIVE OIL (EVOO)
		WHITE RICE FLOUR FOR STRETCHING THE DOUGH AND DUSTING THE PEEL

Sweet, tangy, and salty, this pizza is my secret weapon—the pie I pull out at parties that turns heads and leaves everyone wanting more. Peaches on pizza are a delight, and they are further elevated here by the mild bite of red onion and the briny pop of capers. Use yellow, not white, peaches and make this pie for all your summer gatherings.

If the pizza dough is refrigerated, remove it from the fridge 2 to 3 hours before you plan to bake. Proof the dough on the counter until it's slightly puffy and room temperature. By the end of proofing, it should feel soft and full of gas. While you wait, set up where you'll be stretching and building the pizza **(see Designing Workflow, page 101)** and position a cooling rack, cutting board, and pizza wheel or rocker cutter near the oven. Ready a 9 or 10 in [23 or 25 cm] cake pan half full of white rice flour and set it aside.

An hour before baking, position an oven rack 6 to 8 in [15 to 20 cm] from the top of the oven and set a baking steel or stone on it. Preheat the oven to 550°F [290°C] or as hot as the oven will allow.

Sprinkle a wooden peel with a little white rice flour and set it aside. Slide a dough scraper under the dough round and flip it over into the cake pan of white rice flour. Turn it over two or three times, then transfer it to the peel, handling it gently.

Use your fingertips to indent a ring ¼ in [6 mm] deep all the way around the rim of the dough. Flip the dough over and repeat, pressing an indent around the outer edge. Next, use the pads of your fingers to lightly press down on the inner circle of the dough, going from 12 o'clock at the top to 6 o'clock at the bottom. Flip the dough over

CONT'D

and repeat. Return the dough to the original side up. You'll now use gravity to stretch it into its final shape.

Slide clean, dry hands under the dough and make two fists in the center. Lift your hands and the pizza into the air parallel to your chin. Slowly move your fists in opposite directions to stretch the center of the pizza. Rotate the dough 90 degrees and carefully pull it in opposite directions again. Now arc your hands and let the dough slide down and hang off the back of your knuckles. Guide the dough in a circular motion, keeping it moving over the back of your hands and letting gravity do the final pulling. If the dough is resisting, give it a short rest on the peel and try again.

Lay the dough back on the peel and scatter the mozzarella on top. Distribute the peach slices, red onion, and capers evenly over the pizza. Shimmy the peel a few times to make sure the pizza moves freely and can easily slide off the peel. If the dough is stuck, quickly lift it with the dough scraper and toss a little white rice flour underneath.

Open the oven door and slide the pizza onto the steel by holding the peel at a slight angle and sliding it out from under the pizza in one fluid motion. It can help to match the edge of the peel with the far edge of the steel. Avoid shuffling the peel under the pizza.

Close the oven door and bake the pizza for 5 to 6 minutes. Open the door and check on the pizza. Chances are it will need to be rotated. Spin it 180 degrees with a metal peel or use a pair of long metal tongs to adjust the direction. Close the door and bake for an additional 4 to 5 minutes. The pizza is done when the crust is a burnished red, golden in spots, and the bubbles are slightly charred. The cheese should be melted and browned and the peach slices and red onion slightly charred.

Slide the metal peel under the pizza and transfer it to the wire rack. Dust with the salt and drizzle with the olive oil. Let cool for 5 to 6 minutes, then move the pizza to the cutting board and cut into eight wedges with the pizza wheel or rocker cutter. Serve immediately.

FOR STORAGE AND WARMING INFORMATION, SEE PAGE 271.

ZUCCHINI AND SUMMER SQUASH

MAKES ONE 12 IN [30.5 CM] PIZZA

Squash Topping

Weight	Volume	Ingredient
150 G	1	ZUCCHINI, SLICED
150 G	1	YELLOW SUMMER SQUASH, SLICED
5 G	1 TSP	SALT

Assembly

Weight	Volume	Ingredient
	1	DOUGH ROUND **(any of the doughs in Chapter 2)**
56 G	¼ CUP	ANYTHING GREEN GOES PESTO **(page 181)**
55 G	2 OZ	MOZZARELLA, LOW-MOISTURE, SHREDDED
55 G	2 OZ	FETA, CRUMBLED
	2	GARLIC CLOVES, THINLY SLICED
14 G	1 TBSP	OLIVE OIL (EVOO)
2 G	¼ TSP	SALT
2 G	1¼ TSP	RED PEPPER FLAKES (OPTIONAL)
		WHITE RICE FLOUR FOR STRETCHING THE DOUGH AND DUSTING THE PEEL

Zucchini and yellow summer squash are colorful and fun toppings for pizza but notoriously watery. The key to using them is to salt them lightly and let them sit for a bit to release excess water. This can be done either a day ahead or as the pizza dough is proofing. Choose small, tender zucchini and summer squash and leave the peels on for a pop of green and yellow. I like to slice squashes for pizza with a mandoline to about the thickness of two stacked quarters.

TO PREPARE THE SQUASH TOPPING: In a large mixing bowl, combine the zucchini, yellow squash, and salt and toss with your hands to coat the slices with the salt. Let sit until the squash slices wilt and a little water pools in the bottom of the bowl, about 30 minutes. Transfer the squash slices to a colander and press them against the side of the colander with your hands to force out as much moisture as you can. Transfer to an airtight container and store in the fridge for up to 24 hours. Bring to room temperature before adding to the pizza and drain off any additional water that has been released. **CONT'D**

TO ASSEMBLE THE PIZZA: If the pizza dough is refrigerated, remove it from the fridge 2 to 3 hours before you plan to bake. Proof the dough on the counter until it's slightly puffy and room temperature. By the end of proofing, it should feel soft and full of gas. While you wait, set up where you'll be stretching and building the pizza **(see Designing Workflow, page 101)** and position a cooling rack, cutting board, and pizza wheel or rocker cutter near the oven. Ready a 9 or 10 in [23 or 25 cm] cake pan half full of white rice flour and set it aside.

An hour before baking, position an oven rack 6 to 8 in [15 to 20 cm] from the top of the oven and set a baking steel or stone on it. Preheat the oven to 550°F [290°C] or as hot as the oven will allow.

Sprinkle a wooden peel with a little white rice flour and set it aside. Slide a dough scraper under the dough round and flip it over into the cake pan of white rice flour. Turn it over two or three times, then transfer it to the peel, handling it gently.

Use your fingertips to indent a ring ¼ in [6 mm] deep all the way around the rim of the dough. Flip the dough over and repeat, pressing an indent around the outer edge. Next, use the pads of your fingers to lightly press down on the inner circle of the dough, going from 12 o'clock at the top to 6 o'clock at the bottom. Flip the dough over and repeat. Return the dough to the original side up. You'll now use gravity to stretch it into its final shape.

Slide clean, dry hands under the dough and make two fists in the center. Lift your hands and the pizza into the air parallel to your chin. Slowly move your fists in opposite directions to stretch the center of the pizza. Rotate the dough 90 degrees and carefully pull it in opposite directions again. Now arc your hands and let the dough slide down and hang off the back of your knuckles. Guide the dough in a circular motion, keeping it moving over the back of your hands and letting gravity do the final pulling. If the dough is resisting, give it a short rest on the peel and try again.

Lay the dough back on the peel and spoon the pesto onto the middle. Use the back of the spoon to spread the pesto evenly over the dough, stopping at the indented rim. Scatter the mozzarella over the sauce and then evenly distribute the squash, feta, and garlic on top. Shimmy the peel a few times to make sure the pizza moves freely and can easily slide off the peel. If the dough is stuck, quickly lift it with the dough scraper and toss a little white rice flour underneath.

Open the oven door and slide the pizza onto the steel by holding the peel at a slight angle and sliding it out from under the pizza in one fluid motion. It can help to match the edge of the peel with the far edge of the steel. Avoid shuffling the peel under the pizza.

Close the oven door and bake the pizza for 5 to 6 minutes. Open the door and check on the pizza. Chances are it will need to be rotated. Spin it 180 degrees with a metal peel or use a pair of long metal tongs to adjust the direction. Close the door and bake for an additional 4 to 5 minutes. The pizza is done when the crust is a burnished red, golden in spots, and the bubbles are slightly charred. The cheese should be melted and browned and the squash slices slightly charred.

Slide the metal peel under the pizza and transfer it to the wire rack. Drizzle with the olive oil, dust with the salt, and sprinkle with the red pepper flakes (if using). Let cool for 5 to 6 minutes, then move the pizza to the cutting board and cut into eight wedges with the pizza wheel or rocker cutter. Serve immediately.

FOR STORAGE AND
WARMING INFORMATION,
SEE PAGE 271.

FIG AND GORGONZOLA

Weight	Volume	Ingredient
	1	DOUGH ROUND **(any of the doughs in Chapter 2)**
28 G	2 TBSP	HERBY OLIVE OIL DRIZZLE **(page 182)**
55 G	2 OZ	MOZZARELLA, LOW-MOISTURE, SHREDDED
55 G	2 OZ	GORGONZOLA, CRUMBLED
280 G	7 OR 8	FIGS, SLICED
2 G	¼ TSP	SALT
14 G	1 TBSP	OLIVE OIL (EVOO)
20 G	1 TBSP	HOT HONEY **(page 185)** FOR FINISHING (OPTIONAL)
		WHITE RICE FLOUR FOR STRETCHING THE DOUGH AND DUSTING THE PEEL

Figs are a food of the gods. Their sticky sweet and pulpy interior tastes like a mix of currants, strawberries, honey, and flowers. Their chewy flesh gives way to thousands of tiny seeds and fibers, and when figs are eaten fresh off the tree on a warm day, they already taste like jam. I like the funkiness of the Gorgonzola against the fruitiness of the fig, but you could also use Gruyère, feta, or ricotta. That last one would lend itself well to a sophisticated dessert pizza.

If the pizza dough is refrigerated, remove it from the fridge 2 to 3 hours before you plan to bake. Proof the dough on the counter until it's slightly puffy and room temperature. By the end of proofing, it should feel soft and full of gas. While you wait, set up where you'll be stretching and building the pizza **(see Designing Workflow, page 101)** and position a cooling rack, cutting board, and pizza wheel or rocker cutter near the oven. Ready a 9 or 10 in [23 or 25 cm] cake pan half full of white rice flour and set it aside.

An hour before baking, position an oven rack 6 to 8 in [15 to 20 cm] from the top of the oven and set a baking steel or stone on it. Preheat the oven to 550°F [290°C] or as hot as the oven will allow.

Sprinkle a wooden peel with a little white rice flour and set it aside. Slide a dough scraper under the dough round and flip it over into the cake pan of white rice flour. Turn it over two or three times, then transfer it to the peel, handling it gently. **CONT'D**

Use your fingertips to indent a ring ¼ in [6 mm] deep all the way around the rim of the dough. Flip the dough over and repeat, pressing an indent around the outer edge. Next, use the pads of your fingers to lightly press down on the inner circle of the dough, going from 12 o'clock at the top to 6 o'clock at the bottom. Flip the dough over and repeat. Return the dough to the original side up. You'll now use gravity to stretch it into its final shape.

Slide clean, dry hands under the dough and make two fists in the center. Lift your hands and the pizza into the air parallel to your chin. Slowly move your fists in opposite directions to stretch the center of the pizza. Rotate the dough 90 degrees and carefully pull it in opposite directions again. Now arc your hands and let the dough slide down and hang off the back of your knuckles. Guide the dough in a circular motion, keeping it moving over the back of your hands and letting gravity do the final pulling. If the dough is resisting, give it a short rest on the peel and try again.

Lay the dough back on the peel and drizzle on the herby olive oil, working from the middle to the edge and stopping at the indented rim. Scatter the mozzarella over the dough, then fill in the gaps with the Gorgonzola. Place the figs in a single layer on top. Shimmy the peel a few times to make sure the pizza moves freely and can easily slide off the peel. If the dough is stuck, quickly lift it with the dough scraper and toss a little white rice flour underneath.

Open the oven door and slide the pizza onto the steel by holding the peel at a slight angle and sliding it out from under the pizza in one fluid motion. It can help to match the edge of the peel with the far edge of the steel. Avoid shuffling the peel under the pizza.

Close the oven door and bake the pizza for 5 to 6 minutes. Open the door and check on the pizza. Chances are it will need to be rotated. Spin it 180 degrees with a metal peel or use a pair of long metal tongs to adjust the direction. Close the door and bake for an additional 4 to 5 minutes. The pizza is done when the crust is a burnished red, golden in spots, and the bubbles are slightly charred. The cheese should be melted and browned and the figs gently cooked.

Slide the metal peel under the pizza and transfer it to the wire rack. Dust with the salt and drizzle with the olive oil and hot honey (if using). Let cool for 5 to 6 minutes, then move the pizza to the cutting board and cut into eight wedges with the pizza wheel or rocker cutter. Serve immediately.

FOR STORAGE AND WARMING INFORMATION, SEE PAGE 271.

SAUSAGE AND KALE

Sausage and Kale Topping

Weight	Volume	Ingredient
14 G	1 TBSP	OLIVE OIL (EVOO)
115 G	4 OZ	SPICY ITALIAN SAUSAGE, CASING REMOVED, CRUMBLED
2 G	¼ TSP	SALT
135 G	2 CUPS	LACINATO KALE, STEMMED AND CHOPPED

MAKES ONE 12 IN [30.5 CM] PIZZA

Assembly

Weight	Volume	Ingredient
	1	DOUGH ROUND **(any of the doughs in Chapter 2)**
14 G	1 TBSP	LEMONY ROASTED-GARLIC CREAM **(page 186)**
55 G	2 OZ	MOZZARELLA, FRESH, TORN INTO ½ IN [12 MM] PIECES
5 G	2 TBSP	PARMESAN
2 G	¼ TSP	SALT
14 G	1 TBSP	OLIVE OIL (EVOO)
		WHITE RICE FLOUR FOR STRETCHING THE DOUGH AND DUSTING THE PEEL

Kale on a pizza is a great way to enjoy your greens, but without a little steaming first, you can feel like you're eating a leather boot rather than a light, comforting pizza. Choose Lacinato kale, also known as Tuscan or dinosaur kale, for this recipe. Its leaves are less chewy and firm than the leaves of curly leaf or red Russian kale, and it tastes nuttier, sweeter, and less cabbagey. This is the perfect pizza to welcome fall.

TO MAKE THE SAUSAGE AND KALE TOPPING: In a large skillet, warm the olive oil over medium heat. Add the sausage and salt. Cook, until browned, 3 to 4 minutes. Turn off the heat, add the kale to the pan, cover, and let steam for 8 to 10 minutes. Transfer to an airtight container and store in the fridge for up to 24 hours. Bring to room temperature before adding to the pizza.

TO ASSEMBLE THE PIZZA: If the pizza dough is refrigerated, remove it from the fridge 2 to 3 hours before you plan to bake. Proof the dough on the counter until it's slightly puffy and room temperature. By the end of proofing, it should feel soft and full of gas. While you wait, set up where you'll be stretching and building the pizza **(see Designing Workflow, page 101)** and position a cooling rack, cutting board, and pizza wheel or rocker cutter near the oven. Ready a 9 or 10 in [23 or 25 cm] cake pan half full of white rice flour and set it aside.

An hour before baking, position an oven rack 6 to 8 in [15 to 20 cm] from the top of the oven and set a baking steel or stone on it. Preheat the oven to 550°F [290°C] or as hot as the oven will allow. **CONT'D**

Sprinkle a wooden peel with a little white rice flour and set it aside. Slide a dough scraper under the dough round and flip it over into the cake pan of white rice flour. Turn it over two or three times, then transfer it to the peel, handling it gently.

Use your fingertips to indent a ring ¼ in [6 mm] deep all the way around the rim of the dough. Flip the dough over and repeat, pressing an indent around the outer edge. Next, use the pads of your fingers to lightly press down on the inner circle of the dough, going from 12 o'clock at the top to 6 o'clock at the bottom. Flip the dough over and repeat. Return the dough to the original side up. You'll now use gravity to stretch it into its final shape.

Slide clean, dry hands under the dough and make two fists in the center. Lift your hands and the pizza into the air parallel to your chin. Slowly move your fists in opposite directions to stretch the center of the pizza. Rotate the dough 90 degrees and carefully pull it in opposite directions again. Now arc your hands and let the dough slide down and hang off the back of your knuckles. Guide the dough in a circular motion, keeping it moving over the back of your hands and letting gravity do the final pulling. If the dough is resisting, give it a short rest on the peel and try again.

Lay the dough back on the peel and spoon the garlic cream onto the middle. Use the back of the spoon to spread the garlic cream evenly over the dough, stopping at the indented rim. Scatter the mozzarella evenly over the garlic cream, then evenly distribute the sausage and kale over the top. Shimmy the peel a few times to make sure the pizza moves freely and can easily slide off the peel. If the dough is stuck, quickly lift it with the dough scraper and toss a little white rice flour underneath.

Open the oven door and slide the pizza onto the steel by holding the peel at a slight angle and sliding it out from under the pizza in one fluid motion. It can help to match the edge of the peel with the far edge of the steel. Avoid shuffling the peel under the pizza.

Close the oven door and bake the pizza for 5 to 6 minutes. Open the door and spin it 180 degrees with a metal peel or use a pair of long metal tongs to adjust the direction. Close the door and bake for an additional 4 to 5 minutes. The pizza is done when the crust is a burnished red, golden in spots, and the bubbles are slightly charred.

Slide the metal peel under the pizza and transfer it to the wire rack. Grate the Parmesan on top. Dust with the salt and drizzle with the olive oil. Let cool for 5 to 6 minutes, then move the pizza to the cutting board and cut into eight wedges with the pizza wheel or rocker cutter. Serve immediately.

FOR STORAGE AND WARMING INFORMATION, SEE PAGE 271.

DELICATA SQUASH, SHALLOT, AND GRUYÈRE

MAKES ONE 12 IN [30.5 CM] PIZZA

Delicata Squash and Shallot Toppings

Weight	Volume	Ingredient
200 G	1	DELICATA SQUASH
14 G	1 TBSP	OLIVE OIL (EVOO)
3 G	½ TSP	SALT
15 TO 30 G	1 TO 2 TBSP	UNSALTED BUTTER
56 G	2	SHALLOTS, THINLY SLICED

Assembly

Weight	Volume	Ingredient
	1	DOUGH ROUND **(any of the doughs in Chapter 2)**
15 G	1 TBSP	CRÈME FRAÎCHE **(page 188)**
55 G	2 OZ	MOZZARELLA, LOW-MOISTURE, SHREDDED
55 G	2 OZ	GRUYÈRE, GRATED
5 G	2 TBSP	PARMESAN
3 G	1 TBSP	THYME LEAVES, FRESH
2 G	¼ TSP	SALT
14 G	1 TBSP	OLIVE OIL (EVOO)
		WHITE RICE FLOUR FOR STRETCHING THE DOUGH AND DUSTING THE PEEL

When roasted or baked, delicata squash turns into a golden candy, and it's easy to eat it all before it even gets on the pizza. The small, oblong squash is yellow with green stripes, and its skin is thin and tender enough to eat. Leaving it on adds a nice visual contrast and cuts down on prep time. Warming, creamy, and inviting, this pizza will make you thrilled for squash season.

TO MAKE THE DELICATA SQUASH TOPPING: Preheat the oven to 400°F [200°C]. Line a sheet pan with parchment paper.

Cut the squash in half lengthwise and, using a spoon, scrape out and discard the seeds and stringy fibers. Slice the halves crosswise into thin slices. In a medium mixing bowl, combine the squash, olive oil, and half of the salt and toss to coat the slices evenly. Transfer the squash to the parchment-lined pan, spreading it in a single layer. Bake until lightly browned and tender when pierced with a fork, 20 to 25 minutes. Let cool completely, then use a thin metal spatula to move the squash from the sheet pan to a plate. The squash will keep in an **CONT'D**

airtight container in the fridge for up to 24 hours. Bring to room temperature before adding to the pizza.

TO MAKE THE SHALLOT TOPPING: In a medium skillet, melt the butter over low heat until bubbling gently. Add the shallots, season with the remaining salt and cook, stirring frequently to avoid burning, until soft and deeply browned, 10 to 15 minutes. If the shallots begin to stick to the pan, add a splash of water. Remove from the heat and let cool. The shallots will keep in an airtight container in the fridge for up to 48 hours. Bring to room temperature before adding to the pizza.

TO ASSEMBLE THE PIZZA: If the pizza dough is refrigerated, remove it from the fridge 2 to 3 hours before you plan to bake. Proof the dough on the counter until it's slightly puffy and room temperature. By the end of proofing, it should feel soft and full of gas. While you wait, set up where you'll be stretching and building the pizza **(see Designing Workflow, page 101)** and position a cooling rack, cutting board, and pizza wheel or rocker cutter near the oven. Ready a 9 or 10 in [23 or 25 cm] cake pan half full of white rice flour and set it aside.

An hour before baking, position an oven rack 6 to 8 in [15 to 20 cm] from the top of the oven and set a baking steel or stone on it. Preheat the oven to 550°F [290°C] or as hot as the oven will allow.

Sprinkle a wooden peel with a little white rice flour and set it aside. Slide a dough scraper under the dough round and flip it over into the cake pan of white rice flour. Turn it over two or three times, then transfer it to the peel, handling it gently.

Use your fingertips to indent a ring ¼ in [6 mm] deep all the way around the rim of the dough. Flip the dough over and repeat, pressing an indent around the outer edge. Next, use the pads of your fingers to lightly press down on the inner circle of the dough, going from 12 o'clock at the top to 6 o'clock at the bottom. Flip the dough over and repeat. Return the dough to the original side up. You'll now use gravity to stretch it into its final shape.

CONT'D

Slide clean, dry hands under the dough and make two fists in the center. Lift your hands and the pizza into the air parallel to your chin. Slowly move your fists in opposite directions to stretch the center of the pizza. Rotate the dough 90 degrees and carefully pull it in opposite directions again. Now arc your hands and let the dough slide down and hang off the back of your knuckles. Guide the dough in a circular motion, keeping it moving over the back of your hands and letting gravity do the final pulling. If the dough is resisting, give it a short rest on the peel and try again.

Lay the dough back on the peel and spoon the crème fraîche onto the middle. Use the back of the spoon to spread the crème fraîche evenly over the dough, stopping at the indented rim. Scatter the mozzarella and Gruyère over the dough, then evenly distribute the squash and shallots over the top. Shimmy the peel a few times to make sure the pizza moves freely and can easily slide off the peel. If the dough is stuck, quickly lift it with the dough scraper and toss a little white rice flour underneath.

Open the oven door and slide the pizza onto the steel by holding the peel at a slight angle and sliding it out from under the pizza in one fluid motion. It can help to match the edge of the peel with the far edge of the steel. Avoid shuffling the peel under the pizza.

Close the oven door and bake the pizza for 5 to 6 minutes. Open the door and check on the pizza. Chances are it will need to be rotated. Spin it 180 degrees with a metal peel or use a pair of long metal tongs to adjust the direction. Close the door and bake for an additional 4 to 5 minutes. The pizza is done when the crust is a burnished red, golden in spots, and the bubbles are slightly charred. The cheese should be melted and browned and the squash slices tender and curled at the edges.

Slide the metal peel under the pizza and transfer it to the wire rack. Grate the Parmesan on top. Dust with the thyme and salt and drizzle with the olive oil. Let cool for 5 to 6 minutes, then move the pizza to the cutting board and cut it into eight wedges with the pizza wheel or rocker cutter. Serve immediately.

FOR STORAGE AND WARMING INFORMATION, SEE PAGE 271.

ROASTED CORN AND TUNA

Corn and Tuna Topping

Weight	Volume	Ingredient
28 G	2 TBSP	OLIVE OIL (EVOO)
100 G	1	YELLOW CORN EAR, SHUCKED AND KERNELS CUT FROM THE COB
2 G	¼ TSP	SALT
142 G	ONE 5 OZ CAN	SOLID WHITE TUNA, PACKED IN WATER

Assembly

Weight	Volume	Ingredient
	1	DOUGH ROUND **(any of the doughs in Chapter 2)**
85 G	3 OZ	MOZZARELLA, LOW-MOISTURE, SHREDDED
5 G	2 TBSP	PARMESAN
0.5 G	½ TSP	PARSLEY, DRIED
2 G	¼ TSP	SALT
		SPICY MAYO DRIZZLE **(page 187)** FOR FINISHING (OPTIONAL)
		WHITE RICE FLOUR FOR STRETCHING THE DOUGH AND DUSTING THE PEEL

MAKES ONE 12 IN [30.5 CM] PIZZA

I was first introduced to this pizza while wandering around Tokyo. Shakey's Pizza, a small pizza chain founded in California in the 1950s and popular in Japan, was selling this unusual pizza, and it was *so good*! The original had mayonnaise as the base, but here it's done naked: no sauce and a light stream of **Spicy Mayo Drizzle (page 187)** for a finishing touch. I prefer to use in-season ears of corn and shuck them myself, but you can use frozen corn in a pinch.

TO MAKE THE CORN AND TUNA TOPPING: In a medium skillet, warm the olive oil over low heat until it glistens. Add the corn kernels and salt and cook, stirring frequently, until the corn turns from golden to browned, 5 to 6 minutes. Transfer to a plate to cool.

Drain the tuna. Store the corn and tuna in an airtight container in the refrigerator for up to 24 hours. Bring to room temperature before adding to the pizza. **CONT'D**

TO ASSEMBLE THE PIZZA: If the pizza dough is refrigerated, remove it from the fridge 2 to 3 hours before you plan to bake. Proof the dough on the counter until it's slightly puffy and room temperature. By the end of proofing, it should feel soft and full of gas. While you wait, set up where you'll be stretching and building the pizza **(see Designing Workflow, page 101)** and position a cooling rack, cutting board, and pizza wheel or rocker cutter near the oven. Ready a 9 or 10 in [23 or 25 cm] cake pan half full of white rice flour and set it aside.

An hour before baking, position an oven rack 6 to 8 in [15 to 20 cm] from the top of the oven and set a baking steel or stone on it. Preheat the oven to 550°F [290°C] or as hot as the oven will allow.

Sprinkle a wooden peel with a little white rice flour and set it aside. Slide a dough scraper under the dough round and flip it over into the cake pan of white rice flour. Turn it over two or three times, then transfer it to the peel, handling it gently.

Use your fingertips to indent a ring ¼ in [6 mm] deep all the way around the rim of the dough. Flip the dough over and repeat, pressing an indent around the outer edge. Next, use the pads of your fingers to lightly press down on the inner circle of the dough, going from 12 o'clock at the top to 6 o'clock at the bottom. Flip the dough over and repeat. Return the dough to the original side up. You'll now use gravity to stretch it into its final shape.

Slide clean, dry hands under the dough and make two fists in the center. Lift your hands and the pizza into the air parallel to your chin. Slowly move your fists in opposite directions to stretch the center of the pizza. Rotate the dough 90 degrees and carefully pull it in opposite directions again. Now arc your hands and let the dough slide down and hang off the back of your knuckles. Guide the dough in a circular motion, keeping it moving over the back of your hands and letting gravity do the final pulling. If the dough is resisting, give it a short rest on the peel and try again.

Lay the dough back on the peel and scatter the mozzarella over the dough, then evenly distribute the corn and tuna over the top. Shimmy the peel a few times to make sure the pizza moves freely and can easily slide off the peel. If the dough is stuck, quickly lift it with the dough scraper and toss a little white rice flour underneath.

Open the oven door and slide the pizza onto the steel by holding the peel at a slight angle and sliding it out from under the pizza in one fluid motion. It can help to match the edge of the peel with the far edge of the steel. Avoid shuffling the peel under the pizza.

Close the oven door and bake the pizza for 5 to 6 minutes. Open the door and check on the pizza. Chances are it will need to be rotated. Spin it 180 degrees with a metal peel or use a pair of long metal tongs to adjust the direction. Close the door and bake for an additional 4 to 5 minutes. The pizza is done when the crust is a burnished red, golden in spots, and the bubbles are slightly charred. The cheese should be melted and browned, the tuna sizzling, and the corn charred.

Slide the metal peel under the pizza and transfer it to the wire rack. Grate the Parmesan on top. Dust with the parsley and salt and drizzle with the spicy mayo, if desired. Let cool for 5 to 6 minutes, then move the pizza to the cutting board and cut it into eight wedges with the pizza wheel or rocker cutter. Serve immediately.

FOR STORAGE AND WARMING INFORMATION, SEE PAGE 271.

PITA, FO
AND PIZ
DESSERTS

CACCIA, A-NIGHT

WOOD-FIRED BAKING requires the baker to plan carefully to maximize all the various temperatures of the oven, from a blazing-hot live fire to residual low heat for slow cooking. I suggest you take the same approach whenever you bake. That means piggybacking your bakes, like tossing in some pita after the pizzas are done, or baking fluffy focaccia, then turning up the oven for pizza.

This part is dedicated to those pizza-adjacent bakes—pita, focaccia—that dovetail well with the general flow you're now used to. And, of course, you're going to need an easy birthday cake and some chocolate chip cookies for those memorable pizza parties you'll soon be hosting.

5

PITA

The term *pita* is used in the West as a catch-all name for a variety of Middle Eastern, Mediterranean, and North African flatbreads. Some pitas are baked in a hot oven, puffing up into a pocket that will then be split and filled. Other pitas are cooked in a skillet on a hot stovetop and then folded around a filling like a taco. While the following doughs are wonderful, pita making is more a method than a particular dough. I often use any leftover or unclaimed pizza dough at the end of a pizza night to make pita, flouring it well, rolling it out, and baking it in a still-hot oven.

How to Make Pita Pizza / To turn pita into pizza, roll as directed and dock the dough, or prick all over with the tines of a fork. (This will encourage small bubbles but not a pocket.) Bake on a preheated steel or stone for 1 to 2 minutes, flip the dough with a pair of tongs, and bake for another 1 to 2 minutes. Remove from the oven, top with sauce and cheese, and season with a sprinkle of salt. (Use other toppings sparingly, as it won't spend much time back in the oven.) Slide the pita pizza back onto the steel or stone and switch from bake to broil. Broil until the cheese is browned and bubbly, 2 to 3 minutes. Use a metal peel or a pair of tongs to transfer the pita pizza to a cutting board. Drizzle with olive oil. When cool enough to touch, cut into six wedges. Serve immediately.

Practice with Pita

Pita can be made in a relatively short period of time, one of the great selling points of this versatile flatbread. Both yeasted and naturally leavened versions can be ready to shape in as little as 2 hours. Even if you tack on the time it takes for the levain to ferment, the total time for a naturally leavened pita dough is still within 5 to 6 hours.

That said, pita dough is easier to roll out, more flavorful, and browns especially well when left to rise slowly in the refrigerator overnight. I chill my dough (after a 2-hour spell on the counter) for anywhere from a short stint of 4 to 6 hours to up to 24 hours when I need extra time. Extending fermentation unlocks sugars in the dough, slightly sweetening it, and providing the yeast extra time to gas up the dough, resulting in a pillowy tenderness. When working with chilled dough, bring it to room temperature before shaping.

Pita dough is stiff, between 65 to 70 percent hydration, and uses warm water (about 100°F [38°C]), which results in a sticky but firm dough. Stiff doughs are easy to handle and require little to no flour or water on your hands or work surface. (Flour the dough if necessary but use as little as possible.) When shaping, the tension created between the tacky dough and the work surface helps pull the dough into a ball. When rolling it out, the grip between the dough and the work surface helps it stay extended.

If you want both sides of the pita pocket to have the same thickness, roll out the dough directly after shaping. This ensures that one side doesn't proof more than the other, unevenly trapping gas in the dough that can make one side of the pocket bready and the other side paper-thin.

Pita bread can be temperamental and not open in the oven the way we want. This can occur when the dough is too thick or too thin, or when the oven isn't hot enough. The pocket comes from all the air in the dough rising at once, forming a giant bubble, so it's important that the dough is rolled evenly and the baking surface is fully heated. Pita that doesn't pop is still delicious and can be folded around a filling, rather than split and filled. Also, sometimes pita doesn't puff until it's turned over. Once the pita is fully puffed, poke it with a thin metal skewer or knife tip to release some steam. Otherwise, it may tear from the pressure.

Get your oven blazing hot (500° to 550°F [260° to 290°C]) and bake the pita directly on a preheated baking steel or pizza stone. I preheat my oven for 1 hour and use a baking steel. If you don't have a steel or stone, invert a large cast-iron skillet, place it on the oven rack, and preheat it for the baking surface.

5 Tips for Baking with Children

My four-year-old daughter and I love making pita together. But baking with children is fundamentally different from baking alone, or even with other adults. Children are capable of so much, but they are also unpredictable, a quality that can make baking projects difficult to navigate. Here are my top five tips for successful baking with kids.

1 **TRY THE RECIPE ON YOUR OWN FIRST.** Doing it once yourself before you bake together can be helpful if it's a long recipe or contains techniques you've never tried. If that's not possible, just make sure to tack on some time to the overall process because you will be simultaneously grasping the recipe and guiding your pint-size baker through it.

2 **HANG BACK AND LET THE YOUNG BAKER DO IT.** This includes not rushing. The world will not come to a halt if your pizza is oblong instead of round, but your kid will remember if the experience was fun or not. It is hard to sit back and watch children do things inefficiently or clumsily. But the empowerment and pride they experience fuel confidence that spills over into all areas of life.

3 **EMBRACE THE MESS AND MAKE CLEANUP A DANCE PARTY.** There's going to be flour everywhere (and I mean everywhere). You just can't get around it. If your young ones are too worried about making a mess, they won't be able to concentrate. Dishes and cleanup are a key part of baking, so when it's time tidy up, involve them too. My daughter loves to use a sprayer, so she's in charge of spraying and wiping everything while I sweep and mop.

4 **PREP, PREP, PREP.** It keeps the pace and minimizes the overwhelm when the ingredients are pre-weighed and items like toppings are already done. Kids don't need much to feel a sense of ownership and participation, so I'll often use my kitchen scale to weigh everything out and have my daughter simply mix together the flour and water. If she does want to help with the weighing, I give her cups, tablespoons, and teaspoons to scoop the dry ingredients into a bowl on top of a digital scale.

5 **REPLACE "I CAN'T DO IT" WITH "I CAN'T DO IT YET."** I learned this phrase from a mom I really admire, and I use it on myself and with my kid in and out of the kitchen. Frustration is an inevitable part of baking. Baking is all about troubleshooting, problem-solving, and staying calm when things go wrong. Leading with a positive attitude throughout mishaps sets the tone for how to handle bigger blunders.

EVERYDAY PITA

Baker's Percentage	Weight	Volume	Ingredient
70%	199 G	1⅓ CUPS + 1 TBSP	ALL-PURPOSE FLOUR (11% TO 12% PROTEIN)
30%	85 G	¾ CUP	WHOLE WHEAT FLOUR
60%	170 G	¾ CUP	WATER, WARM (100°F [38°C])
4%	11 G	2¼ TSP	OLIVE OIL (EVOO)
3%	10 G	2½ TSP	GRANULATED SUGAR
2%	6 G	1 TSP	SALT
1%	3 G	¾ TSP	INSTANT YEAST
			ALL-PURPOSE FLOUR FOR SHAPING AND ROLLING OUT THE DOUGH AND DUSTING THE PEEL

MAKES SIX 7 IN [18 CM] PITAS

Pita is mostly flour and water, so even for simple pitas, I add whole-grain flour. Otherwise, they are not very interesting. All-purpose flour lends a tenderness to the bread, but if the dough is not rolled flat and baked on a very hot pizza stone or baking steel, it will struggle to form a singular hole that then becomes a pocket. Pita that doesn't puff can be folded in half around a filling, like a taco, or simply torn and dredged through olive oil.

Example Time Frame	
9:00 A.M.	MIX DOUGH
12:00 P.M.	SHAPE, ROLL, AND BAKE

In a medium mixing bowl, combine the water, olive oil, sugar, salt, and yeast. Whisk together quickly to blend. Add the all-purpose flour and whole-wheat flour to the bowl. Quickly run your hands under warm running water, then use them to grab and squeeze the flour mixture until it forms a shaggy dough and no dry flour is visible. The dough will be sticky and tear easily. Cover with a lid or shower cap and let rest for 10 minutes.

Fill a small bowl with all-purpose flour and set it near your clean, dry work surface. Turn out the dough onto the work surface. Using the heel of your dominant hand, push the top of the dough away from you, then fold it back on itself and rotate it 90 degrees. Push, fold, and rotate again. Repeat this three-step action four or five times. Sprinkle a little flour on the dough and work surface if necessary, keeping in mind that a little stickiness is useful to build tension. Stop kneading as soon as the dough resists. Return the dough to the bowl and re-cover.

For same-day pita, leave the dough on the countertop at room temperature (68° to 72°F [20° to 22°C]) for 2 to 3 hours. I prefer to refrigerate the dough for at least overnight or up to 24 hours. If you decide to refrigerate the dough, bring it to room temperature before continuing with the instructions that follow. **CONT'D**

An hour before you plan to bake the pitas, position an oven rack 6 to 8 in [15 to 20 cm] from the top of the oven and set a baking steel or stone on it. Preheat the oven to 550°F [290°C] or as hot as the oven will allow.

Turn out the dough onto a clean, dry work surface and dust lightly with flour. The dough will shape into a ball easier if it is slightly sticky, so be conservative with the flour. Using a bench knife, divide the dough into six equal portions. (You can simply eyeball this.)

To shape each portion into a round, hold your dominant hand in a C shape and cuddle a portion of the dough between your palm and the work surface. Move your hand in counterclockwise circles, forcing the dough into a ball by applying pressure with your palm where the dough and the surface meet. Set the round aside, seam-side down, and cover with a damp (non-terry cloth) kitchen towel. Form the remaining portions into rounds, slipping each one under the towel as it is ready.

Next, lightly flour a dough round and flatten it between your palm and the dry, clean work surface. Then continue to flatten the dough with a rolling pin: Roll the dough away from you, then rotate it 90 degrees and roll again. Repeat rolling and rotating the dough until it is a 7 in [18 cm] circle about ¼ in [6 mm] thick. If the dough resists, move back and forth among a few rounds, letting one rest while you work another. As each dough circle is ready, run your hand over it to check for any thick sections that may need an extra stroke with the rolling pin. If the pita isn't thin enough, it will fail to form a pocket in the oven. As the circles are ready, cover again with the kitchen towel.

Line a large bowl with a large (non-terry cloth) kitchen towel, letting the towel drape over the sides. Set it near the stove.

Lightly flour a wooden peel (excess flour will burn) and load it with one or two pitas. Shimmy the peel a few times to make sure the pitas move freely and can easily slide off the peel. If a pita is stuck, quickly lift it with a dough scraper and toss a little flour underneath.

Open the oven door. Holding the peel at a slight angle, slip the pitas onto the steel in one fluid motion. Bake the pitas until they puff up, 1 to 2 minutes. Once puffed, poke the pocket in each pita with a thin metal skewer or the tip of a thin, sharp knife. Flip the pitas with long metal tongs and continue baking until the bottoms are deeply browned, 2 to 3 minutes longer. Use the tongs to transfer the baked pitas to the towel-lined bowl, then cover the pitas with the overhang of the towel. Bake the remaining pitas the same way, moving them to the bowl as they come out of the oven. If the pitas stop puffing, give the steel a minute or two to reheat between loads.

Pita is at its best as soon as it is cool enough to handle or within a few hours of baking. Store any uneaten pitas in an airtight container at room temperature for up to 24 hours. To reheat, spritz with water, wrap tightly in aluminum foil, and place in a preheated 350°F [180°C] oven until fragrant and warm, 3 to 5 minutes. After 48 hours, use leftover pitas to make **Za'atar Pita Chips (page 325)**.

YOGURT PITA

Baker's Percentage	Weight	Volume	Ingredient
50%	335 G	2⅓ CUPS + 1 TBSP	ALL-PURPOSE FLOUR (11% TO 12% PROTEIN)
50%	335 G	3 CUPS	WHOLE WHEAT FLOUR
37%	247 G	1 CUP	GREEK YOGURT, PLAIN, ANY FAT CONTENT
28%	187 G	¾ CUP	WATER, WARM (100°F [38°C])
11%	73 G	¼ CUP + 1 TBSP	OLIVE OIL (EVOO)
2%	12 G	2 TSP	SALT
1%	6 G	1½ TSP	INSTANT YEAST
			ALL-PURPOSE FLOUR FOR SHAPING AND ROLLING OUT THE DOUGH AND DUSTING THE PEEL

This pita is special for two reasons. First, it's made with 50 percent whole wheat flour. Second, the hydration is split between water and Greek yogurt. Adding a little fat to the dough inhibits the proteins that form gluten from connecting, making a tender dough. These pitas are bigger and softer than the others in this chapter and may need a few additional minutes in the oven to compensate for the added moisture.

Example Time Frame	
9:00 A.M.	MIX DOUGH
12:00 P.M.	MOVE TO FRIDGE
9:00 A.M. (FOLLOWING DAY)	SHAPE, ROLL, AND BAKE

In a large mixing bowl, combine the yogurt, water, olive oil, salt, and yeast. Whisk together quickly to blend. Add the all-purpose flour and whole wheat flour to the bowl. Quickly run your hands under warm running water, then use them to grab and squeeze the flour mixture until it forms a shaggy dough and no dry flour is visible. The dough will be sticky and tear easily. Cover with a lid or shower cap and let rest for 10 minutes.

Fill a small bowl with all-purpose flour and set it near your clean, dry work surface. Turn out the dough onto the work surface. Using the heel of your dominant hand, push the top of the dough away from you, then fold it back on itself and rotate it 90 degrees. Push, fold, and rotate again. Repeat this three-step action four or five times. Sprinkle a little flour on the dough and work surface if necessary, keeping in mind that a little stickiness is useful to build tension. Stop kneading as soon as the dough resists. Return the dough to the bowl and re-cover. Rest for 2 to 3 hours on the countertop at room temperature.

Move the dough to the refrigerator overnight or for up to 24 hours. Bring it to room temperature before continuing with the instructions that follow.

An hour before you plan to bake the pitas, position an oven rack 6 to 8 in [15 to 20 cm] from the top of the oven and set a baking steel or stone on it. Preheat the oven to 550°F [290°C] or as hot as the oven will allow.

Turn out the dough onto a clean, dry work surface and dust lightly with flour. The dough will shape into a ball easier if it is slightly sticky, so be conservative with the flour. Using a bench knife, divide the dough into twelve equal portions. (You can simply eyeball this.)

To shape each portion into a round, hold your dominant hand in a C shape and cuddle a portion of the dough between your palm and the work surface. Move your hand in counterclockwise circles, forcing the dough into a ball by applying pressure with your palm where the dough and the surface meet. Set the round aside, seam-side down, and cover with a damp (non-terry cloth) kitchen towel. Form the remaining portions into rounds, slipping each one under the towel as it is ready.

Next, lightly flour a dough round and flatten it between your palm and the dry, clean work surface. Then continue to flatten the dough with a rolling pin: Roll the dough away from you, then rotate it 90 degrees and roll again. Repeat rolling and rotating the dough until it is an 8 in [20 cm] circle about ¼ in [6 mm] thick. If the dough resists, move back and forth among a few rounds, letting one rest while you work another. As each dough circle is ready, run your hand over it to check for any thick sections that may need an extra stroke with the rolling pin. If the pita isn't thin enough, it will fail to form a pocket in the oven. As the circles are ready, cover again with the kitchen towel.

Line a large bowl with a large (non-terry cloth) kitchen towel, letting the towel drape over the sides. Set it near the stove.

Lightly flour a wooden peel (excess flour will burn) and load it with one or two pitas. Shimmy the peel a few times to make sure the pitas move freely and can easily slide off the peel. If a pita is stuck, quickly lift it with a dough scraper and toss a little flour underneath. **CONT'D**

Open the oven door. Holding the peel at a slight angle, slip the pitas onto the steel in one fluid motion. Bake the pitas until they puff up, 2 to 3 minutes. Once puffed, poke the pocket in each pita with a thin metal skewer or the tip of a thin, sharp knife. Flip the pitas with long metal tongs and continue baking until the bottoms are deeply browned, 2 to 3 minutes longer. Use the tongs to transfer the baked pitas to the towel-lined bowl, then cover the pitas with the overhang of the towel. Bake the remaining pitas the same way, moving them to the bowl as they come out of the oven. If the pitas stop puffing, give the steel a minute or two to reheat between loads.

Pita is at its best as soon as it is cool enough to handle or within a few hours of baking. Store any uneaten pitas in an airtight container at room temperature for up to 24 hours. To reheat, spritz with water, wrap tightly in aluminum foil, and place in a preheated 350°F [180°C] oven until fragrant and warm, 3 to 5 minutes. After 48 hours, use leftover pitas to make **Za'atar Pita Chips (page 325)**.

POCKETLESS PITA

Baker's Percentage	Weight	Volume	Ingredient
100%	439 G	3 CUPS + 2 TBSP	ALL-PURPOSE FLOUR (11% TO 12% PROTEIN)
55%	241 G	1 CUP	WATER, WARM (100°F [38°C])
4%	18 G	1 TBSP	OLIVE OIL (EVOO)
3%	13 G	1 TBSP	GRANULATED SUGAR
2%	9 G	1½ TSP	SALT
0.8%	4 G	1 TSP	INSTANT YEAST
			ALL-PURPOSE FLOUR FOR SHAPING AND ROLLING OUT THE DOUGH
	15 TO 30 G	1 TO 2 TBSP	UNSALTED BUTTER FOR THE PAN (OPTIONAL)

MAKES EIGHT 7 IN [18 CM] PITAS

Also known as Greek pita, pocketless pita is cooked on the stovetop in a hot skillet and folded around fillings or torn and dunked in oil or hummus. The dough is stretchy and forgiving, and even though it bakes up with no pocket, it might be my favorite pita. It's tender, versatile, and great for warmer seasons when you don't want to turn on the oven. Large and fluffy, these pitas are a real treat.

Example Time Frame

9:00 A.M.	MIX DOUGH
12:00 P.M.	SHAPE, ROLL, AND COOK

In a medium mixing bowl, combine the water, olive oil, sugar, salt, and yeast. Whisk together quickly to blend. Add the all-purpose flour to the bowl. Quickly run your hands under warm running water, then use them to grab and squeeze the flour mixture until it forms a shaggy dough and no dry flour is visible. The dough will be sticky and tear easily. Cover with a lid or shower cap and let rest for 10 minutes.

Fill a small bowl with all-purpose flour and set it near your clean, dry work surface. Turn out the dough onto the work surface. Using the heel of your dominant hand, push the top of the dough away from you, then fold it back on itself and rotate it 90 degrees. Push, fold, and rotate again. Repeat this three-step action four or five times. Sprinkle a little flour on the dough and work surface if necessary, keeping in mind that a little stickiness is useful to build tension. Stop kneading as soon as the dough resists. Return the dough to the bowl and re-cover.

For same-day pita, leave the dough on the countertop at room temperature (68° to 72°F [20° to 22°C]) for 2 to 3 hours. I prefer to refrigerate the dough for at least overnight or up to 24 hours. If you decide to refrigerate the dough, bring it to room temperature before continuing with the instructions that follow. **CONT'D**

Turn out the dough onto a clean, dry work surface and dust lightly with flour. The dough will shape into a ball easier if it is slightly sticky, so be conservative with the flour. Using a bench knife, divide the dough into eight equal portions. (You can simply eyeball this.)

To shape into a round, hold your dominant hand in a C shape and cuddle a portion of the dough between your palm and the work surface. Move your hand in counterclockwise circles, forcing the dough into a ball by applying pressure with your palm where the dough and the surface meet. Set the round aside, seam-side down, and cover with a damp (non-terry cloth) kitchen towel. Form the remaining portions into rounds, slipping each one under the towel as it is ready.

Next, lightly flour a dough round and flatten it between your palm and the dry, clean work surface. Then continue to flatten the dough with a rolling pin: Roll the dough away from you, then rotate it 90 degrees and roll again. Repeat rolling and rotating the dough until it is a 7 in [18 cm] circle about ¼ in [6 mm] thick. If the dough resists, move back and forth among a few rounds, letting one rest while you work another. As the circles are ready, cover again with the kitchen towel.

Line a large bowl with a large (non-terry cloth) kitchen towel, letting the towel drape over the sides. Set it near the stove.

Heat a medium nonstick or cast-iron skillet over medium heat, adding the butter, if desired. If using the butter, let it melt before starting to cook. Carefully lay a pita in the center of the hot pan and cook until browned on the underside, 1 to 2 minutes. Use long metal tongs or a spatula to flip the pita and continue to cook until the second side is also golden with darker spots, 2 to 3 minutes longer, keeping an eye on the pita to avoid burning. Use the tongs or spatula to transfer the pita to the towel-lined bowl, then cover the pita with the overhang of the towel. Cook the remaining pitas the same way, giving the pan a minute or two to reheat between loads and moving each pita to the bowl as it comes off the pan.

Pita is at its best as soon as it is cool enough to handle or within a few hours of cooking. Store any uneaten pitas in an airtight container at room temperature for up to 24 hours. To reheat, spritz with water, wrap tightly in aluminum foil, and place in a preheated 350°F [180°C] oven until fragrant and warm, 3 to 5 minutes. After 48 hours, use leftover pitas to make **Za'atar Pita Chips (page 325)**.

BUTTERMILK PITA

Sponge

Baker's Percentage	Weight	Volume	Ingredient
100%	78 G	½ CUP + 1 TBSP	BREAD FLOUR (12% TO 14% PROTEIN)
75%	56 G	¼ CUP	WATER
1%	1.5 G	¼ TSP	INSTANT YEAST

MAKES EIGHT 7 IN [18 CM] PITAS

Dough

Baker's Percentage	Weight	Volume	Ingredient
80%	221 G	1½ CUPS + 1 TBSP	ALL-PURPOSE FLOUR (11% TO 12% PROTEIN)
20%	55 G	½ CUP	SPELT FLOUR
60%	166 G	⅔ CUP	BUTTERMILK, AT ROOM TEMPERATURE
50%	138 G	¾ CUP	SPONGE
3%	20 G	1 TBSP	HONEY, CLOVER OR OTHER LIGHT, MILD TYPE
2%	6 G	1½ TSP	VEGETABLE OIL
2%	6 G	1 TSP	SALT
			ALL-PURPOSE FLOUR FOR SHAPING AND ROLLING OUT THE DOUGH AND DUSTING THE PEEL

Prefermenting flour, even without the culturing that lactic acid bacteria in sourdough performs, is beneficial. A sponge is a yeasted preferment that has less water than flour, and it can be ready in as little as 2 to 3 hours. Sponges start enzymatic activity, which breaks downs proteins and sugars, softening and sweetening the final dough. The addition of buttermilk to this dough gives the pita a tangy flavor, and the spelt flour contributes a toothy tug. If you don't have spelt on hand, you can swap it out for whole wheat flour with no adjustments necessary.

Example Time Frame	
9:00 A.M.	MIX SPONGE
12:00 P.M.	MIX DOUGH
2:00 P.M.	SHAPE, ROLL, AND BAKE

TO MAKE THE SPONGE: In a pint-size deli or similar container, combine the bread flour, water, and yeast. Stir thoroughly with a spoon. The sponge will be sticky and a little stiff. Try to keep most of it in the container and not on the spoon. Cover with a lid and ferment for 3 hours at room temperature (68° to 72°F [20° to 22°C]). It's ready when it has doubled in size, smells yeasty, and is full of bubbles. **CONT'D**

TO MAKE THE DOUGH: In a medium mixing bowl, combine the buttermilk, sponge, honey, vegetable oil, and salt. Whisk together quickly to blend. Add the all-purpose flour and spelt flour to the bowl. Quickly run your hands under warm running water, then use them to grab and squeeze the flour mixture until it forms a shaggy dough and no dry flour is visible. The dough will be sticky and tear easily. Cover with a lid or shower cap and let rest for 10 minutes.

Fill a small bowl with all-purpose flour and set it near your clean, dry work surface. Turn out the dough onto the work surface. Using the heel of your dominant hand, push the top of the dough away from you, then fold it back on itself and rotate it 90 degrees. Push, fold, and rotate again. Repeat this three-step action four or five times. Sprinkle a little flour on the dough and work surface if necessary, keeping in mind that a little stickiness is useful to build tension. Stop kneading as soon as the dough resists. Return the dough to the bowl and re-cover.

For same-day pita, leave the dough on the countertop at room temperature (68° to 72°F [20° to 22°C]) for 2 to 3 hours. I prefer to refrigerate the dough for at least overnight or up to 24 hours. If you decide to refrigerate the dough, bring it to room temperature before continuing with the instructions that follow.

An hour before you plan to bake the pitas, position an oven rack 6 to 8 in [15 to 20 cm] from the top of the oven and set a baking steel or stone on it. Preheat the oven to 550°F [290°C] or as hot as the oven will allow.

Turn out the dough onto a clean, dry work surface and dust lightly with flour. The dough will shape into a ball easier if it is slightly sticky, so be conservative with the flour. Using a bench knife, divide the dough into eight equal portions. (You can simply eyeball this.) **CONT'D**

To shape into a round, hold your dominant hand in a C shape and cuddle a portion of the dough between your palm and the work surface. Move your hand in counterclockwise circles, forcing the dough into a ball by applying pressure with your palm where the dough and the surface meet. Set the round aside, seam-side down, and cover with a damp (non-terry cloth) kitchen towel. Form the remaining portions into rounds, slipping each one under the towel as it is ready.

Next, lightly flour a dough round and flatten it between your palm and the dry, clean work surface. Then continue to flatten the dough with a rolling pin: Roll the dough away from you, then rotate it 90 degrees and roll again. Repeat rolling and rotating the dough until it is a 7 in [18 cm] circle about ¼ in [6 mm] thick. If the dough resists, move back and forth among a few rounds, letting one rest while you work another. As each dough circle is ready, run your hand over it to check for any thick sections that may need an extra stroke with the rolling pin. If the pita isn't thin enough, it will fail to form a pocket in the oven. As the circles are ready, cover again with the kitchen towel.

Line a large bowl with a large (non-terry cloth) kitchen towel, letting the towel drape over the sides. Set it near the stove.

Lightly flour a wooden peel (excess flour will burn) and load it with one or two pitas. Shimmy the peel a few times to make sure the pitas move freely and can easily slide off the peel. If a pita is stuck, quickly lift it with a dough scraper and toss a little flour underneath.

Open the oven door. Holding the peel at a slight angle, slip the pitas onto the steel in one fluid motion. Bake the pitas until they puff up, 1 to 2 minutes. Once puffed, poke the pocket in each pita with a thin metal skewer or the tip of a thin, sharp knife. Flip the pitas with long metal tongs and continue baking until the bottoms are deeply browned, 2 to 3 minutes longer. Use the tongs to transfer the baked pitas to the towel-lined bowl, then cover the pitas with the overhang of the towel. Bake the remaining pitas the same way, moving them to the bowl as they come out of the oven. If the pitas stop puffing, give the steel a minute or two to reheat between loads.

Pita is at its best as soon as it is cool enough to handle or within no more than a few hours of baking. Store any uneaten pitas in an airtight container at room temperature for up to 24 hours. To reheat, spritz with water, wrap tightly in aluminum foil, and place in a preheated 350°F [180°C] oven until fragrant and warm, 3 to 5 minutes. After 48 hours, use leftover pitas to make **Za'atar Pita Chips** **(page 325)**.

WHOLE WHEAT PITA

Levain

Baker's Percentage	Weight	Volume	Ingredient
100%	39 G	⅓ CUP	WHOLE WHEAT OR HIGH-EXTRACTION FLOUR
100%	39 G	2½ TBSP	WATER
100%	39 G	2½ TBSP	SOURDOUGH STARTER

MAKES EIGHT 7 IN [18 CM] PITAS

Dough

Baker's Percentage	Weight	Volume	Ingredient
100%	290 G	2½ CUPS	WHOLE WHEAT OR HIGH-EXTRACTION FLOUR
72%	209 G	¾ CUP + 2 TBSP	WATER, WARM (100°F [38°C])
40%	116 G	⅓ CUP + 2 TBSP	LEVAIN
8%	23 G	1 TBSP	HONEY, CLOVER OR OTHER LIGHT, MILD TYPE
5%	14 G	1 TBSP	VEGETABLE OIL
2%	6 G	1 TSP	SALT
1%	2 G	½ TSP	INSTANT YEAST
			ALL-PURPOSE FLOUR FOR SHAPING AND ROLLING OUT THE DOUGH AND DUSTING THE PEEL

I love the nutty flavor of a whole-grain pita, and when filled with tuna or egg salad, it's a perfect throwback hippie café lunch straight from the 1970s. However, whole-grain flour can be "thirsty," and water needs to be added slowly over time to achieve the right consistency or the pitas risk ending up dry and chalky. Make this recipe with the amount of water called for and then add more as needed to make the dough pliable and soft.

Example Time Frame

8:00 A.M.	MIX LEVAIN
12:00 P.M.	MIX DOUGH
2:00 P.M.	SHAPE, ROLL, AND BAKE

TO MAKE THE LEVAIN: In a pint-size deli or similar container, combine the whole wheat flour, water, and sourdough starter. Stir thoroughly with a spoon. The levain will be loose and sticky. Try to keep most of it in the container and not on the spoon. Cover with a lid and ferment for 4 hours at room temperature (68° to 72°F [20° to 22°C]). It's ready when it has doubled in size, smells like yogurt, and is full of bubbles.

TO MAKE THE DOUGH: In a medium mixing bowl, combine the water, levain, honey, vegetable oil, salt, and yeast. Whisk together quickly to blend. Add the whole wheat flour to the bowl. Quickly run your hands under warm running water, then use them to grab and squeeze the mixture until it forms a shaggy dough and no dry flour is visible. The dough will be sticky and tear easily. Cover with a lid or shower cap and let rest for 10 minutes.

CONT'D

Fill a small bowl with all-purpose flour and set it near your clean, dry work surface. Turn out the dough onto the work surface. Using the heel of your dominant hand, push the top of the dough away from you, then fold it back on itself and rotate it 90 degrees. Push, fold, and rotate again. Repeat this three-step action four or five times. Sprinkle a little flour on the dough and work surface if necessary, keeping in mind that a little stickiness is useful to build tension. Stop kneading as soon as the dough resists. Return the dough to the bowl and re-cover.

For same-day pita, leave the dough on the countertop at room temperature (68° to 72°F [20° to 22°C]) for 2 to 3 hours. I prefer to refrigerate the dough for at least overnight or up to 24 hours. If you decide to refrigerate the dough, bring it to room temperature before continuing with the instructions that follow.

An hour before you plan to bake the pitas, position an oven rack 6 to 8 in [15 to 20 cm] from the top of the oven and set a baking steel or pizza stone on it. Preheat the oven to 550°F [290°C] or as hot as the oven will allow.

Turn out the dough onto a clean, dry work surface and dust lightly with flour. The dough will shape into a ball easier if it is slightly sticky, so be conservative with the flour. Using a bench knife, divide the dough into eight equal portions. (You can simply eyeball this.)

To shape into a round, hold your dominant hand in a C shape and cuddle a portion of the dough between your palm and the work surface. Move your hand in counterclockwise circles, forcing the dough into a ball by applying pressure with your palm where the dough and the surface meet. Set the round aside, seam-side down, and cover with a damp (non-terry cloth) kitchen towel. Form the remaining portions into rounds, slipping each one under the towel as it is ready.

Next, lightly flour a dough round and flatten it between your palm and the dry, clean work surface. Then continue to flatten the dough with a rolling pin: Roll the dough away from you, then rotate it 90 degrees and roll again. Repeat rolling and rotating the dough until it is a 7 in [18 cm] circle about ¼ in [6 mm] thick. If the dough resists, move back and forth among a few rounds, letting one rest while you work another. As each dough circle is ready, run your hand over it to check for any thick sections that may need an extra stroke with the rolling pin. If the pita isn't thin enough or isn't evenly thin, it will fail to form a pocket in the oven. As the circles are ready, cover again with the kitchen towel.

Line a large bowl with a large (non-terry cloth) kitchen towel, letting the towel drape over sides. Set it near the stove.

Lightly flour a wooden peel (excess flour will burn) and load it with one or two pitas. Shimmy the peel a few times to make sure the pitas move freely and can easily slide off the peel. If a pita is stuck, quickly lift it with a dough scraper and toss a little flour underneath.

Open the oven door. Holding the peel at a slight angle, slip the pitas onto the steel in one fluid motion. Bake the pitas until they puff up, 1 to 2 minutes. Once puffed, poke the pocket in each pita with a thin metal skewer or the tip of a thin, sharp knife. Flip the pitas with long metal tongs and continue baking until the bottoms are deeply browned, 2 to 3 minutes longer. Use the tongs to transfer the baked pitas to the towel-lined bowl, then cover the pitas with the overhang of the towel. Bake the remaining pitas the same way, moving them to the bowl as they come out of the oven. If the pitas stop puffing, give the steel a minute or two to reheat between loads.

Pita is at its best as soon as it is cool enough to handle or within a few hours of baking. Store any uneaten pitas in an airtight container at room temperature for up to 24 hours. To reheat, spritz with water, wrap tightly in aluminum foil, and place in a preheated 350°F [180°C] oven until fragrant and warm, 3 to 5 minutes. After 48 hours, use leftover pitas to make **Za'atar Pita Chips (page 325)**.

ZA'ATAR PITA CHIPS

Weight	Volume	Ingredient
8 G	2 TBSP	OREGANO, DRIED
8 G	2 TBSP	SUMAC
8 G	2 TBSP	SESAME SEEDS
4 G	1 TBSP	MARJORAM, DRIED
4 G	1 TBSP	THYME, DRIED
6 G	1 TSP	SEA SALT, FINE
240 G	3 OR 4	PITAS, 1 OR 2 DAYS OLD
42 TO 56 G	3 TO 4 TBSP	OLIVE OIL (EVOO)

MAKES 48 TO 64 CHIPS

Although pita never lasts long in my house, occasionally we have a few rounds that need new life, at which point they are reincarnated as pita chips. Simple and endlessly "riff-able," pita chips are a blank canvas for a sweet or savory adventure. I began making za'atar for bagels and have loved having this Middle Eastern blend of herbs and spices on hand. Tangy, earthy and aromatic, za'atar calls for three herbs: oregano, thyme, and marjoram. The addition of sumac brightens the flavor and sesame seeds give it a nice crunch. It makes for a great savory chip experience and is also delicious on popcorn.

Preheat the oven to 450°F [230°C]. Have ready a large sheet pan.

In a small bowl, combine the oregano, sumac, sesame seeds, marjoram, thyme, and salt and mix thoroughly. This is your za'atar.

Use a serrated knife to cut each pita into two rounds. Using a pastry brush, brush both sides of each round with the olive oil. Use scissors to cut each round into eight triangles, or use your hands to tear the rounds into various-sized pieces. Hold the pieces over a plate (to avoid a big mess) and season with the za'atar. As they are ready, transfer them to the sheet pan, arranging them in a single layer.

Bake the pita triangles for 5 minutes. Remove from the oven and check the browning and texture. If the pitas were on the thin side, the chips may be done now. If the pitas were on the thick side, the chips may require up to an additional 5 minutes of baking to rid them of excess moisture. They should be golden brown and crack easily when broken in half.

Transfer the chips to a (non-terry) cloth-lined basket or bowl and serve immediately. Store any leftover chips in an airtight container at room temperature for up to 48 hours. Leftover za'atar can be stored in an airtight container at room temperature for up to 1 month.

6

FOCACCIA

Focaccia is a flatbread that is anything but flat. Lofty, bubbly, and golden brown, it is made with stronger flour and more water than pizza dough, straddling the line between pizza and bread while bringing out the best of both. Leavened with yeast, a natural starter, or a combination of the two, focaccia dough is lively and joyful to work with. It's adaptable, resilient, and forgiving, all the qualities we look for in a good dough.

Focaccia Practice

How thick you like your focaccia is a combination of personal preference and practical application. I recommend a thinner focaccia for sandwiches and a thick, tall bread for swooping up spreads or olive oil. Each of the following dough recipes yields about 1.1 kg [2½ lb], enough for one large focaccia. For a focaccia that can be cut in half crosswise, I like to use a Lloyd black steel pan measuring 12 by 12 in [30.5 by 30.5 cm] with 1½ in [4 cm] sides. For a thicker focaccia, fun to pull apart into chunks for bread boards and quick lunches, I use a smaller pan, like a Lloyd 8 by 8 in [20 by 20 cm] with 2 in [5 cm] sides or a standard 9 by 13 in [23 by 33 cm] baking pan.

Many of the doughs that follow can be made in a single day or spread out over 2 to 3 days, using the refrigerator to stop and start the process. For sourdough or other naturally leavened doughs, more time in the fridge will mean more built-up acidity in the dough, which results in a nice cultured, tangy taste. No matter what, remember these two simple rules:

1. Don't move the dough from bulk fermentation to the pan until it feels like a pillow.

2. Don't bake the dough until it has risen and feels full of air again.
   Always wait as long as you need—never rush.

Due to the relatively high amount of water in focaccia doughs (the Fridge Focaccia, **page 332**, is 90 percent hydration), I fold the dough more intensively than I fold pizza dough. I use a slightly modified version of Richard Bertinet's slap-and-fold technique, which I described **under Strengthening in the Techniques section (see page 86)**: Smear a little water on your work surface. Using a dough scraper, gather the dough together in the bowl and, with a quick motion, scoop it up with the dough scraper and flip it out onto the damp work surface. Using your hands, lift the dough off the surface, then slap the bottom half down so it sticks a little while still holding the top. Gently lean back, stretching the dough, and then quickly lean forward, tossing the dough still in your hands over the portion stuck to the surface. Repeat slapping, stretching, and folding three or four times. As you work, the dough will become smooth and pull itself into a ball. Using the dough scraper, return the dough to its container, smooth-side up. Cover and proceed according to the recipe.

A black metal pan will absorb and transfer heat efficiently and steadily, baking the bottom evenly and well, which is why I use the two black steel Lloyd pans described previously. I've also made incredible focaccia in a large cast-iron skillet and, on occasion, in a cake pan. If you use a 10 in [25 cm] cake pan, cut a parchment circle the same size as the base of the pan, lay it inside, and oil the parchment and the pan before turning out the dough. It's a luxury to have a fitted plastic lid on your proofing pan. Find one if you can, or wrap the proofing dough tightly in cling film.

Bake the focaccia on a preheated baking steel or pizza stone to get that boost of conductive heat, helping the water turn into steam and lift the dough one last time. If you don't have a steel or a stone, bake the focaccia on a preheated inverted large cast-iron skillet or on a flat cast-iron griddle. Extra thermal mass in your oven is always good when baking!

Focaccia dough is a great place to experiment with different types of flours. Since the dough is proofed and baked in a pan, you can increase the water and swap around flours, choices that are harder when you need the dough to stand up on its own, such as for pizza or a hearth loaf. Try the recipes that call for whole-grain flour, like the **Poolish Focaccia Dough** **(page 337)** and the **20 Percent Rye Focaccia Dough** **(page 344)**. Source some freshly milled flour or mill your own to include in the **High-Extraction Focaccia Dough** **(page 348)**. Once you're comfortable, you can play around, increasing or decreasing freshly milled and whole-grain flours in any of the doughs.

I try not to drown my focaccia in olive oil. In fact, I use less and less of it as the years go by. I prefer using a decent extra-virgin olive oil and just lightly oiling my pan. I find the less-is-more approach to using olive oil a welcome change after so many grease-stained bread bags and expensive oil slicks in pans. The oil does impart flavor and create the bubbly, golden-brown bread we're all excited to taste, but use only as much as you need.

One of the best things about focaccia is all that surface area. It's like a baguette in that regard! However, all that surface also means it can go stale quickly. I cut my focaccia into squares and keep a few in an airtight container at room temperature for up to 5 days and freeze the rest in a resealable plastic bag. To reheat the focaccia, preheat the oven to 350°F [180°C], preferably with a baking steel or pizza stone. Wrap the focaccia tightly in aluminum foil, place it on the steel, stone, or oven rack, and heat until fragrant, warm, and soft, 5 to 8 minutes.

PAR-BAKE FOCACCIA

Follow the recipes up to the point where the toppings are added. Refrain from topping the dough but do bake it on a preheated baking steel or pizza stone at 400°F [200°C] until it begins to color, 10 to 15 minutes. Remove from the oven, let cool in the pan on a wire rack for a few minutes, and then remove the focaccia from the pan to the rack to cool to room temperature. Wrap tightly in cling film and freeze. The night before you want to finish baking, thaw the frozen focaccia in the fridge, then top and finish baking on a preheated steel or stone at 450°F [230°C] for 10 to 15 minutes.

○ **USING YOUR BAKING STEEL OR PIZZA STONE FOR FOCACCIA /** The juxtaposition of a crunchy bottom and an airy, crisp top makes focaccia irresistible. To achieve this, I start by baking my focaccia on a preheated baking steel or pizza stone and then finish it off on the oven rack under the baking steel. Starting on the hot steel gives the dough an upward boost, then once the crust is set, moving it below the steel directs radiant heat to the surface, with the steel acting as a sort of low-key broiler, finishing off the bake for a nicely set, always springy but never gummy bite.

FRIDGE FOCACCIA DOUGH

Baker's Percentage	Weight	Volume	Ingredient
50%	284 G	2 CUPS	BREAD FLOUR (12% TO 14% PROTEIN)
50%	284 G	2 CUPS	ALL-PURPOSE FLOUR (11% TO 12% PROTEIN)
90%	512 G	2 CUPS + 2 TBSP	WATER, WARM
2%	12 G	2 TSP	SALT
1.2%	7 G	1¾ TSP	INSTANT YEAST

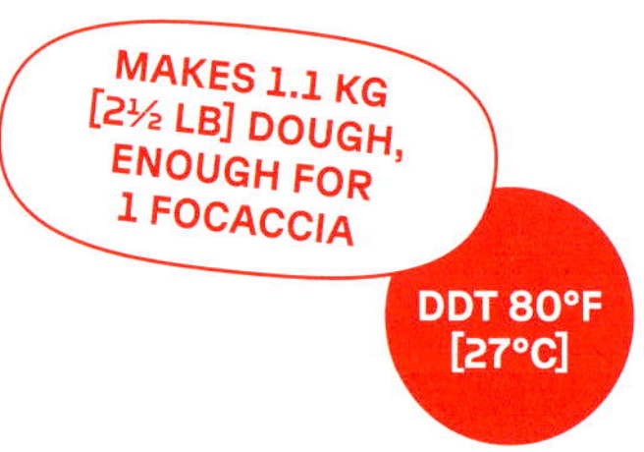

This focaccia dough is as easy as it gets. It is left in the fridge overnight to rise slowly before it's baked into the golden-brown bread pillow we all know and love. Throw it together on a weekday morning and have it for dinner the next day, saving leftovers for cutting into snacks for the rest of the week. Bread flour creates a pleasing chewy texture and helps keep the dough strong in the fridge, but if you have only all-purpose flour, you can swap it in for the full amount.

Example Time Frame	
9:00 A.M.	MIX DOUGH AND MOVE TO FRIDGE
10:00 A.M.	FOLD
3:00 P.M.	FOLD
8:00 P.M.	FOLD

Ready a restaurant-style wide-mouthed water pitcher half full of warm water. **To get the precise temperature, use the chart on page 82**, or just use 80°F [27°C]. You'll use water from this pitcher for mixing the dough and later for wetting your fingers when folding.

In a large mixing bowl, combine the bread flour, all-purpose flour, water, salt, and yeast. Whisk together to blend. Quickly run your hands under warm running water, then use them to grab and squeeze the flour mixture into a cohesive yet shaggy dough with no visible streaks of dry flour. The dough will be loose and sticky, almost like a batter—this is normal. Use a dough scraper to clean off your hands and the inside of the bowl, pressing any extra bits of dough back into the shaggy ball. Cover with a lid or shower cap and immediately transfer to the refrigerator.

The dough is now bulk fermenting, and it will stay in the fridge, coming out for three folds, for up to 24 hours before being proofed in a pan at room temperature.

An hour later, bring out the dough and remove the cover. It will be puffy, almost doubled in size, and covered in tiny holes and dimples. Don't be alarmed—this is OK.

To fold the dough, dip your fingers into the water in the pitcher and smear a little water on your work surface. Using the dough scraper, gather the dough together in the bowl and, with a quick motion, scoop it up with the dough scraper and flip it out onto the damp work surface. Using your hands, lift the dough off the surface, then, while still holding the top, slap the bottom half down so it sticks a little. Gently lean back, stretching the dough, and then quickly lean forward, tossing the dough still in your hands over the portion stuck to the work surface. Repeat slapping, stretching, and folding three or four times. The dough is ready when it is smooth and pulls itself into a ball. Using the dough scraper, return the dough to its container, smooth-side up. Cover and return to the fridge.

Repeat the fold in 5 hours and then repeat it again 5 hours after that. The dough won't look as puffy when you return to as it did on the first fold, but you may see some big bubbles, and it should still be light and airy. For panning, proofing, topping, and baking instructions, **see any of the focaccia recipes starting on page 356**.

SAME-DAY FOCACCIA DOUGH

Baker's Percentage	Weight	Volume	Ingredient
100%	604 G	4¼ CUPS + 1 TBSP	BREAD FLOUR (12% TO 14% PROTEIN)
80%	483 G	2 CUPS	WATER, WARM
2%	12 G	2 TSP	SALT
0.8%	4 G	1 TSP	INSTANT YEAST

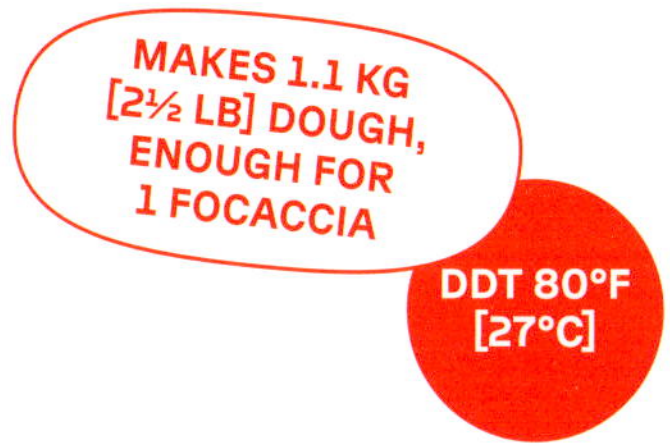

This fluffy and forgiving dough is a cinch to pull together and can be mixed, proofed, and baked all in one day. With no preferment or refrigeration involved, it's an excellent dough to make when you wake up on Saturday morning and want fresh bread for dinner. To encourage efficient fermentation and a lofty rise, use warm water and keep the dough around 80°F [27°C] the entire time.

Example Time Frame

9:00 A.M.	MIX DOUGH
9:45 A.M.	FOLD

Ready a restaurant-style wide-mouthed water pitcher half full of warm water. **To get the precise temperature, use the chart on page 82**, or just use 80°F [27°C]. You'll use water from this pitcher for mixing the dough and later for wetting your fingers when folding.

In a large mixing bowl, combine the bread flour and yeast. Quickly stir with a dry hand to blend and aerate, then add the water. Next, using your dominant hand in the shape of a claw, agitate the flour and water into a dough. You can use your free hand to stabilize the bowl. Once a rough, sticky dough has formed, grab and squeeze it several times to bring it into a cohesive, shaggy mass. Cover with a lid or shower cap and let rest for 10 minutes.

Return to the bowl and sprinkle the salt over the dough. With your hands in the shape of crab claws, pinch in the salt. You'll feel the dough tighten. Stop once you have felt the salt dissolve. Cover and let rest for 30 minutes.

The dough has now entered bulk fermentation, or the first rise, and will be given a single fold before being moved to a pan for proofing. Keep the dough warm, around 80°F [27°C], and away from any drafts. **CONT'D**

To fold the dough, dip your fingers into the water in the pitcher and smear a little water on your work surface. Using the dough scraper, gather the dough together in the bowl and, with a quick motion, scoop it up with the dough scraper and flip it out onto the damp work surface. Using your hands, lift the dough off the surface, then, while still holding the top, slap the bottom half down so it sticks a little. Gently lean back, stretching the dough, and then quickly lean forward, tossing the dough still in your hands over the portion stuck to the work surface. Repeat slapping, stretching, and folding three or four times. The dough is ready when it is smooth and pulls itself into a ball. Using the dough scraper, return the dough to its container, smooth-side up. Cover and let rest for 2 to 3 hours.

The dough has finished bulk fermentation when it is pillowy, has risen about 40 percent in the bowl, and feels full of air when gently pressed. If the dough needs a little more time, give it an extra 30 minutes. You may now move on to panning, proofing, topping, and baking. **For instructions, see any of the focaccia recipes starting on page 356.**

POOLISH FOCACCIA DOUGH

Poolish

Baker's Percentage	Weight	Volume	Ingredient
100%	101 G	⅔ CUP	BREAD FLOUR (12% TO 14% PROTEIN)
100%	101 G	¼ CUP + 2½ TBSP	WATER
1%	1.5 G	¼ TSP	INSTANT YEAST

Dough

Baker's Percentage	Weight	Volume	Ingredient
80%	362 G	2½ CUPS + 1 TBSP	BREAD FLOUR (12% TO 14% PROTEIN)
20%	90 G	¾ CUP + 2 TSP	WHOLE WHEAT FLOUR
88%	398 G	1½ CUPS + 2 TBSP	WATER, WARM
45%	203 G	¾ CUP	POOLISH
8%	36 G	2½ TBSP	OLIVE OIL (EVOO)
2%	9 G	1½ TSP	SALT
0.5%	2 G	½ TSP	INSTANT YEAST

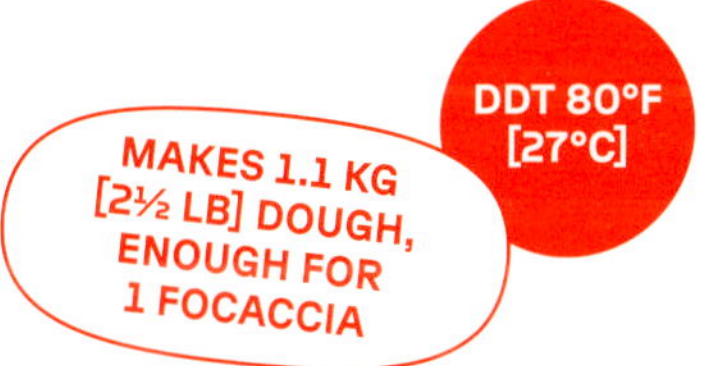

A poolish is a yeasted preferment that rises slowly over 10 to 12 hours at room temperature. Made from equal parts flour and water, it's easy to mix and bubbles away pleasingly. During the overnight fermentation, the stretchy proteins start to break down thanks to the enzyme protease, and the complex sugars are freed up into simple sugars from the work of the enzyme amylase. The final dough is soft, silky, and naturally sweet.

TO MAKE THE POOLISH: In a pint-size deli or similar container, combine the bread flour, water, and yeast. Stir thoroughly with a spoon. The poolish will be loose and sticky. Try to keep most of it in the container and not on the spoon. Cover with a lid and ferment for 10 to 12 hours at room temperature (68° to 72°F [20° to 22°C]). It's ready to use when it has doubled in size, smells yeasty, and is full of bubbles.

TO MAKE THE DOUGH: Ready a restaurant-style wide-mouthed water pitcher half full of warm water. **To get the precise temperature, use the chart on page 82**, or just use 80°F [27°C]. You'll use water from this pitcher for mixing the dough and later for wetting your fingers when folding. **CONT'D**

Example Time Frame

8:00 P.M. (PREVIOUS NIGHT)	MIX POOLISH
8:00 A.M.	MIX DOUGH
8:45 A.M.	FOLD
9:45 A.M.	FOLD

In a large mixing bowl, combine the bread flour, whole wheat flour, and yeast. Quickly stir with a dry hand to blend and aerate, then add the poolish, olive oil, and water. Next, using your dominant hand in the shape of a claw, agitate the flour and water into a dough. You can use your free hand to stabilize the bowl. Once a rough, sticky dough has formed, grab and squeeze it several times to bring it into a cohesive, shaggy mass. Cover with a lid or shower cap and let rest for 10 minutes.

Return to the bowl and sprinkle the salt over the dough. With your hands in the shape of crab claws, pinch in the salt. You'll feel the dough tighten. Stop once you have felt the salt dissolve. Cover and let rest for 30 minutes.

The dough has now entered bulk fermentation, or the first rise, and will be given two folds spaced 1 hour apart. Keep the dough warm, around 80°F [27°C], and away from any drafts.

To fold the dough, dip your fingers into the water in the pitcher and smear a little water on your work surface. Using the dough scraper, gather the dough together in the bowl and, with a quick motion, scoop it up with the dough scraper and flip it out onto the damp work surface. Using your hands, lift the dough off the surface, then, while still holding the top, slap the bottom half down so it sticks a little. Gently lean back, stretching the dough, and then quickly lean forward, tossing the dough still in your hands over the portion stuck to the work surface. Repeat slapping, stretching, and folding three or four times. The dough is ready when it is smooth and pulls itself into a ball. Using the dough scraper, return the dough to its container, smooth-side up. Cover and let rest for 1 hour.

Fold again, repeating the above steps, then cover and let rest for 1 hour.

The dough has finished bulk fermentation when it is pillowy, has risen about 40 percent in the bowl, and feels full of air when gently pressed. If the dough needs a little more time, give it an extra 30 minutes. You may now move on to panning, proofing, topping, and baking. **For instructions, see any of the focaccia recipes starting on page 356.** Or to develop more flavor and a nice rise before continuing, chill it in the fridge for up to 24 hours.

CHEESY FOCACCIA DOUGH

3-Hour Sponge

Baker's Percentage	Weight	Volume	Ingredient
100%	110 G	¾ CUP	BREAD FLOUR (12% TO 14% PROTEIN)
75%	82 G	⅓ CUP	WATER
1%	1.5 G	¼ TSP	INSTANT YEAST

MAKES 1.1 KG [2½ LB] DOUGH, ENOUGH FOR 1 FOCACCIA

DDT 80°F [27°C]

Dough

Baker's Percentage	Weight	Volume	Ingredient
50%	195 G	1⅓ CUPS + 1 TBSP	BREAD FLOUR (12% TO 14% PROTEIN)
50%	195 G	1⅓ CUPS + 1 TBSP	ALL-PURPOSE FLOUR (11% TO 12% PROTEIN)
90%	350 G	1⅓ CUPS + 2 TBSP	WATER, WARM
50%	194 G	1 CUP	SPONGE
20%	78 G	2¾ OZ	CHEDDAR, CUBED
20%	78 G	2¾ OZ	MOZZARELLA, LOW-MOISTURE, SHREDDED
2%	8 G	1½ TSP	SALT
1%	4 G	1 TSP	INSTANT YEAST

What's better than cheese *on* focaccia? Cheese *in* focaccia. The salty, buttery accent of the cheese under the dimpled pockets of olive oil–rich dough makes this bread into a meal all on its own. The recipe calls for mozzarella and Cheddar, but you could try provolone, feta, or Gruyère for a decadent bite. The sponge is a large portion of the dough, and this much prefermented flour contributes a silky crumb texture, a slightly sweeter taste, and a speedy rise.

Example Time Frame	
9:00 A.M.	MIX SPONGE
12:00 P.M.	MIX DOUGH
12:45 P.M.	FOLD
1:45 P.M.	FOLD

TO MAKE THE SPONGE: In a pint-size deli or similar container, combine the bread flour, water, and yeast. Stir thoroughly with a spoon. The sponge will be sticky and stiff. Try to keep most of it in the container and not on the spoon. Cover with a lid and rest for 3 hours at room temperature (68° to 72°F [20° to 22°C]). It's ready when it has doubled in size, smells yeasty, and is full of bubbles.

TO MAKE THE DOUGH: Ready a restaurant-style wide-mouthed water pitcher half full of warm water. **To get the precise temperature, use the chart on page 82**, or just use 80°F [27°C]. You'll use water from this pitcher for mixing the dough and later for wetting your fingers when folding. **CONT'D**

In a large mixing bowl, combine the bread flour, all-purpose flour, and yeast. Quickly stir with a dry hand to blend and aerate, then add the sponge and water. Next, using your dominant hand in the shape of a claw, agitate the flour and water into a dough. You can use your free hand to stabilize the bowl. Once a rough, sticky dough has formed, grab and squeeze it several times to bring it into a cohesive, shaggy mass. Cover with a lid or shower cap and let rest for 10 minutes.

Return to the bowl and sprinkle the Cheddar, mozzarella, and salt over the dough. With your hands in the shape of crab claws, pinch in the cheese and salt. You'll feel the dough tighten. Stop once you have felt the salt dissolve. Cover and let rest for 30 minutes.

The dough has now entered bulk fermentation, or the first rise, and will be given two folds spaced 1 hour apart. Keep the dough warm, around 80°F [27°C], and away from any drafts.

To fold the dough, dip your fingers into the water in the pitcher and smear a little water on your work surface. Using the dough scraper, gather the dough together in the bowl and, with a quick motion, scoop it up with the dough scraper and flip it out onto the damp work surface. Using your hands, lift the dough off the surface, then, while still holding the top, slap the bottom half down so it sticks a little. Gently lean back, stretching the dough, and then quickly lean forward, tossing the dough still in your hands over the portion stuck to the work surface. Repeat slapping, stretching, and folding three or four times. The dough is ready when it is smooth and pulls itself into a ball. Using the dough scraper, return the dough to its container, smooth-side up. Cover and let rest for 1 hour.

Fold again, repeating the above steps, then cover and let rest for 1 hour.

The dough has finished bulk fermentation when it is pillowy, has risen about 40 percent in the bowl, and feels full of air when gently pressed. If the dough needs additional time, give it an extra 30 minutes. You may now move on to panning, proofing, topping, and baking. **For instructions, see any of the focaccia recipes starting on page 356.** Or to develop more flavor and a nice rise before continuing, chill it in the fridge for up to 24 hours.

LEVAIN AND SPONGE FOCACCIA DOUGH

Levain

Baker's Percentage	Weight	Volume	Ingredient
100%	72 G	½ CUP	BREAD FLOUR (12% TO 14% PROTEIN)
100%	72 G	⅓ CUP	WATER
10%	15 G	1 TBSP	SOURDOUGH STARTER

Sponge

Baker's Percentage	Weight	Volume	Ingredient
100%	83 G	½ CUP + 1 TBSP	BREAD FLOUR (12% TO 14% PROTEIN)
80%	66 G	¼ CUP	WATER
1%	1.5 G	¼ TSP	INSTANT YEAST

Dough

Baker's Percentage	Weight	Volume	Ingredient
60%	226 G	1½ CUPS + 2 TBSP	BREAD FLOUR (12% TO 14% PROTEIN)
20%	75 G	½ CUP	ALL-PURPOSE FLOUR (11% TO 12% PROTEIN)
20%	75 G	½ CUP + 3 TBSP	WHOLE WHEAT FLOUR
75%	282 G	1 CUP + 3 TBSP	WATER, WARM
40%	151 G	½ CUP + 2 TBSP	LEVAIN
40%	151 G	½ CUP + 2 TBSP	SPONGE
3%	12 G	2¼ TSP	OLIVE OIL (EVOO)
2%	8 G	1½ TSP	SALT

DDT 80°F [27°C]

MAKES 1.1 KG [2½ LB] DOUGH, ENOUGH FOR 1 FOCACCIA

Example Time Frame	
9:00 P.M. (PREVIOUS NIGHT)	MIX LEVAIN
6:00 A.M.	MIX SPONGE
9:00 A.M.	MIX DOUGH
9:45 A.M.	FOLD
10:45 A.M.	FOLD

This dough is risen and flavored by the combination of an overnight levain and a 3-hour yeasted sponge. These two preferments work in tandem to leaven the dough, creating big, bouncy surface bubbles—a key visual of a well-made focaccia. The blend of bread, all-purpose, and whole wheat flours yields a soft dough with a sweet, nutty flavor that bakes up into a crisp crust. If you have access to freshly milled stone-ground whole wheat flour, use it. If you don't, supermarket whole wheat flour works well too. **CONT'D**

TO MAKE THE LEVAIN: In a pint-size deli or similar container, combine the bread flour, water, and sourdough starter. Stir thoroughly with a spoon. The levain will be sticky and stiff. Try to keep most of it in the container and not on the spoon. Cover with a lid and let ferment for 12 hours at room temperature (68° to 72°F [20° to 22°C]). It's ready to use when it has doubled in size, smells like yogurt, and is full of bubbles.

TO MAKE THE SPONGE: In a pint-size deli or similar container, combine the bread flour, water, and yeast. Stir thoroughly with a spoon. The sponge will be sticky and a little stiff. Try to keep most of it in the container and not on the spoon. Cover with a lid and ferment for 3 hours at room temperature (68° to 72°F [20° to 22°C]). It's ready to use when it has doubled in size and is pillowy.

TO MAKE THE DOUGH: Ready a restaurant-style wide-mouthed water pitcher half full of warm water. **To get the precise temperature, use the chart on page 82**, or just use 80°F [27°C]. You'll use water from this pitcher for mixing the dough and later for wetting your fingers when folding.

In a large mixing bowl, combine the bread flour, all-purpose flour, and whole wheat flour. Quickly stir with a dry hand to blend and aerate, then add the levain, sponge, water, and olive oil. Next, using your dominant hand in the shape of a claw, agitate the flour and water into a dough. You can use your free hand to stabilize the bowl. Once a rough, sticky dough has formed, grab and squeeze it several times to bring it into a cohesive, shaggy mass. Cover with a lid or shower cap and let rest for 10 minutes.

Return to the bowl and sprinkle the salt over the dough. With your hands in the shape of crab claws, pinch in the salt. You'll feel the dough tighten. Stop once you have felt the salt dissolve. Cover and let rest for 30 minutes.

The dough has now entered bulk fermentation, or the first rise, and will be given two folds spaced 1 hour apart. Keep the dough warm, around 80°F [27°C], and away from any drafts.

To fold the dough, dip your fingers into the water in the pitcher and smear a little water on your work surface. Using the dough scraper, gather the dough together in the bowl and, with a quick motion, scoop it up with the dough scraper and flip it out onto the damp work surface. Using your hands, lift the dough off the surface, then, while still holding the top, slap the bottom half down so it sticks a little. Gently lean back, stretching the dough, and then quickly lean forward, tossing the dough still in your hands over the portion stuck to the work surface. Repeat slapping, stretching, and folding three or four times. The dough is ready when it is smooth and pulls itself into a ball. Using the dough scraper, return the dough to its container, smooth-side up. Cover and let rest for 1 hour.

Fold again, repeating the above steps, then cover and let rest for 1 hour.

The dough has finished bulk fermentation when it is pillowy, has risen about 40 percent in the bowl, and feels full of air when gently pressed. If the dough needs a little more time, give it an extra 30 minutes. You may now move on to panning, proofing, topping, and baking. **For instructions, see any of the focaccia recipes starting on page 356.** Or to develop more flavor and a nice rise before continuing, chill it in the fridge for up to 24 hours.

20 PERCENT RYE FOCACCIA DOUGH

Levain

Baker's Percentage	Weight	Volume	Ingredient
100%	88 G	½ CUP + 2 TBSP	BREAD FLOUR (12% TO 14% PROTEIN)
80%	70 G	¼ CUP + 1 TBSP	WATER
10%	9 G	1¾ TSP	SOURDOUGH STARTER

Dough

Baker's Percentage	Weight	Volume	Ingredient
80%	384 G	2⅔ CUPS + 1 TBSP	BREAD FLOUR (12% TO 14% PROTEIN)
20%	96 G	¾ CUP + 2 TBSP	RYE FLOUR
92%	442 G	1¾ CUPS + 1 TBSP	WATER, WARM
35%	168 G	⅔ CUP	LEVAIN
2%	10 G	1½ TSP	SALT
0.5%	2 G	½ TSP	INSTANT YEAST

MAKES 1.1 KG [2½ LB] DOUGH, ENOUGH FOR 1 FOCACCIA

DDT 80°F [27°C]

Rye flour adds incredible flavor to breads and pastries, and breads made with 100 percent rye flour are a delight. But rye doesn't show up often in the world of pizza and focaccia. That's a shame, because the depth of flavor is unparalleled, and once you start tasting it regularly, other doughs will seem uninteresting. Beyond 20 percent rye flour, the volume and bubbles associated with focaccia suffer, so I find 20 percent a happy medium for impact, workability, and flavor. At the supermarket, you'll likely encounter dark rye or simply rye flour. Both will work, as will light rye flour, with the dark rye yielding a slightly denser and more robust result and the light rye a milder and more tender one.

TO MAKE THE LEVAIN: In a pint-size deli or similar container, combine the bread flour, water, and sourdough starter. Stir thoroughly with a spoon. The levain will be sticky and stiff. Try to keep most of it in the container and not on the spoon. Cover with a lid and ferment for 12 hours at room temperature (68° to 72°F [20° to 22°C]). It's ready to use when it has doubled in size, smells like yogurt, and is full of bubbles.

TO MAKE THE DOUGH: Ready a restaurant-style wide-mouthed water pitcher half full of warm water. **To get the precise temperature, use the chart on page 82**, or just use 80°F [27°C]. You'll use water from this pitcher for mixing the dough and later for wetting your fingers when folding.

In a large mixing bowl, combine the bread flour, rye flour, and yeast. Quickly stir with a dry hand to blend and aerate, then add the water and levain. Next, using your dominant hand in the shape of a claw, agitate the flour and water into a dough. You can use your free hand to

Example Time Frame

9:00 P.M. (PREVIOUS NIGHT)	MIX LEVAIN
9:00 A.M.	MIX DOUGH
9:45 A.M.	FOLD
10:45 A.M.	FOLD

stabilize the bowl. Once a rough, sticky dough has formed, grab and squeeze it several times to bring it into a cohesive, shaggy mass. Cover with a lid or shower cap and let rest for 10 minutes.

Return to the bowl and sprinkle the salt over the dough. With your hands in the shape of crab claws, pinch in the salt. You'll feel the dough tighten. Stop once you have felt the salt dissolve. Cover and let rest for 30 minutes.

The dough has now entered bulk fermentation, or the first rise, and will be given two folds spaced 1 hour apart. Keep the dough warm, around 80°F [27°C], and away from any drafts.

To fold the dough, dip your fingers into the water in the pitcher and smear a little water on your work surface. Using the dough scraper, gather the dough together in the bowl and, with a quick motion, scoop it up with the dough scraper and flip it out onto the damp work surface. Using your hands, lift the dough off the surface, then, while still holding the top, slap the bottom half down so it sticks a little. Gently lean back, stretching the dough, and then quickly lean forward, tossing the dough still in your hands over the portion stuck to the work surface. Repeat slapping, stretching, and folding three or four times. The dough is ready when it is smooth and pulls itself into a ball. Using the dough scraper, return the dough to its container, smooth-side up. Cover and let rest for 1 hour.

Fold again, repeating the above steps, then cover and let rest for 1 hour.

The dough has finished bulk fermentation when it is pillowy, has risen about 40 percent in the bowl, and feels full of air when gently pressed. If the dough needs a little more time, give it an extra 30 minutes. You may now move on to panning, proofing, topping, and baking. **For instructions, see any of the focaccia recipes starting on page 356.** Or to develop more flavor and a nice rise before continuing, chill it in the fridge for up to 24 hours.

NATURALLY LEAVENED FOCACCIA DOUGH

Levain

Baker's Percentage	Weight	Volume	Ingredient
100%	50 G	⅓ CUP	BREAD FLOUR (12% TO 14% PROTEIN)
90%	45 G	3 TBSP	WATER
10%	5 G	1 TSP	SOURDOUGH STARTER

Dough

Baker's Percentage	Weight	Volume	Ingredient
50%	250 G	1¾ CUPS	BREAD FLOUR (12% TO 14% PROTEIN)
50%	250 G	1¾ CUPS	ALL-PURPOSE FLOUR (11% TO 12% PROTEIN)
95%	475 G	1¾ CUPS + 3 TBSP	WATER, WARM
20%	100 G	⅓ CUP + 1 TBSP	LEVAIN
3%	15 G	1 TBSP	OLIVE OIL (EVOO)
2%	10 G	1½ TSP	SALT

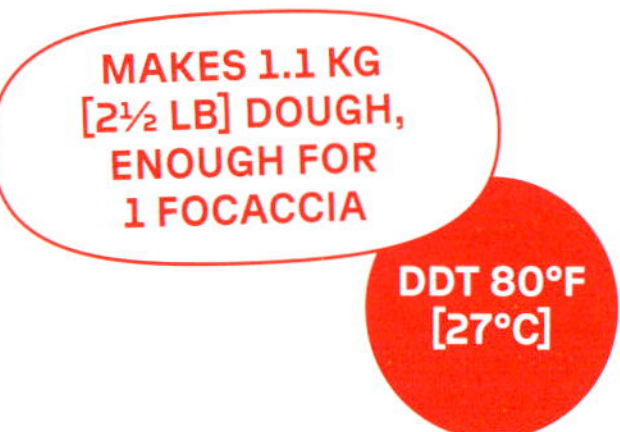

Cultured and slightly fruity, thanks to the levain and olive oil, this focaccia has a pleasant, tuggy chew and a creamy, custard-like crumb. This dough calls for an overnight levain that includes sourdough starter, so you'll need to plan ahead. Once the levain is added to the dough, the dough is given two folds before it is proofed and baked or it is chilled in the fridge for up to 24 hours. Time in the fridge will build up flavor and strength, making a beautifully bubbly dough with a fresh, light taste.

TO MAKE THE LEVAIN: In a pint-size deli or similar container, combine the bread flour, water, and sourdough starter. Stir thoroughly with a spoon. The levain will be sticky and stiff. Try to keep most of it in the container and not on the spoon. Cover with a lid and ferment for 12 hours at room temperature (68° to 72°F [20° to 22°C]). It's ready to use when it has doubled in size, smells like yogurt, and is full of bubbles.

TO MAKE THE DOUGH: Ready a restaurant-style wide-mouthed water pitcher half full of warm water. **To get the precise temperature, use the chart on page 82**, or just use 80°F [27°C]. You'll use water from this pitcher for mixing the dough and later for wetting your fingers when folding.

In a large mixing bowl, combine the bread flour and all-purpose flour. Quickly stir with a dry hand to blend and aerate, then add the water, levain, and olive oil. Next, using your dominant hand in the shape of a claw, agitate the flour and water into a dough. You can use your free

Example Time Frame	
9:00 P.M. (PREVIOUS NIGHT)	MIX LEVAIN
9:00 A.M.	MIX DOUGH
9:45 A.M.	FOLD
10:45 A.M.	FOLD

hand to stabilize the bowl. Once a rough, sticky dough has formed, grab and squeeze it several times to bring it into a cohesive, shaggy mass. Cover with a lid or shower cap and let rest for 10 minutes.

Return to the bowl and sprinkle the salt over the dough. With your hands in the shape of crab claws, pinch in the salt. You'll feel the dough tighten. Stop once you have felt the salt dissolve. Cover and let rest for 30 minutes.

The dough has now entered bulk fermentation, or the first rise, and will be given two folds spaced 1 hour apart. Keep the dough warm, around 80°F [27°C], and away from any drafts.

To fold the dough, dip your fingers into the water in the pitcher and smear a little water on your work surface. Using the dough scraper, gather the dough together in the bowl and, with a quick motion, scoop it up with the dough scraper and flip it out onto the damp work surface. Using your hands, lift the dough off the surface, then, while still holding the top, slap the bottom half down so it sticks a little. Gently lean back, stretching the dough, and then quickly lean forward, tossing the dough still in your hands over the portion stuck to the work surface. Repeat slapping, stretching, and folding three or four times. The dough is ready when it is smooth and pulls itself into a ball. Using the dough scraper, return the dough to its container, smooth-side up. Cover and let rest for 1 hour.

Fold again, repeating the above steps, then cover and let rest for 1 hour.

The dough has finished bulk fermentation when it is pillowy, has risen about 40 percent in the bowl, and feels full of air when gently pressed. If the dough needs a little more time, give it an extra 30 minutes. You may now move on to panning, proofing, topping, and baking. **For instructions, see any of the focaccia recipes starting on page 356.** Or to develop more flavor and a nice rise before continuing, chill it in the fridge for up to 24 hours.

HIGH-EXTRACTION FOCACCIA DOUGH

Levain 1

Baker's Percentage	Weight	Volume	Ingredient
100%	66 G	½ CUP + 1 TBSP	HIGH-EXTRACTION OR SIFTED FLOUR (11% TO 12% PROTEIN)
60%	40 G	3 TBSP	WATER
10%	7 G	1½ TSP	SOURDOUGH STARTER

Levain 2

Baker's Percentage	Weight	Volume	Ingredient
100%	112 G	1 CUP	HIGH-EXTRACTION OR SIFTED FLOUR (11% TO 12% PROTEIN)
100%	112 G	⅓ CUP + 2 TBSP	WATER
100%	112 G	⅓ CUP + 2 TBSP	LEVAIN 1

MAKES 1.1 KG [2½ LB] DOUGH, ENOUGH FOR 1 FOCACCIA

DDT 80°F [27°C]

Dough

Baker's Percentage	Weight	Volume	Ingredient
100%	478 G	4 CUPS + 2 TBSP	HIGH-EXTRACTION OR SIFTED FLOUR (11% TO 12% PROTEIN)
70%	335 G	1⅓ CUPS + 1 TBSP	LEVAIN 2
55%	262 G	1 CUP + 1½ TBSP	WATER, WARM
3%	14 G	1 TBSP	OLIVE OIL (EVOO)
2%	10 G	1¾ TSP	SALT

Freshly milled stone-ground flour is a living ingredient, with the perishable germ still intact and portions of the bran present even when sifted. I prefer to use high-extraction flour when sourcing from a stone mill. This means that most—though not 100 percent—of the wheat berry is still present, with only the roughest, largest bran flakes screened out. Building the dough in two stages curbs unwanted acidity and makes a mild focaccia that elevates the flavor of the flour.

TO MAKE THE LEVAIN 1: In a pint-size deli or similar container, combine the high-extraction flour, water, and sourdough starter. Stir thoroughly with a spoon. The levain will be sticky and stiff. Try to keep most of it in the container and not on the spoon. Cover with a lid and ferment for 12 hours at room temperature (68° to 72°F [20° to 22°C]). It's ready to use when it has doubled in size, smells like yogurt, and is full of bubbles.

TO MAKE THE LEVAIN 2: In a medium mixing bowl, combine the high-extraction flour, water, and the first levain. Mix thoroughly with a spoon until no dry flour is visible. Cover with a shower cap or lid and ferment for 2 hours at room temperature (68° to 72°F [20° to

Example Time Frame	
11:00 P.M. (PREVIOUS NIGHT)	MIX LEVAIN 1
7:00 A.M.	MIX LEVAIN 2
9:00 A.M.	MIX DOUGH
9:45 A.M.	FOLD
10:45 A.M.	FOLD

22°C]). It's ready to use when it has almost doubled in size and has plenty of surface bubbles. If it is going slowly, give it more time.

TO MAKE THE DOUGH: Ready a restaurant-style wide-mouthed water pitcher half full of warm water. **To get the precise temperature, use the chart on page 82**, or just use 80°F [27°C]. You'll use water from this pitcher for mixing the dough and later for wetting your fingers when folding.

In a large mixing bowl, weigh the high-extraction flour. Quickly stir with a dry hand to aerate, then add the water, levain 2, and olive oil. Next, using your dominant hand in the shape of a claw, agitate the flour and water into a dough. You can use your free hand to stabilize the bowl. Once a rough, sticky dough has formed, grab and squeeze it several times to bring it into a cohesive, shaggy mass. Cover with a lid or shower cap and let rest for 10 minutes.

Return to the bowl and sprinkle the salt over the dough. With your hands in the shape of crab claws, pinch in the salt. You'll feel the dough tighten. Stop once you have felt the salt dissolve. Cover and let rest for 30 minutes.

The dough has now entered bulk fermentation, or the first rise, and will be given two folds spaced 1 hour apart. Keep the dough warm, around 80°F [27°C], and away from any drafts. **CONT'D**

To fold the dough, dip your fingers into the water in the pitcher and smear a little water on your work surface. Using the dough scraper, gather the dough together in the bowl and, with a quick motion, scoop it up with the dough scraper and flip it out onto the damp work surface. Using your hands, lift the dough off the surface, then, while still holding the top, slap the bottom half down so it sticks a little. Gently lean back, stretching the dough, and then quickly lean forward, tossing the dough still in your hands over the portion stuck to the work surface. Repeat slapping, stretching, and folding three or four times. The dough is ready when it is smooth and pulls itself into a ball. Using the dough scraper, return the dough to its container, smooth-side up. Cover and let rest for 1 hour.

Fold again, repeating the above steps, then cover and let rest for 1 hour.

The dough has finished bulk fermentation when it is pillowy, has risen about 40 percent in the bowl, and feels full of air when gently pressed. If the dough needs a little more time, give it an extra 30 minutes. You may now move on to panning, proofing, topping, and baking. **For instructions, see any of the focaccia recipes starting on page 356.** Or to develop more flavor and a nice rise before continuing, chill it in the fridge for up to 24 hours.

GRITS FOCACCIA DOUGH

Levain

Baker's Percentage	Weight	Volume	Ingredient
100%	55 G	⅓ CUP + 1 TBSP	BREAD FLOUR (12% TO 14% PROTEIN)
80%	44 G	3 TBSP	WATER
10%	6 G	1¼ TSP	SOURDOUGH STARTER

Dough

Baker's Percentage	Weight	Volume	Ingredient
100%	426 G	3 CUPS	BREAD FLOUR (12% TO 14% PROTEIN)
80%	340 G	1⅓ CUPS + 1 TBSP	WATER, WARM
50%	213 G	1 CUP	GRITS, YELLOW OR RED, COOKED AND COOLED
25%	106 G	⅓ CUP + 2 TBSP	LEVAIN
2%	9 G	1½ TSP	SALT

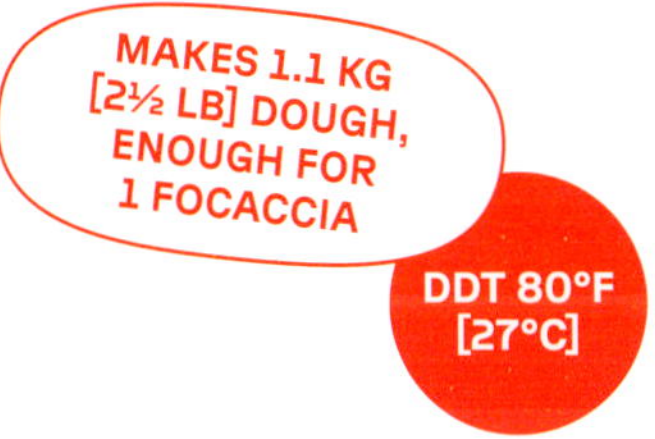

With more water than flour in the dough, this focaccia bakes up into a lacy crumb with a custardy interior studded with bright-yellow cooked grits. I prefer stone-ground grits (see sources on page 405) and switch off among Bloody Butcher red corn, yellow corn, or even purple corn from the Cherokee Nation in the Carolinas. Season the grits as you normally would, with salt, pepper, and butter.

Example Time Frame	
9:00 P.M. (PREVIOUS NIGHT)	MIX LEVAIN
9:00 A.M.	MIX DOUGH
9:45 A.M.	FOLD
10:45 A.M.	FOLD
11:45 P.M.	FOLD

TO MAKE THE LEVAIN: In a pint-size deli or similar container, combine the bread flour, water, and sourdough starter. Stir thoroughly with a spoon. The levain will be sticky and stiff. Try to keep most of it in the container and not on the spoon. Cover with a lid and ferment for 12 hours at room temperature (68° to 72°F [20° to 22°C]). It's ready to use when it has doubled in size, smells like yogurt, and is full of bubbles.

TO MAKE THE DOUGH: Ready a restaurant-style wide-mouthed water pitcher half full of warm water. **To get the precise temperature, use the chart on page 82**, or just use 80°F [27°C]. You'll use water from this pitcher for mixing the dough and later for wetting your fingers when folding.

In a large mixing bowl, weigh the bread flour. Quickly stir with a dry hand to aerate, then add the water and levain. Next, using your dominant hand in the shape of a claw, agitate the flour and water into a dough. You can use your free hand to stabilize the bowl. Once a rough, sticky dough has formed, grab and squeeze it several times to bring it into a cohesive, shaggy mass. Cover with a lid or shower cap and let rest for 10 minutes. **CONT'D**

Return to the bowl and distribute the grits evenly over the dough and then sprinkle on the salt. With your hands in the shape of crab claws, pinch in the grits and salt. The dough may become stringy as you work in the grits. Keep grabbing and squeezing until it reforms. You'll feel the dough tighten and smooth out when it's done. Cover and rest for 30 minutes.

The dough has now entered bulk fermentation, or the first rise, and will be given three folds each spaced 1 hour apart. Keep the dough warm, around 80°F [27°C], and away from any drafts.

To fold the dough, dip your fingers into the water in the pitcher and smear a little water on your work surface. Using the dough scraper, gather the dough together in the bowl and, with a quick motion, scoop it up with the dough scraper and flip it out onto the damp work surface. Using your hands, lift the dough off the surface, then, while still holding the top, slap the bottom half down so it sticks a little. Gently lean back, stretching the dough, and then quickly lean forward, tossing the dough still in your hands over the portion stuck to the work surface. Repeat slapping, stretching, and folding three or four times. The dough is ready when it is smooth and pulls itself into a ball. Using the dough scraper, return the dough to its container, smooth-side up. Cover and let rest for 1 hour.

Fold again, repeating the above steps, then cover and let rest for 1 hour. Fold one more time, then cover and let rest for 1 hour.

The dough has finished bulk fermentation when it is pillowy, has risen about 40 percent in the bowl, and feels full of air when gently pressed. If the dough needs a little more time, give it an extra 30 minutes. You may now move on to panning, proofing, topping, and baking. **For instructions, see any of the focaccia recipes starting on page 356.** Or to develop more flavor and a nice rise before continuing, chill it in the fridge for up to 24 hours.

Naked focaccia dipped into salted olive oil is pure heaven. Toppings should only enhance an already stellar dough. ●

TOPPED FOCACCIA

If too many are used, or if they aren't well prepared, additions to focaccia, even when well intended, can detract from the deliciousness. Just as when building a pizza, keep your toppings simple, seasonal, and fresh and you can't go wrong.

It's worth it to keep a window box of herbs just for focaccia. Rosemary, thyme, oregano, marjoram, and even mint and lavender are beautiful in bubbly, golden dough. When using fresh herbs, coarsely chop them and soak them in a mixture of 1 cup water and 1 tablespoon lemon juice for 20 minutes before using to prevent them from turning brown while baking. Drain well and pat dry before using.

I divide toppings into two categories: ingredients that need to be cooked first and ingredients that can go on uncooked before or after the bake. Hearty or fibrous vegetables, such as potatoes or kale, will need to be cooked before they are added. Softer toppings, such as olives or onions, can go on just as they are. While I don't pull out a ruler to measure the thickness, I do recommend using a mandoline to thinly slice most vegetable toppings.

Precook or roast mushrooms, winter squash, beets, and potatoes and wilt or quick sauté bitter greens, bacon, asparagus, leeks, and zucchini. Toast any nuts to bring out their oils. You can also use the confit method of cooking in oil to tenderize potatoes and garlic. Save the oil to drizzle over the focaccia when it's done.

Focaccia is done when it pulls away from the sides of the pan, shrinking a little due to the evaporation of water. It can still be helpful to run a thin, sharp knife along the sides of the pan to loosen the focaccia. I like to use a metal offset spatula or a pair of tongs to maneuver the baked dough from the pan to the wire rack to cool.

CANNELLINI BEAN, GARLIC, AND HERB

Weight	Volume	Ingredient
	1 RECIPE	FOCACCIA DOUGH **(any of the doughs on pages 332 to 351)**
55 G	¼ CUP	OLIVE OIL (EVOO)
5 G	1 TSP	FLAKY SALT
2 G	1 TSP	BLACK PEPPER
179 G	⅔ CUP	CANNELLINI BEANS, CANNED, RINSED, AND DRAINED OR FRESH COOKED AND DRAINED
27 G	3 TBSP	GARLIC, THINLY SLICED
8 G	2 TBSP	OREGANO, FRESH, CHOPPED
		OLIVE OIL FOR PAN PREP

Cannellini beans, also known as white kidney beans, retain their shape and texture well, making them a good candidate for topping focaccia. Popular in dishes such as minestrone, chili, and white bean dip, these large, kidney-shaped beans are high in fiber and meatier and more flavorful than their two better-known white bean cousins, great northern and navy. If cannellini beans aren't standard in your pantry, maybe this creamy, tangy focaccia will convince you to begin stocking them.

Example Time Frame

9:00 A.M.	TRANSFER DOUGH TO PAN
9:30 A.M.	STRETCH
10:00 A.M.	STRETCH
10:30 A.M.	STRETCH
11:00 A.M.	STRETCH
12:00 P.M.	DIMPLE, TOP, AND BAKE

If you are working with dough from the refrigerator, bring it to room temperature before transferring it to the pan. Using olive oil, lightly grease a 9 by 13 in [23 by 33 cm] pan for a taller focaccia or a 12 by 12 in [30.5 by 30.5 cm] pan for a thinner focaccia. Use a dough scraper to gently turn the dough out of its container into the greased pan.

The dough will proof on the counter for 3 to 4 hours. During this time, you will stretch it at least four times, spacing the stretches about 30 minutes apart. The dough will naturally relax and spread, so you don't need to stretch it aggressively. Instead, dip your fingers into cool water and coax the dough toward the corners of the pan by gently lifting it at the midpoint along the sides, top, and bottom and pulling it in the opposite direction. Look for any mounds of dough and focus your stretching there. If the dough is cold, you may need an extra stretch or two to work it to the edges.

After each stretch, cover the pan tightly with a lid or cling film and let the dough proof at warm room temperature (72° to 78°F [22° to 26°C]). It is ready when it has risen at least 75 percent in the pan, is full of air, has surface bubbles, and feels like a pillow.

Toward the end of proofing, about 45 minutes before you want to bake, set a baking steel or pizza stone on the middle rack of the oven and preheat the oven to 500°F [260°C]. When the oven is ready, you'll dimple and top the dough. Ready a small bowl of cool water for wetting your fingers for dimpling.

To dimple the dough, dip your fingertips into the water and then hold your hands as if you're at a piano, fingers outstretched and hands side by side. Starting at the edge of the pan closest to your body, dimple the dough by pushing your fingers almost all the way to the bottom of the pan. Pick up your fingers and do another line of dimples. Work your way up and down the dough a few times.

Drizzle the dough evenly with the olive oil, then sprinkle with the salt and pepper. Scatter the beans and garlic evenly over the surface of the dough and distribute the oregano on top. Quickly dimple one last time to gently push the toppings into the dough.

Bake the focaccia for 10 minutes. Lower the heat to 450°F [230°C] and continue to bake until the bubbles are perfectly charred, the dough is golden, and the bottom is crispy and well browned, about 10 minutes more. The focaccia is ready when it has pulled away from the sides of the pan. Remove from the oven and let cool in the pan on a wire rack for 5 to 10 minutes. Then, using an offset spatula or tongs, slide and guide the focaccia onto the rack and let cool to the touch.

Cut into squares or other shapes and serve warm.

STORAGE AND WARMING: Any extra focaccia can be stored in an airtight container at room temperature for up to 5 days. To reheat the focaccia, preheat the oven to 350°F [180°C], preferably with a baking steel or pizza stone on the middle rack. Wrap the focaccia tightly in aluminum foil, place it on the steel, stone, or rack, and heat until fragrant, warm, and soft, 5 to 8 minutes.

PARMESAN AND ROSEMARY

Weight	Volume	Ingredient
	1 RECIPE	FOCACCIA DOUGH **(any of the doughs on pages 332 to 351)**
55 G	¼ CUP	OLIVE OIL (EVOO)
5 G	1 TSP	FLAKY SALT
2 G	1 TSP	BLACK PEPPER
55 G	2 OZ	PARMESAN, GRATED
3 G	3 TBSP	ROSEMARY, FRESH, CHOPPED
		OLIVE OIL FOR PAN PREP

MAKES 1 FOCACCIA

Focaccia was made for salt and fresh herbs. Use freshly grated Parmesan to avoid the chalky taste pre-shredded cheeses leave on the tongue. If you don't have rosemary on hand, swap it out for torn fresh basil, thyme, or oregano. And if fresh herbs aren't in your kitchen, substitute dried herbs. They are more potent than fresh, so reduce the amount by one-third.

Example Time Frame	
9:00 A.M.	TRANSFER DOUGH TO PAN
9:30 A.M.	STRETCH
10:00 A.M.	STRETCH
10:30 A.M.	STRETCH
11:00 A.M.	STRETCH
12:00 P.M.	DIMPLE, TOP, AND BAKE

If you are working with dough from the refrigerator, bring it to room temperature before transferring it to the pan. Using olive oil, lightly grease a 9 by 13 in [23 by 33 cm] pan for a taller focaccia or a 12 by 12 in [30.5 by 30.5 cm] pan for a thinner focaccia. Use a dough scraper to gently turn the dough out of its container into the greased pan.

The dough will proof on the counter for 3 to 4 hours. During this time, you will stretch it at least four times, spacing the stretches about 30 minutes apart. The dough will naturally relax and spread, so you don't need to stretch it aggressively. Instead, dip your fingers into cool water and coax the dough toward the corners of the pan by gently lifting it at the midpoint along the sides, top, and bottom and pulling it in the opposite direction. Look for any mounds of dough and focus your stretching there. If the dough is cold, you may need an extra stretch or two to work it to the edges.

After each stretch, cover the pan tightly with a lid or cling film and let the dough proof at warm room temperature (72° to 78°F [22° to 26°C]). It is ready when it has risen at least 75 percent in the pan, is full of air, has surface bubbles, and feels like a pillow.

Toward the end of proofing, about 45 minutes before you want to bake, set a baking steel or pizza stone on the middle rack of the oven and preheat the oven to 500°F [260°C]. When the oven is ready, you'll dimple and top the dough. Ready a small bowl of cool water for wetting your fingers for dimpling. **CONT'D**

To dimple the dough, dip your fingertips into the water and then hold your hands as if you're at a piano, fingers outstretched and hands side by side. Starting at the edge of the pan closest to your body, dimple the dough by pushing your fingers almost all the way to the bottom of the pan. Pick up your fingers and do another line of dimples. Work your way up and down the dough a few times.

Drizzle the dough evenly with the olive oil, then sprinkle evenly with the salt, pepper, Parmesan, and rosemary. Quickly dimple one last time to gently push the toppings into the dough.

Bake the focaccia for 10 minutes. Lower the heat to 450°F [230°C] and continue to bake until the bubbles are perfectly charred, the dough is golden, and the bottom is crispy and well browned, about 10 minutes more. The focaccia is ready when it has pulled away from the sides of the pan. Remove from the oven and let cool in the pan on a wire rack for 5 to 10 minutes. Then, using an offset spatula or tongs, slide and guide the focaccia onto the rack and let cool to the touch.

Cut into squares or other shapes and serve warm.

FOR STORAGE
AND WARMING INFORMATION,
SEE PAGE 357.

GRAPE, GRUYÈRE, AND TOASTED WALNUT

Weight	Volume	Ingredient
	1 RECIPE	FOCACCIA DOUGH **(any of the doughs on pages 332 to 351)**
55 G	¼ CUP	OLIVE OIL (EVOO)
230 G	8 OZ	RED GRAPES
130 G	1 CUP	WALNUTS, CHOPPED AND TOASTED
55 G	2 OZ	GRUYÈRE, SHREDDED
		OLIVE OIL FOR PAN PREP

MAKES 1 FOCACCIA

Grapes turn jammy inside when slowly baked, making this focaccia both sweet and savory. Typically made during the grape harvest in Italy, grape focaccia can stand alone, with just the fruit, or be matched with any number of aged cheeses, drizzles, or herbs. This recipe calls for the semi-hard Swiss-type Gruyère cheese, which contributes a creamy nuttiness. But it can be swapped out for sharp Cheddar, creating a more complex bite, or even for a salty and bright blue cheese.

Example Time Frame

9:00 A.M.	TRANSFER DOUGH TO PAN
9:30 A.M.	STRETCH
10:00 A.M.	STRETCH
10:30 A.M.	STRETCH
11:00 A.M.	STRETCH
12:00 P.M.	DIMPLE, TOP, AND BAKE

If you are working with dough from the refrigerator, bring it to room temperature before transferring it to the pan. Using olive oil, lightly grease a 9 by 13 in [23 by 33 cm] pan for a taller focaccia or a 12 by 12 in [30.5 by 30.5 cm] pan for a thinner focaccia. Use a dough scraper to gently turn the dough out of its container into the greased pan.

The dough will proof on the counter for 3 to 4 hours. During this time, you will stretch it at least four times, spacing the stretches about 30 minutes apart. The dough will naturally relax and spread, so you don't need to stretch it aggressively. Instead, dip your fingers into cool water and coax the dough toward the corners of the pan by gently lifting it at the midpoint along the sides, top, and bottom and pulling it in the opposite direction. Look for any mounds of dough and focus your stretching there. If the dough is cold, you may need an extra stretch or two to work it to the edges.

After each stretch, cover the pan tightly with a lid or cling film and let the dough proof at warm room temperature (72° to 78°F [22° to 26°C]). It is ready when it has risen at least 75 percent in the pan, is full of air, has surface bubbles, and feels like a pillow. **CONT'D**

Toward the end of proofing, about 45 minutes before you want to bake, set a baking steel or pizza stone on the middle rack of the oven and preheat the oven to 500°F [260°C]. When the oven is ready, you'll dimple and top the dough. Ready a small bowl of cool water for wetting your fingers for dimpling.

To dimple the dough, dip your fingertips into the water and then hold your hands as if you're at a piano, fingers outstretched and hands side by side. Starting at the edge of the pan closest to your body, dimple the dough by pushing your fingers almost all the way to the bottom of the pan. Pick up your fingers and do another line of dimples. Work your way up and down the dough a few times.

Drizzle the dough evenly with the olive oil, then scatter the grapes, walnuts, and Gruyère evenly over the surface of the dough. Quickly dimple one last time to gently push the toppings into the dough.

Bake the focaccia for 10 minutes. Lower the heat to 450°F [230°C] and continue to bake until the bubbles are perfectly charred, the dough is golden, and the bottom is crispy and well browned, about 10 minutes more. The focaccia is ready when it has pulled away from the sides of the pan. Remove from the oven and let cool in the pan on a wire rack for 5 to 10 minutes. Then, using an offset spatula or tongs, slide and guide the focaccia onto the rack and let cool to the touch.

Cut into squares or other shapes and serve warm.

FOR STORAGE
AND WARMING INFORMATION,
SEE PAGE 357.

ASPARAGUS, CAPER, AND FETA

MAKES 1 FOCACCIA

Asparagus Topping

Weight	Volume	Ingredient
230 G	8 OZ	ASPARAGUS
5 G	1 TSP	SALT

Assembly

Weight	Volume	Ingredient
	1 RECIPE	FOCACCIA DOUGH **(any of the doughs on pages 332 to 351)**
55 G	¼ CUP	OLIVE OIL (EVOO)
5 G	1 TSP	FLAKY SALT
55 G	2 OZ	FETA, CRUMBLED
36 G	¼ CUP	CAPERS
		OLIVE OIL FOR PAN PREP

Fresh spring asparagus is tender and sweet—nothing like the out-of-season, woody, bitter stalks often sold at supermarkets. Save this focaccia for a springtime trip to the farmers' market when asparagus has just been harvested and you can find long, thin, tender spears. Paired with salty capers and tangy feta, they are earthy and bright.

Example Time Frame

9:00 A.M.	TRANSFER DOUGH TO PAN
9:30 A.M.	STRETCH
10:00 A.M.	STRETCH
10:30 A.M.	STRETCH
11:00 A.M.	STRETCH
12:00 P.M.	DIMPLE, TOP, AND BAKE

TO MAKE THE ASPARAGUS TOPPING: Using a chef's knife, trim the bottoms off the asparagus and discard. If you have pencil-thick asparagus, keep them whole. If they are thicker, cut them in half lengthwise. Place the asparagus in a steamer basket set over (not touching) simmering water in a covered saucepan on the stovetop. Once the asparagus is bright green, tender, and moist, transfer it to a plate, sprinkle it with the salt, then cover and set aside until needed. The asparagus can be prepped up to 48 hours in advance and stored in an airtight container in the fridge. Bring to room temperature before adding to the focaccia.

TO ASSEMBLE THE FOCACCIA: If you are working with dough from the refrigerator, bring it to room temperature before transferring it to the pan. Using olive oil, lightly grease a 9 by 13 in [23 by 33 cm] pan for a taller focaccia or a 12 by 12 in [30.5 by 30.5 cm] pan for a thinner focaccia. Use a dough scraper to gently turn the dough out of its container into the greased pan.

The dough will proof on the counter for 3 to 4 hours. During this time, you will stretch it at least four times, spacing the stretches about 30 minutes apart. The dough will naturally relax and spread, so you don't need to stretch it aggressively. Instead, dip your fingers into cool water and coax the dough toward the corners of the pan by gently lifting it at the midpoint along the sides, top, and bottom and pulling it in the opposite direction. Look for any mounds of dough and focus your stretching there. If the dough is cold, you may need an extra stretch or two to work it to the edges.

After each stretch, cover the pan tightly with a lid or cling film and let the dough proof at warm room temperature (72° to 78°F [22° to 26°C]). It is ready when it has risen at least 75 percent in the pan, is full of air, has surface bubbles, and feels like a pillow.

Toward the end of proofing, about 45 minutes before you want to bake, set a baking steel or pizza stone on the middle rack of the oven and preheat the oven to 500°F [260°C]. When the oven is ready, you'll dimple and top the dough. Ready a small bowl of cool water for wetting your fingers for dimpling.

To dimple the dough, dip your fingertips in the water and then hold your hands as if you're at a piano, fingers outstretched and hands side by side. Starting at the edge of the pan closest to your body, dimple the dough by pushing your fingers almost all the way to the bottom of the pan. Pick up your fingers and do another line of dimples. Work your way up and down the dough a few times.

Drizzle the dough evenly with the olive oil, then sprinkle evenly with the flaky salt. Scatter the asparagus and feta evenly over the surface of the dough and distribute the capers on top. Quickly dimple one last time to gently push the toppings into the dough.

Bake the focaccia for 10 minutes. Lower the heat to 450°F [230°C] and continue to bake until the bubbles are perfectly charred, the dough is golden, and the bottom is crispy and well browned, about 10 minutes more. The focaccia is ready when it has pulled away from the sides of the pan. Remove from the oven and let cool in the pan on a wire rack for 5 to 10 minutes. Then, using an offset spatula or tongs, slide and guide the focaccia onto the rack and let cool to the touch.

Cut into squares or other shapes and serve warm.

FOR STORAGE AND WARMING INFORMATION, SEE PAGE 357.

ROASTED RED PEPPER, PINE NUT, AND RED PEPPER FLAKES

Roasted Red Pepper Topping

Weight	Volume	Ingredient
300 G	2	RED BELL PEPPERS, HALVED, STEMMED, AND SEEDED
28 G	2 TBSP	OLIVE OIL (EVOO)

Assembly

Weight	Volume	Ingredient
	1 RECIPE	FOCACCIA DOUGH **(any of the doughs on pages 332 to 351)**
55 G	¼ CUP	OLIVE OIL (EVOO)
5 G	1 TSP	FLAKY SALT
34 G	¼ CUP	PINE NUTS
5 G	2½ TSP	RED PEPPER FLAKES
		OLIVE OIL FOR PAN PREP

MAKES 1 FOCACCIA

Here, I roast red bell peppers until blistered and charred and then I pop them into an airtight container for about 15 minutes to finish cooking. This process softens the skin, making it easy to peel it away, and further cooks the peppers with residual heat, intensifying their sweetness. In the summer, I like to char the peppers outside on the grill and leave little flecks of black skin on the cut pepper strips for a pleasing bitter taste to match the sweetness.

Example Time Frame

9:00 A.M.	TRANSFER DOUGH TO THE PAN
9:30 A.M.	STRETCH
10:00 A.M.	STRETCH
10:30 A.M.	STRETCH
11:00 A.M.	STRETCH
12:00 P.M.	DIMPLE, TOP, AND BAKE

TO MAKE THE ROASTED PEPPER TOPPING: Preheat the oven to 350°F [180°C]. Line a sheet pan with parchment paper.

Place the peppers cut-side down on the parchment-lined pan and drizzle with the olive oil. Roast until the skin is blistered and charred, 20 to 25 minutes.

Remove from the oven and use tongs to transfer the peppers to an airtight container. Let rest for 15 minutes. Peel off and discard the skins. Cut the pepper halves into strips about ¼ in [6 mm] wide. Set aside until needed. The peppers can be prepared up to 48 hours in advance and stored in the fridge. Bring to room temperature before adding to the focaccia.

TO ASSEMBLE THE FOCACCIA: If you are working with dough from the refrigerator, bring it to room temperature before transferring it to the pan. Using olive oil, lightly grease a 9 by 13 in [23 by 33 cm] pan for a taller focaccia or a 12 by 12 in [30.5 by 30.5 cm] pan for a thinner focaccia. Use a dough scraper to gently turn the dough out of its container into the greased pan. **CONT'D**

The dough will proof on the counter for 3 to 4 hours. During this time, you will stretch it at least four times, spacing the stretches about 30 minutes apart. The dough will naturally relax and spread, so you don't need to stretch it aggressively. Instead, dip your fingers into cool water and coax the dough toward the corners of the pan by gently lifting it at the midpoint along the sides, top, and bottom and pulling it in the opposite direction. Look for any mounds of dough and focus your stretching there. If the dough is cold, you may need an extra stretch or two to work it to the edges.

After each stretch, cover the pan tightly with a lid or cling film and let the dough proof at warm room temperature (72° to 78°F [22° to 26°C]). It is ready when it has risen at least 75 percent in the pan, is full of air, has surface bubbles, and feels like a pillow.

Toward the end of proofing, about 45 minutes before you want to bake, set a baking steel or pizza stone on the middle rack of the oven and preheat the oven to 500°F [260°C]. When the oven is ready, you'll dimple and top the dough. Ready a small bowl of cool water for wetting your fingers for dimpling.

To dimple the dough, dip your fingertips into the water and then hold your hands as if you're at a piano, fingers outstretched and hands side by side. Starting at the edge of the pan closest to your body, dimple the dough by pushing your fingers almost all the way to the bottom of the pan. Pick up your fingers and do another line of dimples. Work your way up and down the dough a few times.

Drizzle the dough evenly with the olive oil and sprinkle evenly with the flaky salt. Scatter the pepper strips evenly over the surface of the dough, then distribute the pine nuts and red pepper flakes on top. Quickly dimple one last time to gently push the toppings into the dough.

Bake the focaccia for 10 minutes. Lower the heat to 450°F [230°C] and continue to bake until the bubbles are perfectly charred, the dough is golden, and the bottom is crispy and well browned, about 10 minutes more. The focaccia is ready when it has pulled away from the sides of the pan. Remove from the oven and let cool in the pan on a wire rack for 5 to 10 minutes. Then, using an offset spatula or tongs, slide and guide the focaccia onto the rack and let cool to the touch.

Cut into squares or other shapes and serve warm.

FOR STORAGE AND WARMING INFORMATION, SEE PAGE 357.

SESAME HONEY

Weight	Volume	Ingredient
	1 RECIPE	FOCACCIA DOUGH (any of the doughs on pages 332 to 351)
55 G	¼ CUP	OLIVE OIL (EVOO)
5 G	1 TSP	FLAKY SALT
27 G	3 TBSP	SESAME SEEDS
40 G	2 TBSP	HONEY
		OLIVE OIL FOR PAN PREP

Sesame seeds are mild, sweet, a bit buttery, and, most of all, crunchy! They work great on top of a fluffy, golden focaccia, adding a layer of texture to the already crispy bubbles and an earthiness to the bites where the seeds have been pushed into the dough dimples. Drizzled with honey, this simple yet decadent treat is delicious split in half and smeared with fresh chèvre or crunchy peanut butter.

Example Time Frame

9:00 A.M.	TRANSFER DOUGH TO PAN
9:30 A.M.	STRETCH
10:00 A.M.	STRETCH
10:30 A.M.	STRETCH
11:00 A.M.	STRETCH
12:00 P.M.	DIMPLE, TOP, AND BAKE

If you are working with dough from the refrigerator, bring it to room temperature before transferring it to the pan. Using olive oil, lightly grease a 9 by 13 in [23 by 33 cm] pan for a taller focaccia or a 12 by 12 in [30.5 by 30.5 cm] pan for a thinner focaccia. Use a dough scraper to gently turn the dough out of its container into the greased pan.

The dough will proof on the counter for 3 to 4 hours. During this time, you will stretch it at least four times, spacing the stretches about 30 minutes apart. The dough will naturally relax and spread, so you don't need to stretch it aggressively. Instead, dip your fingers into cool water and coax the dough toward the corners of the pan by gently lifting it at the midpoint along the sides, top, and bottom and pulling it in the opposite direction. Look for any mounds of dough and focus your stretching there. If the dough is cold, you may need an extra stretch or two to work it to the edges.

After each stretch, cover the pan tightly with a lid or cling film and let the dough proof at warm room temperature (72° to 78°F [22° to 26°C]). It is ready when it has risen at least 75 percent in the pan, is full of air, has surface bubbles, and feels like a pillow.

Toward the end of proofing, about 45 minutes before you want to bake, set a baking steel or pizza stone on the middle rack of the oven and preheat the oven to 500°F [260°C]. When the oven is ready, you'll dimple and top the dough. Ready a small bowl of cool water for wetting your fingers for dimpling. **CONT'D**

To dimple the dough, dip your fingertips into the water and then hold your hands as if you're at a piano, fingers outstretched and hands side by side. Starting at the edge of the pan closest to your body, dimple the dough by pushing your fingers almost all the way to the bottom of the pan. Pick up your fingers and do another line of dimples. Work your way up and down the dough a few times.

Drizzle the dough evenly with the olive oil and the honey. Sprinkle the surface of the dough evenly with the flaky salt and sesame seeds. Quickly dimple one last time to gently push the seeds into the dough.

Bake the focaccia for 10 minutes. Lower the heat to 450°F [230°C] and continue to bake until the bubbles are perfectly charred, the dough is golden, and the bottom is crispy and well browned, about 10 minutes more. The focaccia is ready when it has pulled away from the sides of the pan. Remove from the oven and let cool in the pan on a wire rack for 5 to 10 minutes. Then, using an offset spatula or tongs, slide and guide the focaccia onto the rack and let cool to the touch.

Cut into squares or other shapes and serve warm.

FOR STORAGE
AND WARMING INFORMATION,
SEE PAGE 357.

CASTELVETRANO AND KALAMATA OLIVE

Weight	Volume	Ingredient
	1 RECIPE	FOCACCIA DOUGH (any of the doughs on pages 332 to 351)
55 G	¼ CUP	OLIVE OIL (EVOO)
5 G	1 TSP	FLAKY SALT
115 G	4 OZ	CASTELVETRANO OLIVES, PITTED
115 G	4 OZ	KALAMATA OLIVES, PITTED
		OLIVE OIL FOR PAN PREP

MAKES 1 FOCACCIA

Castelvetranos are Kermit green and have a full body you can sink your teeth into. Crisp and bright, they are considered the ideal snacking olive by many. I like to mix them with salty Kalamatas for the perfect fluffy focaccia studded with flavor-packed green and black olives. Try mixing different kinds of olives to find your favorite combination. Be sure to choose pitted olives to save yourself or your guests any unpleasantly hard bites.

Example Time Frame

9:00 A.M.	TRANSFER DOUGH TO PAN
9:30 A.M.	STRETCH
10:00 A.M.	STRETCH
10:30 A.M.	STRETCH
11:00 A.M.	STRETCH
12:00 P.M.	DIMPLE, TOP, AND BAKE

If you are working with dough from the refrigerator, bring it to room temperature before transferring it to the pan. Using olive oil, lightly grease a 9 by 13 in [23 by 33 cm] pan for a taller focaccia or a 12 by 12 in [30.5 by 30.5 cm] pan for a thinner focaccia. Use a dough scraper to gently turn the dough out of its container into the greased pan.

The dough will proof on the counter for 3 to 4 hours. During this time, you will stretch it at least four times, spacing the stretches about 30 minutes apart. The dough will naturally relax and spread, so you don't need to stretch it aggressively. Instead, dip your fingers into cool water and coax the dough toward the corners of the pan by gently lifting it at the midpoint along the sides, top, and bottom and pulling it in the opposite direction. Look for any mounds of dough and focus your stretching there. If the dough is cold, you may need an extra stretch or two to work it to the edges.

After each stretch, cover the pan tightly with a lid or cling film and let the dough proof at warm room temperature (72° to 78°F [22° to 26°C]). It is ready when it has risen at least 75 percent in the pan, is full of air, has surface bubbles, and feels like a pillow.

Toward the end of proofing, about 45 minutes before you want to bake, set a baking steel or pizza stone on the middle rack of the oven and preheat the oven to 500°F [260°C]. When the oven is ready, you'll dimple and top the dough. Ready a small bowl of cool water for wetting your fingers for dimpling.

To dimple the dough, dip your fingertips into the water and then hold your hands as if you're at a piano, fingers outstretched and hands side by side. Starting at the edge of the pan closest to your body, dimple the dough by pushing your fingers almost all the way to the bottom of the pan. Pick up your fingers and do another line of dimples. Work your way up and down the dough a few times.

Drizzle the dough evenly with the olive oil and sprinkle with the flaky salt. Scatter the surface of the dough evenly with the Castelvetrano and Kalamata olives, making sure to mix the two colors. Quickly dimple one last time to gently push the olives into the dough.

Bake the focaccia for 10 minutes. Lower the heat to 450°F [230°C] and continue to bake until the bubbles are perfectly charred, the dough is golden, and the bottom is crispy and well browned, about 10 minutes more. The focaccia is ready when it has pulled away from the sides of the pan. Remove from the oven and let cool in the pan on a wire rack for 5 to 10 minutes. Then, using an offset spatula or tongs, slide and guide the focaccia onto the rack and let cool to the touch.

Cut into squares or other shapes and serve warm.

FOR STORAGE AND WARMING INFORMATION, SEE PAGE 357.

SAUSAGE, LEEK, AND FENNEL

Sausage, Leek, and Fennel Topping

Weight	Volume	Ingredient
	1	LEEK
250 G	1	FENNEL BULB
10 G	1¾ TSP	SALT
455 G	1 LB	ITALIAN SAUSAGE
14 G	1 TBSP	OLIVE OIL (EVOO)

MAKES 1 FOCACCIA

Assembly

Weight	Volume	Ingredient
	1 RECIPE	FOCACCIA DOUGH **(any of the doughs on pages 332 to 351)**
55 G	¼ CUP	OLIVE OIL (EVOO)
5 G	1 TSP	FLAKY SALT
		OLIVE OIL FOR PAN PREP

Riffing on Thanksgiving flavors, this focaccia delivers a meal that pairs with a red wine or a stout beer for a cool-weather picnic or holiday gathering. Use tender fennel and leeks from the farmers' market and heighten the festive atmosphere even more by adding fresh herbs, such as sage, rosemary, and thyme.

Example Time Frame

9:00 A.M.	TRANSFER DOUGH TO PAN
9:30 A.M.	STRETCH
10:00 A.M.	STRETCH
10:30 A.M.	STRETCH
11:00 A.M.	STRETCH
12:00 P.M.	DIMPLE, TOP AND BAKE

TO MAKE THE SAUSAGE, LEEK, AND FENNEL TOPPING: To prep the leek, using a chef's knife, cut off and discard the tough, dark green tops of the leek leaves. Then peel away and discard the leathery, dark green outer leaves. Cut off the root from the white base, leaving as much white as possible. Slice the leek in half lengthwise and separate the sections. Cut crosswise into half-moons about the thickness of two stacked quarters.

Line a medium plate with a paper towel. Fill a medium bowl with cool water and transfer the leek pieces to the water. With your hands, give them a shake to loosen and remove any dirt. Then lift them out of the bowl and onto the towel-lined plate. (If the water was very dirty, repeat this step with fresh water.) Pat the leek pieces dry with a paper towel and reserve. **CONT'D**

Using the chef's knife, cut the fennel crosswise at the top, cutting the tall stalks and fronds away from the bulb. Using the knife or a mandoline, shave the tender top of the bulb into pieces the thickness of two stacked quarters. Transfer to a small bowl, sprinkle with about half of the salt, and set aside. Pick apart the feathery fronds, dividing them into smaller pieces, and stand them, stem down, in a cup of cold water. Set aside.

Remove and discard the sausage casings and crumble the sausages. In a large skillet, warm the olive oil over medium heat until it glistens. Add the sausage in a single layer and sprinkle with the remaining salt. Cook, stirring occasionally, until browned and cooked through, 3 to 4 minutes. Remove from the heat, add the leek and fennel, cover, and steam for 8 to 10 minutes. The leek and fennel will be tender to the tines of a fork and slightly wilted. Uncover, let cool, transfer to an airtight container, and refrigerate until needed. The topping can be prepared up to 48 hours in advance. Bring to room temperature before adding to the focaccia.

TO ASSEMBLE THE FOCACCIA: If you are working with dough from the refrigerator, bring it to room temperature before transferring it to the pan. Using olive oil, lightly grease a 9 by 13 in [23 by 33 cm] pan for a taller focaccia or a 12 by 12 in [30.5 by 30.5 cm] pan for a thinner focaccia. Use a dough scraper to gently turn the dough out of its container into the greased pan.

The dough will proof on the counter for 3 to 4 hours. During this time, you will stretch it at least four times, spacing the stretches about 30 minutes apart. The dough will naturally relax and spread, so you don't need to stretch it aggressively. Instead, dip your fingers into cool water and coax the dough toward the corners of the pan by gently lifting it at the midpoint along the sides, top, and bottom and pulling it in the opposite direction. Look for any mounds of dough and focus your stretching there. If the dough is cold, you may need an extra stretch or two to work it into the edges.

After each stretch, cover the pan tightly with a lid or cling film and let the dough proof at warm room temperature (72° to 78°F [22° to 26°C]). It is ready when it has risen at least 75 percent in the pan, is full of air, has surface bubbles, and feels like a pillow.

Toward the end of proofing, about 45 minutes before you want to bake, set a baking steel or pizza stone on the middle rack of the oven and preheat the oven to 500°F [260°C]. When the oven is ready, you'll dimple and top the dough. Ready a small bowl of cool water for wetting your fingers for dimpling.

To dimple the dough, dip your fingertips into the water and then hold your hands as if you're at a piano, fingers outstretched and hands side by side. Starting at the edge of the pan closest to your body, dimple the dough by pushing your fingers almost all the way to the bottom of the pan. Pick up your fingers and do another line of dimples. Work your way up and down the dough a few times.

Drizzle the dough evenly with the olive oil and sprinkle with the flaky salt. Scatter the sausage, leek, and fennel topping evenly over the surface of the dough. Quickly dimple one last time to gently push the toppings into the dough.

Bake the focaccia for 10 minutes. Lower the heat to 450°F [230°C] and continue to bake until the bubbles are perfectly charred, the dough is golden, and the bottom is crispy and well browned, about 10 minutes more. The focaccia is ready when it has pulled away from the sides of the pan. Remove from the oven and let cool in the pan on a wire rack for 5 to 10 minutes. Then, using an offset spatula or tongs, slide and guide the focaccia onto the rack and let cool to the touch. Break up some of the reserved fennel fronds over the focaccia and save the rest for salads.

Cut into squares or other shapes and serve warm.

FOR STORAGE AND WARMING INFORMATION, SEE PAGE 357.

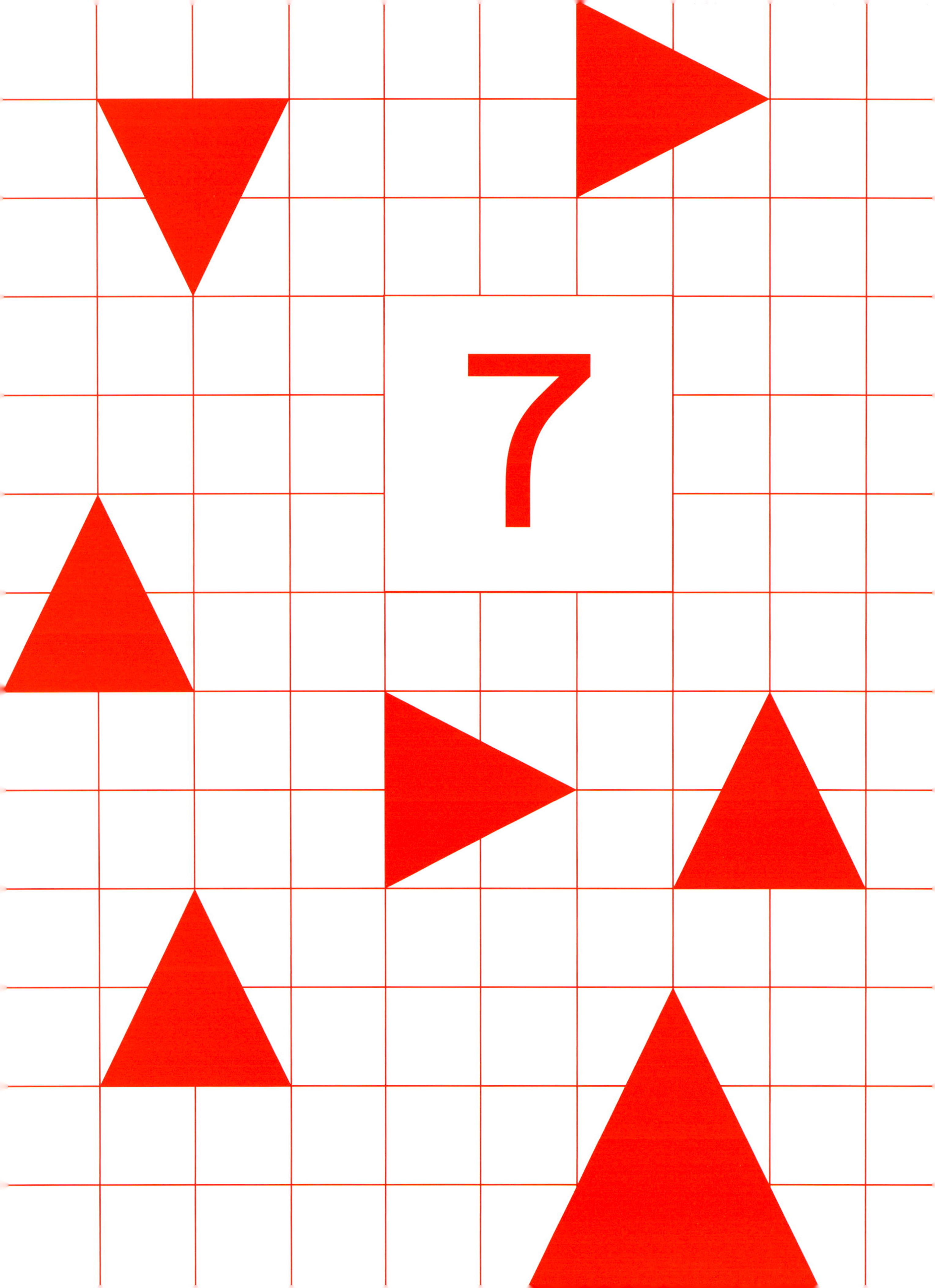
7

PIZZA-NIGHT DESSERTS

Time to Party!

When you're a parent, time for yourself and your relationships is limited. There's always a boo-boo that needs to be kissed, a nose to be wiped, piles of laundry, or mountains of dishes demanding your attention. If you were to flit to and from each need as it arose, there would be no time for anything else. Some days there isn't.

You can lose yourself in the chaos of family, and this anonymity can sometimes feel like a relief. The malaise of my twenties may have simply been selfishness. But if it goes too far, the sacrifices breed resentment. It's important to find something that reminds you of yourself that you can *easily* share with your family. Throwing a pizza-night party is a joy from my pre-parent days that has survived my crossover into being a wife and a mother, and for that I'm grateful.

When our family is having a pizza night, we're in the moment together. It's not me giving my children attention in a one-way-street or me trading time credits with my husband, who doesn't get any "free" time either. Pizza night lifts us up and away from the day-to-day drudgery so we can be in an experience everyone is excited about.

There are rules for pizza-party desserts: They must be mixed in one or two bowls, they must be able to be prepared at least a couple of days in advance, and they must be bite-size or handheld. For these reasons, I've settled on square pan cakes, bars, cookies, the occasional cobbler, and, of course, no-churn ice cream. The best part of nearly all these treats is that they are wonderful vehicles for exploring freshly milled whole-grain flours and seasonal fruits.

In my kitchen, I use spelt flour and all-purpose flour interchangeably. Spelt is tender and nutty, and unlike brawny whole wheat flour, it's delicate. I generally do not adjust the liquid when swapping out all-purpose for spelt. I also love rye flour in sweets. Grassy and fluffy, rye adds an earthy dimension and makes a light batter. In our family, our most-beloved desserts are the **Citrus Olive Oil Snack Cake (page 387)**, which we make every year for my mom's birthday, and the **Brown Butter Chocolate Chip Cookies (page 390)**.

RELAXED BAKING (NO SCALE!)

I'll be frank. I don't pull out a digital scale for my snack cakes. I make them with my kids, and we use cups and tablespoons for ease. I have taught them how to use the spoon-and-sweep method for measuring flour, and although **I have included the directions for working with flour using this method on page 65**, I will repeat it here so you have it for close reference: Spoon flour, granulated sugar, or similar fine or granular ingredients into a cup measure until mounded in the middle and almost spilling over the sides. Using the spine (straight back edge) of a knife, level off the ingredient by sweeping the knife across the top of the cup. (You may need to do a few sweeps.) Never pack down or shake the cup, or you will compact the ingredient and end up with more than you need. If using measuring spoons for salt, baking powder, baking soda, cornstarch, or the like, use the scoop method for measuring: Dip the spoon into the ingredient, overfilling it slightly, and then level it off with the spine of a knife.

Swapping Pans / For these cakes, you can use any of the following pans:

One 9 by 9 in [23 by 23 cm] square pan

One 10 in [23 cm] round pan

Two 6 in [15 cm] round pans

FLOUR FOR CAKES

Cake flour is made from low-protein soft red or white wheats and milled to a fine texture. Appalachian White and Sonora are two soft wheats that make nice cake flour. Typical store-bought cake flour contains 7 to 9 percent protein, making it too fragile for bread or even cookies but perfect for a fluffy, moist cake. Commercial cake flour may be bleached to further weaken the proteins, so check your flour bags and stay clear of bleached or brominated flour. Commercial cake flours are milled to a powdery texture and should be mixed gently. Freshly milled flour may need a few additional strokes to become fully incorporated. Because it is difficult to find well-made cake flour, I call for all-purpose flour in my snack cakes, but if you can find high-quality cake flour then you may use that rather than the all-purpose, or try making your own!

Using Flour Milled at Home

I love milling spelt berries for cake flour. The resulting flour is fluffy and has beautiful freckles of reddish bran, and a cake made from it is toothy, nutty, and flavorful. When using freshly milled flour ground at home, you will need to account for the inherent coarseness of the flour. Soak just the flour and the liquids for the cake, without the leavening, for 10 to 15 minutes. This rest will allow the moisture to begin to penetrate the chunky starches. You may notice a cake is denser when it is made with home-milled whole wheat flour, but what it lacks in looks it makes up for in deliciousness. Freshly milled flour is notoriously sticky, too, so mill it a day or two ahead of when you want to bake so it can stabilize and better absorb the moisture.

Make Your Own Cake Flour

Cornstarch is ultrafine, and when mixed with all-purpose flour, it can make a suitable substitute for store-bought cake flour. To make cake flour at home, measure 140 g [1 cup] all-purpose flour or 116 g [1 cup] whole spelt flour and carefully remove 18 g [2 Tbsp]. Sift the flour into a medium mixing bowl, then sift in 10 g [2 Tbsp] cornstarch. Sift the flour and cornstarch into a second medium bowl. You can make up to three times this amount at once and store any unused homemade cake flour in an airtight container in a cool, dry place for up to 1 month or in the freezer for up to 2 months. Bring to room temperature and sift again before using.

BAKE SCHEDULE

Make sure all your ingredients are room temperature before you start, so bring out the eggs, buttermilk, and the like a few hours before you plan to mix. Although you can bake and frost or glaze the cakes in this chapter all within the span of a few hours, I prefer to bake the cakes, let them cool completely, and then tightly wrap them in cling film and let them rest on my counter, where they keep well for up to 3 days. If you want to serve the cake from the pan, let it cool in the pan completely and then wrap the pan in cling film. I often make the frosting or glaze up to 3 days in advance of baking the cake, bringing it to room temperature and stirring it well to smooth it out before using.

Freezing Cake

These snack cakes disappear fast, but should you need to bake far in advance or something comes up, you can certainly freeze them. (Some bakers even swear that freezing cake improves the flavor and makes the cake more stable.) To freeze a snack cake, double wrap it in cling film and then wrap it in aluminum foil and freeze it for up to 3 months. Thaw it in the refrigerator overnight before topping with frosting or glaze and serving.

Number or Letter Cakes

The snack cakes are baked in a 9 by 9 in [23 by 23 cm] square pan, which makes them perfect for cutting into big, blocky numbers and letters for a birthday or other special event. Here's how to make a number or letter cake: Draw the number or letter on stiff cardboard, such as the back of an empty cereal box, and then cut it out with scissors. (You can also buy plastic letter or number stencils or print a large letter or number to use as a template.) Bake the snack cake of your choice. When the cake has completely cooled, usually after 1 to 2 hours, transfer it to a cutting board, lay the cardboard stencil on top, and cut around the stencil with a small knife. (Save any cake scraps for snacks.) Frost the top with swoops of buttercream and garnish with sprinkles or candies of your choice.

Sunken Middles

Cakes can sink in the middle for all kinds of reasons, and it can drive a baker crazy trying to troubleshoot the problem. I typically use 5 g [1 tsp] baking powder and 1 g [¼ tsp] baking soda to 140 g [1 cup] all-purpose flour in a cake. Too much leavening can cause a cake to rise and fall, so check that first, as well as the expiration date on your baking powder and baking soda. I usually swap mine out every 6 months. Cakes can also fall because the oven door was opened too soon (keep it shut for at least the first 15 minutes of the bake) or the pan was overfilled. In general, cake pans should be filled only half full; occasionally very wet cakes can go to two-thirds full.

Other Tips

You can make your own buttermilk by stirring together 1 cup [240 g] whole milk and 1 Tbsp [15 g] white vinegar. Let sit to thicken. Use a full-fat milk, if possible, and make the buttermilk a day ahead of time and store it in the fridge so it has time to thicken. If it still seems thin, use 30 g [about 2 Tbsp] less than the recipe calls for.

Although these cakes aren't fussy, do yourself a favor and refrain from opening the oven door for the first half of the bake (15 minutes).

Some shrinking is normal as the cake cools. That's because the air inside the cake cools down and contracts. If the middle falls or the cake bakes unevenly, it may be underbaked, have too much leavening, or the oven door was opened too often or too soon during the bake.

Try These Mix-Ins and Swaps / A handful of chocolate chips / A cup of rainbow sprinkles for a Funfetti look / Lemon, grapefruit, or orange zest (in the vanilla cake) / Swap out buttermilk or yogurt for sour cream / Swap out butter for oil, or swap out oil for butter

CHOCOLATE SNACK CAKE WITH PEANUT BUTTER GLAZE

Cake

Weight	Volume	Ingredient
140 G	1 CUP	ALL-PURPOSE FLOUR (11% TO 12% PROTEIN)
25 G	⅓ CUP	DUTCH-PROCESS COCOA POWDER
5 G	1 TSP	BAKING POWDER
1 G	¼ TSP	BAKING SODA
4 G	½ TSP	SALT
116 G	2	LARGE EGGS
200 G	1 CUP	GRANULATED SUGAR
55 G	¼ CUP	VEGETABLE OIL
248 G	1 CUP	YOGURT, FULL-FAT, PLAIN
4 G	1 TSP	VANILLA EXTRACT
30 G	2 TBSP	WATER, BOILING

MAKES ONE 9 BY 9 IN [23 BY 23 CM] SINGLE-LAYER CAKE

Peanut Butter Glaze

Weight	Volume	Ingredient
115 G	1 CUP	POWDERED SUGAR
32 G	2 TBSP	PEANUT BUTTER, CREAMY
64 G	⅓ CUP	HEAVY CREAM
14 G	1 TBSP	OLIVE OIL (EVOO)
15 G	1 TBSP	WATER, BOILING
4 G	1 TSP	VANILLA EXTRACT
1 G	¼ TSP	SALT

Moist, classic, and easy to dress up, this is my answer for dinner parties, playdates, picnics, or holiday get-togethers when a chocolate cake is on the menu. You'll want to use a full-fat yogurt, either Greek for a more custard-like interior or regular for a lighter bite. For a kid-friendly version, toss a big handful of chocolate chips into the batter or decorate the glaze with a dusting of sprinkles. If a whole-grain option appeals, swap out the all-purpose flour for spelt flour.

TO MAKE THE CAKE: Preheat the oven to 350°F [180°C]. Make a parchment paper sling for a 9 by 9 in [23 by 23 cm] pan: Cut a piece of parchment paper that is at least 9 in [23 cm] wide and about 20 in [51 cm] long. Center the parchment in the pan and crease and fold wherever there is an edge so it sits nicely on the bottom and doesn't slouch or slide down the sides. You want about 1½ in [4 cm] overhang on either end. Remove the sling and trim off any excess so it will lie flat. Lightly spray the bottom and sides of the pan with nonstick cooking spray, then return the parchment sling to the pan and lightly coat the sling with cooking spray.

In a medium mixing bowl, sift together the all-purpose flour, cocoa powder, baking powder, baking soda, and salt. In a separate medium bowl, whisk together the eggs, granulated sugar, vegetable oil, yogurt, and vanilla. Add the boiling water while whisking constantly, then whisk for a few more strokes to ensure the mixture is well blended.

Using a flexible spatula, fold half of the flour mixture into the egg mixture until fully incorporated. Add the remaining flour mixture and fold in gently until well mixed and the batter is smooth. Pour the batter into the prepared pan.

Bake the cake until a toothpick inserted into the center comes out clean, 25 to 30 minutes. Let cool in the pan on a wire rack for 8 to 10 minutes. Then, using the parchment overhang, lift the cake from the pan and set it on the rack to finish cooling.

WHILE THE CAKE COOLS, MAKE THE PEANUT BUTTER GLAZE: In a medium mixing bowl, whisk together the powdered sugar, peanut butter, cream, olive oil, boiling water, vanilla, and salt until well blended and smooth.

When the cake is completely cooled, invert it onto another wire rack and carefully peel away the parchment. Return the cake to the wire rack right-side up and set the rack on a sheet pan to catch any drips. Drizzle the glaze evenly over the top of the cake, allowing it to drip down the sides. Let sit until the glaze sets, 25 to 30 minutes.

Transfer the cake to a serving plate. Using a sharp knife, cut the cake into nine squares and serve.

The unglazed cake will keep, tightly wrapped in cling film on the counter, for up to 3 days. The glazed cake can be stored on the counter in an airtight container, for up to 4 days. For the best flavor and texture, wait until the day of serving to cut the cake. The unglazed cake can be tightly wrapped first in cling film and then in aluminum foil and stored in the freezer for up to 3 months. Thaw overnight in the refrigerator before glazing and serving.

BIRTHDAY CAKE WITH AMERICAN BUTTERCREAM

Cake

Weight	Volume	Ingredient
210 G	2 CUPS + 1 TBSP	SPELT FLOUR
5 G	1 TSP	BAKING POWDER
1 G	¼ TSP	BAKING SODA
3 G	½ TSP	SALT
2 G	¼ TSP	GROUND TURMERIC
116 G	2	LARGE EGGS
200 G	1 CUP	GRANULATED SUGAR
227 G	1 CUP	BUTTERMILK
32 G	¼ CUP	VEGETABLE OIL
9 G	2¼ TSP	VANILLA EXTRACT

MAKES ONE 9 BY 9 IN [23 BY 23 CM] SINGLE-LAYER CAKE

Buttercream

Weight	Volume	Ingredient
115 G	1 CUP	POWDERED SUGAR
55 G	¼ CUP	UNSALTED BUTTER, AT ROOM TEMPERATURE
15 TO 30 G	1 TO 2 TBSP	WHOLE MILK
8 G	2 TSP	VANILLA EXTRACT
2 G	¼ TSP	SALT
		SPRINKLES FOR DECORATING

Spelt flour is fluffy, slightly sweet, and turns lightly golden when baked, making it perfect for cake. If you don't have spelt flour in the pantry, you can use all-purpose with no other changes to the recipe. The addition of turmeric to the batter gives this cake a sunny color, but if there's no turmeric in your spice rack, you should still make the cake! The buttermilk adds a nice cultured flavor.

TO MAKE THE CAKE: Preheat the oven to 350°F [180°C]. Make a parchment paper sling for a 9 by 9 in [23 by 23 cm] pan: Cut a piece of parchment paper that is at least 9 in [23 cm] wide and about 20 in [51 cm] long. Center the parchment in the pan and crease and fold wherever there is an edge so it sits nicely on the bottom and doesn't slouch or slide down the sides. You want about 1½ in [4 cm] overhang on either end. Remove the sling and trim off any excess so it will lie flat. Lightly spray the bottom and sides of the pan with nonstick cooking spray, then return the parchment sling to the pan and lightly coat the sling with cooking spray. **CONT'D**

In a medium mixing bowl, sift together the spelt flour, baking powder, baking soda, salt, and turmeric. In a separate medium mixing bowl, whisk together the eggs and granulated sugar until smooth and deep yellow. Pour in the buttermilk and the vegetable oil while whisking constantly. Finally, whisk in the vanilla, then whisk for a few more strokes to ensure the mixture is well blended.

Using a flexible spatula, fold in half of the flour mixture until fully incorporated. Add the remaining flour mixture and fold in gently until well mixed and the batter is smooth. Pour the batter into the prepared pan.

Bake the cake until a toothpick inserted into the center comes out clean, 25 to 30 minutes. Let cool in the pan on a wire rack for 8 to 10 minutes. Then, using the parchment overhang, lift the cake from the pan and set it on the rack to finish cooling.

WHILE THE CAKE COOLS, MAKE THE BUTTERCREAM: In a medium mixing bowl, whisk together the powdered sugar, butter, milk, vanilla, and salt. Start with the minimum amount of milk and add splashes as needed to achieve a smooth, spoonable consistency.

When the cake is completely cooled, invert it onto another wire rack and carefully peel away the parchment. Transfer the cake right-side up to a serving plate and spoon the buttercream on top. Use an offset spatula first to smooth and then to create swoops and swirls in the buttercream. Top with the sprinkles. Using a sharp knife, cut the cake into nine squares and serve.

The unfrosted cake will keep, tightly wrapped in cling film on the counter, for up to 3 days. The frosted cake can be stored on the counter in an airtight container, for up to 4 days. For the best flavor and texture, wait until the day of serving to cut the cake. The unfrosted cake can be tightly wrapped first in cling film and then in aluminum foil and stored in the freezer for up to 3 months. Thaw overnight in the refrigerator before frosting and serving.

CITRUS OLIVE OIL SNACK CAKE

Weight	Volume	Ingredient
140 G	1 CUP	ALL-PURPOSE FLOUR (11% TO 12% PROTEIN)
60 G	½ CUP	ALMOND FLOUR
5 G	1 TSP	BAKING POWDER
2 G	½ TSP	BAKING SODA
5 G	1 TSP	SALT
124 G	½ CUP	ORANGE JUICE
5 G	1 TSP	VANILLA EXTRACT
2 G	½ TSP	ALMOND EXTRACT
8 G	1 TBSP	GRATED ORANGE ZEST
150 G	3	LARGE EGGS
130 G	⅔ CUP	GRANULATED SUGAR
110 G	½ CUP	OLIVE OIL (EVOO)

MAKES ONE 9 BY 9 IN [23 BY 23 CM] SINGLE-LAYER CAKE

This is a *perfect* snack cake! It comes together easily (I do use a stand mixer to help incorporate the olive oil), doesn't require any frosting, and can be eaten right out of the pan. For the best flavor, use an extra-virgin olive oil that is not too robust or spicy. Because olive oil stays liquid at room temperature, this cake remains delicious for up to a week on the counter—though you'll be lucky if there's any left over after even a day! I love to make this one for my mom, whose birthday falls in citrus season.

Preheat the oven to 350°F [180°C]. Make a parchment paper sling for a 9 by 9 in [23 by 23 cm] pan: Cut a piece of parchment paper that is at least 9 in [23 cm] wide and about 20 in [51 cm] long. Center the parchment in the pan and crease and fold wherever there is an edge so it sits nicely on the bottom and doesn't slouch or slide down the sides. You want about 1½ in [4 cm] overhang on either end. Remove the sling and trim off any excess so it will lie flat. Lightly spray the bottom and sides of the pan with nonstick cooking spray, then return the parchment sling to the pan and lightly coat the sling with cooking spray.

In a medium mixing bowl, whisk together the all-purpose flour, almond flour, baking powder, baking soda, and salt until well blended. In a small bowl, whisk together the orange juice, vanilla, almond extract, and orange zest. Set aside. **CONT'D**

In a stand mixer fitted with the paddle attachment, beat the eggs on medium speed until the whites and yolks are fully blended and slightly aerated. This should take just a few strokes. Add the sugar and continue to beat on medium speed until the mixture is light yellow and fluffy, about 3 minutes. Stop the mixer and use a flexible spatula to scrape down the sides of the bowl and underneath the mixture. On low speed, drizzle in the olive oil and then continue to mix until fully incorporated. The mixture will thicken, take on a sheen, and become homogenous.

Increase the speed to medium and drizzle in the orange juice mixture, beating just until incorporated. This should take only a few strokes of the paddle. Stop the mixer and use the flexible spatula to scrape down the sides of the bowl and underneath the mixture. On low speed, add the flour mixture in three additions, beating after each addition just until blended, then stop the mixer. Using the flexible spatula, fold the batter several times to ensure all the ingredients are incorporated. Pour the batter into the prepared pan.

Bake the cake until the top is deeply browned, the center is firm to the touch, the sides have pulled away slightly from the pan, and a toothpick inserted into the center comes out clean, 30 to 35 minutes. Transfer the pan to a wire rack to cool.

My family prefers to eat squares of the cake directly from the pan, so I let it cool completely in the pan. Should you wish to serve the cake on a serving plate, let it cool in the pan on the rack for about 10 minutes, then, using the parchment overhang, lift the cake from the pan and set it on the rack to finish cooling. When the cake is completely cooled, invert it onto another wire rack and carefully peel away the parchment. Transfer the cooled cake right-side up to a serving plate. Using a sharp knife, cut the cake into nine squares and serve.

The cake will keep, tightly wrapped in cling film on the counter, for up to 3 days. For the best flavor and texture, wait until the day of serving to cut the cake. To freeze the cake, wrap tightly first in cling film and then in aluminum foil and place in the freezer for up to 3 months. Thaw overnight in the fridge before serving.

BROWN BUTTER CHOCOLATE CHIP COOKIES

Weight	Volume	Ingredient
227 G	1 CUP	UNSALTED BUTTER, CUT INTO 1 IN [2.5 CM] CHUNKS
150 G	¾ CUP (PACKED)	LIGHT BROWN SUGAR
116 G	2	LARGE EGGS, COLD
19 G	1	LARGE EGG YOLK, COLD
4 G	1 TSP	VANILLA EXTRACT
140 G	1 CUP	ALL-PURPOSE FLOUR (11% TO 12% PROTEIN)
160 G	1½ CUPS + 1½ TBSP	SPELT FLOUR
6 G	1 TSP	BAKING SODA
4 G	½ TSP	SALT
340 G	2 CUPS	SEMISWEET CHOCOLATE CHIPS
115 G	4 OZ	BITTERSWEET CHOCOLATE, CHOPPED INTO PEA-SIZE CHUNKS

MAKES ABOUT 48 COOKIES

This is a chocolate chip cookie adults will love and kids won't scoff at. Made with browned butter, spelt flour, and an extra egg yolk, these cookies are chewy and toothy and have a caramel flavor that pairs deliciously with chocolate chunks. The dough is soft and sticky just after mixing, but once it is chilled, it's a dream to scoop. If you like spelt flour, you can swap out all the all-purpose for more spelt with no adjustments. The cookies can be baked the same day the dough is made, or the dough can mellow in the fridge for up to 3 days.

Put the butter into a light-colored medium skillet and place over medium heat. (A light pan makes it easier to see when the milk solids turn into toasty brown bits.) Stir the butter with a heat-safe flexible spatula to encourage it to melt. Once it has melted, it will sizzle on the sides of the pan and become foamy. Cook gently, continuing to stir, until brown flecks appear on the bottom of the pan, 5 to 8 minutes. The butter will smell nutty and like caramel. Transfer the hot butter to a small heatproof mixing bowl, using the spatula to get all the toasty bits into the bowl too.

Let the butter cool for 30 minutes to 1 hour. You want it soft but not hot when you mix the cookie dough.

In a large mixing bowl, whisk together the cooled butter, brown sugar, eggs, egg yolk, and vanilla until well blended and smooth. Add the all-purpose flour, spelt flour, baking soda, and salt and fold in gently with a flexible spatula until the dough is a uniform consistency and no streaks of dry flour are visible. Finally, add the semisweet chocolate chips and fold in just until evenly distributed throughout the dough. Cover the bowl and refrigerate the dough until well chilled, about 4 hours. (You can chill the dough in the fridge for up to 3 days. I do that and then take it out and scoop a few cookies to bake fresh after school each day.)

Preheat the oven to 375°F [190°C]. Line two sheet pans with parchment paper.

Using a small cookie scoop or a spoon, scoop the dough into balls of about 2 Tbsp each and stagger the balls, with the flat side down and the domed side up, at least 1 in [2.5 cm] apart on a prepared sheet pan. You should get about eight cookies on the pan. The warmer the dough is when you start, the more the cookies will spread, so don't be tempted to put too many on the pan.

Press two or three pieces of bittersweet chocolate into the top of each cookie.

Bake the cookies until they are browned on the edges, golden in the center, slightly puffed, and smell nutty, 8 to 10 minutes. Remove from the oven and let cool on the pan on a wire rack for a few minutes, then, using an offset spatula, transfer the cookies to the rack and let cool completely.

While the first batch of cookies is in the oven, load the second prepared sheet pan with scoops of dough the same way, then slip the second batch into the oven when the first batch comes out. Repeat the scooping and baking until all the dough is used, letting the pans cool down a bit before loading them so the cookies don't spread too much in the oven.

The baked cookies will keep in an airtight container at room temperature for up to 4 days or in the freezer for up to 2 months. You can also scoop the cookie dough into balls onto a parchment-lined sheet pan, add the bittersweet chocolate chunks, freeze the balls on the pan, and then transfer the frozen balls to a large resealable plastic bag and return them to the freezer. Bake the frozen cookie dough directly from the freezer on a parchment-lined sheet pan, adding an additional 2 to 5 minutes to the bake time.

WHITE CHOCOLATE BLONDIES

Weight	Volume	Ingredient
140 G	1 CUP	ALL-PURPOSE FLOUR (11% TO 12% PROTEIN)
120 G	1 CUP + 2 TBSP	RYE FLOUR
2 G	½ TSP	BAKING POWDER
4 G	½ TSP	SALT
116 G	2	LARGE EGGS
213 G	1 CUP (PACKED)	LIGHT BROWN SUGAR
5 G	1 TSP	VANILLA EXTRACT
170 G	¾ CUP	UNSALTED BUTTER, CUT INTO 1 IN [2.5 CM] CHUNKS
115 G	4 OZ	WHITE CHOCOLATE, ROUGHLY CHOPPED

MAKES 9 BLONDIES

A blondie is a butterscotch version of a brownie, elevated here with browned butter and coarsely chopped white chocolate. This recipe is endlessly adaptable, so if you're not a white chocolate fan, trade out the chopped chocolate for macadamia nuts, pistachios, or shredded coconut. Like white chocolate but want a bit of variety? Mix in one of these alternatives along with the white chocolate.

Preheat the oven to 350°F [180°C]. Make a parchment paper sling for an 8 by 8 in [20 by 20 cm] pan: Cut a piece of parchment paper that is at least 8 in [20 cm] wide and about 19 in [48 cm] long. Center the parchment in the pan and crease and fold wherever there is an edge so it sits nicely on the bottom and doesn't slouch or slide down the sides. You want about 1½ in [4 cm] overhang on either end. Remove the sling and trim off any excess so it will lie flat. Lightly spray the bottom and sides of the pan with nonstick cooking spray, then return the parchment sling to the pan and lightly coat the sling with cooking spray.

In a medium mixing bowl, sift together the all-purpose flour, rye flour, baking powder, and salt. In a separate medium mixing bowl, whisk together the eggs, brown sugar, and vanilla until well blended and smooth.

Put the butter into a light-colored medium skillet and place over medium heat. (A light pan makes it easier to see when the milk solids turn into toasty brown bits.) Stir the butter with a heat-safe flexible spatula to encourage it to melt. Once it has melted, it will sizzle on the sides of the pan and become foamy. Cook gently, continuing to stir, until brown flecks appear on the bottom of the pan, 5 to 8 minutes. The butter will smell nutty and like caramel. Remove from the heat.

Begin whisking the egg mixture, then slowly and steadily stream in the hot browned butter. When most of the butter is in the bowl, put the whisk down and use the flexible spatula to get all the toasty bits from the pan into the bowl. Give the egg mixture a few good strokes with the spatula to mix everything well. Add the flour mixture to the egg mixture and fold in gently until no dry flour is visible. Finally, fold in the white chocolate pieces, distributing them evenly, and then pour the batter into the prepared pan.

Bake until the edges are set and a toothpick inserted into the center comes out clean, 20 to 25 minutes. (If you like blondies on the gooey side, bake until the edges are set and the center is slightly jiggly but puffed up.)
Let cool in the pan on a wire rack for 5 to 10 minutes. Then, using the parchment overhang, lift the blondie square from the pan and set it on the rack to cool completely. Once fully cooled, starting at the edges, gently peel away the parchment.

Transfer to a cutting board and, using a sharp knife, cut into nine squares to serve. These blondies are moist and deeply flavorful, perfect on the second or third day after baking, so make them ahead of pizza night. Any leftover blondies can be stored in an airtight container at room temperature for up to 4 days or in the freezer for up to 2 weeks.

RYE BROWNIES

Weight	Volume	Ingredient
140 G	1⅓ CUPS	RYE FLOUR
20 G	¼ CUP	DUTCH-PROCESS COCOA POWDER
4 G	1 TSP	BAKING POWDER
4 G	½ TSP	SALT
116 G	2	LARGE EGGS
200 G	1 CUP	GRANULATED SUGAR
14 G	1 TBSP	OLIVE OIL (EVOO)
2 G	½ TSP	VANILLA EXTRACT
115 G	4 OZ	DARK CHOCOLATE, CHOPPED
115 G	½ CUP	UNSALTED BUTTER, CUT INTO PATS
30 G	2 TBSP	WATER, VERY HOT

MAKES 9 BROWNIES

Brownies should be decadent and deeply chocolaty without being so boldly flavored that you can't enjoy a whole square in one sitting. To tone down the intensity and add some lightness, I use earthy rye flour in my brownies, which helps round out the usual richness and sweetness associated with brownies. Plus, because the rye berry is naturally high in starch, the flour contributes a pleasingly fluffy texture.

Preheat the oven to 350°F [180°C]. Make a parchment paper sling for an 8 by 8 in [20 by 20 cm] pan: Cut a piece of parchment paper that is at least 8 in [20 cm] wide and about 19 in [48 cm] long. Center the parchment in the pan and crease and fold wherever there is an edge so it sits nicely on the bottom and doesn't slouch or slide down the sides. You want about 1½ in [4 cm] overhang on either end. Remove the sling and trim off any excess so it will lie flat. Lightly spray the bottom and sides of the pan with nonstick cooking spray, then return the parchment sling to the pan and lightly coat the sling with cooking spray.

In a medium mixing bowl, sift together the rye flour, cocoa powder, baking powder, and salt. In a separate medium mixing bowl, whisk together the eggs, sugar, olive oil, and vanilla until well blended. **CONT'D**

Fill a medium saucepan half full of water and set it on the stovetop over medium-high heat. Combine the chocolate and butter in a medium stainless-steel or tempered-glass bowl and set the bowl over (not touching) the water in the pan. As the water heats, it will warm the bottom of the bowl and gently melt the butter and chocolate. Stir occasionally with a heat-safe flexible spatula until melted and smooth. If the water begins to sputter out of the pan, lower the heat to maintain a gentle simmer. Remove the bowl from over the heat. Reserve 30 g [2 Tbsp] of the hot water for the brownie batter.

Begin whisking the egg mixture, then slowly and steadily stream in the chocolate mixture. When most of the chocolate mixture is in the bowl, put the whisk down and use the flexible spatula to scrape out all the chocolate mixture into the bowl. Add the reserved hot water and whisk until smooth. Add the flour mixture to the chocolate-egg mixture and fold in gently until no dry flour is visible. Pour the batter into the prepared pan.

Bake the brownies until the edges are set and a toothpick inserted into the center comes out clean, 20 to 25 minutes. (If you like brownies on the gooey side, bake until the edges are set and the center is slightly jiggly but puffed up.) Let cool in the pan on a wire rack for 5 to 10 minutes. Then, using the parchment overhang, lift the brownie square from the pan and set it on the rack to cool completely. Once fully cooled, starting at the edges, gently peel away the parchment.

Transfer to a cutting board and, using a sharp knife, cut into nine squares to serve. These brownies only get better over the next 24 hours, so make them ahead of pizza night. Any leftover brownies can be stored in an airtight container at room temperature for up to 4 days or in the freezer for up to 2 weeks.

ANY-FRUIT OAT BARS

Dough

Weight	Volume	Ingredient
240 G	1⅔ CUPS	ALL-PURPOSE FLOUR (11% TO 12% PROTEIN)
70 G	½ CUP	OAT FLOUR
90 G	1 CUP	OLD-FASHIONED ROLLED OATS
100 G	½ CUP (PACKED)	LIGHT BROWN SUGAR
2 G	¼ TSP	SALT
2 G	½ TSP	GROUND CINNAMON
2 G	½ TSP	BAKING POWDER
170 G	¾ CUP	SALTED BUTTER, COLD, CUBED

MAKES 12 BARS

Filling

Weight	Volume	Ingredient
300 G	2 CUPS	CHOPPED OR WHOLE FRUIT (SUCH AS BLUEBERRIES, STRAWBERRIES, CHERRIES, APPLES, OR PEARS)
15 G	1½ TBSP	CORNSTARCH
4 G	1 TSP	LEMON JUICE
50 G	¼ CUP	GRANULATED SUGAR
2 G	¼ TSP	SALT

I love using oat flour in recipes that also call for rolled oats. It increases the oaty flavor and the delicate flour tenderizes the dough. The dough can be made up to 3 days in advance and stored, tightly wrapped, in the fridge, then brought to room temperature before using. Swap out the fruit depending on what is in season. Blueberries, cherries, and cubed apples are my favorite fruit toppings. It's necessary to cool the bars fully before cutting. You may even want to pop them into the freezer for a short stint to get them very firm.

Preheat the oven to 350°F [180°C]. Make a parchment paper sling for an 8 by 8 in [20 by 20 cm] pan: Cut a piece of parchment paper that is at least 8 in [20 cm] wide and about 19 in [48 cm] long. Center the parchment in the pan and crease and fold wherever there is an edge so it sits nicely on the bottom and doesn't slouch or slide down the sides. You want about 1½ in [4 cm] overhang on either end. Remove the sling and trim off any excess so it will lie flat. Lightly spray the bottom and sides of the pan with nonstick cooking spray, then return the parchment sling to the pan and lightly coat the sling with cooking spray. **CONT'D**

TO MAKE THE DOUGH: In a food processor, combine the all-purpose flour, oat flour, rolled oats, brown sugar, salt, cinnamon, and baking powder and pulse two or three times to mix well. Scatter the butter over the flour mixture and process on high speed until a dough begins to form. If your food processor has only on, off, and pulse settings, use the pulse setting in short bursts several times. Stop the processor and turn the dough out onto a lightly floured work surface. Gently knead for a few strokes to bring the dough together. Eyeball it into a 60-40 split, reserving 60 percent for the bottom crust and 40 percent for the crumble topping. Transfer the crust dough to the parchment-lined pan and wrap the rest of the dough in cling film and move it to the fridge.

Working gently but firmly, press the dough evenly onto the bottom of the pan, making sure you extend it into the corners. Transfer the pan to the freezer while you work on the fruit filling. If you're using berries or another fruit that doesn't need to be chopped, freeze the dough for at least 10 minutes before proceeding.

TO MAKE THE FILLING: Put the prepared fruit into a medium mixing bowl. Add the cornstarch, lemon juice, granulated sugar, and salt and toss together to coat the fruit evenly. Remove the doughs from the freezer and the fridge. Spread the fruit filling across the bottom crust, then break up the cold topping dough with your hands, scattering the pieces to cover the fruit filling.

Bake until the edges are deeply browned, the topping is slightly puffed, and you can see the fruit bubbling, 40 to 45 minutes. Transfer to a wire rack and let cool for 10 to 15 minutes. Then, using the parchment overhang, lift the oat bar square from the pan and set it back on the rack to cool completely. Once fully cooled, starting at the edges, gently peel away the parchment.

Transfer to a cutting board and, using a sharp knife, cut into 12 bars to serve. The bars are crumbly when warm, so if you need to cut them early, pop them into the freezer for 5 to 10 minutes and cut them directly from the freezer.

As the bars cool, the filling gets jammy and the crust develops a melt-in-your-mouth texture, so I prefer to eat them the day after they are baked and typically make them ahead of pizza night. Any leftover bars can be stored in an airtight container at room temperature for up to 4 days or in the freezer for up to 2 months. Thaw in the fridge overnight before serving.

NO-CHURN VANILLA ICE CREAM

SERVES 4

Weight	Volume	Ingredient
397 G	ONE 14 OZ CAN	SWEETENED CONDENSED MILK
8 G	2 TSP	VANILLA BEAN PASTE OR VANILLA EXTRACT
28 G	2 TBSP	OLIVE OIL (EVOO)
2 G	¼ TSP	SALT
357 G	1½ CUPS	HEAVY CREAM

No-churn ice cream starts with a base made from sweetened condensed milk, which works as a concentrated, low-moisture dairy base (in place of eggs) and as the primary sweetener. Whipped cream is then folded into the base to mimic the air that would typically be introduced through churning. Easy, fun, and delightful, this ice cream is a breeze to make. Keep in mind that it is not as stable as traditional ice cream and will melt a little faster.

Flavor Options

Warm spices, such as cinnamon or coriander; grated citrus zest; or even a spoonful of instant espresso powder for a bold coffee flavor.

Add mix-ins / Stir in nuts, dried or fresh fruit, caramel sauce, pumpkin purée, or chocolate chips by layering them into the ice cream as you spoon it into the loaf pan.

Steep ingredients / Warm the cream until hot, add fresh mint leaves, coffee beans, or fresh ginger slices, and let steep for 15 to 20 minutes, then strain the cream, let cool, and chill well before whipping.

Make it chocolate / Heat the cream and stir in chopped semisweet or dark chocolate until it melts. Let cool, then chill well before whipping.

Place a medium metal mixing bowl in the freezer for 15 minutes. (A cold bowl will help the heavy cream aerate faster and with increased volume for a better final texture.)

In a separate medium mixing bowl, whisk together the sweetened condensed milk, vanilla, olive oil, and salt until well blended.

Remove the cold bowl from the freezer and pour in the heavy cream. Using a handheld mixer or immersion blender, whip the cream until soft peaks form. Using a flexible spatula, fold the whipped cream into the condensed milk base until fully incorporated.

Spread the ice cream into a 9 by 5 in [23 by 13 cm] loaf pan. Cover with a tight-fitting lid or with a piece of parchment paper pressed directly onto the surface of the ice cream and secured to the pan. Freeze until firm before serving, at least 4 hours or preferably 8 hours or up to overnight. Any leftover ice cream (is that even a thing?) will keep in the freezer for up to 1 month.

PEACH AND BLACKBERRY COBBLER

MAKES 9 SQUARES

Fruit Filling

Weight	Volume	Ingredient
400 G	2	PEACHES, SLICED
285 G	2½ CUPS	BLACKBERRIES
140 G	¾ CUP + 2½ TBSP	GRANULATED SUGAR
6 G	1 TSP	VANILLA EXTRACT

Topping

Weight	Volume	Ingredient
250 G	1¼ CUPS	GRANULATED SUGAR
175 G	1¼ CUPS	ALL-PURPOSE FLOUR (11% TO 12% PROTEIN)
50 G	¼ CUP + 3 TBSP	WHOLE WHEAT FLOUR
9 G	2 TSP	BAKING POWDER
2 G	¼ TSP	SALT
325 G	1⅓ CUPS	WHOLE MILK

This cobbler comes together quickly and is *almost* equal parts berries, sugar, and milk, making it the delicious cousin of snack cake. Switch out the fruit seasonally: strawberries and rhubarb in spring or pears and apples deep into fall. I make this all summer long and enjoy a cold slice in the morning with coffee.

Preheat the oven to 350°F [180°C]. Grease a 9 by 9 in [23 by 23 cm] pan with nonstick cooking spray.

TO PREPARE THE FRUIT FILLING: In a medium mixing bowl, fold the peaches, blackberries, sugar, and vanilla together with a flexible spatula and coax the fruit into the pan.

TO MAKE THE TOPPING: Using the same bowl, whisk together the sugar, all-purpose flour, whole wheat flour, baking powder, and salt. Add the milk and gently beat with the whisk until no dry flour is visible. Pour the batter over the fruit.

Bake until the topping has puffed, the edges are browned, and a toothpick inserted into the center comes out clean, about 1 hour. Let cool on a wire rack for 1 hour and serve warm.

To store, cover the pan with aluminum foil and keep in the refrigerator for up to 3 days. Or live on the wild side and leave the cobbler on the counter covered with a kitchen towel and eat the cobbler square by square throughout the week.

TOOL AND EQUIPMENT SUPPLIERS

BAKING STEEL

The Original, the company's 16 by 14 in [40.5 by 35.5 cm] steel, is the only one you'll need and is worth the investment.
bakingsteel.com

GI.METAL USA

This subsidiary of a Tuscan-based company carries an amazing selection of high-quality pizza peels, oven brushes, and other pizza tools.
gimetalusa.com

GOZNEY

Gozney makes high-quality outdoor pizza ovens and tools. I use the Roccbox and the Dome.
us.gozney.com

LLOYDPANS

Based in Washington state, these black, pre-seasoned steel pans are my favorite for making pan pizza and focaccia.
lloydpans.com

WEBSTAURANTSTORE

A commercial restaurant-supply company that will deliver to your home. This is where I buy my dough boxes, pizza tools, parchment paper, cling film, sheet pans, and other equipment.
webstaurantstore.com

WHERE TO FIND GOOD FLOUR

ANSON MILLS
South Carolina
1922C Gervais Street, Columbia, SC 29201
ansonmills.com

BAKER'S FIELD FLOUR & BREAD
Minnesota
1401 Marshall Street NE #120
Minneapolis, MN 55413
bakersfieldflour.com

BARTON SPRINGS MILL
Texas
16604 Fitzhugh Road Building B
Dripping Springs, TX 78620
bartonspringsmill.com

CAIRNSPRING MILLS
Washington
11829 Water Tank Road, Burlington, WA 98233
cairnspring.com

CAMAS COUNTRY MILL
Oregon
90472 Woodruff Street, Eugene, OR 97402
camascountrymill.com

CAPAY MILLS
California
capaymills.com

CAPUTO FLOUR
Italy
caputoflour.com

FARM & SPARROW
North Carolina
farmandsparrow.com

FARMER GROUND FLOUR
New York
farmergroundflour.com

GRIST & TOLL
California
990 S. Arroyo Parkway #1, Pasadena, CA 91105
gristandtoll.com

GROUND UP STONE MILLED FLOURS
Massachusetts
4 North Bridge Street, Holyoke, MA 01040
groundupgrain.com

HAYDEN FLOUR MILLS
Arizona
932 N Colorado St, Gilbert, AZ 85233
haydenflourmills.com

JANIE'S MILL
Illinois
405 N. 2nd Street, Ashkum, IL 60911
janiesmill.com

KING ARTHUR BAKING COMPANY
Vermont
135 US Route 5 South, Norwich, VT 05055
kingarthurbaking.com

MAINE GRAINS
Maine
42 Court Street, Skowhegan, ME 04976
mainegrains.com

ACKNOWLEDGMENTS

This book wouldn't have been possible without my husband's support. Thank you, *Marley*, for protecting my time to create, for investing in it, and for lending your own skills to these pages. And thank you to *my mom*, who always had a yeasty pizza dough rising on the counter for Saturday-night pizza. Many of the front matter details, like the baker's math, friction factor, and sifted flours sections, were the result of in-depth conversations with my colleague and friend *Andrew Janjigian*. Andrew, you are too generous! *Katie Parla*, you are an inspiration. Thank you for your commitment to cookbooks and for writing such a bold foreword. And thank you to my team at *Chronicle Books*! It was a joy to work with *Sarah Billingsley* and *Jessica Ling*. *Sharon Silva*, your copyedits read like a love letter. Thank you to *Lizzie Vaughan* and also to *Scott Suchman* and *Lisa Cherkasky* for gorgeous photos and creative styling. And finally, praise *God* from whom all blessings flow. xo

INDEX

A

B

C

D

E

F

G

H

I

J

K

L

M

N

O

P

S

T

Z

Photo by Ilana Freddye

Tara Jensen is one of the preeminent bread bakers, baking instructors, and bread-baking cookbook authors in the United States. Her previous books are *Flour Power* (2022) and *A Baker's Year* (2018), a memoir and cookbook based on her bakery in the mountains of North Carolina, Smoke Signals. She lives in Virginia with her family and many pizza ovens.

Scott Suchman is a food, lifestyle, and travel photographer based in Washington, DC.

Chronicle Books publishes distinctive books and gifts. From award-winning children's titles, bestselling cookbooks, and eclectic pop culture to acclaimed works of art and design, stationery, and journals, we craft publishing that's instantly recognizable for its spirit and creativity. Enjoy our publishing and become part of our community at www.chroniclebooks.com.